A Rusty Gun

A Rusty Gun

NOEL 'RAZOR' SMITH

VIKING
an imprint of
PENGUIN BOOKS

VIKING

Published by the Penguin Group

Penguin Books Ltd, 80 Strand, London WC2R ORL, England

Penguin Group (USA) Inc., 375 Hudson Street, New York, New York 10014, USA

Penguin Group (Canada), 90 Eglinton Avenue East, Suite 700, Toronto, Ontario, Canada M4P 2Y3

(a division of Pearson Penguin Canada Inc.)

Penguin Ireland, 25 St Stephen's Green, Dublin 2, Ireland (a division of Penguin Books Ltd)

Penguin Group (Australia), 250 Camberwell Road, Camberwell, Victoria 3124, Australia

(a division of Pearson Australia Group Pty Ltd)

Penguin Books India Pvt Ltd, 11 Community Centre, Panchsheel Park, New Delhi – 110 017, India

Penguin Group (NZ), 67 Apollo Drive, Rosedale, North Shore 0632, New Zealand

(a division of Pearson New Zealand Ltd)

Penguin Books (South Africa) (Pty) Ltd, 24 Sturdee Avenue, Rosebank, Johannesburg 2196, South Africa

Penguin Books Ltd, Registered Offices: 80 Strand, London WC2R ORL, England

www.penguin.com

First published in 2010
1

Set in 12/14.75 pt Bembo MT
Typeset by Ellipsis Book Production Limited, Glasgow
Printed in Great Britain by Clays Ltd, St Ives plc

A CIP catalogue record for this book is available from the British Library

ISBN: 978-0-670-91549-1

www.greenpenguin.co.uk

This book is dedicated to my son – Joseph Stephen Smith.
May you always walk in sunshine.

And for my parents –
Noel Stephen and Bernadette Mary Smith.
Thank you.

'I have been studying how I may compare
This prison where I live unto the world.'
Richard II, Act V, William Shakespeare

'If you ever have occasion to chop a body up in the bath,
never saw the arms off first, otherwise the torso will keep spinning
as you cut the rest. It makes it awkward.'
Advice from Brian, a Grendon inmate

You can't con a con.
Prison proverb

A Rusty Gun is based on true events, but all persons appearing in the book have had their names and identifying characteristics changed to protect their privacy.

Contents

Acknowledgements

I would like to thank my friend and agent Will Self for all his hard work on my behalf. Also, my editor, Tony Lacey, for having the patience of a saint. I first signed the contract to supply this book in late 2004, but due to the contents being somewhat 'controversial', at least as far as HM Prison System is concerned, I have been unable to complete the manuscript until quite recently. Let's hope it is worth the wait! So a big thank you for all at Penguin. As usual I would like to thank my family for their support and love during some very trying decades.

And finally, to everyone, inmates and staff, who have shared the Grendon experience since 1962. It's not something you forget.

Author's Note

Much has been written and recorded about HMP Grendon in its two-score plus years of existence. There have been various newspaper and magazine articles, half a dozen television documentaries, numerous official reports and pamphlets on the workings of this unique prison, and fourteen published books. Former governors have explained their approach to running Grendon from the top, HM Chief Inspectors of Prisons have reported on the conditions and regime they found there, criminologists and psychiatrists have pontificated on the treatment available to the inmate volunteers, and a German ex-bunny girl with a degree in criminology was given access to the prison for a year in order to produce a book about it. And, while each one of these publications no doubt adds something to the constant and ongoing debate about criminal rehabilitation and the psychology of persistent offenders, there seem to have been very few words written by the men who have passed through the Grendon experiment themselves. As far as I can ascertain, not one word about Grendon has ever been commercially published by an ex-inmate. Governors, therapists, screws, facilitators, psychiatrists and criminologists can come and go at Grendon, but the prisoners themselves are a constant. The prisoners who volunteer for Grendon live the regime twenty-four hours a day, seven days a week, 365 days a year, and their lives, problems, phobias and offending history make up the fuel that drives the engine of this therapeutic machine. For the professionals HMP Grendon is work, but for us, the people down at the sharp end with a desire to change our lives and a long history of failing, Grendon is usually our final shot of red-eye in the last-chance saloon. So, with *A Rusty Gun*, I hope to redress the balance slightly.

Over a period of almost five years I witnessed first-hand and participated in the therapeutic regime at Grendon. As a Grendon volunteer I was one of the men of violence, with a long criminal record, looking for answers and possibly a way to change my entrenched criminal thinking and behaviours. At daily group therapy sessions and in psychodrama I heard the oft-times horrific life stories of my fellow offenders. I have been a violent criminal for most of my life but even I was shocked by some of the things I heard. I have come to realize that the world can be a cruel and terrifying place for some people. For this reason I have changed the names of the people featured in this book. Regrettably, all of the case details are as accurate as I heard them.

Preface: The Rise and Fall of the Grendon Experiment?

Her Majesty's Prison Grendon is a category B male prison near Aylesbury in Buckinghamshire which holds up to 244 prisoners. The prisoners are, on the whole, long-term violent recidivists who have volunteered to enter the jail's therapeutic regime and take part in daily group therapy sessions with the aim of searching for genuine rehabilitation. Grendon volunteers have all been diagnosed as suffering from various anti-social personality disorders, or psychopathy. To put it simply, an anti-social personality disorder can be described as a set of behaviours that, when repeated, will harm the perpetrator and others – i.e. serious criminal acts. Before volunteering for Grendon, prisoners must be prepared to sign an agreement to refrain from violence, drug-taking and sex, and forgo any chance of parole or early release for the duration of their therapy. The therapy at Grendon is based on the neo-Freudian concept of group therapy developed in Britain in the 1930s and now used widely around the world. Grendon operates in a social-democratic framework unheard of in the mainstream prison system, by giving prisoners responsibility for themselves and their actions and a chance to vote on matters that may affect their daily lives. The prison was opened as an experiment over four decades ago and the fact that it is still open and running, despite the many recent changes in penal policy and prison regimes, is a testament to the fact that Grendon actually works. HMP Grendon has the lowest reconviction rates of any comparable category B prison with a largely violent recidivist population.

The 'Grendon experiment' is ongoing, but with the tide of public opinion turning towards more punishment for prisoners and less rehabilitation, who knows how much longer it may last? I spent nearly five years at HMP Grendon, from July 2003 until May 2008, and the prison I entered was almost unrecognizable from the prison I left. Prison overcrowding, a Home Office in serious disarray and being spooked and steered by the media, the opening of other, less committed therapeutic units within the prison system, and a governing team with a greater interest in budgets and avoiding publicity than in therapy and rehabilitation, have all combined to drag Grendon back into the mainstream prison system from which it once stood proud and separate. There are plans to build a 600-bed category B prison within the grounds of HMP Grendon, and many believe this will be the death knell of the Grendon experiment. For some in the Home Office and Prison Service this is a prospect to relish because, despite doing exactly what it says on the tin for the past forty-eight years, Grendon has never been everyone's cup of Darjeeling.

It is an interesting fact that when HMP Grendon opened, in 1962, it was the first jail where inmates were allowed to wear wristwatches. Letting prisoners wear watches was seen as 'mollycoddling' by the rest of the prison system and some prison staff and governors believed that this could be setting a 'dangerous precedent'. Over the next four decades the regime at Grendon was to set many more 'dangerous precedents', none of which turned out to be dangerous at all. In 1965 Grendon became the first category B jail to host a football match against a team from outside: a mixed team of Grendon staff and inmates thrashed a team from Stoke Mandeville Hospital, cheered on by a mix of inmates, staff and civilians. In 1969 a pre-release hostel was set up at the prison, which allowed men coming to the end of their sentences to go out to work in the local community. In 1972 staff at Grendon began to use the word 'Mister' to promote equality among staff and inmates. In 1990 the practice of issuing psychotropic drugs and night sedation, customary in most prisons, was ended at Grendon. Also in 1990 the whole population of the prison was relocated temporarily to other prisons for six months while electrical repairs were carried out, and then returned to the jail, having been kept together and committed to their therapeutic regime. In 1992 in-cell electricity and televisions were allowed and Family Day visits were initiated for the whole prison, Grendon being the first jail to do so. The central kitchen, standard in every other jail, was scrapped in 1994 in favour of an individual cooking area for each wing, meaning meals are fresh and served hot. Also in 1994 Robert Kilroy-Silk hosted a television debate live from the gymnasium inside the jail, in which thirty Grendon inmates and thirty victims of crime took part, the first live broadcast from a British prison. So HMP Grendon was very much a beacon of innovation among British category B prisons. Add to this the low reconviction rates, and to say that Grendon's 'maverick' reputation irked prison hard-liners in the rest of the prison system would be putting it mildly.

The reason for some prison and Home Office staff's dislike for Grendon was simple. For decades the majority of British jails operated very harsh and brutal regimes, some even up to the present day. The policy was 'Stick-'em-and-nick-'em': if prisoners step out of line give them a good beating and charge them with breaking any prison rule. The dinosaurs among prison staff, some of whom obviously progressed through the ranks to Prison Service HQ, and even the lower reaches of the Home Office, were great believers in heavy discipline when it came to dealing with prisoners. When Grendon opened, the hard-liners predicted that treating convicted criminals with respect and giving them any sort of responsibility would inevitably lead to a breakdown in order and discipline that would end in disaster. They chuckled at the very idea that prisoners would be capable of understanding even the concept of trust. So when Grendon actually started working, on men who, in a lot of cases, the conventional prison system had discarded as violent subversive no-hopers, they began to get a bit worried. It soon became apparent that the re-habilitation of criminal recidivists, that long sought-after holy grail of liberal prison campaigners to which the conventional prison system had been paying no more than lip-service for many decades, was actually viable under the Grendon regime. Not only did Grendon have low reconviction rates but it also had the lowest rate of incident reports. At Grendon there were no riots, stabbings, scaldings, persecution of sex offenders or assaults on staff or inmates – in fact, the prison does not even have a punishment block! So the obvious implication was that the Grendon way might actually be the right way, and the rest of the system was stumbling around in the dark making bad people worse. Of course that was not what the dinosaurs wanted or expected. It is much easier to punch someone in the face and lock them in solitary than it is to sit down with them and try to help sort out their problems. But the staff and inmates at Grendon were a pretty dedicated bunch.

The trouble for the hard-liners was that very early on in its life some important people started to notice that Grendon was working and became interested. In 1963 a Dr Snell presented the first paper on Grendon to the Medico-Legal Society, and in 1970 the first book about the prison – *The Frying Pan* by Tony Parker – was published to much interest and acclaim. The Grendon Experiment was soon being talked about wherever prison campaigners, criminologists, psychologists, therapists, lawyers, judges, penologists, and anyone interested in the rehabilitation of prisoners, gathered. To this day HMP Grendon plays host to groups of visitors from many countries every year. Law students from America, penologists from Russia, psychologists from Japan, criminologists from Australia – it seems everybody wants to come and study Grendon. So, as Grendon became known worldwide, the British prison system was lumbered with it – a unique prison that actually did the job that every other prison was supposed to do but couldn't. How bad did that make the rest of our system look? The answer to that question is – pretty bad. You might suppose that the most logical solution to this dilemma would be to go with the model that has been proven to work. To look at the majority of prisons, with their harsh inhumane regimes and their incredibly high rates of violent incidents and reconviction, and then look at Grendon, with the exact opposite, and ask yourself: which is better for society as a whole? Do we want more criminals or fewer? More victims or fewer? It's obvious, isn't it? Well, apparently not to those who make prison policy in Britain. It took four decades for the Home Office finally to decide to use what they had witnessed at Grendon in the rest of the system, and even today the process has only just started.

Obviously no prison can be perfect. In 1982 Grendon had its first escape: an A-wing man who was the store's red-band (trusty) scaled the wall and was at large for five days. And then in 2002, the year before I arrived, Grendon suffered its worst catastrophe: three prisoners from D-wing, two lifers and a determinate (with a fixed release date), cut their way through the fence on the sports field during an exercise period and escaped. They were all recaptured within eighteen hours, but a multiple breakout from a category B prison is about as serious as it can get. Those who had been waiting for Grendon to fail had their patience rewarded. This was the perfect opportunity for the hard-liners to drag this prison, which had been embarrassing them for nearly forty years, back into the fold. Within a few short months of the escape, only the second in Grendon's history, a new governor, who would change the fabric, regime and part of the ethos of Grendon during his tenure, was installed. It was my misfortune to be at Grendon as most of the things that had made the prison work since its inception were systematically dismantled.

The week the new governor arrived, Grendon was ripped apart in the most destructive search the jail had ever seen. Staff were told to remove every piece of 'unauthorized' furniture from the cells, search every inch of the prison for contraband, and send a message to the prisoners that things were going to change from then on. After locking all the inmates in their community rooms, they set to work. When I arrived at Grendon, 'the Big Search', as it has become known, was still being talked about by staff and prisoners who witnessed it.

At Grendon inmates had been allowed to decorate and customize their own cells by painting, putting down scraps of carpet and rugs bought cheaply from catalogues. Some men were skilled in woodwork and would make their own cell furnishings – wooden tables, chairs, chess boards, pelmets for their curtains and shelves – out of scrap wood. During the search all of these things were deliberately ripped from the cells and smashed. Under the guise of 'security' the wings were stripped of everything that made daily life in Grendon that bit different from other prisons. On each landing there was a decorative tile with the landing's number embossed on the surface which had been in place since the prison was built, but some bright security screw took a crowbar to these tiles and smashed them out 'just in case anything was hidden behind them'. So much furniture was broken and so many belongings ruined that the prison had to pay for ten industrial skips to remove the wreckage over the next several weeks. Many old hands, both prisoners and staff, believe that it was after the Big Search that the life started to go out of Grendon, that it started on a downhill slope that could only end in disaster.

Over the next four years the wall came down and dozens of security fences went up, dividing what was once an open-plan prison with a feeling of freedom into a series of gated cages. Prisoners no longer had free access inside the main buildings either. Whereas before you could just ask and be let off your wing to visit other wings or go to the library or education, now prisoners were not allowed to leave the wing without permission from 'control'. Everybody had to carry photo ID cards and, if they were not prominently displayed, you could get a nicking. Therapy visits, where prisoners could be escorted to see their families in times of emergency, were cancelled, as was 'The Grendon Roadshow'. The Grendon Roadshow involved a group of prisoners and staff visiting other prisons for a day and explaining what went on inside Grendon and having a Q&A session. These roadshows helped to recruit many men to try the Grendon experience. And while the roadshow did make a brief comeback in 2005, it was short-lived.

During the new regime almost the whole governing team were replaced with more hard-line staff, many recruited from young offenders' institutes and Special Security Units in other jails where discipline and tight security were the bywords. The governors who came from youth prisons seemed obsessed with petty rules and wanted to run Grendon as though it were a borstal, and those who came from the units brought an obsession with security. In my five years at Grendon I had many dealings with these men, both as part of my various rep jobs and sometimes on a more personal level whenever I was in trouble for my journalism work. Though they pretended that therapy was still at the forefront of the Grendon ethos, I sincerely believe that most of them didn't give a fuck about it.

When it came right down to it though, the governing team were just civil servants under orders from the Home Office, who seemed to follow the whims of tabloid editors. Or so it appeared to us at the sharp end. As successive New Labour home secretaries jerked their knees and turned prisons and prisoners into a political football that could safely be kicked in any direction that took their fancy and might please the public, Grendon suffered the backlash. The public, or so the headlines would have us believe, didn't want convicted criminals to be treated with respect or compassion. Human rights? How dare we demand such things! They wanted us hanged, right now! And if not hanged, then certainly locked into cells for the rest of our lives with no hope of ever seeing daylight. In this climate of tabloid-whipped punishment frenzy a prison like Grendon, which openly treated convicted criminals with respect and tried to rehabilitate them through the carrot rather than the stick, could be a massive embarrassment for the Home Office. All it needed was the press to point an accusing finger in Grendon's direction, maybe a headline about 'murderers, rapists and robbers' living it up in a 'holiday camp jail', and jobs could easily be lost in the ensuing panic and arse-covering exercise that would inevitably follow – governors' jobs. So the governing team at Grendon tried to make sure that there were no obvious benefits for inmates that the press could point that finger at. In the process they succeeded in dismantling a good part of what had made Grendon work in the first place. Grendon inmates were no longer given any trust or responsibility. For a prison whose uniqueness was based on precisely that trust and responsibility this was a major shift in policy. We were just category B prisoners in a category B prison. The only difference between Grendon and the dozens of other category B prisons was that we were participating in voluntary therapy. But soon even this distinction was to become blurred.

Another thing that had a major impact on Grendon was the spreading of the therapy ethos to other jails, which should have been a positive move, and would have been if handled right. But the government treated it like another Band-Aid they could stick over the festering wounds of a failing prison system. Many of these therapeutic units in other jails were abused by prisoners who saw them as no more than a stepping stone to recategorization, days out and parole. The units were springing up everywhere and those who ran them knew that, in order to survive, they had to be filled with inmates. So the selection process, which had been such a huge part of keeping the Grendon population stable and going in the right direction, became the first casualty in the rush to get bodies on seats. Instead of a prisoner having to sit several interviews, including one with a psychiatrist, and completing an IQ test to ascertain if he was intelligent enough and genuinely committed to benefit from therapy, entrance to these units became as simple as sticking your name down on an application form. Everyone was welcomed with open arms and this meant that manipulators easily slipped in under the radar. A therapeutic community can only really operate if the environment is safe enough for honesty and challenge, and if the majority of the community commit themselves to change; it needs only a hard-core minority to upset the balance and subvert the process. On occasion this happened on various wings at Grendon, usually around illegal drugs. If a couple of the more dominant characters in a community became compromised, then a per-centage of weaker characters would follow, until, pretty soon, there would be safety in numbers and open challenge of the culture would become dangerous – which is exactly how other jails were happy to operate. Luckily, at Grendon, the therapeutic dynamic was so strongly and historic-ally ingrained in the volunteers that it seemed to inspire moral courage in many of the men, and compromise could not go unchallenged for long. The newer therapeutic units had no such history nor a stringent selection process, so they suffered a surfeit of fakers, spoofers and predators, who had no real interest in changing their lives through therapy but only in reefing the system for whatever they could get out of it.

Inevitably, this sudden proliferation of therapeutic units led to a kind of aggressive marketing strategy designed to entice prisoners into therapy, and this was bound to have a knock-on effect on Grendon. In 2001 HMP Dovegate, a privately run category B prison in Staffordshire, opened with space for 200 inmates in its therapeutic units. At that time the number of prisoners who had applied for Grendon and were on the waiting list stood at just under 200, and these men were encouraged to go to Dovegate, which was being touted as the 'new Grendon' and had no waiting list. Most of them took up the offer. If Grendon was to survive then it too would have to lower its strict criteria for acceptance of inmates, and by 2005 this is exactly what had happened. In order to compete with other therapeutic units and keep its numbers up, the Grendon entry process was quietly dumbed-down. Gone were the numerous interviews by professionals, the IQ test, and the six-month drug-free period – getting to Grendon was now as simple as expressing a mild interest. Men began arriving at the prison still under the influence of drugs and carrying them secreted about their person and this was no longer cause for them to be refused entry and returned to the sending establishment. Other men arrived with no interest or inclination for therapy but because they had been told by staff in the sending establishment that Grendon was an easy ride to recategorization and parole. Still more came looking for a safe hideout, men who would be seriously assaulted in other prisons for their crimes or for informing on other inmates or running up debts, and Grendon, with its no-violence rule, gave them sanctuary without the shame of going on to a VP (vulnerable prisoners) wing. Some of these men did eventually become interested in the therapeutic process and engaged in changing their lives while they were at Grendon, but many just played along with the process in public and took whatever advantage they could get from the regime. Inevitably, all this had the effect of diluting the ethos of Grendon, which was keenly felt by me and others, including some staff, who had witnessed first-hand the real work that could be done without these distractions.

HMP Grendon has, since its inception, been a prison dedicated to change – change for the better in the worst and most sickeningly un-attractive characters imaginable – and at the same time the prison itself has been constantly evolving. Since 2002 this evolution has been shaped by interference from outside influences and subversive elements within. Almost everything that made this prison a success story when compared to the other 140-odd jails in Britain is now being eroded and dismantled. Yet it struggles on, a shadow of what it once was, but still clinging to its original brief to rehabilitate through therapy some of the most dangerous and violent criminal predators society has produced. And despite the many changes that were imposed on Grendon during my time there, there always remained a hard-core of inmates, staff and civilian professionals who firmly believed in the power of the therapeutic process to effect change and genuine rehabilitation in men who had previously been judged untreatable lost causes.

I am proud to say that I was one of the men who benefited from the Grendon experiment. I started my journey as a violent, ignorant man, severely damaged by almost three decades of brutality, perpetrated by me and on me, both inside and outside the prison system, and the story of this journey and how it ended is documented in this book. Is there a future for Grendon? That is debatable. But one thing I do know – there is now a future for me, and many others like me, and Grendon has played a huge part in that.

1. Getting There

HMP Whitemoor
A-wing, Red spur
6 July 2003

HMP Whitemoor is a top-security dispersal jail that holds some of the most dangerous and notorious prisoners in Britain. Murderers, terrorists, robbers, drug barons, rapists and cut-throats of every hue and creed have stalked its unhallowed halls. Though it is the newest of the dispersal prisons, its electronic gates having opened for the first van-load of desperate convicts in 1991, the jail has a reputation for prisoner violence that is unsurpassed in the British prison system. Its short but bloody history is littered with deaths, maimings and serious 'unrest' (which is official-speak for rioting). In its first year of operation there were several mini-riots, the first one being over the use of CCTV cameras in the visiting hall. In 1992 a notorious child-killer, whom the press had nick-named 'Catweazle', was murdered by fellow prisoners, choked to death in his cell. In 1994 five IRA prisoners and a well-known London robber escaped from the so-called 'escape-proof' Special Security Unit, shooting two prison officers in the process. In 1996 two prisoners stormed the central control centre on D-wing and assaulted several prison officers. They caused thousands of pounds of damage to computers and alarm systems during the eight-hour siege that followed. In 1997 a prisoner, already serving life for murder, retired two prison officers by throwing a pot of boiling fat over them. Add to this the almost daily round of prisoner-on-prisoner stabbings, coshings and beatings, and you can hand-on-heart say that HMP Whitemoor was not a place for the faint-hearted.

By the time I reached Whitemoor, on 4 July 2000, it had quietened down a bit. Many of the prisoners were of a more mature nature and all were serving very long sentences. The average on A-wing was twenty-five years, and most of us were serious and persistent violent offenders who had terrible prison records but were now content to just get on with our bit of bird with minimum fuss. That's not to say that the prison had become a retirement home for old cons, far from it. Except at this time the stabbings and coshings were more for special occasions rather than daily events.

In July 2003 I was just over four years into a life sentence. I had received my 'L plates' (con-speak for a life sentence) not for murder, but for eight counts of bank robbery. The sentence had been automatic as I had fallen foul of the Crime (Sentences) Act 1997, or the 'two-strike Act' as it became known, which meant a life sentence for anyone convicted of a second violent offence. I couldn't really complain as I had a history of violent offences dating back to 1975. Though it did rankle that I had actually been sentenced on my past record, for which I had already served my time once, rather than my present crimes. I had been expecting the judge to throw the book at me. After all, I was a prolific robber who had committed my crimes while on parole from a previous nineteen-year sentence imposed for almost identical offences, but I had been expecting something more along the lines of a Reader's Digest Condensed Book, not the complete set of *Encyclopaedia Britannica*. Still, as an old fence of mine used to say, 'You've got to take the shit with the cream' – and I'd certainly had the cream.

My record, both in and out of prison, is pretty bad. I have fifty-eight previous criminal convictions for armed robbery, possession of firearms, GBH, prison escape, theft, burglary, fraud and deception, car theft, criminal damage and possession of offensive weapons. I started my criminal career at the age of fourteen, and I was then forty-two. My disciplinary record while serving my sentences also left a lot to be desired. I had been done for causing gross personal violence to prison officers, escape, attempted escape, inciting others to riot, assault, being in possession of unauthorized articles and weapons. It would be fair to say that I was not a well-balanced individual. I had become entrenched in a cycle of crime and imprisonment.

Whitemoor was easy for me. The screws rarely gave me any trouble and, due to my previous prison sentences and past deeds, I was one of the boys, a 'face'. I spent three years just marking time. I no longer involved myself in prison politics, and as I was not a drug user I had no need to get involved in all the bollocks that goes along with that culture. A lot of the violence that occurs in prison is over heroin: either people get themselves into debt and have to be given a beating or a slashing, or dealers fall out with each other and violence is the result of the ensuing power struggle. I have never used heroin, and everyone knew my views on it. I believe heroin did, in less than a decade, what the prison system couldn't do in 150 years: it destroyed the solidarity among prisoners.

Many of my friends in prison are heroin users. I don't judge them for it; they made their choice and they live with it. Some of them I would trust with my life. But I wouldn't trust a single one of them around a bag of tackle.

In con-speak 'having it' means being in someone's company. The people I was having it with in Whitemoor were some of the most infamous prisoners in the system. Men whose crimes and deeds are legendary behind the high walls and razor-wire fences of the British penal system. You have to bear in mind that prison is a completely different world from that in which the straight-goer lives. We have our own language, customs and history. You may remember the year 1987 for the massive storms that swept the country, or for the horrific fire that claimed so many innocent lives at King's Cross tube station, but in prison history it is remembered as the year that Andy Russell landed a hijacked helicopter on the yard at Gartree top-security prison and flew off with Johnny Kendall and Sid Draper. Perhaps, for you, the abiding memories of 1989 are the fall of the Berlin Wall and the collapse of Communism, but for the denizens of prison it was the fire-bomb exploding in the TV room on A-wing at HMP Albany, causing major damage and almost burning sixty prisoners to death in their cells. Different worlds, different history.

So, though the majority of the straight-going world may not have heard the names or legends of men such as John 'Shotgun' Shelley, Greg 'Houdini' Crabtree, Vinnie Bradish, Johnny Kendall, Frannie Pope, Charlie Tozer or Staggsy, in the world of prison they are faces. And these, and a few others, were the people I was having it with at Whitemoor. On the whole we were all experienced career criminals who had spent many years making our presence felt, both in and out of prison. In our world there were rules that had to be followed and a code that had to be adhered to. We would not suffer a grass or a nonce to live on the same spur as us, and if one were to slip on undercover, and be found out, he would be 'tea-bagged' (left with many perforations) in short order. If the screws tried taking too many liberties they knew we would fight back, either all-out physically or in a war of attrition.

I had lived in this world and followed the code for nearly three decades. But now I was about to take a step that would radically alter my life and make me question and eventually abandon all that I had held as truth. The seed of my search for change had started to germinate during my last period of freedom – 5 August 1997 to 7 August 1998. Though I had been hard at it in my chosen criminal profession of armed robbery, I began to have doubts about my lifestyle. I loved being a criminal, it was a buzz being out there on the sharp end, gun in hand, masked and taking the prize. But suddenly robbing banks was no longer the great game I had once thought it. This feeling didn't arrive full-blown, but crept up on me insidiously when I wasn't looking. I was waking up on the morning of a planned robbery feeling anxious and edgy, whereas, in the past, I would have been jumping out of bed with excitement and anticipation. We always referred to our criminal activities as 'work', and that's exactly what it was starting to become for me – a dead-end job. And when you are putting your life and liberty on offer every time you punch in, these kinds of feelings are not good. Robbing banks calls for 100 per cent concentration.

When I was finally arrested in a Flying Squad ambush I guessed that my life might effectively be over and that I should have listened to those nagging doubts. On 24 July 1999 in Court 2 at the Old Bailey, I was sentenced to eight life sentences, plus eighty years concurrent. My tariff was a minimum of eleven years to serve. Three years later my minimum was reduced to eight years by the Court of Appeal. I had always abided by the old adage 'If you can't do the time then don't do the crime', so I took it on the chin. What other choice did I have? I spent the first two years at HMP Belmarsh as a category A prisoner. And then, once I was downgraded to category B, I was shipped to HMP Whitemoor – a category A prison!

It was while I was at Whitemoor that I received the most devastating news of my life. On 24 October 2001 my youngest son, Joe, was found dead in suspicious circumstances. He was nineteen years old. For a long time I was in free fall, my emotions ranging from grief and black despair to rage and even temporary madness. Joe's death had a profound effect on me. The security governor at Whitemoor refused me permission to attend my son's funeral. I was told that he could not 'risk' the safety of his staff to escort me outside the prison. Ironically though, he allowed me to go to the Chapel of Rest – double-cuffed, with a four-screw escort and shadowed by the police. I found out later I was allowed that only because it was the minimum required by law. In the aftermath of Joe's death I thought a lot about my own wasted life. Uncomfortably, I began to recognize the victims I had left in my destructive wake. Not least of which were my children. It was time for me to grow up. Six months after my beautiful son was laid to rest I applied for Grendon.

HMP Grendon, set in the gently rolling landscape of Buckinghamshire, is unique among the 149 prisons in Britain. Its regime is therapy-based, and it has the lowest reconviction rate of any British prison. Opened in 1962, Grendon sprang from an experiment in 'democratic living' called Q Camp. In 1936 Q Camp in Essex opened for a small group of male offenders aged between sixteen and twenty-five, who had moderate behavioural problems. The camp aimed to study and treat their anti-social behaviour using a range of techniques, including psychotherapy. Each member of the camp had a role in its government. Q Camp closed in 1940, but this idea of shared responsibility is still a major feature of the community at Grendon today.

I read all the official bumf on Grendon that I could get my hands on, but I also sought the unofficial skinny on the place from men who had been there. Before I committed myself to such a life-altering step I wanted to be sure I was doing the right thing. I remembered I had first heard of Grendon while serving my previous sentence. My brother-in-law, Tony, a mandatory lifer who has now served over eighteen years for murder, had told me of his experiences at Grendon. Tony had been there three times, failing each time, and his views on the gaff were mixed. He said the regime was more relaxed than at other jails, and that the therapy was easy, but the real test was in having to mix with 'wrong-uns': kiddy-fiddlers, granny-bashers and blatant grasses. This information was of no help to me as what I really wanted to know was whether the place actually worked or not. Judging by Tony's continued unrepentant incarceration, it would seem the answer to that question was a resounding no.

On my spur at Whitemoor was a well-known villain, whom I shall call 'Giggsy', who, it was rumoured, had spent some time at Grendon. Over a cup of sticky he told me his views. In his opinion Grendon was definitely the place to aim for if I genuinely wanted to change my life. He told me that though on the surface Grendon might appear as a 'doss' (con-speak for something easy), it was actually the hardest bit of bird he had ever done. The reason he had failed to capitalize on his time at Grendon was because he was a heroin addict who was still too much in love with the brown powder to give it up. At Grendon there are three strict rules: no drugs, no violence, no sex. I was pleased with what Giggsy had to tell me, and the rules did not bother me. I had given up smoking cannabis three years before, I was mature enough to no longer feel the need to express myself through violence, and, unless some of the prisoners were nubile young females, I was definitely off sex for the duration of my sentence.

I filled in the initial application form with a feeling of decisive optimism. The truth was that I believed I was already rehabilitated. I had made the decision to put my long life of crime and punishment behind me. Grendon would be a consolidation of this decision, and a tangible piece of evidence to offer to the system as proof of my intention. The hardest part of Grendon for me, I believed, would be having to mix with the kind of men I had spent the most part of my previous incarcerations hunting down and trying to kill. I would have to swallow my ingrained disgust and revulsion and keep my mind focused on my own addictions rather than other people's.

The road to Grendon was long and mined with all sorts of tests and interviews. First I had to see a psychiatrist. The psychiatrist was a caricature of how I imagined someone of his profession to be. He was mostly bald, but with tufts of white hair over his ears, and wore small, round glasses. His dark, three-piece pinstripe suit looked to be *circa* 1930, and he even had a gold chain looping from the fob-pocket of his tightly buttoned waistcoat. When he spoke I somehow expected to hear a trace of an Austrian accent, and I was slightly disappointed when I recognized the flat vowels of Birmingham. More Black Country than Black Forest. He looked at my breeze-block-thick prison file and hmphed a lot before asking me if I had ever wet the bed. It was not a question I had been expecting, but I gave it some thought before answering. 'I assume that I must have done when I was a baby. But the only time I can remember doing it was after a particularly bad three-day bender, which ended with me knocking back a litre of Fine Fare gin.'

He hmphed again and scribbled something in my file. 'Why do you want to go to Grendon?' he asked. 'Is it to deal with your alcoholism?' I sighed. I could spend half an hour explaining that I was not an alcoholic as such, just a geezer who sometimes liked to push the boundaries a bit. But I thought, Fuck it, I wanted to get back to the wing, I was cooking a spaghetti bolognese for my food-boat and I needed to book space on the wing cooker. So I nodded. He seemed satisfied. He scribbled in my file again, then closed it. 'Send the next one in, please,' he said, without looking up.

My next interview was with a trainee psychologist. She was quite an attractive woman in her mid-twenties, with long chestnut hair and luminous green eyes. I sat in the chair across from her and waited. Her first question was about my alcoholism. I was quite enjoying looking at her and I had no other pressing engagements, so I explained that I was not an alcoholic, and the main reason I wanted to go to Grendon was to deal with issues surrounding my offending behaviour. She was very interested in what had happened to all the money I had stolen during my life of crime, and seemed inordinately disappointed when I told her it was all spent. She brightened up somewhat when I told her about my son's death as the reason for my change of heart about crime and prison. 'That's something we can get our teeth into,' she said, almost gleefully. Suddenly I didn't find her quite so attractive. I endured the rest of the interview with gritted teeth.

My next step was an interview with my 'personal officer'. The personal officer scheme was brought in so that the prison system could save a few quid by not employing welfare officers as a separate job. In the old days prisoners would go to the welfare officer if they had family, or other, problems. Prisoners' welfare was a full-time job, and, on the whole, the WO did a very good job, sorting out extra visits, phone calls, letters and counselling prisoners in times of family illness and bereavement. You were always guaranteed a kindly face and a sympathetic ear from the WO. So the prison system scrapped it, and gave each landing screw the responsibility instead. This meant that the same person who was screaming abuse and rushing to lock you in your cell every day, would be the person you would have to approach if you had a personal problem.

In my three years at Whitemoor I'd had nine personal officers. Some good, some bad, some indifferent. They had a pretty easy job with me as I would rather eat my own feet than go to a screw with my personal problems. But in order to get my move to Grendon I would now have to approach my latest PO. He was a tattooed, gum-chewing, barely literate son of Yorkshire, complete with sloping brow and a half-sovereign ring. I had once witnessed him sneeringly question a fellow screw's sexuality because he happened to be reading a copy of the *Guardian*. I approached him in a no-nonsense manner and told him he would have to interview me and write a report for Grendon. I could see he wasn't too pleased, (a) because he would have to do some writing, and (b) because he could tell by my face that I wouldn't tolerate any of the disparaging comments that came limping into his brain in response to my statement. I knew that if I had been 4 inches shorter and 5 stone lighter, and without a track record for throwing digs at screws, he would have ripped the piss out of me unmercifully. Sometimes, being a bad-un has its perks.

Next on my agenda was getting a mandatory drug test to prove that I was drug-free. This was not as easy as you might think. In 1995 the prison system introduced the Mandatory Drug Testing scheme, 'in order to combat the drug problem in our prisons, and identify those prisoners with drug problems'. Fair enough, I suppose, but, like every other weapon in the system's arsenal, they couldn't help but abuse it. In the first two years after the introduction of MDT, over 70 per cent of the prison population had been tested, and 41 per cent had proved positive for drugs. At first the prison system was delighted that they had managed to catch, and prosecute by means of Governor's Adjudication, so many obvious drug users. But their delight turned a bit sour when they realized the implications of this. Those in high places began to wonder how so many prisoners were able to smuggle in, and use, so many drugs right under the supposedly vigilant gaze of prison officers. And there was the expense of it all; each test cost between £90 and £120 to process, depending on which part of the country the prison was in. Each Governor's Adjudication was resulting in an average of twenty-one days being added to the sentence of everyone who tested positive, which meant they had to be kept in an already overcrowded and expensive prison system for longer. And now more money would have to be spent on security budgets in order to combat the problems highlighted by MDTs. The upshot of all this was that every year since 1997 the number of MDTs has been tailing off, purely due to cost.

At Whitemoor I had one MDT in my first two and a half years. They seemed to target only those suspected of heroin use. Now I had to ask for a test as tangible proof that I was drug-free. Typically, when I requested an MDT, I was viewed with outright suspicion. Their logic was that if I was asking for a test it must be because I was planning a drug binge in the near future and I wanted to take my test now while I was drug-free! Sometimes I think the worst thing about the prison system, worse even than the brutality and the stupidity, is the paranoid propensity to see plots and schemes in every word and move a prisoner speaks and makes.

After a couple of months of constant applications for an MDT, without success, I decided to play them at their own game. One morning I rubbed a little bit of soap into both my eyes and left it in for five minutes. When I washed the soap out, my eyes were as red as Little Red Riding Hood's socks. I went up to the wing office and began mumbling, stuttering, scratching and acting irrationally. Within an hour two screws came to my cell and told me that my name had been randomly selected for a mandatory drug test. Once again the system had forced me into using subterfuge in order to get something done. I sometimes wonder if the system is actually designed to perpetuate our criminal mindset, thus keeping them in business. Or is that just my prison-induced paranoia kicking in?

My final interview was with the prison probation officer. Even though I was a lifer and it was essential that I forge close links with the Probation Service, as they would have to make reports for my eventual release and supervise me, on licence, for the rest of my natural life, I had spoken to only one probation officer in the previous five years; and that was a twenty-minute post-sentence interview. I was registered as a born-again atheist, but I had seen more of the chaplaincy than I had of the Probation Service. The trouble lay in the fact that following the introduction of the two-strike Act in October 1997, the lifer population in British prisons leapt from 1,800 to just under 6,000 by 2003. Every single one of those lifers, with the exception of those who die in prison, will have to have reports written on them and be supervised for life, and the Probation Service just do not have the staff or resources to carry out the job. If you are reading this on a weekday, chances are that somewhere in this country another five men and women are being sentenced to life imprisonment. Britain has the largest population of lifers in the Western world, with the exception of the USA, from whom we take our lead in matters of incarceration and punishment. So getting an interview with a real, live probation officer was a bit of an exciting prospect. This was what my life had been reduced to.

The female probation officer was very nice and understanding, and supportive of my application. We spoke at length about my attitude towards my offences, why I had committed them, and what I now hoped to achieve by going to Grendon. I came away from the interview feeling, for the first time, that I was really making some progress. Within three days I was handed a copy of the probation officer's report: it was excellent. She recommended that I should be offered a place at Grendon.

My final hurdle was the IQ test. The IQ test was to establish whether or not I was bright enough to be able to understand the therapeutic regime

I was committing myself to. It seemed a bit muggy to have this test last, as surely it would have made more sense to take it first before going through all the other interviews and reports? What would now happen if the test said I was too stupid? I was about to find out.

The IQ test, administered by a different trainee psychologist, was called the Ravens Test, named, I assumed, after the person who invented it rather than the large, black birds. I was handed a book of 100 puzzles; each one involved identifying certain shapes and where they would fit in the overall picture. The trainee sat there and timed me as I attempted to match the various shapes with their rightful spot on the pattern. After about twenty pages I grew bored with it, and my mind began to wander. After forty pages I just wanted to finish it, so guessed the rest, figuring that the law of averages would allow me to get enough right. I handed back the hastily completed test and was told that they would get back to me with the results within 'a few days'.

It was now thirteen months since I had made my initial application to be considered for Grendon. Sometimes it seems as though the prison system is a machine with only two gears – dead slow and stop – but I was fairly optimistic that I would get my move eventually. In the meantime, life went on at what passes for normal in a top-security prison. There were a couple of particularly bad stabbings which led to the whole prison being put on lock-down. Both the incidents happened on the spur of the wing that I was living on. One was pretty straightforward, in prison terms. A nasty piece of work had moved in four cells away from mine, but was quickly found out. He was serving ten years for a particularly brutal attack on an old woman, in which she was raped and battered with a table leg. This excuse-for-a-man was soon identified as a nonce, and a contract was put on his head. As I've explained, the residents of A-wing's Red spur were mostly men who had done plenty of bird and had done more than their share of 'wet-work' over the years, but there were also a handful of young bloods on the spur who were always looking for a chance to enhance their own reputations. The contract was taken up by two of these youngsters, but, lacking experience, they got a bit carried away and very nearly ended up on a murder charge.

After the granny-basher had been rushed to an outside hospital, the lock-down and police investigation began. Having spent many years as a resident on top-security prison wings, and having dished out a good few nonce-beatings myself, I was very blasé about the whole incident. But when my door was unlocked for the evening meal, which was being delivered by four screws as nobody was allowed to leave their cell until the investigation was completed, one of the screws made a comment that made me think. As he handed me my pre-packed meal he was talking to one of the other screws about the incident: '. . . he's in a bad way, might even be dead by morning'. I knew that letting me overhear this conversation was a standard ploy by which they hoped to elicit a response from me that they might be able to use as evidence. I said nothing, but as I took my meal I smiled. The screw shook his head in disgust. 'You won't be smiling if you get to Grendon,' he said. 'Nonces rule the roost there. See how you like being in the minority.' Then he slammed the cell door shut.

I thought a lot about what the screw had said. I hated sex offenders; they made my skin crawl, and I had spent large portions of my previous sentences hunting them down. I had even gone so far as joining a secret society within prison, called DAAGAN (Direct Action Against Grasses And Nonces). DAAGAN was just a collection of like-minded ODCs (ordinary decent criminals) who made it their business to give wrong-uns a little taste of what their victims had suffered. Of course, we never for one moment considered what our own victims had suffered. Founded in Albany prison on the Isle of Wight in 1995, DAAGAN quickly spread to other jails, as members 'ghosted' on suspicion of administering beatings and setting fire to cells began recruiting. DAAGAN was a short-lived phenomenon as hard-core members had to spend months in punishment blocks when they were found out. By the time I came back to prison on my life sentence, DAAGAN was finished.

Now I had to wonder if I really would be able to live on the same landing as nonces and wrong-uns, listen to their stories and excuses, and treat them as though they were 'normal' people. It's difficult to explain just how hard this was going to be for me. I would be breaking the unwritten code that I had lived my life by and pissing on all that I believed in. It would be a massive step for me, and I wrestled with it for weeks. I had known when I first applied for Grendon that I would have to live with these people, as enough of my friends had pointed it out whenever I broached the subject of my application, but now I had actually made the move it all began to seem real. After much mental struggle I decided that I had to go through with it, not only for myself but for my family. All these years, nearly three decades, I had done the selfish thing and taken my family for granted. I couldn't count the number of times I had sat in prison visiting halls and told my mother, father, sister, brother, wife and children that I had learned my lesson and this would be the last time. I never meant it; I just said it to keep them happy. I loved the thrill of crime too much to give it up. This time it was different, but like the boy who cried wolf, it would take more than a few words to make people believe me. I would have to place my head in the wolf's jaws.

When I finally arrived at this momentous decision it was almost rendered academic by my results from the Ravens IQ test. The psychology department informed me that my test had proved that I was 'of below average intelligence'. This meant that I would not be acceptable to Grendon. I was gutted. I had always considered myself as smarter than the average bear, and here was evidence that I was no more than a run-of-the-mill div. I had an A level in law, an honours diploma from the London School of Journalism, I had won four Koestler Awards for my writing, and written articles for magazines and broadsheets, and yet I had come unstuck with a book of shape puzzles. The more I thought about it, the more pissed off I got. I demanded to see someone from the psychology department. After a week of arguing my case, it was decided that I could take a different test. This time I would keep my mind on the job.

A week later I was informed that the new test put me just above average intelligence, and I was now on the waiting list for HMP Grendon. I breathed a sigh of relief. That morning the two youngsters who had almost killed the granny-basher were both sentenced to life imprisonment for it. One of them was my brother-in-law, Jimmy Hogan. He had been serving eight years, and now he would be lucky if he didn't spend the next fifteen years in prison. What a waste. I took it as a sign I was doing the right thing.

The whole process of applying for Grendon had taken fifteen months. On 6 July 2003 I was called to the wing office and informed that I was being transferred to Grendon the next morning. I went back to my cell and packed my belongings. I was on the verge of taking a step that might alter my entire future. Was I looking forward to it? Sort of.

2. Second Thoughts

On the morning of 7 July 2003 I climbed aboard a sweatbox and waved goodbye to HMP Whitemoor through the darkly tinted window. I had received the traditional 'dispersal cheer' as I had left Red Spur, prisoners on the landings shouting funny comments and advice as I was escorted off the wing by two screws. Part of me was gutted to be leaving this life behind me. It had certainly had its moments over the years, and there was also something comforting about belonging in such a hard and macho environment. I was heading into what was uncharted territory for a con with my pedigree. And I couldn't help but feel a tingle of trepidation.

The journey was about as uncomfortable as any other journey I'd taken in a sweatbox since 1975. These vehicles are designed for security and not comfort, and you can feel the truth of this with every crack and bump in the road as it vibrates through you. Imagine, if you can, being locked into a steel cell, seven feet high and three feet wide, with a moulded plastic seat and one twelve-inch tinted Perspex window through which the world seems to be in perpetual twilight. You cannot stretch your arms out, nor can you stand up when the vehicle is moving. There are no hand holds, so when the vehicle brakes or goes around bends and corners you are bounced off the smooth cold walls. In the summer these cells are swelteringly hot – hence the nickname 'sweatbox' – but in winter they are colder than a High Court judge's heart. Some journeys in this nightmare on wheels can take up to eight hours, depending on which prison you are being transferred to. But I was lucky, the driver made the journey from Cambridgeshire to Buckinghamshire in only an hour and a half.

My first sight of Grendon was the big white perimeter wall that sur-rounded the prison. The wall was high, but it didn't look unbeatable for a man with my escape experience. Of course, I had no intention of attempting an escape. I had escaped and attempted to escape many times on previous sentences and it had brought me nothing but grief. But there was still an ember of a freedom-loving spirit somewhere deep inside me that made me weigh up every prison I entered for opportunities, rather like an old boxer who cannot help but judge each jaw he meets for the susceptibility of a right hook. Purely academic.

The reception area was small and brightly painted, and had the most relaxed atmosphere I've ever encountered in a prison. The norm for a prison reception area is hustle and bustle, harassed screws and anxious prisoners. In the reception area of local prisons such as Belmarsh or Brixton an average weekday can see up to 150 prisoners passing in and out. The reception area was usually the epitome of organized chaos and noisier than the M25 on a Bank Holiday Friday. But at Grendon you could have heard a jaw drop.

I was greeted with a warm 'Hello, there' by the first screw I saw on arrival. I had come a long way since my reception at Send Detention Centre in 1975, when my greeting on stepping from the van had been a punch in the face. 'If you could just wait in here for a while until we've unloaded your property from the van. And then we'll get you processed.' I was shown into a pastel-shaded room, with soft chairs and a small coffee table covered in magazines.

Sitting there reading a copy of *Country Life*, the burglar's bible, was another prisoner. I knew he was a prisoner by the shifty look in his eyes and the fact that he was wearing a 'Spiderman suit', which is what prisoners call the moody acrylic, blue and red tracksuits issued by the system for those who choose not to wear their own clothes. This was my first test. As far as I knew, this fella could be a right nonce. He certainly had the look of a kiddy-fiddler, like an oil slick in human form. I sat in one of the chairs and looked at him. It was very quiet in the room. I had to make a move here. 'Been here long, mate?' I asked. He closed his magazine and looked at me with watery blue eyes. 'Amph twen mensute,' he said. An alarm bell began to ring very loudly in my head.

All the gossip I had heard about Grendon flashed through my mind: it's full of nutters, dangerous psychotics who will open you up like a tin of beans, bad nonces who've spent years on the numbers buggering each other, monsters of every description. The paranoia was taking over as I stared at the man before me, wondering which of those categories he belonged in. He leaned forward in his seat, glanced around the room suspiciously and said, 'Ith geen gof gi medjiction gor tix mongs gow!' I didn't know whether to clump him or not. I gave him the benefit of the old slow-burn, which, along with my 17-stone frame and bad reputation, was usually enough of a warning for anyone. But this bloke seemed oblivious. He actually smiled at me, showing a mouthful of teeth that looked like Sugar Puffs.

I was aware that the prisoners at Grendon were going to be different from those I had known in the dispersal system, but I never for one minute thought they would speak a different language. I was gutted. I had been in the nick only five minutes and already my worst fears had been confirmed. I suddenly realized what I had let myself in for. If this man was the kind of prisoner I would be expected to mix with, then my stay here would be a short one. What I didn't realize that day was that I still had plenty of that strange inverted snobbery that professional prisoners carry about with them.

This geezer looked strange and he spoke funny, therefore he must be a bad wrong-un. This is how we judged people in the world I had lived in. We were worse than the screws for categorizing people on the slightest evidence. I had once been in an exercise cage in Wandsworth punishment block, speaking through the wire-mesh wall to a legendary London robber who was exercising in the next cage, when the block screws escorted another prisoner past us and into a cage further along. 'Fucking nonce!' my companion spat. I was curious. 'What's he in for?' I asked. My companion shrugged. 'Fuck knows,' he said. 'Well, how do you know he's a nonce, then?' I asked, genuinely interested. 'Well,' said my pal, 'look at the fucking glasses he was wearing. Proper fucking bacon bins!' I nodded, and accepted his logic. And that's how people are judged in jail.

Back in the waiting room at Grendon I was wondering what I should do next, when the door was opened and a screw beckoned to my strange unintelligible companion. The bloke stood up, still flashing his rotten railings in my direction, and with a little nod ambled off to be processed. I was relieved that he had gone. This was becoming all too strange for me. I knew that my years in jail had made me institutionalized. I felt uncomfortable when my routine was interrupted, and I now craved the familiarity of Whitemoor. How sad was that? I hadn't even made it off reception yet, and already I was missing the confines of my top-security cell. I picked up a magazine from the table in front of me, but I couldn't focus, my mind was reeling.

In the system I had few real worries, I knew the rules, the dodges and the scams. I knew who everyone was, and everyone knew me. My biggest challenge was whether to have an ounce bet on the inter-wing football match every Sunday morning. I had spent almost three decades reaching this comfort level, wading through hip-deep shit and blood to get there. I had done my share of time in punishment blocks, nursing my physical and mental injuries, and feeding my bitterness and hate. And I had reached the stage where conventional jail time was a doss for me. Now I was getting the feeling that things were going to get tough again.

In the system the lines are clearly drawn and everything is black and white. Everyone knows what side they're on, there's no blurring. If someone is a wrong-un, or takes a liberty with me or mine, they can expect a clump, or worse. Divs and hobbits knew to keep their distance, and if they needed a reminder then a look or a growl would be enough. There is a definite pecking order, and everyone knows their place in it. In the system I chose the people I would have it with, and they were the types I felt most comfortable with: professional criminals, robbers and a handful of murderers. Men who were staunch, loyal and game, the qualities that are prized above all others in the twilight world of the career criminal. And now, here I was in Grendon, with its nicey-nice reception screws, pastel-coloured waiting room, and a Stig-of-the-Dump lookalike who spoke in tongues and was probably an example of the men I would be living alongside. What the fuck had I volunteered for?

I waited for another twenty minutes, pacing and thinking. I believed I was a mature and reasonable man. Maybe I was a bit off-key and out of synch with most of the world, but that was a dot on the cards after the kind of life I'd led. I reminded myself that this was my reason for coming to Grendon in the first place. I had never refused a challenge, and this was going to be the biggest one I'd ever faced. I was here to change my ways; I had to keep an open mind.

In a while a screw came and led me out to the reception desk. There was a radio playing softly in the background and the whole atmosphere was one of unhurried indifference. The two screws who were running reception had the uniforms and key-chains of normal system screws, but there was something different about them. It took me a moment to realize what it was: their faces were open, they didn't have the pinched and paranoid look, or the spiteful eyes, of the system screws. The one who was filling in my reception record smiled at me, a novelty in itself, and said, 'Sorry for taking so long to get you out here, Noel. We're a bit snowed under today.' I looked closely to see if he was taking the piss. He wasn't. I was a bit uncomfortable with his use of my first name, but I let it pass. I was used to being addressed as 'Smith, 872' by the authorities, and 'Razor' by my family and friends.

The normal practice in reception is to let you pass through into the prison itself with as little as possible by way of in-possession property. It's almost like a game for most reception screws. Things that you had in possession in previous establishments, with no concern whatsoever, suddenly take on sinister connotations when you move prisons. It has become one more way in which the screws, and the security department in particular, can keep prisoners off balance. Being an old hand, I knew about this, so, before leaving Whitemoor, I bagged up a lot of my property and allowed it to be sent off to the prisoner's property storage depot at Branston. Now I was wishing I hadn't. The reception screws were not interested in confiscating any of my property, or trying to provoke an argument over any item. This really was a new experience.

There was no humiliating strip-search, no barked orders and no sarcastic comments about my inch-thick disciplinary file. I started to relax a bit. The officers were chatting away, and I was even allowed to smoke while I waited for them to fill in my paperwork. 'Ever assaulted a prison officer, Noel?' I was asked, but the tone was neutral. It was a standard reception question. I nodded. 'Yeah,' I said, my own voice neutral. 'A few times. But not lately. I'm getting a bit too old for all that.' The officer nodded and ticked the box on the form.

There was no sign of the inarticulate lump I had shared the waiting room with, so I decided to enquire about him. It was a worry to me that he might be typical of the Grendon con. 'Er, that other geezer I was in the waiting room with, he all right, is he?' A look passed between the officers. 'Bit of a sad case,' one said. 'He's stone deaf, so it makes it very hard to understand what he's saying.' It all clicked into place. His strange, guttural words, the way he stared at my face, probably in order to read my lips. I felt relieved, but I also felt a twinge of guilt. I had done it again: judged someone on appearance, without stopping to look further. It was something I would have to watch, especially here.

When I, and my property, had been processed, and my photo taken, I was ready to be escorted to the induction wing. I had two, blue, standard-size prison property boxes with my kit, and in most jails I would have had to struggle along behind a screw. But this was Grendon. One of the reception staff got on the blower to F-wing, the induction wing, and asked for a couple of inmate volunteers to come and help carry my boxes!

Within five minutes a female officer and two big inmates strolled into the reception area. I studied the prisoners, looking for some sign that they might be sex offenders. One was a stocky Geordie, with a horrific scar down his face starting at the tip of his left eyebrow and ending at the corner of his mouth. He introduced himself as 'John'. The other was a stocky, shaven-headed Londoner, and his name was Andy. After the introductions and a bit of hand-shaking, they each picked up one of my boxes and we headed for F-wing.

On the short walk from reception to F-wing, I studied everything. The grass verges were neat and well maintained, as were the myriad flowerbeds. There was none of the detritus that is normal in the grounds of a prison, no rubbish littering the paths, no plastic remains of prison-issue disposable razors, broken open for their blades and then casually dropped out of cell windows, no prison socks or Y-fronts hanging from coils of rusting razor-wire, no shit-parcels, and no scabrous pigeons huddled in piles of their own excrement waiting patiently for the most inedible bits of prison meals to be thrown from windows. Everything was clean, and that, in itself, was a novelty.

The female officer was happy and chatty and sharing a bit of banter with the two lads who carried my luggage. She asked me what prison I had come from, and when I told her she raised an eyebrow. 'Well, I think you'll find this place a pleasant change then.' Outwardly I smiled, but inside my head I was still reserving judgement. The two lads seemed pretty relaxed and had the confidence I would associate with the kind of prisoners who have nothing to hide. If either of them turned out to be a wrong-un I would be very surprised. But, so far today, I didn't exactly have a 100 per cent track record. Inside I was suspicious and mistrustful of everything.

F-wing was the induction and observation wing, and any new transfer to Grendon had to spend time there being assessed for therapy. The usual stay on F-wing was between eight and twelve weeks, but when I arrived Grendon was under pressure from the Home Office because of the much publicized overcrowding in our prisons, and the assessment period was being cut short. I was to become grateful for this Home Office crisis, because, I found out later, without the drive to fill Grendon I might have been waiting another year for my transfer. And also, I might have ended up spending even longer than I did on F-wing, which was a shithole of the highest order.

The first thing I noticed as I walked through the gates of F-wing was a crowd of prisoners hanging about. And every one of them was looking at me. It was obvious that they had known someone was coming from reception. This was more familiar territory for me. In every prison the entry of newcomers is closely observed – for many reasons. Men watch for old friends, old enemies, or those who might be carrying news or messages from the outside or other parts of the prison system. But mostly they watch to judge. How you carry yourself in prison, how you walk and talk, and what you look like enables others to define and pigeonhole you. I knew the steps of this dance and I quickly performed them.

I straightened my back, standing tall and pushing my chin out slightly to show that I had the right to be here. I put a half-scowl on my face to show that I was not intimidated or impressed. I met every gaze, unblinking, and shot the mental message to them, Fuck with me, and you *will* get hurt. Most of them picked up the message straight away, and either looked away or sent the same message back. I noted the couple who didn't look away; they had the look of eagles about them, and I knew they were ex-dispersal prisoners without even knowing anything else about them. I now realized that not all the men at Grendon would be hobbits, and that eased my mind somewhat.

The crowd of prisoners drifted away now that they had seen me and decided my place in the pecking order. I was called into the wing office and told that my cell was upstairs on the 2s landing. I should go and unpack and settle in, and at 5.30 a bell would be rung to summon the community to the dining hall for roll-check and the evening meal. I waited for a moment, expecting to be escorted by a screw, but then realized this was not Belmarsh or Whitemoor and I was free to make my own way about.

The wing itself was pretty manky, with paint peeling from the ceiling and ranks of ugly pipes. At the bottom of the metal staircase was an old ship's bell that I assumed, rightly, was to summon the denizens for meals, roll-checks and group meetings. I didn't like the idea of the bell; it brought back bad memories of HMP Wandsworth, which had a daily routine governed by the ringing of a similar bell. Wandsworth prison, or 'the Hate Factory', as it is known to those who have spent time there, was a sore point for me. I had suffered a terrible beating at the hands of the screws there on a previous sentence.

Up two flights of stairs there were a couple of dimly lit corridors, and

I chose the one directly facing the stairwell. I could hear loud rave music coming from it, and guessed this must be where the cells were. I was right. At the start of the spur there was a large recess, con-speak for bathroom and toilet, with four steel sinks, urinals, three toilet stalls with half-doors and two shower cubicles. It stunk of piss. As I walked further into the spur I passed a couple of cells with the doors wide open. They were smaller than the average prison cell, about three inches longer than the length of the iron bed they contained, and the same again in width. The ceilings were low enough to touch without stretching, and there was a large, square, barred window on the back wall. The cells I passed had been made as comfortable as the situation allowed, with colourful posters on the walls, family photographs and curtains at the windows. I found cell number 20, which I had been informed was to be my own personal kennel for as long as I was on F-wing, and opened the door with the key I had been handed in the wing office.

Giving prisoners their own keys is not a new concept. I had first come across it in Dover borstal in 1977, and it was also a feature of HMP Albany, when I was there in the 1990s. All you actually get is the key to what is known as the 'courtesy lock'. The cell door has two locks: one is a proper security lock that can only be opened by the keys that screws carry, and the courtesy lock, which allows the prisoner to lock his own door against entry by other prisoners. In Grendon the cells are actually locked and unlocked by a computer. Some prisons have had to install this electronic locking system because the cells are too small to fit a toilet and sink inside. Since the ending of the horrendous practice of slopping out in our prisons in the late 1990s, every prisoner must have twenty-four-hour access to sanitation. Prisons whose cells are too small for toilets have a computer system called 'Night San', which allows prisoners to press a button in their cell and have their door unlocked in order to use the toilet during the night. This system has many disadvantages, but it's a lot better than pissing and shitting in a plastic bucket and leaving it in the corner of your cell all night.

My new cell had an iron bed, with a Rizla-thick foam mattress and pillow, a cupboard on one wall, a small Formica-topped table and a tubular chair – and that was the lot. My two property boxes were on the bed where the lads had left them. I took a quick look out of the window, and was pleasantly surprised to see the perimeter wall about sixty feet away across the exercise yard. In top-security prisons like Whitemoor you rarely get to see the actual perimeter wall, as the cells are usually in the centre of the prison to make it harder to plan an escape. Another thing about the wall at Grendon that was new to me was that there was no anti-grapple dome and no coils of razor-wire; it was just a wall.

It took me about thirty seconds to explore my new cell, and then I opened one of my property boxes and dug out the makings of a cup of tea. As I dropped a Happy Shopper teabag into my plastic cup I was aware of movement in my open doorway. I reached into my prop box and casually picked up my steel-bodied Parker pen, an essential, and legal, 'tool' carried by most prisoners in the dispersal system, and turned towards the door. I wasn't really expecting any trouble at Grendon, but my prison-induced paranoia dictated that I should always be ready to defend myself. 'All right, mate?' The accent was deepest Blackburn. The man behind the accent was quite obviously a Nazi skinhead. I deduced this from the fact that his head was shaved and his shirtless upper torso was adorned with a huge swastika tattoo. But his face was friendly and open. I nodded. The man stuck his hand out. 'I'm Kevin,' he said. 'Welcome to the nut-house.' I shook his hand.

After the introductions Kevin slipped off to make us both a cup of coffee, so I ditched my tea. He was only gone for five minutes as there was an electric kettle plugged into a socket on the landing for prisoners' use. In the meantime, another man walked past my door and then came back and looked in. He was mixed race, in his mid-thirties, and carrying an electric guitar. 'Hello, lad,' he said, the accent pure Liverpool. 'Just got in?' I nodded. He stuck his hand out. 'I'm Tel, nice to meet you.' I shook his hand and told him my nickname. His eyes lit up. 'Not Razor Smith? The one who does the writing for *Inside Time*?' I nodded again. *Inside Time* is the only national newspaper for prisoners, and I had been writing articles for it, usually slagging the prison system off, for some years. 'Fucking hell, lad! I always read your stuff!' I was just putting my modest face on when Kevin came back with the coffee. He gave Tel a sour look and walked into the cell. Tel looked uncomfortable with Kevin's presence. 'Nice to meet you, Razor,' he said. 'I'll talk to you later.' Then he was gone. I sensed the tension between the two, and I assumed it was racial. I sat on my bed and sipped my coffee. 'So,' I said, 'what's the apple on this gaff then?'

I took to Kevin straight away. At this stage I knew nothing about him except what my instincts told me. I sensed he was a straightforward man with little to hide, not afraid to speak his mind. There are many secret racists in prison, as in society as a whole, but, no matter what my own views are, I have to admire a man who has the courage to say, This is me, take it or leave it. Kevin's swastika tattoo was just such a statement. He told me that he was doing five years, seven months for burglary on a 'Paki's house'. He had spent half of his twenty-eight years in and out of prison, usually for violence and racial attacks. He had taken a screw hostage in HMP Deerbolt, suffered the inevitable beatings and the liquid cosh (forced tranquillization), and had been at Grendon for six weeks. Kevin was here to try to sort his life out and to examine the beliefs by which he had lived so far.

According to Kevin, F-wing was 'just like that film, *One Cuckoo Flew Over the Rest*'. He said that half the wing were wrong-uns, and three-quarters were 'fookin' off-key'. The screws were the same. 'See that geezer, who were just at your door? The half-coon? He's a bad fookin' rapist, mate. And ye've got cunts like that walking around here like they've got the right to mix wi' us. It burns me fookin' 'ead out, mate.'

'Any Londoners here?' I asked. Kevin nodded. 'Yeah, a few. All good lads. There's a couple on this landing. See that fella, Andy, who carried your boxes over? He's a cockney.' All Northern prisoners referred to Londoners as 'cockneys', just like we called anyone from outside London 'carrot crunchers' and 'Northerners'. It was pointless trying to explain that not all Londoners are cockneys, just as it was a waste of time trying to tell us that Birmingham was not in the North but in the Midlands.

As I spoke to Kevin another man came to my door. He was in his thirties, athletic-looking and wore a pair of small designer glasses. He looked very familiar but I couldn't place him for a moment. He smiled. 'Hello, Raze,' he said. 'You look a bit different from when I last saw you. What happened to the bald head and the mad beard?' I wracked my brain for his name. Then it came to me. 'Ray!' I exclaimed. 'How are you, son?' I had served time with Ray on a previous sentence at HMP Highdown. Then he had been an up-and-coming south London face, one of the new breed of young criminals, children of the Thatcher era, ruthless around a bit of business and a good money-getter. I remembered that he had been a promising boxer at one time and game as a brace of lions, but sensible with it. He was the first familiar face I'd seen since arriving and I was glad to see him.

It turned out that Ray was now serving a ten-year sentence for smuggling illegal immigrants into the country in the back of a lorry. He had staged a spectacular escape from Folkestone Magistrates' Court, where he had taken a security guard hostage with a syringe full of blood. He had also glassed a couple of wrong-uns at HMP Dovegate, and narrowly escaped a two-strike life sentence. HMP Grendon was the end of the line for him, and he expressed his determination to give up crime for good. I was delighted to hear a hard-core prisoner like Ray speaking like this. It gave me hope and confidence.

Ray and Kevin were already pals, having been on F-wing together for some weeks. This intrigued me. The Nazi skinhead and fervent nationalist palled up with a man who had smuggled illegal immigrants into his country. I made a mental note to explore this relationship further when I had settled in; it was bound to be interesting. Ray told me that there were other people on F-wing that I knew from other jails. Ritchie, a young hothead doing life for murder, who had been part of a sit-down protest I had organized in HMP Belmarsh soon after being sentenced to life. And Toby, another ex-Highdown face and good fella. Ritchie was in his mid-twenties, facing at least fifteen years in the system. He was a ball of furious anger that tended to explode in violence every now and again. But he was also a staunch kid with a heart of gold. Ritchie had done five years of his life sentence and had come to Grendon looking for answers, as we all had.

Now that I knew I would not be the only ODC on the wing I felt a lot happier and more relaxed. Even better was the fact that everyone seemed to be here for the right reasons: no one was going to scoff and point the finger when a seasoned con like me expressed the desire to change my life. I had been a bit worried about this, though I would never have admitted it to anyone.

By the time the bell was rung for the evening meal I had met about half the men on the wing. They turned up at my cell door and introduced themselves. After they walked away Ray and Kevin gave me their potted biography. Just the juicy bits. From what I heard, the balance on the wing between ODCs and wrong-uns seemed to be about 50/50. I had to remind myself that I should keep an open mind about the men here. Even the worst of them had, at least, accepted their guilt and admitted they needed help. They were no different from me in the eyes of society. Just because some of them had been driven to commit their crimes by unnatural urges, rather than through greed and laziness like me, it didn't make me any less culpable.

Grendon was the only adult prison I had ever been in where the prisoners actually ate their meals in a dining hall. In other jails you eat in your cell, five feet from the toilet. In the dispersal prisons you can eat where you like, but no dining hall is provided. The reason the authorities do not usually promote the idea of communal dining is because they have realized through experience that a lot of the mutinies and concerted indiscipline of the past have been over the poor standard of prison food. Gather a large group of hungry prisoners in one spot and serve up the kind of slop a pig would turn his nose up at, and you have a recipe for mutiny on a grand scale.

When I saw the quality of meals they were serving on F-wing, I realized why they felt able to risk a dining hall. The food was well prepared and well presented, and for the first time in five years I sat down to a hot dinner. Of course it was hot, because I didn't have to carry it up three flights of stairs in order to eat it. I met up with Ritchie and Toby in the dining hall and, after effusive greetings, we all sat down and had an enjoyable meal.

Also at our table was a fella I didn't yet know who had been transferred from Long Lartin with Ray and Ritchie. He was tall, clean-cut and had a vaguely military air about him. He was introduced to me as 'Daran'. He was well spoken compared to the rest of us, and seemed a very pleasant man with a good sense of humour. My instant feeling was that I liked him. I had picked up the fact that he was doing a life sentence, and anyone who can keep a sense of humour while wearing L plates is okay by me.

After the meal we were free to do whatever we liked until lock-up at 8.30. My induction would start the next day, but for now I was left to acclimatize myself. I plotted up in Kevin's cell with the lads, drank coffee, smoked roll-ups and exchanged gossip and war stories until it was time to lock up for the night. Kevin's cell, as was to be expected, was plastered in Union Jacks and flags of St George, as well as Nazi and skinhead posters and flyers. By the time I left I felt as though I had overdosed on both British and German patriotism. Once I was in my cell, with an obscenely cheery 'Good night' from the screw who locked me in, I made up my bed, unpacked my boxes and began to write. I had already written my autobiography while at Whitemoor, and it was due to be released by Penguin in June 2004. I found the rhythm of writing as soothing as any sedative; I decided I would keep a diary. That way I would be able to look back and check if there had been any change in me. I jotted down the day's highlights. And after I put my pen away I took a good long look around my tiny cell. I was almost forty-three years old and all my possessions fitted neatly into two cardboard boxes. It was 9 p.m. and all I had to look forward to was bed. Beyond that distant wall people were living full lives, and I, for all my bravado and one-of-the-chaps mentality, was trapped in a bleak and barren landscape of my own making. I felt depressed. I prayed that Grendon would be what I had been searching for. One thing I knew, things were going to get a lot harder in the months to come. I had come here to face up to the unpalatable truths about myself. I hoped I was going to be strong enough to handle it.

I climbed into bed and turned the light out. I was just drifting off to sleep when I heard Kevin's voice out on the landing. He was singing 'England Belongs To Me' at the top of his voice. Fuck it! I had forgotten all about the Night San computer.

3. In the Hot Seat

The summer of 2003 was the hottest since 1976, and one of the worst places to spend it was in a cell the size of a shoe box. Conventional cells are bad enough, but the cells at Grendon were a torture all their own. Not a puff of air circulated in the tiny living space, but as soon as it got light outside swarms of flies descended on the cells and buzzed around the ears of the sleeping occupants. Most British prisons are built on land that is undesirable, and in some cases uninhabitable, and HMP Grendon is no different in this respect. Just outside the walls is a landfill site where the rubbish from surrounding towns is deposited, and this attracts some of the biggest, most irritating bluebottles I have ever come across. Also, in hot weather the stench that permeates the prison turns it into a sulphurous antechamber of hell.

I was rudely pulled from my slumber at first light by a swarm of well-fed flies determined to fly into my ears and party. I was still tired as I hadn't been able to get to sleep until nearly 1 a.m., due to the Night San. Though the cells were locked up for the night at 8.30, the computer that unlocked the doors did not actually kick in until ten o'clock. Then, as each cell occupant pressed a button on a panel inside the cell, the computer put him on a waiting list. From 10 p.m. onwards, there was a constant stream of men being let out on to the landing, one at a time, and each one felt the need to mark his temporary freedom vocally. Officially, each man was allowed three releases per night, for a maximum length of six minutes per go; just enough time to use the toilet and wash his hands. But, in reality, some men stayed out on the landing, laughing, joking and talking to their mates through the gap in the cell doors, for as long as twenty-five minutes. And there was little that could be done about it as the controller was over in the gatehouse of the prison.

I couldn't believe the noise men were making on the landings so late at night. In dispersal jails, where the cons mainly police themselves, there would have been a spate of stabbings on the morning after that night's work. It is hard enough to get to sleep in prison, with constant light from the grounds and the noise of patrolling screws, but the Night San added a new hellish dimension. I vowed to have a quiet word with the loudest individuals I had identified to make sure they were made aware of how much of a frightening growler I can be when I'm tired.

The Night San débâcle did provide me with one nugget though. Tel, the mixed-race scouser rapist, was ensconced in the cell opposite mine, and, around midnight, I could hear Kevin, his voice unmistakable, talking to him through the gap in his door. I listened to their conversation, intrigued.

KEVIN: I've got to tell you, I fookin' hate you. Stick a teabag under the door, will you, I'm having a brew. Cheers. Do you know why I hate you so much? Two reasons, one, you're a fookin' coon, and two, 'cos you're a fookin' rapist. I'd string you up, mate. No problem whatsoever. What do you think of that?

TEL: (*sounding a bit frightened and eager to please*) I know what you mean, Kev. I'd feel the same if I was in your position, lad. I don't like rapists either. Or coons.

KEVIN: You got any sugar sachets? Yeah, if I met you in the system, I'd rip your fookin' 'ead off, d'ye know that? Clean fookin' off.

TEL: Here's a couple of sachets, Kev. I don't blame you for that, Kev. I know I'm the scum of the earth, lad. But I'm here to try and change that.

KEVIN: I know. And that's the only reason I'm not steaming into you every time I see you.

TEL: Nice one, Kev.

KEVIN: Cheers for the teabag and the sugar. See you in the morning. I'm off for a brew.

Kevin then made his way back to his cell, singing 'One More For The Gallows' at full volume.

I lay there and thought about what I'd heard. I'd never heard a conversation like that in the system. Kevin had spoken matter of factly, never raising his voice, just laying his hate out in the open. I don't think for one minute that his aim was to frighten or intimidate Tel, although it was obvious that he did. It was my first taste of 'Grendon honesty', the ethos of 'if you have something on your mind, bring it out and we'll deal with it'. Of course, you were supposed to bring it out in the groups, not on the landing, but I had the feeling that Kevin would not be shy about making his feelings known in any situation.

The meat of the therapy at Grendon was done in group work. Each man was allocated to a small group, usually of about eight men, and they would meet three mornings a week, with a facilitator sitting in, a therapist or prison officer who was trained in the basics. There was also the big group, which was held two mornings a week and involved the whole community. Attendance at all groups was compulsory, and to miss more than two groups in a row could lead to the offender being 'voted out'. Each member of the community, i.e. the prisoners, had a vote in everything, from whether to tape a film for the community video to sending a fellow member back to the system for a serious breach of the rules.

The daily routine on F-wing was: unlock 8 a.m., breakfast 8.30, group work 9 till 10.30, exercise 12 till 1 p.m., lunch 1.15, tea 5.30, lock-up 8.30. Unlike most other prisons, there was no in-cell television on F-wing, but there was a communal television room. There were also rooms containing a pool table and bar football. Everyone on the wing had an area to clean daily, for which we were paid £7 per week, and we could spend our wage in the most overpriced canteen in the prison estate.

I never partake of breakfast, so, after a quick shower in the piss-smelling recess at the end of the landing, and a cup of tea, I took a mooch about. I ran into Daran in the lower spur and got chatting to him about things in general. He was a very easygoing and likeable chap. It turned out that he had spent time in both the Royal Navy and the French Foreign Legion. I've lost count of the number of hobbits I've met in prison who claim to have been in either the Legion or the SAS in an attempt to make themselves seem more windswept and interesting, but I got the feeling that Daran was the real McCoy. There was a quiet confidence about him, and I had to look really close in order to see the glint of steel below his affable surface, but it was there all right. It turned out that Daran was the present vice-chairman of F-wing, and he was a valuable source of information about its routine for a new boy like me.

One of the features of the Grendon community culture was the election every three months of a chairman and a vice-chairman for each wing. They would chair the big group meetings, put the issues into the arena, and generally referee the meetings when things got heated, as they invariably did. A good chairman could control a community meeting like a good sheep dog can control a flock of agitated sheep. But a poor chairman made for group chaos.

The bell was rung at 9 a.m. on the dot, and I made my way upstairs to the community room for my first day of therapy at Grendon. I was more than curious to see this much talked-about system in the flesh, so to speak. This is what I had spent the last fifteen months trying to get to. Now the road to my new life was about to hove into view. And I was ready to take the first step.

The group room was large enough to seat over fifty people, and the chairs were arranged around the walls, leaving an open space in the centre of the room. I found a chair and watched the rest of the community file in. The chairman and vice-chairman sat at the head of the room but everyone else just sat wherever a seat was available. The chairman was a yellow-skinned man with slightly aboriginal features whom I had not met, but I had heard he was doing twelve years for rape. When everyone was in the room the chairman called the group to order and began the official introductions. Each group meeting started by everyone in turn saying who they were, how long they were doing, and what they were in for. I listened closely as each man stated his legend: '. . . murder', '. . . rape', '. . . buggery', '. . . arson', '. . . attempted murder', '. . . grievous bodily harm', '. . . burglary', and on it went, a litany of serious crimes direct from the lips of the perpetrators. When it was my turn I gave my details: 'Razor Smith, two-strike life, armed robbery and possession of firearms with intent'. I sat back and listened.

I noticed that when Kevin made his introduction he stressed the word 'burglary'; I assumed this was so no one could mistake it for 'buggery'. In the present company I couldn't fault him for that. The meeting was not at all what I had been expecting. I thought we would get straight into some heavy therapy and I was certainly fired up for it. But the meeting was mainly taken up with discussing such mundane topics as whose job it was to clean the showers and whether there were going to be extra gym sessions at the weekend. I left feeling slightly disappointed. Out in the corridor Daran pulled me over. 'So, what do you reckon on it?' he asked. I shrugged. 'Bit fucking lightweight, weren't it? I was expecting to witness a bit of therapy.' Daran smiled. 'We don't really start the actual therapy until we get over on to the wings. This wing is all about observing how you react and interact with others. Don't be fooled by the bovine look of the screws on here, they are watching every move we make and writing reports on it.' I saw the sense in that.

After the meeting I went down to Daran's cell for a cup of coffee, and we were soon joined by Kevin, Ray and Ritchie. The lads kept referring to Daran as 'Psycho', and he seemed okay about it, so I had to ask what the nickname was in aid of. Daran explained matter of factly that he was serving life with a twenty-year minimum, for a particularly brutal and gruesome murder. It turned out that he had been on the piss with a mate of his one night and they had got into the company of another man and ended up going back to his flat to continue the drinking session. The man proved to be a homosexual, and duly made a drunken pass at Daran's friend. So Daran killed the man by beating and stabbing him to death. Then he spent quite a while mutilating the body. He popped out the eyeballs, cut off the genitals, ripped out the intestines and scattered them around the room, and, most bizarrely, inserted household items into the man's body, including a pocket calculator in the man's stomach cavity. As Daran concluded his story and got to the bit about the calculator, the lads in the cell, who had obviously heard this story before, let out a burst of semi-horrified laughter. 'Tell Razor what the judge said in his summing up, Daz,' piped in Ritchie, gleefully. Daran smiled. 'He said, "This murder was a cold and calculating act."' The lads yukked it up, and so did I, but I was also looking at him with a new fascination.

I wondered if Daran was a real live psychopath. I had met many men throughout my years in prison, not all of them prisoners, who I guessed were seriously mentally ill, but never one like Daran. He looked and sounded so . . . normal! I decided to ask him. 'So, are you a psychopath then, or what?' It was hardly a subtle approach, but I am renowned for my bluntness. Daran shrugged. 'I don't think so,' he said. 'I just don't like queers.' The conversation then turned to Kevin.

Kevin had grown up in a fervently nationalist family. All his brothers were leading lights in extreme right-wing organizations, and they walked the walk as well as talking the talk. For Kevin, racism, nationalism and patriotism had been a way of life, and he believed with a passion that I have rarely encountered outside of religious fanatics and football fans. The burglary that he was serving his present sentence for had not been motivated by gain; it had been committed for racial reasons. He had broken into the home of a prominent Blackburn Asian, wrecking the house and spraying racist graffiti on the walls. He had stolen nothing.

I was interested to find out how Kevin equated his patriotism with his love of the Nazis. I put it to him that surely there was a big contradiction there? How can you say you love your country and yet at the same time worship the ideology, and proudly display the symbols, of an organization that was responsible for the deaths of so many of your countrymen? How does being a Nazi sit with being 'English and proud of it'? I could see from the look on the faces of the other lads in the cell that I had opened a can of worms. Kevin didn't even take a breath, he launched straight into a ten-minute sermon on National Socialism, the gist of which was that the Nazis and the British people were all on the same side, with common goals and aims, and it was only the politicians who had fucked it all up by taking England and Germany to war against each other.

Kevin was an eloquent and articulate speaker who possessed a logic all his own. I could see he had been brainwashed since birth and arguing with him would be pointless. So I let him finish what he had to say and then asked him the obvious question. Why had he come to Grendon? He went quiet for a moment, and the light of fanaticism faded out of his eyes. 'I want to change,' he said simply.

Exercise on the yard was a pleasant experience. The sun was shining and I didn't have to submit to a full search and metal detecting before getting out there. Grendon is built on the slope of a hill, and the F-wing exercise yard is the highest point. So from one side, looking downwards, I could see open, green countryside. By standing still and focusing on the horizon I could almost convince myself I was not inside a prison exercise yard but out in the country. Some of the lads jogged around the perimeter of the yard, lost in their own thoughts, while others played chess or just sun-bathed on a grass verge that ran the length of the yard. I sat down on the grass and built myself a roll-up. It was 12.30. If I was in Whitemoor now I would already have had lunch and been banged up in my cell for the past fifteen minutes. I took a deep breath. This really was a different world.

I felt strangely light-headed and it took me a moment to realize that I was relaxing, for probably the first time in five years. I was starting to see that there was no danger here. There were no enemies plotting a bit of payback for any real or imagined reason. No hard-faced screws looking for an excuse to show how tough they were. No paranoid gangsters, strutting drug dealers or twitchy, desperate junkies to be avoided. I felt at peace. And it was then that I fully understood how much living in the system had been taking out of me. In the system you must be in a heightened state of awareness for every minute of every day. Even when I was locked inside my cell I knew I wasn't safe. The screws can, and do, come for you at any time of the day or night. It might be a 'spin' (con-speak for a cell and body search), or they might be coming with riot shields and batons to move you to the punishment block, or another prison, because they suspect you might be up to something. You learn to live on the edge and after a while you don't even realize that you're doing it.

Violence and danger are always just a whisper away, no matter who you are. Maybe some young gun will decide to stab you to enhance his own reputation. Or maybe one of your circle of friends has insulted someone or reneged on a drug deal, and you become a target by association. Or maybe you don't say 'Good morning' to one of the many paranoid lunatics you are living with, and he decides that this is a sign that you've got a 'problem' with him, and wants to get you before you get him. You watch every face and you listen to every word and you are always aware of who's behind you. You look at every object for its potential to be used as a weapon, and you judge your distances by how far you are away from the nearest weapon if it should 'go off' (con-speak for violence). And this is how you live for years, sometimes decades, on end.

As I sat there smoking in that sunny yard I felt some of that great weight leaving me. I felt intoxicated, as though I had been puffing on a skunk joint. I couldn't suppress a laugh. Toby and Ritchie looked in my direction. 'You all right, Raze?' asked Toby. I nodded. 'Yeah, mate,' I said. 'I've never felt better.' And I meant it.

One of the things that bothered me about F-wing was the lack of bang-up. In the system prisoners are trained to expect to be locked into their cells at certain times of the day. In local and remand jails the time spent in-cell can be as long as twenty-three hours per day. In dispersal, category B training prisons and category C prisons, the routine of bang-up is basically uniform. After the midday meal you are locked in your cell for up to two hours, and the same after the evening meal. This is to allow prison staff time to get their own meals. But at Grendon there was no bang-up during the day. In the system I looked forward to my bang-up time, it was when I could do a bit of thinking or a bit of writing, or just listen to music. My life's routine was built around the bang-up time, and now I had none I felt a bit lost. I now realize that this craving for routine bang-up was a symptom of my institutionalization. Just one more strange bit of baggage I had picked up over the years.

As a result of having no structured routine on F-wing, the days seemed interminably long. There was little to do, so I wandered the gloomy corridors, stared out of barred windows for long periods or perched in front of the communal television and tried to get interested in the mundane fare of daytime TV. I was like a bear in a circus cage, pacing and stretching but unable to settle in one spot for very long. I decided that the best way to beat the restless boredom was to get involved. I would make it my business to visit every man on the wing and see whatever there was to see.

I was still very wary about approaching any of those in for sex offences. I was afraid one of them might start talking about the details of his crimes, and then my ingrained instincts might force me to act in a violent way. So first I went to see John, the Geordie with the scar who had carried one of my boxes from reception. He lived in the first cell on my spur, and I found him just making himself a cup of coffee. I sat on the chair and he sat on his bed, the cell being so small that with the two of us there it was almost overcrowded. When there were more than four of us in a cell, at least one person had to stand in the doorway or sit on the floor.

John's cell was full of photos of his family and Newcastle FC posters. On a cupboard was a picture of a smiling young man who bore a remarkable resemblance to John himself. Around this photo were cards and objects, arranged so as to give the impression of a shrine, with the picture as the focal point. I asked about it. 'It's ma cousin, we were like brothers. He died last year. Stabbed to death in a gang fight up the road.' 'Sorry, mate,' I said, knowing how fresh his grief must be. My son, Joe, had been dead nearly two years and it was still unbearably painful to be reminded of it. I decided to change the subject. 'How did you end up here?' I asked. John shrugged. 'Violence,' he said. 'Pure fucking violence. I've got previous for fighting, both down here and up the road. I used to think it was just a laugh, sticking blades in people, glassing them in the face, you know? Just a bit of crack. I should be doing life for some of the things I've done. But I was lucky. I got eight years this time, for stabbing a guy over nothing, a silly argument. After ma cousin died, I was a couple of years into this sentence when it happened, I just lost it. I done this.' He pointed to the huge, raw-looking scars across his wrists. 'Tried to top maself.' I had assumed that his scars had been inflicted by someone else. I could only imagine what a state he must have been in. It's not easy to slash your own wrists, and I could tell by the scars that this had been no half-hearted effort.

John was young, in his early twenties, and despite his denials, violence was still a big part of his make-up. He had an outstanding court case in Sunderland for a separate slashing, and the day before I arrived at Grendon he had almost come to blows in the community meeting after the chairman made a remark about him. He reminded me a bit of myself when I was his age. The world had him baffled and he covered his ignorance by striking first. Deep down he was scared and confused.

After talking to John, I went back to my cell and thought about what I had heard. When we spoke about violence in the system it was always to enhance our own legends, or in a jokey way that allowed us to avoid the full horror of the things we had done. I had never sat down and had a serious discussion about the futility of our violence and how it affects us and others. I had done some seriously nasty things to people in the past and I rarely gave them a second thought. I wondered how many people are walking around with scars I've inflicted on them over the years. It's not a comfortable thought.

In the next few days I completed the first part of my induction into Grendon. There were more forms to fill in and more tests. I was interviewed by the psychology department, the drug counsellor, the wing therapist, the medical staff and the education department. It seemed like everyone in the jail had to write a report on some aspect of my personality and abilities. The psychologist asked me to estimate how many crimes I had committed and not been caught for! My reply was 'About half.' I scored 73 per cent in the English test set by the education department, and 3 per cent in the maths test. I knew enough to count my share of the loot and calculate how many years of my prison sentences I would serve, and I had figured that was all the maths I would need.

The drug counsellor wanted to know if I had a problem with drugs. When I replied in the negative, he pointed out that I had two adjudications against me for failing mandatory drug testing in HMP Belmarsh. They were both for cannabis, and I explained that even though I had not smoked a joint for over four years, I did not consider the smoking of cannabis to be a 'drug problem'. He was one of those ex-junkies who, having realized the error of his ways and managed to kick the habit, sees addiction in everyone. 'Cannabis is not a minor matter,' he said, a bit too pompously for my liking. 'I started on cannabis and ended up on heroin.' I shrugged, but I was becoming annoyed. 'Yeah, well, not everyone who has a puff is stupid or weak-willed enough to get involved in skag.' He bristled. I carried on. 'I've smoked puff since I was twenty-seven, and I've never even been tempted to try skag. Do you know why? Because I didn't fucking fancy it, that's why. "Gateway drug" my arse!' He was shaking with rage. 'Well,' he said, through clenched teeth, 'you'll obviously have no need of my services while you're here. You seem to be an expert in your own right.' I got up to leave, but I couldn't resist having one last dig. 'You should lay off the skag, mate. It's obviously fucking your head up.' I know it was a cruel and childish thing to say to a reformed addict, but I couldn't stop myself.

The whole drug issue bores the shit out of me. For years I have been writing articles for prison magazines and newspapers, warning of the heroin epidemic that is sweeping our jails. I even had one of my articles published in the *Guardian*, but all I got was verbal from the junkies, and more red writing on my page 16 from the outraged authorities ('red writing' is disparaging and damaging comments, usually highlighted in red ink, and 'page 16' is an inmate's security file). My anti-heroin views are common knowledge within the system. But it only got up my nose in the first place (forgive the unintended pun), because it fucked up the cannabis trade in prison. Anyway, I didn't foresee my having any use for a drug counsellor in the future. My big addiction was crime.

It sounds strange admitting that I was actually addicted to crime. I was addicted to the power and excitement I got from committing crimes. I was an 'adrenaline junkie'. I got into serious crime at an early age, and by the time I was sixteen I was standing in the dock of the Old Bailey, convicted of armed robbery and looking forward to a future of crime and imprisonment. I was never more alive than when I was jumping over the edge with a gun in my hand. When you're young and strong and you can afford to throw away a decade or two in some pisshole prison and still have plenty of life left to live, it's all a big laugh. Then you wake up one morning and see a strange face staring back at you from the shaving mirror. Some old geezer with bitter, weary eyes where there used to be a devil-may-care twinkle. And suddenly it ceases to be funny. You want to change but don't know how. And you realize that you have become one of those old lags you used to stare at with a mixture of pity, horror, and the smug certainty that you would never still be doing bird at that age. Sure, a life of crime can have its moments, but the price is high.

After I had been on F-wing for a couple of weeks I was thinking more and more about my past and future. The group work still left a lot to be desired as far as actual therapy was concerned. We were warned not to open up with any personal details about our lives, because there was a chance that some of us could still be deemed 'unsuitable for therapy' and sent back to the prisons we had come from. It would be very damaging if someone let loose some startling revelation about himself, and then someone who heard it was sent back to the system where he might feel free to tell all. I could see the logic in the warning. But the strange thing was, there was a lot of what could be called therapy going on in the cells and on the landings. Men were talking to each other. Barriers were being broken down every day. I was no longer making the distinction between sex offenders and others. I spoke to everybody and everybody spoke to me.

Prison overcrowding was all over the news throughout July, and the Home Office was pressuring every prison in the country to make space. In the local prisons, which always bore the brunt of overcrowding, men were being housed three to a cell built for two, and cells that had long been used as temporary office space and storage cupboards were being fitted out for permanent habitation. Grendon, despite its special status, was not immune. At Grendon they like to take as much time as possible in assessing and observing, so as to be sure that every individual is right for therapy and therapy is right for him. Nothing is rushed. The average stay on F-wing was twelve weeks, but in some cases as long as twenty. But under direct orders from a Home Office that was squirming in the spotlight of media attention, F-wing staff were forced to expedite matters. Men were being sent directly up to the main wings and into therapy after as little as two weeks of assessment. None of the staff was happy about this, and not shy about saying so.

Due to this unseemly rush to therapy, by the time I had been on F-wing for three weeks most of the people I knew had gone. Kevin was still there, and I suspected this was due to his frequent outbursts. He was a nice fella, but he could not take criticism, nor resist a tirade. I began to suspect that he was going to have to show spectacular evidence of his desire to change if he was to make it into therapy. It was a shame really, because if anyone was in dire need of sorting their head out it was Kevin. I got on great with him, and I saw a side of him that the staff rarely did. He was generous and kind-hearted to a fault, and a man of honour. I, being more left-wing than Josef Stalin, argued politics with him all day long and pointed out the inconsistencies in his arguments. Though the discussions sometimes got heated enough to attract a crowd, Kevin and I stayed friendly and spent a lot of time in each other's cells.

The new intake of F-wing inductees brought a few more familiar faces. Whispering Mick, who I had done time with in HMP Albany on the Isle of Wight, turned up. I was as surprised to see him at Grendon as he was to see me. Mick was an old-fashioned con, all scams and dodges, and talking out of the side of his mouth, which earned him his nickname. Any man who went through the juvenile and borstal system pre-1980s had to learn to talk from the side of his mouth without moving his lips so the screws couldn't hear or see. Talking on parade could earn you seven days in the punishment block. Whispering Mick was doing ten years for aggravated burglary, which differs from ordinary burglary in that the occupants are tied up or threatened with violence. In con-speak aggravated burglary is known as either 'aggy' or a 'tie-up'. Whispering Mick had previous convictions for aggy dating back to the 1970s, and it was only because he used a knife rather than a gun that he wasn't serving a two-strike life.

Also in the new intake was a mandatory lifer named Nick, doing life for murder and manslaughter. An ex-Hell's Angels 'prospect', and well known in the system, Nick was a strange guy. He came to Grendon from Parkhurst and brought greetings from my brother-in-law, Tony, he of the three unsuccessful stays at Grendon. Nick looked and walked like the old vaudeville comedian Max Wall. He was going bald at the front but had flowing locks at the back, and a pugnacious jaw. He had long arms that swung loosely when he walked, giving him a vaguely simian air. Nick was hyperactive and spoke so fast and for so long without taking a breath, you would think he had been mainlining amphetamine. He had stabbed to death his girlfriend and a love rival in a fit of jealous passion, and then had a nervous breakdown while awaiting trial. Nick felt genuine remorse for what he had done, and seven years into his sentence he carried guilt and shame like a backpack, for all to see. Unfortunately prison, like any macho environment, can be a cruel place, and due to his oddness Nick became the butt of many jokes.

Another familiar face was Jay, doing six years for possession of Class A drugs. Jay was one of those men who now fill me with frustration. An immensely talented singer/songwriter, he squandered his life and gifts in the pursuit of drugs. A heroin and crack addict, Jay had once been offered a chance to record some of his own compositions for a major record label. All he had to do was turn up at the studio. Instead he stopped off at a crack house for a 'livener', and ended up leaving three days later, minus his guitar, which he had sold for crack, and his handwritten book of original songs, which ended up being burned for pipe-ash or some such. Jay never did get to record his songs professionally, but he earned a living playing guitar for numerous bands and selling small amounts of drugs to feed his habit. Now he told me that he had been clean for almost nine months, and he was looking to change. I was pleased for him.

Another new arrival was a bloke named Don, 6 foot 2, with long sandy-coloured hair and a Jason King moustache. When we heard that he had been in both the SAS and the Foreign Legion we nicknamed him 'Chuck Norris'. Don was a strange cat. He looked as though he had stepped straight out of a 1970s porn film, and there was an air of something not quite right about him. He had a habit of letting slip little bits of information that were obviously designed to enhance his own reputation, the SAS and Foreign Legion stuff for example, but when questioned on the details he would get all secret squirrel on us. I didn't trust him one bit, and I was forever trying to catch him out. I wished Daran was still on the wing so he could question him about the Foreign Legion, but I couldn't even get a message to him on C-wing. My suspicions about Don would have to wait.

Right next door to Grendon is another prison, HMP Springhill. Springhill is a category D, open prison, for mainly white-collar criminals or men who are coming to the end of very long sentences and are in need of resettlement. The inmates of Springhill go out into the community to work, and are allowed home leaves when they can visit their families. I have never made it to an open prison as my face and record do not fit, and never have, but these are the kind of prisons that the tabloids often present to the public on a slow news week as 'holiday-camp' prisons, engendering public outrage and forcing the Home Office to crack down on all prisons. With Springhill being right next door, it is convenient for them to send any of their rule breakers, whom they feel might need a reminder of what it feels like to be behind bars and walls, over to Grendon. It happens infrequently but, when it does, the Springhill offender is placed in a cell on F-wing, either for a 'cooling-off period' or to await transfer back to the system. These men are known on F-wing as 'lodgers'. One such lodger, who came on to F-wing when I was there, had been having marital difficulties and decided to go AWOL from Springhill in order to save his marriage. He didn't get far, and when recaptured, less than a mile from the prison, he was brought to F-wing to await transfer. I noticed him around the wing and in the dining hall, exuding an air of gloom and melancholy. He struck me as a man in deep depression. But I was struggling with my own feelings, so I didn't spare him too much thought. After all, what could he have to worry about? Even with the standard twenty-eight-day loss of remission for his attempt to abscond, he would still be back with his family by Christmas. I had a decade left to serve.

After the lodger had been on the wing for a couple of days he faded into the background. Then, one dinnertime, he didn't come down for his meal. No one noticed. I was eating at a table with Kevin, and he was giving out his usual Adolf Hitler vibe. I wasn't really in the mood, so I told him in no uncertain terms to fuck off. Kevin picked up his plate, with a wounded martyr's look on his face, and went upstairs to eat in his cell. At mealtimes the cells and landings are deserted, as everyone is expected to eat together. Immediately he was gone I felt bad about fucking him off, and I resolved to go and make peace after dinner.

Kevin had been gone five minutes when the quiet murmur of the dining hall was drowned out by the screeching-whooping of the general alarm bell. Everybody froze. In the system that sound usually heralds only one thing: trouble. Buttons for the general alarm bell, or 'riot bell', are situated at regular intervals throughout every prison and are pressed by staff to summon help. It could be a member of staff being attacked, or prisoners fighting among themselves or a hostage situation, but it is always something serious. On hearing the bell, prison staff are trained to rush *en masse* to its source, which the control room will immediately inform them of over their personal radios. The staff at Grendon were not used to hearing the bell go off, and it was a long moment before they remembered their training and began keying their radios for a location.

As the staff ran out of the dining hall I wondered if the bell had anything to do with Kevin. I hoped he hadn't chinned somebody, or worse, because of what I had said. I took a fast walk up the corridor towards the stairs. The gates at the end of the wing crashed open and about fifteen red-faced and hyped-up screws piled in and up the staircase. I started to run. If Kevin had kicked off I at least wanted to see if I could lend him a hand. Several other men had come out of the dining hall and headed for the stairs. As I rounded the bend in the staircase a female officer, with a panicked look on her face, was shouting for an ambulance. There was a throng of uniforms blocking the corridor leading to the games rooms. I tried to push my way through, but more uniforms were coming up the stairs behind me and a large PO (principal officer) took control. 'Get the prisoners banged away!' he shouted over the bell and the panic. Several of the screws started ushering us down the spur that contained the cells. 'Bang up! Bang up!' the cry was echoed all over the wing. This was serious.

The screw who tried to steer me into my cell was an F-wing regular. I stood my ground and refused to go in. 'What the fuck is going on?' I demanded. 'Is it Kevin?' The screw shook his head. 'No,' he said. 'It's the lodger, he's tried to kill himself.' I went into my cell and allowed him to lock my door. I was relieved it wasn't Kevin. But the thought of someone attempting suicide on the wing brought up a lot of bad memories for me. You cannot get away from suicide in prison; it's a part of the landscape. An average of 115 people take their own lives in custody every year, and hundreds more make the attempt.

After a while the wing went quiet. I washed my face in the plastic washbowl. I was drained, both emotionally and physically. I sat down to write my diary, hoping that I could get the incident on to the paper and out of my head. I had just put my pen away when I heard the click of the electronic cell locks. I went out on to the landing and saw others on the spur emerging from their own cells. Some looked shell-shocked, but most were just annoyed that they had been locked up for so long. The emergency was over. I went to Kevin's cell, but he wasn't in there so I went downstairs to find him. I pulled Whispering Mick on the ground floor and asked him if he had seen Kevin. 'He's in the office with the therapist,' he told me, *sotto voce*. 'It was him who saved the lodger from going brown-bread [dead].'

Whispering Mick had gleaned most of the story by standing with his ear against the gap in his cell door and earwigging on the screws talking in the office, which was close to his cell. It appeared that Kevin, after his exit from the dining hall, had gone upstairs and decided to watch a bit of telly. As he was walking past the room that housed a bar-football table, he heard strange sounds and went in to investigate. And there was the lodger. He had made a noose from a sheet, and pulled the bar-football table into a corner of the room so he could reach a pipe on the ceiling. When Kevin found him he was close to death. Acting instinctively, Kevin ran into the corridor and pressed the nearest alarm button, and then ran back into the room and grabbed the lodger's legs, holding him up as high as he could to relieve the pressure from the noose. At this stage the man was already unconscious and a dead weight.

This had been no cry for help but a serious attempt at suicide. The lodger had picked mealtime when he was sure there would be no one there to stop him. It was a million-to-one shot that Kevin happened to be upstairs then. The lodger had been rushed to an outside hospital. It was touch-and-go whether he would suffer brain damage if he survived.

Kevin spent over an hour in the therapist's office, and when he came out he still looked in shock. I took him up to my cell for a cup of coffee. 'You done good, Kev,' I said. He looked at me with haunted eyes. 'The noise I heard were his heels banging against the wall,' he said. 'I thought it were someone tap-dancing on the table. But it were his heels.' I put a comforting hand on his shoulder. I felt the tears well up in my eyes again, and turned away to make the coffee. We drank it in silence. Finally Kevin sighed. 'I'm glad I saved him,' he said. 'But I don't know what I'd of done if he were a fookin' Paki!' I knew it was just bravado.

Two days later Kevin was accepted for therapy and moved up to C-wing. I was pleased for him and hoped he would make the best of his opportunity. I was also hoping that I would be next.

4. House of Pain

The day after Kevin went to C-wing I was called in for a chat with Ian, the therapist. Ian was the real power on F-wing and all the staff answered to him. He was casually dressed, in sports jacket and slacks, and a pair of those shoes that look like Cornish pasties and are much beloved by social workers everywhere. In his early forties, Ian had the half-quizzical smile worn by all the best interrogators. It was the kind of smile that said, 'I know you're lying, but carry on anyway and we'll see where this goes.' His hair was dark and short, a bit like the rest of him, and he had a habit of sitting perfectly still at all times – as befits a man who could probably write a book on interpreting body language. He greeted me with a warm handshake and told me to take a seat. I wasn't worried about this little 'chat', it was standard procedure in Grendon.

'How are you settling into F-wing?' was Ian's opening gambit. A fairly innocuous question, to which I gave the stock answer: 'Yeah, okay.' There was a long silence. I have been interrogated many times over the years, usually by Scotland Yard's finest, and I prided myself on knowing most of the tricks. The long silence was known as the 'give-'em-enough-rope routine' by the CID, and it fazed me not at all. The idea is that most people are uncomfortable with silence and they will fill it out of embarrassment, babbling on with the first thing that comes into their mind. This is great for coppers and psychologists, as they are able to pick useful information from the verbal diarrhoea. I waited him out, concentrating my mind on the lyrics to 'Riot In Cell-Block Number 9' by the Robins. I was also conscious of my body language. I sat leaning slightly forward, with my hands loose in my lap. This was an indication that I was open and relaxed with nothing to hide.

I had studied the basics of body language, and viewed it as a useful tool in police interrogations and while giving evidence at trial. I knew that to fold my arms over my chest would be construed as 'closing up', and it was always best to be 'open'. Body language was also useful on the landings and yards of prison. It was great for intimidating anyone who might try and take a liberty – a narrowing of the eyes and a roll of the shoulders can work wonders. And it worked in other ways too. I am a big card player – usually kaluki, a form of rummy played with two packs of cards – and I always watch the body language of my opponents. I've taken many a pot down to a twitch or a tap of the fingers by an opponent.

Finally Ian realized that I was not a babbler, so he broke the silence himself. 'Do I call you Noel, or Razor?' he asked. I had been expecting this. I knew that my nickname would be a bone of contention in Grendon, where image was not tolerated. I had spoken to a friend of mine, Will Self, the novelist, about it when he had visited me in Whitemoor. Will is also my literary agent, and he was instrumental in getting my autobiography out of me and on to the bookshelves. So, on my arrival at Grendon, I had made a conscious effort to ditch the 'Razor' tag. I introduced myself to people as Noel. Unfortunately, because there were people at Grendon who had known me for many years as 'Razor', it wasn't as easy as I had hoped.

My nickname had become an indelible part of me, and no matter how often I corrected people about the use of it, it just would not go away. Before I had made the decision to come to Grendon, I hadn't given the nickname a thought. I no longer noticed it, just like the tattoos on my neck and hands. It was only when meeting people for the first time that I was sometimes reminded, if they happened to comment. I never thought of 'Razor Smith' as any different from 'Noel Smith'; it was not some alter ego that existed separately in my mind, we were one and the same. There was nothing that 'Razor' would do that 'Noel' wouldn't. I didn't do 'bad' things and blame them on Razor, I wasn't that fucked up!

I had been given the name in the mid-1970s, when, as a young Teddy boy, I had taken to carrying, and sometimes using, a cut-throat razor. We all had nicknames back then, it was part of the culture of gang warfare we had adopted. There was 'Cut-throat' John from Brixton, who also carried a razor, Joe 'The Blade' from Battersea and 'Hatchet' Harry from Balham. A scary nickname was *de rigueur* if you were in a gang. It was an edge, a way of striking fear into the enemy before they even laid eyes on you. The only reason I was still being called 'Razor' into middle age was that, unlike most of my contemporaries, I had spent most of my life in an environment where an edge was still useful: prison.

Razor was also my pen-name. When writing articles for publication, which I had been doing since 1993, I always signed myself as Razor Smith.

My writing, which was usually about the prison system, was full of vitriol in the early days. A type of self-therapy if you will.

Ian was still waiting for an answer. I knew he had obviously noted that I had introduced myself as Razor at the first community meeting. That had been a slip of the tongue which I now regretted, if only because it gave him an angle to come at me. You have to remember that I was new at this therapy game, and I still did not completely trust the therapists. I was going at it the way I had always gone at authority, treating it like a battle of wills. This was my criminal mindset, still to the fore. I smiled and spread my arms. 'It's Noel,' I said. Ian smiled back at me. 'How do you think you are perceived by the rest of the community?' he asked, with a nifty change of direction. I shrugged. He had wrong-footed me. 'I don't really know,' I said. He was on me like a robber's dog. 'Do you think that some members of the community feel . . . intimidated by you?' I shook my head. 'Surely not,' I said. 'Why would they be?' He moved in for the kill. 'Perhaps it could be because of your size, demeanour and reputation. Or maybe because you are known as "Razor" Smith? That's a pretty intimidating name, isn't it?'

I explained it all to him: how difficult it was proving to be to leave the name behind, and, to be honest, how I would still carry on using it as a pen-name. I told him how I had come to Grendon to shake off my image and change my life, and that, if he thought losing the nickname was important, then I would redouble my efforts in this endeavour. By the end of my explanation I'm not sure if I was babbling, but it was close. I left Ian's office feeling as though I had managed a score draw from our first close encounter. But looking back now I can see that I was just fooling myself. It would be a while longer before I realized that these sessions were not supposed to be gladiatorial contests. I had a lot to learn.

Among the new intake to F-wing was a Scouser by the name of Mark. He was stocky, with close-cropped black hair and a fierce-looking scar on his cheek. He moved in on my spur, a couple of cells away from me, but I didn't really speak to him much. We just nodded to each other when we passed on the landings. I knew he was a burglar and was doing five years. When I was a kid I did my share of burgling, but the last time had been in 1977. I didn't particularly like or respect burglars, especially since I had been burgled myself on one occasion. It may sound strange, but there is a definite pecking order among criminals, a class system if you will, and burglars are looked down on, just as the upper class would look down on the middle class.

At the lowest end of the scale are petty criminals, shoplifters, sneak thieves, joyriders, muggers (or 'street robbers', as they are now called) and gas-meter bandits. Up a step are burglars, car thieves, fraudsters and drug dealers. And at the top end of the scale are armed robbers, GBH merchants, some murderers and organized gangsters. That's the pecking order in a nutshell, but there are some exceptions. For example, the average dwelling-house burglar can move up a notch by branching into commercial burglary (the burgling of shops and business premises). There is even more kudos to be had for a burglar who gets into 'creeping', 'creeper' being the criminal term for a cat burglar. In fact, the more daring and lucrative the burglary, the more respect the burglar is afforded by the criminal fraternity. Someone who breaks into council flats to nick the telly and video is classed as a 'mug' and a 'toerag', but a burglar who scales the balconies of Mayfair to cop for a parcel of tom (tom-foolery = jewellery) is one of the chaps.

As a rule, the blokes at the top of the burglars' pecking order are the aggy men. They go for the richest prizes and bring an element of physical violence to burglary. Armed, sometimes with guns, they usually work to a plan and research their targets. It's a dangerous game, as most of the time the occupants of the house have to be tied up and this calls for the element of surprise. I have never taken part in an aggravated burglary; it never appealed to me as a crime. I robbed banks because I convinced myself that it was a victimless crime. I was in and out in four minutes, I didn't physically touch anyone, and the money I stole was fully insured. This was how I stilled my occasional twinges of conscience. What I did was business. Going into someone's home with a gun was too personal for me.

You may have noticed that I do not include sex offenders anywhere in the pecking order. This is because the criminal fraternity do not class them as criminals. In the world I once inhabited, they are lower than anybody, an underclass. Non-people.

One day I got talking to Mark the Scouser in the canteen queue. It turned out that he knew a few of the same people I knew in other nicks, having done a previous sentence in Full Sutton dispersal prison in the 1990s. Mark was very well read, favouring history and autobiographies. I took to him when I found out he also had a sense of humour. One thing I can't have around me in jail is miserable bastards. It's bad enough being there in the first place, without having to look at glum faces every day.

Mark was a 'quality' burglar, travelling all over the country to hit his targets. Unfortunately, he was also a heroin and crack addict. He had stolen a small fortune during his burglary career, but it had all gone up his nose. Realizing how serious his problem was – both the drugs and the crime – he decided to come off the gear and give Grendon a try. He told me how hard it was for him to give up drugs, and that he believed giving up the criminal lifestyle would be pretty easy compared to that.

By now all the men who had been on F-wing when I arrived had gone up to the wings. Ray, Kevin and Daran had ended up on C-wing, along with Tel, the Scouse rapist. Ritchie, Toby and Geordie John had gone to D-wing, which was rumoured to be the worst one in the prison. I was hoping for A-wing myself, as one of my best pals was already over there and giving it good reports. Steve, from the Old Kent Road, doing a two-strike life for bank robbery, had been at Grendon for almost a year by the time I arrived. I had served time with him in Pentonville, Belmarsh and Whitemoor over the years and, in the vernacular of the underworld, he was one of your own.

Steve was a strange character. At first glance he seemed a typical villain: 6 feet tall, broad-shouldered, with a craggy face and a broken nose. He was heavily tattooed, including on his neck and shovel-sized hands, and he spoke in a gruff voice. But he had a professorial knowledge of English history, in particular the monarchy. He was a nationalist, but, unlike Kevin, not a racist.

I had first met Steve on the yard in Pentonville in 1987, where I had witnessed him bashing the granny out of a man who had been bullying some of the younger and weaker cons. Since then he and I had been bumping into each other in the system. Steve had started his life sentence at Wormwood Scrubs, from where he had been allocated to the brand-new lifers' wing at HMP Swaleside. Unfortunately, the lifers' wing left a lot to be desired from an inmate's point of view, and the cons made their feelings known by withdrawing their cooperation and refusing to work. There were a couple of fires and some general unrest, and many lifers were ghosted to other nicks. Steve ended up at Belmarsh, where we teamed up again. He was also on Red spur at Whitemoor when I was there, and applied for Grendon before me. He had a history of drug abuse and came to Grendon determined to knock the drugs on the head. Conventional prisons are awash with heroin, which makes kicking the habit that much harder for anyone with a mind to. Grendon's zero-tolerance drug policy was a welcome relief for men who were serious about getting clean.

Steve came up to F-wing to see me. He was looking a lot healthier now that he was off the skag, and he was very enthusiastic about Grendon, and A-wing in particular. A-wing was the only one in the prison that was actually accredited, which means that it was recognized by the Home Office for its work as a therapeutic community. Steve urged me to do my best to get on to A-wing, though I wouldn't have much say in the matter as it was decided by the head therapist. I told Steve I had heard that A-wing was stricter than the other wings, with few second chances given to anyone who stepped out of line. He laughed it off. 'Yeah, a lot of the bods over there are therapeutons, but the likes of us have got fuck all to worry about. It's only the snides who get dug out.' It was the first time I'd heard the word 'therapeuton', a disparaging term for someone who was so far into therapy that everything had to be examined for its 'therapeutic value'.

Grendon has its own language, which I came to think of as 'therapese'. It was not in use on F-wing as nobody was really doing any serious therapy, but therapese was common throughout the rest of the jail. Therapese words and phrases were used so often that they became clichés. Examples of therapese are 'bad space', as in 'I'm in a bad space at the moment', or 'owning it', as in 'I know I've done terrible things, but I'm owning it'. Others that equally jarred the life out of me were: 'flagging it up', 'buying into it', 'running with it', 'comfort zone' and 'I'm not doing this justice'. Later I would come to detest certain phrases spoken in therapese and it made me cringe to hear these banal clichés used over and over again. At one small group meeting I counted twenty-seven bad spaces and nine owning its, in an hour and a half. I was determined not to 'buy into' therapese, and waged a one-man campaign to obliterate it.

I was talking to Jay one day when the subject of drugs came up. Jay was a serious addict who committed crimes only to fund his addiction, and he had said that he was determined to give up drugs. Now he told me that he had smuggled a couple of grams of coke in on his first visit at Grendon. I was outraged. I couldn't believe that, knowing how drugs had fucked his life, he was putting his place in Grendon at risk by snorting coke. I ripped into him, but his attitude was 'It's only a bit of charlie! It's not crack or smack! What's the big deal?' In the end I had to just shrug my shoulders. I was well aware how devious and self-deceiving junkies can be; I had lived among enough of them. But later on it bothered me when I thought about it. Why go through all the performance of getting to Grendon, which was no walk in the park, if you had no intention of taking it seriously? It just didn't make sense. I suppose that is the nature of serious addiction.

The misuse of both legal and illegal drugs was taken very seriously at Grendon. Under the rules of Grendon's constitution, inmates who were accused of drug misuse could be voted out by members of the community and be returned to their previous prison. Before reaching Grendon every prisoner had to sign a compact committing them to voluntary drug tests. VDTs were done weekly, and the whole prison had to submit to them. In most jails 90 per cent of the drugs come in on visits, usually swallowed or secreted in the prisoner's anus (known as 'bottling', bottle and glass = arse), and there is always a heavy security presence in the visiting room. But Grendon had the most relaxed visits I have ever experienced. The staff in the visiting room were very low key and unobtrusive; there were no black paramilitary-style jump-suited screws waiting to jump on any prisoner who might raise his hand to his mouth or scratch his arse, as in other jails. There were CCTV cameras in the visiting room and enough staff for safety, but the atmosphere was great. Unfortunately this meant it was pretty easy for someone to take advantage and smuggle a parcel in, and there were people who did.

I like a puff (cannabis) as much as anyone, and probably more than most, but it seemed pointless to put in fifteen months of effort to get here only to be kicked out after the first piss-test. If all I had wanted was to get high I could have saved myself the hassle and stayed in the system, where all manner of drugs are available on every landing. A couple of days after I spoke to Jay, he failed the weekly VDT and was straight on a van back to Swaleside.

One of the blokes on my landing, Shaun, was serving seven years for rape. He was a nervous little man with bright ginger hair, and he didn't speak much. One day he was called down to see the wing therapist for an assessment. When he came back on the landing he seemed in shock, so I asked him what had happened. He told me that he was going back to Dartmoor. It turned out that the woman who had accused him of rape had been to the police and admitted that she had been lying all along, but because the criminal justice system, though very quick to jail people, has no swift remedy for those who are unjustly incarcerated, Shaun's case had to be referred to the Criminal Cases Review Committee, who would then recommend a retrial, and this would take months. In the meantime, Shaun had been judged unsuitable for therapy as the rape conviction was the sum total of his criminal record, so he had to go back to the prison he had come from, Dartmoor. At this stage he had already served over two years, most of it on protection wings, and had been beaten and abused by other prisoners for being a rapist. I knew that if I had run into Shaun anywhere but Grendon and had found out he was in for hairy (hairy ape = rape), I would have had no hesitation in clumping him, or worse. Everyone knows that there are innocent men and women in our prisons – more than anyone cares to admit – but they have to take their chances like everyone else.

One man who was not so innocent was Roy, a big Brummie with a shaved head and a good line in bullshit. Roy came on to F-wing from Wakefield prison, known as 'Monster Mansion' for its large population of sex offenders. At first I was suspicious of Roy, for three reasons: one because he was a Brummie, two because he wore dark glasses, and three because he had come from Wakefield. Each of those reasons would be a cause for concern by itself, but all together they were louder than a four-alarm fire.

Roy seemed to latch on to me straight away and, maybe because I was beginning to change, I didn't spot him as a bad wrong-un. Usually I have a sixth sense, a jail radar, that warns me about people like Roy long before they get within ten feet of me. It doesn't always work, and I have been fooled before, as we all have, but Roy was good. He established the groundwork like a pro, growling at the suspects on the wing while showing the right amount of respect to the obvious ODCs. He contrived to get next to me in the dinner queue and coated all nonces and wrong-uns, finishing with an exasperated 'What the fuck are people like us doing in a gaff like this, Raze?' Once we had our food he sat down at my table to eat, engaging Whispering Mick in a conversation about crime. I kept a wary eye on Roy, but it was more out of habit. I analysed my initial suspicion of him thus: okay, so he's a Brummie, but there must be a few sensible people from there – though I'd never met one. The dark glasses screamed 'nonce!', but that was just stereotyping. After all, Roy Orbison had worn shades, and look at the great music he'd produced, and not a hint of kiddy-fiddling. And Wakefield was not all nonces, there were some ODCs unlucky enough to end up there. I decided to give Roy the benefit of the doubt, but not until after he had stated his crime in a group meeting.

The next morning we had a community meeting that started, as usual, with everyone introducing themselves. When it got to Roy he gave his name, his sentence of fourteen years, and his crime, GBH. That sealed it for me, as I knew that honesty was the cornerstone of Grendon, and I was sure that if anyone gave the wrong legend they would be pulled by the staff and made to rectify it. So Roy was an ODC. At this stage, though I was still finding it hard to deal with my ingrained revulsion towards sex offenders, I was learning how to deal with my prejudices. If Roy had said he was in for rape, I would not have blanked him, though I certainly would not have welcomed him into my company with open arms. The only people I still could not bring myself to be near were actual kiddy-fiddlers, men who had committed crimes against children, but, thank fuck, there were none of these on F-wing at this time. Or so I thought.

Roy joined our little firm. There was me, Scouse Mark, Peter, who was a Manchester armed robber, Whispering Mick, Lindsay and Paul. We weren't a 'firm' in the usual prison sense of the word, we just knocked about together on the wing, playing cards and pool and taking coffee in each other's cells. Being ODCs we all had crime and prison experiences in common. Lindsay was a robber from Hull, in his late forties, who was always moaning about something or other, and we would rip the piss out of him, but it was just banter. Paul was also in his forties, but he had aged worse than the rest of us and looked about sixty-five. He was from Manchester and was serving seven and a half years for a commercial burglary. He was a bit strange. I could never tell whether he really was as thick as two short planks or whether it was just an act. One day in a community meeting he said he only committed his crimes in order to 'punish the sinners'. I pulled him afterwards and questioned him about uttering such an outrageous statement, and he looked puzzled. 'I thought that's the kind of stuff they want to hear,' he said.

Roy soon made a name for himself on the wing with his constant slagging of the sex offenders and his bursts of violent temper during meetings. He didn't scare any of our firm, but I could see that a few of the lads on the wing were a bit intimidated and shied away from him. He was a big fella and could talk a good fight; at Grendon that made him a fair-sized fish in a small pond. Roy was always respectful to me, and he had a good line in patter and plenty of funny stories about the Birmingham underworld, such as it is, so I swallowed his story about why he was in jail. Hook, line and sinker.

According to Roy, he had been one of the top drug dealers in Birmingham and also ran a firm of nightclub doormen with his twin brother. They had sold a parcel of disco-biscuits to another firm in Yorkshire and been stiffed for their bit of dosh. So Roy had gone further north to recover the parcel and administer suitable punishment. He had caught up with a couple of the other firm and, when recompense was not forthcoming, he exacted some swift and merciless retribution. With a baseball bat. We had no reason to disbelieve Roy's tale, and it was not unlike many I had heard before on the yards and landings of a lot of jails. Besides, if he was lying, the staff would have surely had a quiet word and given him directions: tell the truth or go back to Wakefield. There's no point starting off in therapy with basic lies. But things were not that straightforward. I found out afterwards that Roy had been called into meetings with the therapist and wing staff on many occasions and was strongly advised to reveal the truth about himself but had refused. As he was seen as a prime candidate for therapy, it was decided to give him time to reach the right decision himself. In the meantime, me and Roy had some long chats about why we had come to Grendon, and life in general, and I found I quite liked him.

By then I had been on F-wing for five weeks and seen plenty of men come and go, and I was getting pissed off. I was tired of the lack of activity. Every day was the same as the last, and seemed longer than a week in Wandsworth chokey. The meetings were nothing more than gripe sessions where people constantly whinged about everything from having no telly to the price of budgie seed in the canteen. I was bored, and there was little to stimulate me on the wing. I wrote when I could, but it was hard to get into a routine with very little lock-up time. The cell doors opened at 8 a.m. and didn't shut again until 8 p.m., and the heat and noise were stifling. Some blokes had £400 stereo systems that could kick out more wattage than a Black Sabbath concert, and they weren't shy about hitting the volume button. The screws wouldn't say a word to them; it wasn't the Grendon way. We were supposed to police ourselves and sort out any disputes in a non-violent way. I knew that if I was to go around clumping the owners of the noisy stereos I would be back in Whitemoor before most of them hit the ground. So I tried speaking to them. The trouble with this was that they too were aware of the no-violence rule and were ready to milk it. The best I could do was give them my mad-eyed stare, and start dropping hints that I might be thinking of going back to Whitemoor. And if I was going to leave Grendon I might as well go out with a bang. This got them worried enough to start lowering the volume.

I was called in for my initial wing assessment. This was a meeting with wing staff and the therapist, and it was usual to be told which wing you would be going on and when. I went into the meeting bright-eyed and bushy-tailed, ready to answer all questions and get my posting to a therapy wing. I nodded and smiled in all the right places, but at the end, instead of the good news I was hoping for, Ian said, 'Okay, you're doing well. Just carry on.' And that was it. To say I was disappointed would be like saying Billy Bunter liked the occasional cream cake. I was fucking gutted. All I could see stretching out before me was more endless days on F-wing. I tried my best not to show it though, and just cracked on. I reminded myself that I had spent longer in solitary confinement, in a lot worse conditions, than I had spent on F-wing. Fuck! I had spent longer in prison canteen queues!

There was a portable television on the wing, which was really for the night staff to use, but the office where it was kept was open during the day and it became okay for prisoners to take it upstairs to watch if they wanted to see their evening soap operas instead of the video that was provided in the communal TV room. I was aware that Roy had been organizing a rota for the lads who were on the 1s to have the telly in their cell every night. It was against the rules to have the telly in a cell after bang-up, but the screws knew nothing about it. Up on the 2s we never got a crack at the telly, so I decided to put this right. I pulled Roy and told him that we were joining the coup, and that I was having the telly that night. He was sweet with this, but he said that Sap, a rapist on the 1s, wouldn't be happy because it was his turn. With my usual charm and grace I replied, 'Fuck him, I'm having it tonight. And if he kicks off tell him to come and see me.'

Roy sneaked the telly into my cell under a prison blanket. Why he bothered with the blanket I don't know, as if a member of staff were to have seen him it wouldn't have taken much working out that the blanket-draped telly-shaped object was actually a telly. But some people just have to make a performance about everything. Roy said that Sap was 'screwing' over me having the telly on his night, but he didn't have the minerals to come up and front me about it. I stashed the telly under my bed until bang-up, and looked forward to a night of *Football on Five* and a decent film.

At 8 p.m. the staff came around and locked up for the night. Inside every cell, as part of the Night San, is a tannoy system with which the staff in the downstairs office can call people down without having to run up and down the stairs all the time. I was just pulling the telly out from under the bed when the tannoy crackled loudly to life. It was Myra, a sour-faced old biddy, who was on duty in the office. 'Will whoever has the staff television get on their cell bell and give it back. If this is not done in the next five minutes, there will be no Night San for F-wing tonight.' My heart sank. I had been lollied up, good and proper, and I could guess who had done it. Sap had made sure that if he wasn't getting the telly, then no one was.

I was cursing my luck. The scam with the telly had been going for weeks without a hitch, but the one time I got it I was captured bang to rights. I had no choice, I had to get on the bell and stick my hands up. If they left us without Night San they would simply open the cells one at a time and search till they found the telly. I got on the bell and was opened up by Myra, a triumphant look on her crone-like features, and I handed the telly back. 'What do you expect?' I said in reply to her look. 'I'm a fucking criminal!'

I knew that I was going to be 'winged' for having the telly. That meant that I would have to explain my actions to the whole community, who would then decide on my punishment. But, to tell you the truth, I was quite looking forward to it. I knew that at least half the wing had had the telly in their cells at one time or another, and it would be fascinating to hear what they would have to say about my punishment.

The next day there was a full community meeting. I had spent the night planning what I was going to say. Being winged was not to be taken lightly. In extreme cases it meant you could be put to a 'commitment vote', and voted out of Grendon for your behaviour. I didn't think it would come to that, but I was prepared for every eventuality. I had toyed with the idea of writing a speech to read at the meeting, but in the end I decided to play it by ear.

After the meeting had been brought to order and the introductions had been made, the chairman announced that there was a disciplinary matter in the book that had to be dealt with. He read the brief details of the entry that had been made by Myra. Then Myra herself gave an account of what had happened. As she said that taking the telly had been a 'breach of trust that betrayed the whole community', I looked around the faces of that community. Some of those faces, those who had never had the telly in their cells, were wearing suitable looks of disappointment and betrayal or glowing in righteous indignation. Others, who had been part of the coup, seemed to find things of the utmost fascination on the tiled floor and would not meet my eyes. I was amused. This was more like it! At last, after weeks of boredom and inactivity, I was in my element again, about to enter the arena for a verbal combat with the forces of the system. This is what I craved.

Myra made it plain that because I had been caught red-handed with the telly I had no defence, and she said that as punishment the staff were of the mind that it should be confiscated for a month, therefore depriving the whole wing of a telly in order to force on me the realization that my actions had an effect on others. Myra finished her evidence and sat back with a satisfied look on her leathery face. The chairman nodded judiciously and turned the spotlight on to me. 'Noel, what have you got to say about this?' I cleared my throat and launched my attack.

'Firstly,' I began, 'I do not deny that I had the telly in my cell. I took it because I am bored being stuck on this wing 24/7 with nothing to do but stare at the walls. I know this is not much of an excuse, but it is the truth. I am a criminal; I steal things. I've come here to try and change that, but it's early days and I can't just wipe out a lifetime of learned behaviour in a few weeks. I would expect you to be aware of that. Secondly, in mitigation I will say this. The Nazis were a bunch of horrible bastards.' At this unexpected statement all heads came up and everyone began to look interested. I continued. 'If one of their men was killed in occupied territory, they would wipe out whole villages in reprisal, men, women and children. This is known as collective punishment; the punishment of many for the deeds of the few. And I've always thought that the prison system is very Nazi-like in its approach to punishment.' The uniformed staff in the room looked uncomfortable. Myra was staring daggers at me, but Ian, the therapist, looked very interested. 'Someone scales a wall at HMP Durham, and cons as far away as HMP Exeter will be locked down in the ensuing panic. Collective punishment. But I was led to believe that Grendon was different from "the system". Grendon is supposed to be a "community", a "democracy", where each individual must take responsibility for his own actions and be accountable to the community. No blanket punishments, and each case judged on its own merits. And yet, all that appears to be no more than a sham, smoke and mirrors. Grendon is no more than "the system" wearing different clothes. The worst thing about prison, far worse than the brutality and the mind-numbing boredom, is that it strips us of responsibility. It makes babies of us, reliant on the system for everything and refusing to take charge of our own lives. Well, today I want back some of what the system has taken from me over the years. I want to be responsible for my own actions. Yes, I took the telly, so punish me. Me. Not everyone else. Just me. Prove to us that Grendon is different, and all you say it is, and start right now. That's all I have to say.' I sat back in my chair.

There was a silence that seemed to last for ever. Then Nick, who was sitting next to me, his simian features contorted in empathy, clapped once and said, 'Yeah, good stuff.' Ian, the therapist, nodded slightly. Most of the staff wore neutral looks, but Myra's face made it plain that she was not impressed. Mark, the Scouser, leaned forward. 'Raze, do you think that you only took the telly because you wanted to be caught?' he asked. I saw Ian nod again in agreement with the question. I looked thoughtful for a moment before answering. 'Maybe,' I conceded. 'It could be that I'm pissed off wasting time on this wing, and maybe I want the decision to move on, one way or the other, to be taken out of my hands.' Mark leaned back and winked at me as if to say 'well caught'. Paul scratched his head and looked confused. 'So where do the Germans come into it?' he asked.

The staff asked the community to decide what my punishment for taking the telly was to be, and they voted, to a man, for a caution. Myra wasn't happy with that. After a heated discussion it was decided that there should be a token ban of seven days with no telly, for me alone. I was happy, it had been a result all round. I had enjoyed the meeting for a change and the hour and a half had seemed to fly by. Afterwards I was called down to the wing office. Ian was there, along with two members of staff and the wing probation officer. The atmosphere was light and relaxed, so I sat and waited. Ian smiled. 'A place has become available on A-wing,' he said. I was over the moon but kept my face neutral. 'Nice,' I said. Ian smiled. 'We're thinking of sending you over this weekend. How do you feel about that?' I allowed a smile to creep out. 'I'm ready,' I said. And that was that. I had made it through F-wing.

*

It was not until after I had left F-wing that Roy decided to reveal himself. It turned out that far from being a drug-dealing Birmingham hard man, in for GBH on a rival, Roy was no more than a kiddy-fiddler, who had beaten and sexually abused two eight-year-old girls. Apparently, it was as nasty a case as you could get. When I found out, I was sick. I had trusted him and invited him into my company, when I should have been poking his eyes out with a dirty pencil. His crime revolted me, but, if I am to be honest, what enraged me more was the fact that he had taken me for a mug. He had deliberately sought me out and inveigled his way past my defences, knowing who I was and my reputation for hurting people like him. I couldn't get my head around it.

As soon as Roy came clean about his offences he was allocated to G-wing, which is the semi-isolated wing where the worst type of sex offenders are kept. I did not see him again for months, and by then my rage had dissipated and I was content to blank him. Roy was not the first wrong-un to fool me, and I don't suppose he'll be the last.

5. A Different Planet

I never did get to A-wing. It turned out that the space that was due to be available fell through because of an administration error. Instead, I was reallocated to C-wing. I didn't really mind as C-wing would have been my second choice anyway. I knew a few of the lads on there.

It's a tradition at Grendon that before moving on to one of the therapy wings you should go to the wing and take a meal there. This is so you can be introduced to the community and get a feel of what the wing is like. You are shown the cell you will be moving into, and if you want to paint it, now is the time. You stay for a couple of hours before going back to F-wing for the night and moving down properly the next day.

On the Saturday I was ready to go and take my meal on C-wing. I was picked up by the C-wing vice-chairman, a big, fat, dour Welshman doing a two-strike life for arson, and the C-wing rep, a black guy from the south coast, doing life for murder. The VC, Dean, didn't say much, but Mikey, the rep, was very chatty. He said a lot of the community were quite pleased about having me on C-wing, as my reputation as a prison face and a writer of some notoriety added a bit of kudos to the wing. I wondered if what they were actually looking forward to was dismantling my image. But I was ready for anything.

The walk from F-wing to C-wing was a long one, along cream-coloured corridors and past the chapel, the MDT suite, the gym, the kitchen, the canteen, the Bhudda grove, G-wing, where the serious sex offenders were housed, A-wing, B-wing and finally, downhill, to where C- and D-wings sat opposite each other. On the wall outside them was a huge well-painted mural of a scene from the London Underground at the turn of the twentieth century. It certainly brightened the gaff up. The only things you see on most prison walls are obscene graffiti and blood stains.

The entrance to C-wing was the standard prison double-barred gates in front of heavy wooden doors. Dean rapped on the door, and within a couple of seconds the gates and doors were unlocked by a relaxed-looking screw. 'This must be the infamous Razor Smith,' he said, but I detected no malice in his voice. I said nothing. As I stepped through the gate I was greeted by a welcoming committee consisting of Kevin, Daran and Ray. The lads were as glad to see me as I was to see them, and there was a lot of hand-shaking and back-slapping all round.

The lads took me up to Kevin's cell for a cup of coffee. Kevin lived on the 3s landing, up five flights of stairs. On every landing were well-kept potted plants, and the railing of the stairs was painted brilliant white. Everything seemed clean and bright. Compared to F-wing, it was very quiet. On each landing was a small alcove with soft chairs, a small coffee table and a fish tank. I had never seen such things on a prison wing. I was already impressed by the surroundings.

Kevin's cell was no surprise. Resplendent with Union Jacks, crosses of St George and posters of grim-faced, big-booted, bald-headed skinhead bands. If anything, there was even more of it on display than there had been in his cell on F-wing. The big difference was the level of what passes for luxury in a prison cell. The floor was carpeted, there was a small television set in one corner, and all the cell furniture was intact. In most cells there will be items of furniture either missing or broken. For example, you may have a cupboard in which to keep your clothes, but no shelves inside it. Or a locker, but with no door on it. The higher the turnover in the cell, the more damage the furniture will receive over the years. If you lock stressed-out men in a room the size of the average bathroom for long periods of time, the cell furnishings tend to be the first things they take their frustrations out on.

I was happy to listen to the lads extolling the virtues of C-wing. The one thing that struck me was the genuine pride they seemed to take in the wing. Time and again I was told that C-wing was the best one in the nick. In dispersal jails prisoners only ever take a kind of perverse pride in their wings, if at all. Someone might point out that their wing has had the most stabbings, or the most skag for sale, or the most nutters on the loose. I had never heard a prisoner publicly praising the wing staff, or the community. Even Kevin had good things to say.

While we were in the cell a screw appeared in the doorway with a smile on his face. I tensed slightly, but the lads were all relaxed and started a bit of banter with him. He gave as good as he was getting, greeting the lads by their first names. He stepped into the cell and stuck his hand out to me. I was caught off guard and was shaking hands with him almost before I realized I was doing it. I had never shaken hands with a screw before; it was unheard of in the nicks I had been in. In fact, I had known men who had been stabbed by other prisoners just for being seen in conversation with screws. I felt my face grow hot with the shame and confusion of what I had just done. I quickly looked at the others to see if any of them was eyeing me with suspicion or disgust, but they seemed genuinely unfazed by it. I gripped my coffee cup in both hands and bowed my face into the steam issuing from it to cover my extreme embarrassment.

'I'm Keith,' said the screw. 'It's nice to finally meet you, Razor. I've been following your writing career for years. I've got all the stuff you've done for *Prison Writing* and *Inside Time*, some of which I agree with and some I don't. But we'll talk about that later. I used to work with Deborah, who knows you quite well from when you were on your last sentence . . .' He was chatting away and mentioning some of the people I had met through my writing. He seemed to know most of them. I felt myself begin to relax now that we were in familiar territory. He mentioned a recent article I had written for *Inside Time* about heroin addiction in prison, and I soon found myself in a debate with him about a couple of points I had made. We talked for about fifteen minutes before Keith said he had to go and take the roll-check. As he left he winked at me. 'We'll talk more later. I'll be interested in hearing your opinion on several other matters. In the meantime, welcome to the wing.'

After Keith had left, Daran nudged me. 'I knew you'd get on with Keith,' he said. 'He's been dying to meet you.' Kevin nodded. 'You know me, Raze,' he said, flexing the swastika tattoo on his chest. 'I fookin' hate screws, but some of 'em on this wing are proper diamonds. And Keith's one of 'em.' This place really was a different planet compared to any other nick I had been in. It was hard to get my head around the things that were happening here, but I found it all very encouraging.

The evening meal took place in a large dining hall, just like on F-wing. But, unlike in F-wing, everyone seemed happy and relaxed. I lost count of the number of complete strangers who stopped to say hello to me and welcome me to the wing. The food was great and the room was buzzing with quiet conversation. I sat at a table with Daran, Ray and Kevin. I had to ask the obvious question, I couldn't help myself: 'How many sex cases on this wing, then?' Kevin wasn't shy about answering. 'Too fookin' many!' he said. Ray nodded. 'Yeah, but let's have it right, even one is too many. You've just got to accept them. You knew they was going to be here when you applied to come, so it's pointless driving yourself mad over them.' I could see Kevin getting his argumentative face on, so I jumped in. 'You're spot on, Ray,' I said. 'I only asked out of curiosity. I'm not planning on weighing any of them in, it took me too long to get here.' Kevin grunted and attacked his battered fish. Daran smiled. 'Anyway,' he said, 'there's no kiddy-fiddlers here. It's mainly about four or five rapists, and a couple of other undesirables. Most of us on this wing are normal criminals. This is the best wing in the prison.' Ray nodded again. 'Amen to that,' he said.

After the meal the lads took me to meet a few of the more sensible cons on the wing. Every prison wing has got its prisoner hierarchy, and Grendon was no different from any other jail in this respect. Top of the pecking order in most jails are the serious career criminals, some of whom will have achieved notoriety in the outside world as well. In Grendon the faces are ODCs who have gained a reputation through their deeds in other jails. One on C-wing was Fred. Fred was well known in the system as one of the boys; game and subversive, he wouldn't back down from anyone, con or screw. I had never met Fred, even though he came from the same manor as me, but I had heard a lot about him over the years.

Kevin took me up to Fred's cell and introduced me. When he was still in his teens Fred had been sentenced to eighteen years' imprisonment for various charges of robbery and violence. He had served over a decade in some of the hardest prisons in the country, including a long spell in Parkhurst from the age of twenty-one, where he mixed with the most violent and infamous prisoners in the system. Fred, at 5 foot 8 and weighing in at 9 stone, more than held his own in the violent arena of the dispersal system, mainly due to the fact that he was an excellent boxer, able to hit equally hard with either fist. He had many bouts, both gloved and bare-knuckle, in prison and it was rumoured that he had never lost a fight. As for most of us who had come to prison for long periods in our formative years, extreme violence became the norm for Fred. After his release it wasn't long before he was back in prison, this time for a brutal hammer attack on his older brother. He received a life sentence for GBH under the two-strike Act. And it was his sentencing judge who recommended he should come to Grendon.

I liked Fred straight away. He was very sensible but also had a good sense of humour, and we knew many of the same people. What impressed me was the lack of guile in him. He spoke about therapy in a serious way and seemed up for it. Grendon had obviously helped him a lot. At thirty-three he appeared older and wiser than his years, and I tried to equate this relaxed and personable man with the stories I had heard. Fred's reputation was pretty fearsome at one time, but at Grendon no one felt the need to prove themselves and past reputations were surplus to requirements. I was now starting to grasp that fact.

Fred took me up to the 3s landing to introduce me to his best mate on the wing. John was a big fella who had also gained a reputation in the dispersal system before coming to Grendon. Fourteen years into a life sentence for murder, he had spent a good portion of it knocking screws up in the air and generally causing mayhem until he had his moment of clarity and realized he could be doing exactly the same thing for another couple of decades. He had been at Grendon for over two years and had also benefited from therapy.

John came from Corby but was Scottish and still retained his accent. Everything in his cell, from the cups to his bathrobe, was in the green and white hoops of Celtic FC. John was kind of the daddy of the wing, not because he was old – he was in his late thirties – but because he was so calm and steady and people trusted him. Fred and John were a very funny double act, bouncing the banter off each other in such a way that I could tell they had been doing it for a long time.

Soon it was time for me to head back to F-wing for the night. The lads walked me down to the gate of C-wing, where I was taken along the endless corridors once again, but this time by a screw. F-wing was depressing, and I really was looking forward to moving on. As soon as I got back to my cell I packed everything into my two blue boxes, in preparation for the morning.

The following day I was ready bright and early for my move. Once again I was picked up by Dean and Mikey, this time with a trolley to carry my boxes on the long journey to C-wing. I had told Steve that I wouldn't be moving to A-wing after all, but I would get to see him in the exercise yard. F-wing had its own exercise yard for its inmates only, so we couldn't mix freely with prisoners from other wings until we actually got into therapy. But now I would be able to associate with everyone except the inmates on F-wing. The more I thought about it the more I realized that my time spent on F-wing had been just like time spent in a punishment block, but without the beatings and the screams in the middle of the night.

My cell was on the 1s landing, number 119, and the lads had painted the walls for me before I moved in so it was clean and fresh. Kevin had also laid out ½oz of snout for a bit of carpet for the cell floor, which I greatly appreciated. The cell was of the same small dimensions as the ones on F-wing but cleaner, and had a small television in one corner and an extra shelf on the wall. I had a bed, a window, a pisspot and a cupboard – all the essentials that make up the modern prison cell.

It took me less than thirty minutes to unpack my boxes and get the cell looking the way I wanted it. I'd guess I've probably been in more than a thousand cells in my life. When I was a category A man I had to change cells every twenty-one days for 'security reasons', so I had cell decoration off to a fine art. I would never personalize a cell like a lot of prisoners do, sticking up loads of family photos, or posters, and most times I didn't even bother with curtains, I would just hang a prison blanket over the windows to cut out the light. At best I would stick up a picture of my kids and unpack a few books. In the old days this was because I was such a bad troublemaker I knew it wouldn't be long until I did something that would have me removed to a punishment block or another prison altogether. I didn't like to get too settled in any prison as it would seem as though I was surrendering to incarceration. Personalizing a cell and sticking up photos sends a message to the screws that you are here to stay and have something to lose. The most subversive prisoners in the system live out of cardboard boxes, ready for a move at a moment's notice.

Once I had sorted out my cell I went on the mooch to have a closer look at my new wing. Up on the 2s landing was a large room with a tatty-looking pool table and a bar-football table, and a darts board with no darts. On the ground floor was the large community meeting room. It was brightly painted, with three big curtained windows and blue soft chairs lined around the walls and facing into the room. It would hold forty-two inmates and up to six staff during the twice-weekly community meetings. There was a square, brightly coloured rug in the centre of the room and a television on a dais at the back wall for when the room was used for evening association. I stood in the empty room and imagined what it would be like full of personality-disordered prisoners. I would know soon enough I guessed.

I arrived on C-wing during the summer therapy break. Therapy breaks happen three times a year – Christmas, Easter and summer – and usually last for a fortnight. In those two weeks there are only two meetings, one each Wednesday morning, lasting for no more than thirty minutes, just as a sort of check-in with the community. Therapy, I had heard, was so intense that if there were no regular breaks then people's heads would be exploding and imploding all over the place. Personally, I thought that was exaggerated, just a fanny so everyone could have a bit of a holiday, but I was later to find out the truth of it.

As I came out of the community room I noticed an odd-looking individual staring at me. He was about thirty, with a head like a cannon-ball and one of those vacant faces that you often see on High Court judges or psychopaths. I nodded to him. 'All right, mate?' I asked. Something that might have been distantly related to a smile flitted across his rubbery-looking lips. Jesus Christ! I thought to myself. This is what happens when cousins marry. He pointed a podgy finger in my direction. 'Are yis a cockney, like?' I recognized his accent as pure Geordie. I've met quite a few Geordies in prison and they are usually good stuff if you catch them when they're not in the depths of a 'roid rage. I nodded again. 'South London,' I said. His Brillo-pad eyebrows seemed to knit together in concentration. 'D' yis kna a gadjee named Johnny Broon? He's from your way.' I shook my head. 'Don't ring any bells,' I said. 'Whereabouts is he from in south London exactly?' There was more movement from his eyebrows, which I assumed was an indication that he was wracking his brain cell. 'Milton Keys!' he suddenly blurted, looking pleased with himself.

I was still chuckling when John came downstairs to see if I wanted a coffee. 'What was Biff saying to you?' John asked. 'I'm not really too sure,' I said. He smiled. 'He's not the full shilling.' I shook my head. 'I don't even think he's sixpence!' John told me there were a few bods like Biff in the nick, their shoe size about the same as their IQ. I wondered how they had managed to pass all the tests to get to Grendon, especially the IQ test. John shrugged. 'Some people are special cases,' he said. 'They may be a couple of sparks short of a fuse box, but that doesn't mean they can't benefit from therapy. Biff is pretty harmless. He just comes from a very deprived background and he's never really had a chance.'

It turned out that, like myself, Biff was serving a two-strike life sentence for bank robbery, and it was not his first crack at 'the Heavy', as we used to call blagging in my distant youth. Unlike me, Biff had a penchant for using a household implement on his robberies instead of a firearm. He would wrap the plastic pipe section of a 'Henry' Hoover in a paper bag and pretend it was the barrel of a shotgun. Then, wearing a hat as a disguise, he would enter a bank or building society and have a demand-up.

A couple of times he managed to pull it off and escape with a couple of grand in till money, which he promptly spent on class A drugs. The first time he was caught he was given seven years' imprisonment. The second time, as a persistent offender, he was sentenced to life imprisonment under the two-strike Act.

It was sad really. There was never any chance of Biff shooting anyone with his Hoover pipe – at worst he might have given the bank carpets a quick going over – but under British law an imitation firearm carries exactly the same sentence as a real loaded gun. The cashiers in the banks must have believed that Biff was in possession of a real gun or they never would have handed over the cash, and there is no doubt that staff and customers were put through a traumatic ordeal while innocently going about their business, but people like Biff do not belong in high-security prisons and they should certainly not be serving life sentences.

This country now has the highest population of life-sentenced prisoners in the whole of Europe, and the life sentence has been cheapened and trivialized by successive vote-hungry governments whose knee-jerk policies pander to the moral panic about crime that has been whipped up by tabloid editors as a sales tactic. There are now four different types of life sentence available to the judiciary: mandatory life, which replaced hanging and has to be given on conviction for murder; discretionary life, which can be given for a first serious offence, such as manslaughter, arson, GBH, armed robbery or rape; Her Majesty's Pleasure, detention for life, which can be given to anyone under the age of eighteen who is convicted of murder; and, the newest and most contentious, automatic life, known as 'two-strike' life, which can be given for a long list of 'second violent offences'.

The two-strike life, or, to give it its official title, 'Automatic Life Sentence under section 2 of the Crime (Sentences) Act 1997', was one of the ideas that Michael 'Something of the Night' Howard nicked from America when he was Home Secretary. In America it was three strikes, but Howard, wanting to show how tough on crime he was, made the British version two strikes. On the face of it, two-strikes is a pretty simple and effective piece of legislation but, if you look more closely, the flaws are obvious. Here's how it works in reality. Example: B, an eighteen-year-old, full of raging hormones and the stupidity of youth, gets into a fight at a party or football match and punches another youth, causing his victim a broken nose or chipped tooth. B is charged with grievous bodily harm and appears before the courts, which deal with him by way of a short spell of youth custody. Thirty years later, having led an exemplary life as a fully paid-up member of society, B has all but forgotten his youthful indiscretions. But the courts have not. Let's say that B gets into a heated boundary dispute with his neighbour and during the argument he utters the words 'I'll kill you'. B is now in imminent and real danger of being sentenced to prison for life on conviction of a 'second violent offence', i.e. threats to kill. Anyone with an ounce of sense might think that B might deserve a good ticking off, or at worst a stiff fine, but the two-strike life is automatic. And that is the problem.

The example I've used above is an actual case and B is now four years into his life sentence.

After a cup of coffee with John it was time for exercise. The exercise yard was massive compared to the one outside F-wing and also contained a fenced-off tarmac area for football matches. It was a hot day and it seemed as though everyone had decided to come out on the yard to catch a bit of sun. I spotted Steve from A-wing, and made my way over to him. He introduced me to his pal. Lee was a stocky little Scouser with a sarcastic sense of humour and an infectious laugh, doing life for murder. 'How's it goin', Razor lad? I've read some of your stuff in *Inside Time*, fair play to ya. I never thought I'd see you in a gaff like this.' I shook his hand. 'You know the apple, mate,' I said, 'I'm a lifer now, got to make the effort, or they'll never let me out.'

We took a slow amble around the yard just inside the perimeter wall and chatted. Ritchie and Toby, who had both gone to D-wing from F-wing, came up to shake hands and say hello. Toby was pretty relaxed but Ritchie was as hot-headed as ever. 'Fucking nonces everywhere!' was his opening gambit. 'They make my fucking skin crawl. If I had a machine-gun I could wipe out half the monsters in the prison system!' 'Yeah, nice to see you too, Rich,' I replied. Ritchie grinned and shrugged. 'Sorry, Raze,' he said. 'I'm still not used to this gaff. The bacons proper jar me. I'm thinking of going back to Long Lartin.' I shook my head. 'You knew what this nick was all about before you volunteered to come here, Rich,' I said. I liked Ritchie, he was a good kid too, but sometimes he could be just a little bit impetuous for his own good.

Ritchie had been convicted of murder and given a mandatory life sentence alongside his father. They beat and stabbed a man to death in an argument over a woman. It hadn't been Ritchie's fight but he became involved out of loyalty to his dad, and it didn't do Ritchie's head any good when his father found religion at the start of their Old Bailey trial and tried to put all the blame for the murder on to Ritchie. By the time the jury came back with two guilty verdicts both father and son had vowed never to speak to each other again. Ritchie was too wild and headstrong to settle down in prison and do his bird, and he seemed to stumble from one row to another. He had only served six years of his lengthy tariff and I personally thought there was plenty of trouble left in him before he would be able to settle down and get the full benefit of Grendon.

The sun was hot on the yard so we stopped walking and sat down on a grass verge to talk. It was the usual trip down felony lane: who was now dead, who was doing life, who had had it off in a big way, and who had got a result in court. I turned to Steve. 'What do you think then, mate? Have we made the right move coming here, or what?' Steve stared up at the clear, blue sky for a moment before answering. Then he rubbed his flat hooter with a sausage-like tattooed finger and smiled. 'That depends,' he said, 'on whether you've got plans on goin' back on the pavement when you finally get out.'

I shook my head. 'Not me,' I said. And I meant it. Grendon was my last chance, and I was seizing it with both hands.

Three weeks later Ritchie kicked off on the wing, threatening sex offenders, taking drugs and refusing to come to meetings. One morning, when we were all still locked in our cells, they came for him. He was shipped back to Long Lartin top-security prison. Grendon was no easy ride and if you weren't fully committed to it, it could be even harder. We had a couple of letters from him, full of bravado about how glad he was to be back with 'real people' again, but we all knew that at some stage in his future Ritchie would be coming back to Grendon. He needed it.

My first community meeting on C-wing came on Wednesday morning. I got to the community room at 8.55 and plonked myself down in one of the blue chairs. By nine everybody had filed in and taken their seats. 'Slick', the wing therapist, who had a penchant for expensive suits and handmade shoes, was sitting opposite me. My first impressions of him were that he was a very clever and manipulative man, as you might expect from a therapist, but essentially decent and approachable. The chairman opened the meeting by putting me in the spotlight, which was standard with new arrivals. 'We have a new man on the wing, whom most of you have already met, so we'll start with introductions.' Everyone introduced themselves one by one. When it was my turn I said, 'Noel Smith, two-strike life, armed robbery and possession of firearms. Good to be here.' I noticed the fleeting look of approval that crossed Slick's face. 'Razor' was no more.

After the introductions the chairman called for 'minutes' and about half a dozen men stuck their hands up. Bill, a potato-faced serial rapist from Yorkshire, began to speak. 'Yeah, I'd just like to say to the thieving fucker who stole my yoghurt out of the 2s' fridge, I hope you fookin' choke on it.' There was a moment's silence while people digested this, then the chairman pointed at another man who had his hand up. 'Yes, Pete.' Pete wanted to know why the canteen had added 25p to their already overpriced tins of tuna, and this led to a debate on canteen prices. I sat back in my chair and sighed. What sort of therapy is this, I wondered. It was no different from a whinging session on the landing of any other nick. I was disappointed.

The meeting seemed to drag on for half the day, and I stopped listening when one hobbity-looking geezer launched into a passionate plea about people cleaning the toilets after they'd used them. This was all bollocks. I studied the faces and mannerisms of some of the men in the room. Most of them seemed strange, the kind of men whom I would notice as odd if I saw them on the out, but maybe I was attributing to them a strangeness they didn't deserve because of where they were. I watched Slick as he watched everyone else. He had come to interview me on F-wing to see if I'd be suitable for C-wing. Why had I robbed so many banks, he had asked me. I thought about it for a moment and replied, 'Because I'm greedy and lazy.' I think it was the honesty of my answer that impressed him enough to choose me for C-wing.

The community meeting finally dragged to an end and I was out of my chair like a ferret up a drainpipe. Outside Fred approached me. 'I could see you were bored by all that,' he said. 'But don't be put off. Therapy break meetings are just a chance for everyone to do a bit of moaning. The real work is done in the small groups. Have they told you what group you're on yet?' I shook my head. 'I think you might be coming on group 3,' he said. 'My group.' I asked him what the group was like and who was on it. 'It's probably the strongest one on the wing. We do a lot of good work on some very important issues. And there's no hobbits in group 3.'

Back in my cell I was struck by the heat as I opened the door and made a mental note to order myself an electric fan from Argos. I was wondering whether I should switch the telly on and numb my brain with a dose of daytime TV, or write a letter. In Whitemoor I would already have finished my cleaning job for the day – another 95p in the bank – and be settled in front of my trusty old manual typewriter. I missed my writing routine. I hated writing in longhand as, though I am ambidextrous, I suffered broken bones in both hands at different stages of my life and holding a pen could get painful. I had to leave the typewriter behind at Whitemoor as, even though I had appropriated it and had it in my possession for three years, it wasn't on my official property card and would have been confiscated on reception. Or so I had thought. When I arrived on F-wing I found out that Grendon does not allow items to be sent in from family and friends. In most prisons, including the top-security dispersals, prisoners are allowed to receive items through the post, paid for by family and friends, which include postage stamps, CDs and music cassettes, underwear, clothing and books. At Grendon, however, the rule was that any item needed by a prisoner must be purchased by him from a small number of catalogues approved by the governor, and the cost, including postage and packing, had to be paid for by the prisoner out of his maximum wage of £10 per week. There was no specific reason for this ridiculous rule that I could discover, other than it had been implemented by a previous governor who 'wanted to make his mark on Grendon'. This is a major pain in the arse for prisoners, and meant that volunteering to come to Grendon and genuinely trying to rehabilitate ourselves put us under financial constraints not seen anywhere else in the prison system. To get a typewriter would mean saving up all my wages for around eight weeks, going without tobacco, toiletries, stamps and phone credits. But that problem was academic anyway because none of the approved catalogues contained typewriters.

On F-wing someone told me about a dodge that could be used to get goods sent in. The trick was to get someone on the out to buy whatever you needed – tracksuit, trainers or, in my case, a typewriter – and send it to the prison you had come from. The prison would forward the items to Grendon. Because they had come from another prison, Grendon would then issue them. I got in touch with Will Self and asked him to buy me a manual typewriter and send it to Whitemoor. Unfortunately, he couldn't find anywhere that sold manual typewriters any more and by the time I settled for an electric typewriter the Grendon loophole had been closed.

So I had a brand-new electric typewriter sitting in reception, which was marked NFI (not for issue), and in the meantime I was working in longhand whenever the pain would permit me.

While I was pondering my lack of writing machine, there was a tap on my cell door. I opened it to find the bloke who was living in the cell opposite me. I had noticed him around and he looked pretty sensible, compared to some of the odd bods on the wing. He was about 6 foot 2, athletic looking, military-style crop and small round glasses. He stuck his hand out. 'Hello, mate, I'm Taff. I live opposite,' he added, needlessly. When I heard the Welsh accent I almost winced. I had met plenty of Welshmen in jails like Albany and Dartmoor and, as a rule, I didn't think much of them. They were either steroid-abusing bodybuilders doing bird for 'roid rage attacks on their wives or neighbours, or 'joyriding' car thieves who didn't have the sense to earn a pound note from their crimes. I had met the odd decent one, like Rob in Highdown, who was a great artist and could sniff out a ½oz deal in the worst puff drought, or Jammo, the mad Cardiff skinhead, who had a bad joke for every conceivable occasion, but on the whole I found the Welsh a bit trying. Still, putting aside all my stereotypical notions, I shook hands with Taff and gave him a warm welcome.

We exchanged pleasantries and I was just warming to him when his face went a funny shade of red and he stumbled over what he was saying. I wondered if he had some kind of affliction, like a mild brain embolism or something, because his eyes started shifting all over the place and he completely lost track of the conversation. 'Are you okay?' I had to ask. He shook his head and pointed behind me to the window ledge where I had stacked my small book collection. I couldn't see anything. 'What?' I asked. Taff swallowed hard. 'Is that a book on the IRA?' he asked. His question must have been rhetorical, because it was obvious by the huge letters that the book was indeed *The IRA* by Tim Pat Coogan, but I answered anyway. 'Yeah,' I said. 'Do you want to borrow it?' He ignored my question and came back with one of his own. 'Are you a Provo, then?' I bristled, not so much at his question as at the aggressive tone in which he asked it. 'Why?' I asked, with equal sharpness. He tore his gaze from the book and looked at me as if for the first time, eyes glaring. 'I was in the fucking army, and I served in Northern Ireland,' he snarled. 'Yeah,' I said. 'So fucking what?' I wondered how we had gone from sniffing each other out in a friendly manner to facing each other down with growls and bristling fur. 'I don't fucking like Paddies,' he muttered, turning on his heel and marching from my doorway. I could feel my anger mounting. 'I don't particularly like the fucking Welsh either,' I shouted after him. 'Or brown-nosing suck-up Celts who join the English army. Fucking traitor!' He stopped in his tracks and turned, eyes blazing. 'It's not the English army, it's the British army.' I felt like sticking something in his eye, and if we'd been anywhere else I might have done just that, but I managed to retain some control over myself. 'Nice to meet you,' I said. 'Don't hurry back.' And I slammed my cell door.

I was fuming. Who was this mug that thought he could have a pop at me over what books I chose to read? It was a fucking liberty! The thought crossed my mind that I should break a coffee jar and go over to his cell and do a bit of 'wet work' on him. It's usually after an argument like this in prison that my paranoia kicks in. I figure that if I'm contemplating violence on him, he must be doing the same on me, so I should get in first and put him out of the game. That was how I had always thought in the past, but now I stopped and tried to rationalize things. Okay, I'm in Grendon, which has a no-violence rule, and if I attack him, or he attacks me, we'll both be kicked out. I don't know anything about the fella, but just the fact that he's here tells me something. He must have applied to come and gone through the same tests as me, so that means he must have some capacity for rationalization himself. And if it was going to come to violence, then surely it would have happened on the spot? There was a knock on the door. I opened it and Taff was standing there. 'Can I have a word?' he asked, calmly.

Taff apologized for his outburst. I apologized for mine. We shook hands. We told each other not to worry about what had happened, but I knew, and he knew, that some sort of war had been declared between us under the guise of truce. Taff and me were never going to be friends; at best we would tolerate each other, and somewhere down the line there would be a reckoning. I knew all this in the two minutes it took to mouth our platitudes and disappear into our respective cells. I had made my first enemy on C-wing, and it had taken less than a week.

Later that day I was having a cup of coffee with Fred and John, and brought up the subject of Taff. They told me that he was a strange cat, super paranoid and always pulling people for perceived slights. He was considered to be a bully, and was in for a proper naughty crime that would have got him run off most wings back in the system. Nobody knew the full story yet, but he was a Schedule 1 offender, which is a prisoner who has committed a crime against a child under the age of sixteen. Taff claimed he got his Schedule 1 status from a misunderstanding: he said he came out of a pub, drunk and pilled up, when a load of youths started taking the piss out of him and his mate, so he chased them, caught one, and gave him a hiding. It turned out his victim was only fifteen. But that wasn't Taff's Index Offence (the most serious charge on the indictment), which was far more sickening. He had suspected his girlfriend of sleeping with another man, so he had tortured her with a household iron, burning her and then cutting off one of her fingers. When I heard this I felt like opening him up on the spot. I had never had to live with this kind of scum on normal prison wings, or if I did I would never have known it. And if I'd suspected it I would have made sure they got a bit of what was coming to them.

I returned to my cell at bang-up time, managing to avoid Taff. Once my door was locked I switched on the telly and tried not to think of what was living less than ten feet away from me. I had known there were going to be monsters at Grendon, and that I would have to mix with them, live with them and hear their stories. It was all part of showing the system that I was rehabilitated. That I could take any shit they threw at me and keep smiling, not lash out like I used to. But it was hard.

I had a restless night, but by morning I'd resolved that I wasn't going to let Taff stay in my head. I decided the best course of action would be not to see him, even when he was right there in front of me. He, and all the others of his ilk on the wing, would be non-persons to me. I wouldn't talk to him, but if he spoke to me I would be polite. In this way I hoped to avoid any sort of confrontation that might lead to violence. It was the best I could do.

The two-week therapy break seemed to fly by. Every day I went on exercise and walked around with Steve, Lee, Ritchie and Kevin for my allotted hour. The afternoons I spent with Daran and Ray, drinking coffee and shooting the shit in the alcove on the 1s. I was starting to create a routine for myself, instead of relying on a ready-made routine that existed in other jails. I was given a wing job, which was, once again, cleaning out the offices. I wasn't best pleased with getting the same job I had detested so much on F-wing, but I gritted my teeth and cracked on with it.

Jobs in Grendon are not only to supply the men with work as per Home Office regulations for convicted prisoners, but also to test 'commitment' to the therapeutic regime. In order to show commitment to the wing, newcomers must serve at least three months as a wing cleaner before they can apply for any other job. If someone is not doing their cleaning job, they will be pulled about it, first by the cleaner's foreman, and then, if they still persist in slacking, in front of the entire wing during a community meeting. If the wing so decide, dodging work can lead to a commitment vote, which is very serious. You can actually be voted out of the community for persistent lack of commitment.

The cleaners' foreman when I started my commitment job was a black guy named Abs. Abs was an ex-crackhead, from north London, serving four years nine months for theft and burglary. He was a devout Muslim and had one of the loudest voices on the wing. At first I didn't like him. I've always disliked loud people and go by the adage of 'empty vessels make the most noise', but he was good pals with Fred, so he must have had something going for him. After a week of cleaning offices I'd just about had enough. I detested having to go into the offices and work around the staff who were invariably in them, and I still had a lot of hatred for the uniform. Even though most of the staff at Grendon were different from what I had been used to in the system, I still had a deep-seated neurosis about them. I had taken so many beatings at the hands of those who wore that hated uniform that it was hard for me to be around them. I decided to approach Abs and see if I could get a job change.

Abs listened to what I had to say and told me he'd see what he could do. In the meantime, I did my office cleaning job with as much bad grace as I could muster, deliberately running the Hoover over the screws' feet and knocking over piles of paperwork and files under the guise of dusting the desks. The next day Abs appeared at my cell with a big smile on his face. 'I've got good news and bad news,' he said. 'The good news is you're no longer the office cleaner.' I was delighted, it was like a weight had been lifted off my shoulders. I really did feel uncomfortable with that job. I thanked Abs as I knew he must have put himself out in order to get me a change. I was starting to warm to this fella, though I still considered him to be loud and a bit arrogant. 'The bad news,' he said, his smile seeming to grow larger, 'is that you are now the 3s recess cleaner. Good luck!' I sighed in resignation.

'Recess' is prison-speak for toilet. Cleaning the average family toilet can be an unpleasant chore, but imagine what it's like to clean a prison recess that's used by an average of twenty men. And there are some proper nasty bastards in prison. Still, the way I saw it, cleaning toilets meant I wouldn't have to come into contact with staff unless it was on my own terms. I rolled my sleeves up and got to work. I got a bit of ribbing from the lads but nothing I couldn't handle.

Sure enough I was soon informed that I was to be on group 3, so I sought to find out everything I could about it before starting. The facilitator on group 3 was a prison officer named Brian, and he was also pretty new in the group. I had seen nothing of Brian since I'd been on the wing as group facilitators were also on therapy break, but from what I could gather he was one of the good guys. I would make my own mind up about that one in time but the news was encouraging nonetheless. The facilitator's job is to sit in on every meeting and referee the group. He has to tread a fine line between letting the men arrive at their own therapeutic conclusions and making sure things don't get dangerous for the group as emotions can run high when unstable men are dealing with heavy issues. A good facilitator makes for a good group.

There were seven other men in group 3, including Fred and Abs. There was Deke, a Scotsman from Birmingham with a long criminal history of violence, serving seven and a half years for cocaine smuggling; Mel, a huge Yorkshireman with a history of serious prison violence, fourteen years into a life sentence for murder; Caveman, a big dopey Northerner with a nasty snide streak, twelve years into a life sentence for murdering a four-year-old boy; Dave, a wide boy from Milton Keynes serving eight years for running a large drug-dealing network; and the Scouse rapist from F-wing, Tel.

Tel had only been on C-wing for a few days when he had a serious heart attack during which he 'died' twice and was resuscitated. He spent the next three months in hospital and convalescence so I didn't really see a lot of him. Which I have to say was no great loss to me.

On the first Monday after therapy break I made my way to the group 3 meeting room, which was an office on the ground floor, and took my seat. Brian was there, an open-faced man of medium build, going a bit thin on top, and he started by welcoming me to the group. It was just like introductions in the community meetings and everyone in the group gave me a potted history of their crimes and told me how long they had been at Grendon.

Mel was the senior member of group 3, having been in therapy for over three years. He was a quietly spoken man, which was at odds with his huge frame and head. When he moved, even slightly, I could see the muscles rippling in his body. He made Arnold Schwarzenegger look like a 9-stone wimp and I don't think anything short of both barrels of a 12-gauge shotgun would have stopped him if he lost his temper. Luckily, therapy had had a calming effect on his previous violent outbursts. He told me that he had been involved in a 'door-war' in Leeds, that's the periodic battles that break out between bouncers from various firms and clubs, usually power struggles that involve drug distribution in the clubs and takeover bids for lucrative doors to mind. At the age of nineteen Mel was at the top of his game when he stabbed a man to death in a fit of rage.

Deke was next in seniority, having been in the group for two and a half years. He had the typical Glasgow hard-man persona, an aggressive way of doing everything from walking to talking. He could make the mildest of enquiries sound like a challenge. Of below average build, he had a wizened face that made him look older than his thirty-five years. He had moved from Glasgow to Birmingham in his teens and that was where he had been based. With previous convictions for everything from GBH and possession of firearms to shoplifting and theft Deke had been through the system from borstal to many different prisons. He was loud and opinionated and couldn't string two words together unless at least one of them was 'fuck'. Known as Deke the Sneak behind his back because he was so slippery and snide, he was serving his sentence for smuggling 2 kilos of liquid cocaine back from Jamaica in brandy bottles. He was one of those bitter and twisted people who can spot the cloud in every silver lining. I quite liked Deke.

Fred was next, with two years under his belt. Fred was good stuff but could have his volatile moments like everyone else, the proof being that he was serving his two-strike life sentence for a particularly brutal hammer attack that almost killed his stepbrother. Fred was a bit of a pessimist and was always worrying about his size and weight. If he thought anyone was taking the piss or trying to take a liberty with him he could become very dangerous, plotting up on them. He was well liked and respected by almost everyone on the wing, including staff, but he went through stages of paranoia and depression when he would take to his bed and not be seen for days. In the system Fred had dealt with any slight with severe violence, but at Grendon he knew that option was not available which is why he tried to sleep his rage away.

Next up was Caveman, to whom I took an instant dislike even before I heard he was in for killing a child. Though I think he did show genuine remorse for his crime, he was a big arrogant bully who used his sarcasm to try to browbeat people. He was one of those ape-like men covered in hair and able to grow a full beard in about ten minutes after shaving. He had a penchant for ridiculous hairy affectations, such as mutton chop side-burns, strange Victorian-looking beards and walrus moustaches. He had been on C-wing for a year, having previously been thrown out of A-wing over a drug scandal which he was still denying any part in. He got his life sentence after moving in with a girlfriend who already had a couple of kids by a previous relationship. He was left to look after one of them, a four-year-old boy. Drunk and high on drugs, he punched the kid to death for making too much noise. When Caveman had finished his story it took all my strength to stay in my seat. I wanted to leap on him and give him a few hard digs to see how he liked it, but I managed to contain myself through an almost superhuman effort.

Abs had been in the group for eleven months and was serving the shortest sentence on the whole wing. He had a very violent past, having been found not guilty on at least one murder charge, and had been beaten, stabbed and blasted in the head with a sawn-off shotgun on different occasions. Abs's main problem was crack cocaine. He had been heavily addicted, as are most people who try it. He was committing crimes in order to fund his habit and taking liberties with the wrong people when he was high. Though he was very loud and loved the sound of his own voice, Abs was also a naturally good-natured and happy kind of fella and I could not help but like him. He still had a few shotgun pellets lodged in the side of his face and head and was always dabbing his eye with a tissue as he had nearly lost it when he was shot and it still gave him trouble. Abs was very genuine about therapy. Given his short sentence, if he had stayed in the system he could already have been in open conditions; instead he chose to subject himself to the restrictions of a high-security jail in order to undergo therapy.

Dave was serving his eight-year sentence for possession of class A and class B drugs. He was one of those men for whom doing the deal, whether it be for drugs or a lorryload of stolen toilet paper, was the buzz. If there was something you needed, then Dave was sure to know a geezer who could get it quicker and cheaper, and most of the time he didn't even want to earn off it. For him, just putting the deal together was enjoyment enough. If he'd been born into a slightly more advantaged background he would have made a great straight businessman. His word was his bond and you could always count on him to deliver. He was fast, always seeming to be moving at 100 miles an hour but managing to juggle everything in the air without dropping a thing. Even when sitting perfectly still in group meetings he had a look of speed and movement about him. Dave had started out selling a couple of ounces of puff, but it wasn't long before his love of a deal had made him one of the biggest suppliers of cocaine, ecstasy and cannabis in Milton Keynes and surrounding areas, which brought him to the attention of the boys in blue. As well as dealing drugs through a network of street-level dealers, Dave was also buying and selling parcels of stolen goods on a large scale, so the police mounted a year-long surveillance operation on his business and the result was a guilty plea and an eight-year sentence for his sins. He had a genetic disorder that caused a deformity of his hands and stopped them growing with the rest of his body. He was very sensitive about them.

This then was group 3, the unit that I would be involved with until the day I left Grendon. I would listen to their innermost secrets, hear their life stories and watch each of them be broken down and built back up again by the therapeutic process. They, in turn, would witness the same in me. This was going to be interesting.

The first session was taken up discussing an incident where Dave had volleyed off one of the gym instructors and come close to throwing a dig at him. It seems that he felt the gym screw was taking the piss. I sat back and listened as the more experienced members dissected Dave's anger. Using a series of softly asked but pertinent questions from the group, Dave was able to reach the conclusion that the real reason for his dislike of the gym screw, and therefore his angry outburst, was that the man bore a striking resemblance to a former friend of Dave's who had attempted to move in on his girlfriend when Dave was jailed.

Dave and his childhood sweetheart had been together for a long time and had three kids together. Though he had started to take the relationship for granted before he received his prison sentence, he was nevertheless desperately in love with his girl and thought the world of his kids, but he was now coming to realize that being a provider did not only mean being able to give his family expensive items, it also meant providing them with a husband and father who was actually there for them and not off organizing the next deal. Or off in prison. When Dave heard that his girl had a brief fling with one of his friends it nearly destroyed him. At the time of my first group 3 meeting he was still suffering from this revelation and trying to patch up his relationship.

I knew exactly how Dave was feeling and could empathize with him – my first taste of real 'empathy', a word that figures large in the lesson that Grendon teaches people like me. I had been through something similar to Dave's experience on my previous prison sentence. Me and Denise had met in 1979, when I was on the run from borstal, and by 1981 we were living together and she was pregnant with our first child. I loved Denise as much as I could have loved anyone and we stuck by each other through some very rough times. We ended up having three kids together, but I was the world's worst father and husband. I was too selfish and immature for a long-term serious relationship. I cheated on Denise with other women at every possible opportunity, I was rarely at home, either out drinking, fighting or robbing, or in prison. It was a wonder we stayed together for as long as we did. In 1982 I embarked on a serious affair with a wild young woman from Limerick, named Miriam, and she fell pregnant.

After surviving the fallout from Denise finding out that another woman was having my child, I figured that our relationship could survive anything so I continued taking her for granted, sure that we would still be together in old age. Little did I know! In 1992 I escaped from prison again and moved in with a girl I had known since we were kids and started a very public affair with her while continuing to see Denise. It was the last straw for Denise. When I was recaptured and sent back into jail with a further fifteen years added to my sentence, she got her revenge. She told me we were finished and hinted she had started a relationship with someone else. I was devastated. Despite everything I had put Denise through, I never once dreamed that she might give me a taste of my own medicine. One of the things that had attracted me to her in the first place and made me stay with her so long was her loyalty. She would take my side against anyone in public no matter what fights we might have been having in private and I trusted her 100 per cent.

I've watched a lot of men go to pieces in prison when their relationships inevitably break down due to their incarceration. I've seen big hard villains break down in tears and even attempt suicide when they get the 'Dear John' letter telling them that what they thought they had outside has gone. The most dangerous and yet melancholy night in any prison is New Year's Eve, when every incarcerated man and woman knows that at twelve o'clock the odds are that their partner will be kissing a stranger. Being in prison tends to breed jealousy and mistrust in most relationships. But I always trusted Denise and knew how lucky I was. When it finally did happen to me I was totally unprepared for it.

Our break-up was long and bitter, much as most of our relationship had been, and once again it was my fault. I refused to accept that 'my' Denise would ever leave me for someone else and I wasn't going to let it end without a fight. It was all done via letter and phone as there was no way she was going to visit me and I couldn't make her. It all got very messy with me doing silly and spiteful things like threatening and abusing her on the phone and sending back all her photos with the eyes cut out. I'm not proud of how I acted and I have no excuses. I should have given in gracefully and accepted the inevitable.

I think what hurt most was my pride and self-image. I was Razor Smith, top armed robber, slasher and all-round tough guy, veteran of hundreds of tear-ups where, even when I lost, my opponents knew they'd been in a fight, being taken for a 2-bob mug by some stranger whose face I couldn't even imagine. Some fucking wanker who had dared try to take what was mine while I was locked up and unable to even defend my corner. That was what burned me just as much as losing Denise, if not more. I had always been a fighter and I needed someone to fight in order to vent my spleen. I turned my rage on the prison system and, by proxy, myself.

By the time the group meeting finished at 10.30, I had seen real therapy in action and made my first emotional link. I could identify with Dave's anger and therefore listening to what other group members said to him had helped me as well. Dave may not have been 'cured' but at least he had managed to talk through his anger and gain an insight into some of the reasons behind it. He left the room in a better frame of mind, and so did I. Therapy was not as confusing and complicated as I had first thought.

After the group meetings there was a five-minute break for people to grab a smoke, use the toilet and gather their wits before we all came together in the community room for 'feedbacks'. Feedbacks were designed to keep the whole community in the loop as to what was going on. There is no such thing as confidentiality in Grendon. If you don't want something fed back to the community, then you shouldn't talk about it. One member of each group takes it in turn to do the group's feedback. The only men exempt from this process are new members who have not yet had their first group assessment.

The chairman called the community to order and began with group 1. A summary of what had been discussed in group 1 that morning was fed back to the community, with special attention being asked for any individual who had 'had a bad group', which could mean anything from discussing the death of a loved one to delving into the sexual abuse he had suffered as a child. Listening to the feedbacks over the next few months made me aware of just how many of the men at Grendon had been physically, sexually or emotionally abused in their lives. Some of the stories were truly horrific.

Feedbacks were feared and hated by a lot of the men who had to do them. For some, being in the spotlight and having to speak about someone else's delicate and disturbing issues in front of the whole community was a nightmare. Others took it in their stride and were confident enough to handle it well. I had stage fright for the first couple of feedbacks I had to do but I quickly learned to dissociate myself from what I was talking about and not seem callous and uncaring at the same time. In the end I quite looked forward to doing them.

After each group had fed back, the chairman called for final minutes and several people put their hands up to ask various questions. And that was the end of therapy for the day. Or so I thought. When I came out of the community room and headed up the stairs to the alcove for a smoke and a cup of coffee, I found it was busier than I'd ever seen it during the therapy break. Fred, Ray, John, Kevin, Daran and a couple of others were in the alcove and I joined them. Ray had the kettle on and was making coffee for everyone and all the talk was about the groups that morning. At first I thought it was just idle gossip, but as I listened I realized that people were seriously discussing some of the therapeutic issues that had been raised that morning. I sat back amazed. The conversation was just so different from anything I'd ever encountered from a bunch of long-term cons on a prison wing. It was then that I realized another truth about Grendon – the therapy never really stops.

6. Bug-eyed Bob

Having now had my first taste of real therapy it didn't take me long to settle into the routine of C-wing and group 3. I know that logic dictates that time is a constant that moves neither quickly nor slowly and that the speed of its passing is relative to each person and situation, but the most oft-heard remark on C-wing was that the days there seemed to fly by. In most nicks every second seems like a month and each hour crawls by like a crippled millipede. You hardly ever get out of your cell, and trying to fill the long days and nights with something of interest can often lead to brick-counting becoming a bit of a hobby. I've probably counted every brick in every cell I've ever had the misfortune to occupy. But at Grendon a lot of my time was spent observing the traits and antics of the strange characters that surrounded me. And, such is human nature, I found myself fascinated by the most repellent. It was really no wonder that head-shrinks of every grade and discipline were queuing up to work at Grendon, it was a veritable cornucopia of broken ids and shattered psyches.

Bug-eyed Bob was a strange cat and, in a place as dedicated to strangeness as Grendon, that was really saying something. He was a big body-builder type with protruding eyeballs and a lisp. He came from Kendal and was serving a mandatory life sentence with a seventeen-year tariff for murder. There was something ever so slightly off-key about Bob, and his attempts to fit in with the lads on the wing were not very well received – he tried a little bit too hard. I had first met him on F-wing when he had been transferred in from HMP Kingston, a lifers-only nick in Portsmouth with a reputation for a dodgy clientele. He gave me the creeps. It was nothing I could really put my finger on but I've learned to trust my prison radar and Bug-eyed Bob was coming up as a big blip. There was something vaguely effeminate about him despite, or maybe because of, his muscle-beach stance. Maybe it was the lisp, or the way he couldn't help but preen and admire himself in every reflective surface, but it was obvious enough for comment on the wing. On F-wing I was having it with Mark, the Scouser, one day and, in the pits of boredom, we decided to rip the piss out of Bug-eyed Bob to pass the time. We set out to get him to admit, by fair means or foul, that he was in fact a closet homosexual.

Unfortunately for him, Bob was about as bright as a 20-watt bulb and didn't even have the sense to walk off and deprive us of our entertainment. We ripped him unmercifully, and Bob was like a deer caught in the headlights, eyes bugged out even further, sweat beading his top lip, a look of fear and confusion contorting his features as he struggled to lisp replies to our impertinent questioning. After a mere five minutes we had him on the ropes, and after thirty he was ready to throw the towel in. He stormed off to his cell, slamming the door behind him. Mark and I were pleased with our performance and had a cup of coffee to celebrate a job well done. It had livened up what otherwise would have been a pretty dull afternoon. And this is how grown men amuse and entertain themselves while incarcerated, by verbally assaulting the weak-minded.

By the evening I had all but forgotten the incident and was sitting in the TV room watching the News when Mark sought me out. He had been approached by Bob, who, now he had got over his confusion, was very pissed off and had told Mark in private that he was not happy with our banter. He explained that it brought up a lot of bad feelings for him as he detested homosexuals. The man he had murdered had made sexual advances to him, and that was the reason Bob had killed him. To be accused in public of being a closet homosexual was Bob's worst nightmare made flesh. He had asked Mark to ask me not to bring it up again. What could I say? We discussed it and decided to give Bob a break and not mention it any more. We soon found other victims for our acid wit and dropped Bob out.

One of the strange things that was to surprise me at Grendon was a thing rarely, if ever, heard of in the rest of the system, and this was known as 'confession fever', though even at Grendon it is not that common. What happens is that men get so into therapy that they lose all their natural caution and start confessing to things that they needn't have mentioned and which otherwise would have remained secret. In some cases confession fever had serious consequences.

One officer, who had been at Grendon for over fifteen years, told me about several cases that had led to further prison sentences for the confessees, including a man who made a living by conning his way into pensioners' houses to rob them. Already serving five years for three such burglaries, he confessed, first in his therapy group and then in court, to a further twenty-five and was given another seven years on top of his sentence. One infamous case which is still dusted off with some regularity in the Sunday tabloids involves a character, whom I shall call 'Billy', who, after being tried and acquitted for the murder of a nineteen-year-old girl, went on to confess to the crime while at Grendon. While I was on C-wing a man on A-wing who was already serving life for murder confessed to another killing some years earlier and is currently awaiting trial for that case. Therapy is not covered by the rules of the confessional and if you admit to further crimes it is the duty of staff to inform the relevant authorities.

As I became more in tune with my surroundings my mood about Grendon lightened but there were still things about the prison that had a tendency to jar me. I realize now that by seizing on petty infringements of the prison rules by staff and management I was deflecting. Instead of looking at the bigger picture, I had this ingrained desire to fight the system. In the past it had been a mainly physical fight but after hitting the age of forty I gradually lost the desire to swap punches with prison staff, though I still had an insane urge to strike a blow in other ways. Every now and again I would get my teeth into some small detail of prison life in which I thought the system was trying to take liberties and I would not unclench until I had made my mark. This was how it was with the Grendon canteen.

In every prison in the country, and probably in the whole civilized world, there is a 'shop' where prisoners are allowed to spend their pittance of a wage, usually on a set day once a week. Since privatization started to creep into the prison system in the mid-1990s, such shops have become a lucrative target for profiteering by private companies. They usually close the shop down and hire a handful of minimum-wage employees to bag up prisoners' pre-ordered goods. With very few overheads, no business rent to pay and being able to buy wholesale and sell at higher than retail price these firms manage to turn a nice profit. The problem is that, though monopolies are supposed to be banned in the real world, prisoners have no choice as to where they can shop. The 'canteens' (which is what they are known as in prison-speak) usually operate on a take-it-or-leave-it basis and don't bother with all the niceties of consumer law. You cannot return a purchase for any reason whatsoever, you cannot avail yourself of any of the now widespread 2-for-1 offers, you cannot examine the items before you purchase them and you have no choice in what goods or brands the canteen chooses to stock. On the whole it's a pretty piss-poor service but it's all we've got. Whenever anyone asks me if I know what it feels like to be robbed I just point at the prison canteen, who have been robbing me on a weekly basis for many years. The only difference between me and them is that they don't wear a mask and carry a gun in pursuit of their larceny.

At Grendon the canteen was one of the few that had not yet been closed down in favour of the bagging system but that didn't mean it was any better. It's situated halfway down the long central corridor of the prison and occupies a space equivalent to about three cells knocked into one. Every Thursday afternoon at around 3.30 the men of C-wing would queue up to sample the delights of this grocery emporium, though we were allowed only two steps inside the door before being met by the insurmountable barrier of a wooden counter and two bullish female canteen staff. The first time I went to the canteen at Grendon, to purchase toiletries and tobacco, I asked for a receipt for the goods and was told by a female who bore a striking resemblance to Martin Clunes that they did not 'supply receipts'. When I got back to my cell and totted up my purchases I found I had been overcharged by 23p. Now 23p may not sound a lot, but when your weekly wage is £6.37 it becomes quite a sizeable chunk to be fleeced of. The next week I complained bitterly to the same woman and was met with a shrug. I decided to make a stand.

I made a written complaint to the governor in charge of the canteen and pointed out that he was legally obliged to supply every prisoner with a receipt. His reply, which came some weeks later, was like a slap in the face. He might just as well have attached a photo of himself laughing uproariously and sticking two fingers up at me. He wrote that he was not going to supply receipts and if I thought he was breaking the law maybe I should phone the police! He suggested that if I wanted receipts with my purchases then I shouldn't have broken the law and come to prison in the first place. I must admit, I couldn't fault his logic. I decided to take his advice. I put in an application to make a phone call to the local police in order to report a crime committed by the canteen. I had to tread carefully because, knowing the staff on C-wing, it was likely that my request to phone the police would be granted and the last thing I wanted was to be forced to go through with what was essentially a bluff. The police have no powers to act in consumer law. So I made sure that a copy of my request went to the canteen first. That very afternoon a memo arrived on the wing from the canteen governor stating that from now on prisoners would be issued with receipts for their purchases. I withdrew my request.

The whole canteen receipt thing might seem petty and of little consequence but any victory against the system is to be treasured. There is a terrific addictive buzz in taking on the might of bureaucracy and winning, no matter how tiny the victory. A large percentage of people who come to prison are so overwhelmed by the size and obvious power of the system that they become automatons. They follow the rules and any order given to them unthinkingly. They lose every shred of individuality, and because they are treated no better than cattle they are defeated almost from the moment they step off the sweatbox. A lot of it stems from fear since you soon learn what the consequences are for stepping out of line. There are boots, batons, strip cells, solitary confinement, loss of visits and privileges, the liquid cosh, constant transfers on the prison ghost train and in some extreme cases even death for those who dare to buck the system. But there are people, and I was one of them, who refuse to be impressed or cowed by it all. Whether it's through stupidity, pride or just plain stubbornness a few of us just will not conform. And knowing the cost of it makes any victory that little bit sweeter. So my stand against the canteen was small potatoes in the overall scheme of my life but part of my make-up nonetheless.

Grendon is a place where men go to change – that is a given – but I think you have to be clear in your own head just what it is you want to change. I knew before I applied that the things I wanted to change were my offending behaviour, my lifestyle and most of my attitudes. They had led to me spending most of my life in jail and I had grown weary of it all. I didn't want to be a criminal or even a professional prisoner any more, but the thing I found hardest at Grendon was sorting out my own values from my adopted criminal values. For example, my criminal values told me that to inform on anyone was a bad thing, but my personal values told me the same thing and I was never going to be comfortable with the Grendon ethos of challenging this view. Certain men can come to Grendon from a system background, just like me, and very quickly turn turtle and embrace the other side with open arms. I've witnessed so-called staunch cons come into Grendon full of piss and vinegar and boasts of how they've fought the system and, within a few months, the next thing you know they're going round grassing people up for the slightest infringement of the rules and siding with the screws as a matter of course. I can only assume that this kind of behaviour was always latent within them, waiting for a chance to show itself. Rather like your true personality can make an appearance under the influence of drink or drugs.

On C-wing informers were known as 'feedbackers' as a nod towards the effect therapy can have on some people. I was determined never to become either a feedbacker or a therapeuton but that didn't mean I couldn't embrace the therapeutic regime in my own way. For my first three months on C-wing I kept a close observation on what was going on around me. I spoke to everyone on a casual level but I cherry-picked the people I would really have it with. Some men come to Grendon and rush into therapy, throwing caution to the winds, and usually come unstuck very quickly. I witnessed many men opening their hearts and the deep dark closets of their minds when they had been in therapy for only a matter of weeks. These men believe they are going to get a quick fix and think that Grendon offers them a cure-all that will make their lives beautiful. It was sad to watch them explode and implode at the same time and take that long ride on the next bus out more ruined and confused than when they arrived. The great thing about Grendon was that when this sort of thing did happen they were well looked after and given the opportunity to return when they felt better able to handle therapy. I rarely saw anyone abandoned in those early days.

One group 3 member who rushed in was Silver. Silver was twenty-three and came from west London. At the age of fifteen he had been recruited into a Chinese youth gang and, even though he wasn't Chinese, he had worked his way up through the ranks until he became a 'soldier' on the fringes of a Triad organization. Influenced by martial arts and action videos, Silver took his position very seriously. He later described his recruitment and induction into the gang as a kind of 'brainwashing'. From petty theft and drug-dealing he progressed to a Chinatown protection racket and carrying out punishment beatings for his Triad masters. It was because of one such beating, where his victim was chopped near to death with machetes, that Silver found himself serving fifteen years. When he got to Grendon he was overcome by the impatience of youth and the need to unburden himself. I pulled him to one side and warned him to take his time with therapy but he wouldn't have it. He was in my group and I had to watch him lay his soul bare and have all his beliefs questioned and his self-image challenged until he could barely open his mouth without bursting into tears or verbally abusing someone. Silver didn't last. He put in his papers about six months after coming into the group and left Grendon drained both mentally and emotionally. Silver would return to Grendon and group 3 eighteen months after leaving for HMP Swaleside.

My own policy was to take things slowly. After all, with eight life sentences plus eighty years to serve, I had nothing but time. I started to understand the dynamic of group 3. Brian, our facilitator, was brilliant at his job. Mostly he would just observe and listen to what we had to say, letting the group have its head and coming in only when he had a genuine question. Sometimes, when Brian had to take time off, we had a 'guest' facilitator, often a member of the uniformed staff, and the effect it had on the group dynamic was almost palpable. Whenever Brian missed a group the mood became somewhat sombre and the topics of conversation very general: we talked about things such as the state of the prison system or world politics. It was never a strategy planned between us, and just happened naturally because it was understood by all of us that guest facilitators were not to be trusted with our sensitive issues or innermost secrets as Brian was. I soon came to recognize that Brian, though he wore the uniform of the Prison Service, was a fully fledged and valuable member of group 3.

The first time I spoke of anything of consequence in the group was in October. Up until then I had given a short account of my criminal career and spoken about my life in prison, but October was a bad month for me. It was the second anniversary of my son's death. It was in October 2001, soon after his release from Feltham Young Offenders Institution, that he had been found dead in an alley. Joe's death was still very raw and painful for me and I had no intention of discussing it with anyone, but I was starting to trust group 3 and they were getting to know me. Though I thought I was doing a good job of concealing my moods and feelings, the group quickly picked up on it. It was Fred who brought it up. He commented that I seemed to be a bit down; was there any particular reason for this? I looked around the group and saw the genuine interest on their faces and suddenly it felt safe to open up. I started to tell them about Joe, explaining the guilt I had been feeling over his death, the fear I had that I had contributed to it by not being around when he so desperately needed me. I spoke about how painful it was to know that I couldn't even comfort my family, the despair that comes with knowing I couldn't even reach out a comforting hand to my children except across a prison visiting-room table. I spoke about my son and all the things I would have loved to say to him and the things I missed about him. And I broke down in tears.

I don't think I had ever cried in front of another man before. Even when I first heard about Joe's death when I was at Whitemoor, I went and locked myself in my cell before the tears came. It had been two years since Joe's death and I hadn't been able to grieve in any real sense. I had been refused permission to go to his funeral, and I had never seen the place where he died, never placed flowers where his ashes lay. To me it was just all so unreal. I knew that Denise, Dean and Lianne and all Joe's friends would be doing something to mark the anniversary, just as they had the first year, and I couldn't be part of it and that was very painful. So I told the group about Joe and my feelings about everything to do with his life and death. And all through it I was crying like I was never going to stop. I know it's a terribly overused cliché but it really did feel as though something inside me had broken open, some dark and brittle container in which I had sealed my grief, and it came out in a gush.

The group were very supportive and I was relieved. It was the first time I'd ever sat in a room with eight other prisoners and a member of uniformed staff and poured my heart out. It could never happen in any other jail. There would always be someone to snigger or see it as a sign of weakness to be used against me at some later date. At that moment I felt closer to these men than I did to my family. That morning I managed to shed the first layer of the armour I had spent my whole life donning. I began to care less about presenting a tough and uncaring image to the world. My dried and shrivelled heart had taken its first drop of emotional moisture and a change began to grow in me. It would be a long and arduous journey but I had taken the first step. In the past I had never stinted on the amount of effort I had put into being a criminal and a bad bastard and now I would do no less for change. It was then that I really started in therapy.

That morning was when I really found out some of what Grendon is all about. It's about being safe enough to be yourself, being able to unburden yourself to men who, in most cases, have been to some of the places you have been and will not rush to judge you. It's about being honest with yourself and not being afraid to show your feelings. Most people who deliberately set out on a life of crime, knowing all the baggage that comes with it, are running from something. I had always believed I was quite comfortable with myself and I did what I did because I enjoyed it. In truth, I've never liked myself. And that's a hard thing to admit. After talking about Joe I came out feeling a lot better. I had been able to share the weight of a heavy burden and was able later to think clearly about the issues surrounding my son's life and death. It was a powerful incentive to carry on.

So, I had made a start, but old habits die hard and one hymn doesn't make a saint. I felt a great warmth towards my group, but the rest of the community were still sale-or-return for me and I couldn't just drop my guard around them. There may have been only forty-two men on the wing but there seemed to be a couple of hundred personalities between them. I carried on observing, making mental notes on who to avoid for reasons of instability and learning as much as I could. I set no time limit on myself, I would stay at Grendon for however long it took. I was eager for more therapy but my natural caution told me to proceed slowly and not rush into anything. I was coming to realize that therapy is a process of evolution rather than revolution.

7. The Vote

Fred was a big help to me. He knew exactly what to say in order to empathize with people and just listening to his logical and reasoned arguments was enough to soothe the most savage breast. Fred was the peacemaker of the wing, always ready and able to sort out people's problems and pour oil on troubled waters. But there was another side to him, the side that had caused him to beat his brother half to death with a 2lb hammer and the side he showed when he was boxing or fighting. In those moments he was like a machine that had been programmed with only one instruction – hurt your opponent, badly.

One of the men that Fred had a lot of time for on C-wing was a lifer named Paul. I had spoken to Paul on a couple of occasions and found him to be almost painfully shy but a very nice fella. He was the only soft-spoken Geordie I've ever met. He was serving a discretionary life sentence for stabbing his girlfriend's mother, by accident – he had meant to stab her father. I didn't know all the details, but from what I did hear it could have been a crime of passion. Other than what he was in for, Paul had never committed an act of violence before or since. He was a couple of years over his tariff, which is the minimum time a lifer has to spend in prison before being released on life licence, because he had refused to comply with sentence plans or participate in any of the course work that the parole board sets such store in. When it came right down to it, Paul was still horrified over his crime and believed he deserved to spend more time in prison. It may come as a surprise to some people but there are prisoners in the system so wracked by guilt that they have no desire to be released. We are not all brutal animals impatient to get out and wreak our vengeance on society.

Paul had come to Grendon looking for an outlet for his grief and guilt that he would never find in the conventional prison system, but he was struggling with himself every day and had on numerous occasions expressed the desire to jack it all in and head back into the system. Fred had recognized Paul's struggles and would sit and talk to him whenever things were getting too much. Paul was also friendly with Dean, the wing chairman, who lived in the cell opposite him. The big Welshman would often hold court in Paul's cell, surrounded by a few of the real inadequates of the wing. Dean had the reputation of being half a bully whenever the opportunity presented itself and as such he liked to have a few acolytes around him that he could ridicule and order about but in a subtle and covert way. Paul had confided to Fred that he was afraid of Dean and didn't really want him in his cell but was scared to tell him to fuck off. Fred advised Paul to pull away from the Welshman gradually and let him know that he wasn't happy with him coming to his cell. But Dean, being a brash and ignorant man, didn't take the hints. Fred spoke to me about the situation one afternoon when we were having a coffee in my cell. He was worried that Paul might use the situation with Dean as an excuse to put his papers in and leave Grendon. In my ignorance, I offered to go and have a quiet word with Dean, maybe threaten to cut him if he started to get lemon. This was never going to be an option but at this stage I had enough of the system mentality left in me to still be thinking in this way. Fred laughed at my suggestion. 'You're quite sick, aren't you? You ain't in Parkhurst now, Raze. You can't just slash problems out of the way.' I shrugged. 'Yeah, I suppose you're right.'

That evening after bang-up I pondered on Fred's comments. Even though he had made them in a jokey manner he was right. I had been quite sick in the past and I had believed I could solve my problems in one way only, by attacking them head on, all guns blazing. I reached the conclusion that a lot of it stemmed from my inability to argue verbally. My voice had a tendency to become slightly high-pitched whenever I got into an argument and this made me feel ridiculous. Feeling ridiculous made me embarrassed and the more embarrassed I felt the more ridiculous I thought I looked. I had learned early on that the best way to avoid this situation was to attack straight away – physically and with plenty of force. That way nobody would get a chance to take the piss. When I thought about it I realized that I didn't even like the violence. I liked the fighting, the fist, head and boot fighting of a straightener against someone else who was up for it. Maybe that was the Irish in me. But the over-the-top slashing and coshing people was not enjoyable. This was a revelation to me. I had always convinced myself that hurting people didn't bother me, that I was hardened to it and even enjoyed it, but that was bollocks. I realized that violence actually made me sick, but I had become very good at hiding my true feelings, even from myself. Once I accepted that the violence sickened me, the next step was to look at why I did it anyway. This was something I wanted to bring to the group.

The situation between Paul and Dean came to a head at one of their group meetings a couple of days after Fred had told me about it. Paul felt safe enough to confront Dean in a group situation and tell him that he thought he was a bit of a bully. Dean didn't take it well and called Paul a few choice names. Paul's frustration got the better of him and he stormed out of the room pausing only to put his fist through a window on his way out. Dean, taking this somehow as a personal insult, ran after him and began throwing punches. Dean was around 6 foot 4 and over 20 stone, so getting a clump from him was no walk in the park. Paul tried to fight back, but he had severed a nerve and some veins in his hand when he punched the window so there was little he could do against the bigger man. It all got a bit nasty and several members of the group tried to break it up. It took six of them and the female facilitator, Sue, to drag Dean to the floor and hold him until he calmed down.

The riot bell was pressed and several prison officers rushed to the scene and took Dean to his cell and Paul to the hospital. We heard the commotion in our group room but figured it was just someone getting it all off their chest in one of the other groups. Therapy is not always a quiet affair, especially in a prison. It wasn't until the break before feedbacks that we heard exactly what had happened. This was a serious matter for all concerned and it would definitely lead to a commitment vote. The feedbacks that morning were a subdued affair, since violence at Grendon was not a common occurrence and it affected everybody. In the system this sort of incident would have passed without comment. Blood, violence and riot bells were everyday, sometimes more than once a day, happenings. I had learned over many years to take them in my stride, but even I was out of practice by this time. Bearing in mind that almost every man in Grendon has a seriously violent past, and that it has more than its fair share of psychopaths, it is odd that when violence occurs we should be shocked. It is a testament to the atmosphere and regime of the place that we are not all stabbing and coshing each other every minute of the day.

Paul needed sixteen stitches in his hand. He also had a black eye where Dean had caught him with a punch. Sue had a badly bruised arm, and several other members of the group had various bruises. The word was that it was going to be a commitment vote for both Paul and Dean. This was something I had been dreading ever since I came to Grendon. A commitment vote meant that every member of the community had to publicly vote on whether the offender would stay at Grendon or be shipped out, usually back to the prison he had come from. Voting someone out was not something that could be taken lightly by anybody, but particularly by me. I had lived my whole life abiding by that strange criminal code of honour that meant I did not act as judge and jury on any other criminal for doing something that I could easily have done myself. The criminal justice system acting on behalf of society had tried me on many occasions and I had always held it in contempt, but now I was being forced to take its role against those who were my fellow criminals. To me it stank of betrayal – whether of the men involved or of my own twisted values I didn't yet know. This was going to be a serious struggle for me. I decided to speak to Fred about it.

Fred was right in the middle of everything. He felt as though he should have done something about the situation before it got out of hand. It was he who had advised Paul to deal with it in the safe setting of his group. He had been up to see Paul at the hospital and came back wanting to give Dean a proper doing. He was white with anger as he sat in my cell and vented some of his feelings, and for the first time our roles were reversed. As Fred talked about getting a tool and 'weighing that fat Welsh cunt in', I spoke to him the way he had spoken to me when I was raging. I told him how silly it would be for him to jeopardize all the work he had put in, not to mention risk another life sentence on top of what he already had to serve. I told him how gutted his family would be when they heard, how all the nasty screws and governors and coppers would have a good chuckle at his expense. But Fred wasn't listening, he was in the zone that violent people enter when they are on the verge of doing something mad. I needed something drastic to pull him out of it, so I dropped the bombshell that I knew would hurt him the most. 'Nah, fuck it! You're right, Fred. Let's go and weigh the cunt in. I'm coming with you, just give me five minutes to make a tool.' I took a brand-new disposable razor and began to break it apart to get at the blade. My actions had the desired effect. I saw the rage leave his face and I breathed a sigh of relief. I spent the next five minutes letting Fred talk me out of making a tool that in reality I had no intention of making. It was interesting to hear him use the same arguments on me that I had used on him only a short time before. It had been a very serious matter but a great lesson in using reverse psychology.

After he had 'calmed' me down, we got into a discussion about the upcoming commitment vote. I explained to Fred how I saw it as a betrayal to vote anybody out. I wanted to change myself but not so much that I became the complete opposite of what I was, which would be what I despised. I was looking for a middle ground. Fred told me straight out that I could only do what my conscience allowed me. I had been in therapy for just three months, and if I wasn't yet ready to take such a big step then that was my business. But he was going to vote Dean out. I told him I'd have to think about what I was going to do. Fred left my cell in a lot better frame of mind than when he had entered.

I had a good feeling about myself for managing to prevent Fred from committing an act of serious violence on Dean. In the past I would have been breaking open that razor for real and buzzing on the thought of imminent trouble. I would have put the consequences from my mind in seconds and would have been reinforcing my rage in order to push myself to commit the violence. I really was changing. I tried this thought on like a new coat and felt pretty comfortable with it. It was a good fit.

The wing was quiet and tense for the next couple of days. Dean kept mostly to his cell and Paul was still up at the hospital. There was a lot of talk about the upcoming vote and how hard it was going to be. Paul was well liked on the wing and even Dean had a few supporters. The consensus of opinion was that either both went or both stayed; there would be no in between. The wing constitution, a lengthy document drawn up by inmates and staff, was consulted. It was pretty clear that any act of violence was a ship-out offence and both Paul and Dean had committed violence. This would be my first experience of a commitment vote so I made sure to talk to all the senior members of the community to find out as much as I could. Every member of the community had to vote, there could be no abstentions. Not voting in a commitment vote was a commitment issue and would lead to the abstainer being put to the vote himself. The more I heard about it the more I thought it sounded like a seventeenth-century witch trial. I wasn't looking forward to it.

On the morning of the commitment vote there was an expectant air in the community room as everyone filed in. I took my seat next to Fred. I still hadn't made up my mind how I was going to vote but decided I would play it by ear. Dean had been the wing chairman but had been immediately relieved of his office after the offence and Big Ritchie, a quietly spoken lifer in for the manslaughter of his brother, had been voted in temporarily. Big Ritchie called the meeting to order and briefly outlined the events that had led to the commitment vote and then asked for Paul and Dean to explain their actions to the community. Dean went first. He said that on the morning of the fight he had been in a bad mood from the moment he woke up having spent the previous day wrestling with some tough therapeutic problems concerning his childhood. He had been shocked when Paul had called their friendship into question and accused him of mental bullying, but he said he had become angry only when Paul punched the window through and he saw a piece of glass hit Sue in the face. He claimed that his own violence stemmed from his outrage at Paul's blatant disregard for Sue's safety and this was why he had lost his temper. He finished by apologizing to everyone concerned and saying that he now had no bad feelings towards Paul or anyone else in the community. Dean hung his head and looked suitably contrite, but the real criminals among the community recognized his virtuoso performance for what it was – an act. We had spent many years pulling off the same kind of stunt ourselves in front of judges, juries and magistrates, with varying degrees of success. In my head I applauded him and gave him eight out of ten for performance, but a bit heavy on the false sincerity.

There was a moment's silence before the chairman called on Paul for his explanation. Compared to the huge, confident and unmarked Dean, Paul cut a rather pathetic figure. He was pale and slight, his right hand swathed in bandages and cradled in his lap, his face creased with worry and nervousness and his eyes tearful. He spoke hesitantly but with simple honesty as he explained how he felt he was being psychologically bullied by Dean long before he confronted him in the group. He said he had punched the window through as both an act of frustration and self-harm. He didn't want to be at Grendon, it was all too much for him. Being here was the hardest thing he'd ever had to do because he had to face himself and his own inadequacies every single day. He admitted he had fought back when Dean attacked him and that this was a clear act of violence as defined by the constitution. He apologized to Sue for any injury she had suffered and ended by saying he was ready to take his punishment. I made up my mind there and then that I would be voting for Paul to stay, but that was the easy part for me. My difficulty lay with Dean. He was a less sympathetic prospect, and I knew that Fred would be voting him out so my loyalties were torn. On the one hand, I had the criminal code that was etched with acid into my psyche and said that voting anyone out would be a traitorous act akin to siding with authority, almost as bad as grassing. But on the other hand, I had my personal loyalty to Fred, a friend who I knew would back me in any situation. It was going to be a close call and no matter which way I voted I would have to live with myself.

The chairman asked Sue about being struck by the broken glass from the window as this had not been mentioned before. Sue said she had no injuries other than the bruise on her arm where she had tried to restrain Dean and she did not recall being struck by glass. This looked bad for Dean as his whole explanation for attacking Paul was based on his outrage at Sue being hurt. The chairman then asked if anyone had any questions before the vote. Fred stuck his hand up. 'Yeah, I've got something to say to Dean.' I looked at Fred and saw the struggle on his face. 'I think what you did was well out of order. You're a bully and a fraud. You ain't here for the right reasons, and I think if we vote for you to stay, then Paul will have to go and I think that would be a shame, because, unlike you, Paul is a genuine fella and he needs Grendon more than most. It will be a fucking sad day if he gets shipped out down to you. I'm voting for Paul to stay and I'm voting for you to go. I'm not trying to influence anyone, people will vote how they feel, but I just wanted to make my own feelings known.' I looked around the room and wondered how many votes would be influenced by Fred's words. Though he had denied he was trying to affect the vote, he knew he had a lot of respect in the community. The chairman explained that there would be one man, one vote and no abstentions. He put Paul to the vote first. 'All those who think Paul should remain in the community raise your hands.' I raised my hand. Thirty-one men voted for Paul to be given a second chance; eleven voted for him to go. Paul looked very relieved and then burst into tears. Then it was time for Dean's vote. 'All those who think Dean should remain in the community raise your hands.' My mouth felt dry and my arm twitched and got halfway up before I forced it back down. I felt as if everyone was watching me and my face was burning with the shame of what I was doing. The votes were counted and I heard the chairman announce that there were seven votes for Dean to stay. Then came the vote for him to go and I raised my hand.

It was done. I had voted someone out of Grendon and it left me with a deep sense of shame. I felt as though I had betrayed everything I had ever stood for and I felt a sense of loss. I went to my cell and lay on the bed. I didn't want to talk to anyone. In time I would realize that this was the moment I began to burn the bridges behind me that led back to what I once had been. Once all of those bridges had been reduced to ash I could go nowhere but forward. But for now I just felt like a rat. A couple of weeks later Dean was returned to Wormwood Scrubs and Paul was back in therapy. The summer was well and truly over.

8. Carrot Top

The most hated man on C-wing was Carrot Top. A pale and skinny, ginger-headed creature who wore thick-lensed glasses and spoke as though he had a nest of frogs permanently lodged in his throat, he was serving a discretionary life sentence for arson and manslaughter. He had been homeless when he managed to secure a room as a lodger in return for becoming an informal childminder for a single mother who had two young daughters but needed to work. Though I don't like to speak ill of the dead, I can only assume that the mother of the kids was, at best, a fucking moron. If Carrot Top had knocked on my door and asked to look after my children in exchange for board and lodging I would have been loading my shotgun as I chased him down the street. But, apparently, this woman took one look at this imperfect stranger and turned her kids over to him. It is indeed a funny old world. According to Carrot Top's own account, he moved in and things went great for a few months. The mother spent long hours working while Carrot Top fed, bathed and took care of her children as per their arrangement. All the while he was growing disillusioned. He began to have feelings towards the mother, which were not reciprocated, and when she said she would have to charge him a token rent on top of his child-minding duties he became depressed. One night, when the mother and her two young daughters, aged five and eight, were asleep, Carrot Top got a can of petrol and splashed it all over the house. He then lit a match to the petrol and walked out, locking the door behind him. The family burned to death.

Carrot Top handed himself in to the police a couple of days after the fire. At his trial he pleaded not guilty due to diminished responsibility. He had been examined by several psychiatrists while in prison awaiting trial and all agreed that he had not been in his right mind when he started the fire. He was found not guilty of the three murders, but guilty of manslaughter and arson. The judge sentenced him to a discretionary life sentence with a minimum tariff of eight years. As a child-killer, Carrot Top was seriously assaulted by other prisoners at every opportunity until he was placed on a protection wing with others of his ilk. He spent around five years at HMP Wakefield before coming to Grendon. In the system child-killers are fair game for any prisoner with a blade or a pot of boiling fat, and even at Grendon they are barely tolerated and know that if things go wrong for someone they will be top of the target list.

In my first few months at Grendon the thought entered my head that if I was ever to be voted out or just decided to leave I would not miss the opportunity of weighing in a few of the worst wrong-uns before I went. And Carrot Top would have been top of my list. I hated him, on several levels. Mostly for his crime, but for his appearance and demeanour too. It also galled me that he could take the lives of three people, including two young girls, and be given an eight-year tariff by a judicial system that gave me an eleven-year tariff for robbing banks. Carrot Top's sentence served to reinforce in me the hatred and distrust of the British judicial system that had festered for most of my life. Though it was not really his fault that he had been dealt with leniently, I still could not help but blame him for it. Every time I looked at him I got this irrational feeling of rage over the disparity between our tariffs. There were many moments in my first six months on C-wing that I toyed with taking a blade to Carrot Top. But as I got further into therapy I began to become more tolerant of other people, even him.

I began to wonder how it would be to go through life looking like Carrot Top, let alone all his other problems, and realized it would be difficult even for a strong-willed person. Carrot Top was not strong-willed; if anything, he was weak in almost every way. He had no friends on the wing and almost everyone treated him with contempt. On the few occasions I'd had reason to speak to him I was civil, but barely so, and I guessed he could see the hatred in my eyes. I knew I had reached a turning point in my therapy when I was able to empathize with someone like Carrot Top. I didn't like the fella and I still felt anger and disgust at his crime but I no longer saw him as a target for my hate. I wouldn't want him as best man at my wedding if I ever tied the knot, but I figured that given different circumstances and chances in life he would not have burned those kids to death any more than I would.

Of course, Kevin never missed an opportunity to bait men like Carrot Top. Kevin had changed a lot from the loud, opinionated Nazi I had first met on F-wing, but not so much that he was afraid to say out loud what everyone else was thinking. He still hated a lot of people for a lot of reasons, but he reserved the worst of his vitriol for child-abusers. He no longer stomped around shouting his opinions at the top of his voice; he had learned to state his hatred and the reasons behind it in a calm and fairly reasonable manner that, though no less offensive to some people, was a lot less aggressive and frightening. Therapy was working for Kevin, but it would be a slow process. I was his best mate on the wing. I think he saw me as a father figure as he had never known his own father. Whenever he had a problem, which was often, he would come to me and talk it through. I tried my best to steer him in the right direction but I needed a lot of patience with him. I would sit him down and give him the benefit of my advice and he would be contrite and promise to take it on board. Then, ten minutes later, he would be doing the same thing over again as if we'd never spoken. His loyalty to his friends was extraordinary and slightly frightening. When he found out about my feud with Taff he came and spoke to me. 'Listen, Razor,' he said, 'I'm only doing a short sentence compared to you and I know you can't afford to get nicked again as you're already a lifer, so just give me the word and I'll go in and stab Taff for you. I'll do a good job on him, I swear. I mean it, mate, the worst they can do to me is put me in a mental hospital, so I'd gladly do this for you.' He was deadly serious. It took me an hour to talk him out of it and I managed it only by appealing to the very sense of loyalty that made him offer in the first place. I told him that if he did stab Taff I would no longer class him as a friend because he would have betrayed me by not letting me handle my own battles. This worked, but I had to be careful what I said to Kevin in the future, he had an almost hero-worship for me which made him want to attack anyone I had the slightest disagreement with. Kevin would have been a great fella to have around me in the dispersal system but in Grendon he was more of a liability than an asset.

Kevin was also friendly with Mel, the gigantic ex-bouncer from my group, because he had known him on a previous sentence in HMP Nottingham. Mel had dabbled with right-wing thuggery in his youth and had battles with black and Asian gangs in Leeds and Bradford. Though Mel was not as rabid on racial issues and fascist politics as Kevin, he would lend a sympathetic ear to the latter's racist rantings. One day they were in Mel's cell on the 3s landing talking in right-wing slogans when they were overheard by Deke the Sneak. Deke was pretty friendly with the only Asian guy on the wing, a mandatory lifer named Bal, who was in for shooting his girlfriend, so he took offence for Bal by proxy. Deke was one of those people who take pleasure in stirring things up whenever they can and he liked nothing better than to get someone in a community meeting for a good roasting, so he called a meeting in his cell and invited Bal and a black youngster, who could be pretty volatile, named Damian. He told the lads that he suspected there was a racist conspiracy on C-wing and that Kevin was trying to recruit people into it. This was absolute nonsense as C-wing was probably the least racist point in the whole prison system. But, after Deke had primed the lads, they decided to sit on it for a couple of days and keep their eyes and ears open for more proof before bringing it to the community.

In the meantime group 3 had been joined by a new member. Tony was a podgy, bespectacled ex-submariner. He had joined the navy straight from school and spent the next eighteen years on submarines, becoming a chief petty officer. He was also the most infamous stalker in the country and was the main reason for the introduction of the Protection from Harassment Act 1997. The original stalking case was very complicated but I'll try to put it in simple terms: Tony claimed that he had a six-month relationship with a married woman with whom he worked. The woman, who was also in the navy, denied that any such relationship had existed but complained that she could no longer work with Tony as he would not leave her alone. The subsequent official investigation found in the woman's favour. Tony, incensed that he had not been believed, left the navy and set out on a campaign of harassment of the woman and her family that would last for over eight years.

Tony devoted his every waking moment to the harassment. He kept watch on his victim's home and followed her everywhere. He created a meticulous log on her every move, made nuisance phone calls to her and rendered her life a misery in other ways. He would order taxis by the dozen and send them to her address, along with everything else from pizzas to bouncy castles. He festooned her front garden with hundreds of condoms and slept in his car right outside her house. As the years went by, Tony's obsession with this woman merely seemed to grow. The police were called on many occasions, but there was little they could do as no law actually covered what Tony was doing. Eventually a sympathetic magistrate issued an injunction banning him from going within 100 yards of his victim on pain of imprisonment. This was no deterrent to a man so in the grip of an obsession that he had sacrificed his own marriage, job and home for it. He broke the injunction at every opportunity and served several small prison sentences. During one of his spells in prison he was celled-up with a burglar and proceeded to pick his brains. On his release Tony took his harassment one step further and began breaking into his victim's home while she and her husband were out. He would sit on their sofa with a drink and a sandwich and watch the couple's wedding video, which he eventually stole. He would use their phone to ring foreign countries and then leave it off the hook, running up massive bills. God only knows what else he got up to in the house but you can bet it was off-key. By now Tony was a very sick man, consumed by his obsession and drunk with the feeling of absolute power he had over his victim's life.

Tony's constant harassment was picked up, first by the local press and then by the national dailies. It turned out that Tony was not the only man to dedicate his life to this sort of behaviour and other women came forward with stories of harassment by men. It became a hot political issue when Prime Minister John Major was taunted by Tony Blair, then leader of the opposition, about it in 1996. Major's government wanted to deal with the harassment issue by way of a private member's bill but Blair pressed for it to become a government bill. The Protection from Harassment Act was born in July 1997. Tony, whose actions had done so much to bring about the act, was the first man jailed under it. While he was in prison psychiatrists queued up to interview him. He was released at the end of his sentence and finally gave up stalking his victim, having managed to break up her marriage and a subsequent relationship.

It wasn't long before Tony met another woman, but the relationship once again foundered and Tony reverted to his previous behaviour and started stalking his new victim. This time he didn't hang about. After a few months of harassment he decided to go out with a bang and take his victim with him. He broke into her house, armed with a butcher's knife and a pair of handcuffs, and after handcuffing himself to the victim and swallowing the key, he proceeded to cut her wrists. Then he cut his own. The victim's teenage son tried to get in the house to save his mother but Tony had everything locked up tight. The police were called and a siege developed, with Tony refusing to come out or let his victim receive medical attention for her injuries. Eventually he gave himself up and allowed his victim to be rushed to hospital, where her life was saved. This time Tony was charged with attempted murder. He was convicted and received a life sentence under the two-strike rule. After rattling around the system for a few years he was accepted for Grendon. When he came into group 3 we knew we were going to have trouble with him. He was pompous and arrogant, officious and secretive, and he didn't see himself as a common criminal like the rest of us. He looked down his nose at everybody, which earned him the nickname 'Lord Tony'. But how he ended up tied into Deke the Sneak's racist conspiracy was pure accident.

A couple of days after the meeting between Deke the Sneak, Bal and Damian, while they were all being extra vigilant about any racist remarks that might prove Deke's theory, Tony was standing in the dinner queue engaged in an innocuous conversation about German names with Kevin. The name of film star Arnold Schwarzenegger came up and Tony trans-lated it as Arnold 'Blackman'. Unfortunately for him, Deke the Sneak and Bal were behind him in the queue. They heard the words 'schwarz', 'negger' and 'black man' and this was enough for them. C-wing was obviously a hotbed of racism and probably an outpost of the BNP, and Kevin, Tony and Mel were the grand wizards of this coven. If it wasn't stopped right away there would surely be crosses burning on every landing and lynchings in the community room. Of course they did have a sound base for their conspiracy theory. It had never been a secret that Kevin was an out-and-out racist and fascist, as witnessed by the huge swastika tattooed on his chest and the words 'Anti-Paki League' on his forearm, but the rest of it was pure bollocks. Bal, who had been at Grendon for three years and knew the procedure inside out, put Kevin in the book for 'fostering a climate of racism on C-wing, along with others'. The 'book' was a ledger used by the vice-chairman of the wing to record all events of the wing. Group feedbacks were written into the book, as were the salient points of community meetings, wing assessments and commitment votes. If you wanted to put someone up for a commitment vote, suggest a topic for open discussion or report a complaint about any community member, the first step was to put it in the book. Issues in the book would be read out by the chairman at every community meeting and then be put up for discussion. By entering the racism issue in the book Bal knew it would be read out at the next meeting.

Anyone could walk into the office and take a look at the book, and there were men who did so regularly, either to check whether any of their own infractions had been noted or just so they would know of any upcoming issues in advance. It wasn't long, therefore, before men on the wing were discussing Bal's contribution. When I heard about it I sighed. I knew there was going to be trouble in the community meeting because Kevin was not the sort to roll over and play spaniel, especially when it came to his beliefs. I also knew that, as Kevin's best mate on the wing, I would be suspected of being part of the racist conspiracy. I wasn't looking forward to having to explain myself to the community. If I was a racist then it was my fucking business until I made it otherwise. I didn't think religion, politics or sexual preferences were the community's business unless they directly affected another member or were part of our offending behaviour. Obviously, in Kevin's case – he being in jail for race-hate crimes in the first place – this was relevant. But my own stubbornness would brook no questioning on this matter and I made my mind up that if I was asked about my views I would tell them to fuck off.

All this made me examine where I stood on racial matters. I had been involved in a lot of racial battles over the years. I had grown up in Brixton, south London, which has a large Afro-Caribbean population. I had plenty of black friends in the 1970s, but this was before I became a Teddy boy. There was a handful of black Teddy boys, just as there were some black skinheads, but on the whole we didn't really mix. When I first went into the borstal system at the age of sixteen, the lines were clearly drawn. Much of the unrest in the juvenile jail system was racial. Black v. white riots were quite common in borstal and I played my part in more than one of them. Fighting the black kids was *de rigueur* but I didn't have any deeply held racial beliefs. I never had any desire to join organizations like the National Front or the British Movement – simply because I never saw myself as British. I was Irish, and proud of it. The NF and BM regarded the Irish as one more immigrant group to be looked down on and dealt with once they had achieved their 'white Utopia'. I made a few black friends over the years in the world of crime and prison, men who I would back to the hilt in times of trouble. No, I didn't think I was a racist.

On the morning of the community meeting I took my seat in the big room with nervous anticipation. Once the wing minutiae had been dealt with, the chairman read out the book issue and called on Bal to elucidate further. Bal explained how Deke had overheard racist conversations on 'several occasions' and they had come to the conclusion that there were men on the wing who were hiding racial issues, and that Bal himself, as well as Damian, no longer felt safe in the community. 'If there are people on here who are secret racists, then how am I expected to work through my own issues knowing they hate me for my skin colour?' he asked. Throughout Bal's oratory I watched Deke the Sneak and noted the look of smug satisfaction on his features. I knew that Deke was in his element and saw him as a malignant puppet-master pulling the strings behind the scenes and causing a major issue where none really existed. I knew that he had instigated the whole thing because he had taken a dislike to Kevin from the moment he met him. It was more about personalities than racism.

The chairman turned to Kevin and asked if he had anything to offer. Kevin, who was volatile at the best of times, turned into a raging lunatic on the spot. With fists clenched, face contorted with fury and words cascading from his spit-flecked lips, he launched into a tirade that would have been funny under other circumstances. 'It's no secret that I'm a fookin' racist and a fascist. Have I ever denied it? Have I? No, I fookin' haven't! So what do you think, that I'm going to change overnight? You're living in a fookin' dream world, youse cunts! I thought this place was about tolerance and understanding. But no, it's only about tolerance and understanding as long as you're not a fascist. Youse lot say that racism is a bad thing, yeah? That digging someone out because they're different and in a minority is a terrible thing to do? Well, I'm in the fookin' minority here, I'm fookin' different! So what if I still use the words "Paki" and "nigger" in private? Less than a year ago you'd have heard me shouting them around the wing and proud to take on any bastard who wanted to fight over it. I'm a white nationalist and I'm proud of my race and my country and my heritage. Why has that become such a dirty thing over the last few years? You lot treat rapists, child-killers and serial abusers with plenty of understanding, you shake your heads in sympathy when they tell you what a hard life they had as kids and comfort them when they explain how the abuse they suffered themselves as kids led to them becoming what they now are, but has anyone ever fookin' wondered what sort of abuse I might have suffered to make me like this? No, you just fookin' point the accusing finger. Yes, I'm a fookin' racist. Yes, I don't like niggers and Pakis. But don't try and bring my mates into it and claim there's a fookin' conspiracy going on, 'cos that ain't right!'

Mel, who was sitting next to Kevin, pulled him back to his seat as he rose. Mel kept a tight grip of Kevin's arm and tried to calm him down. Anyone who left their seat in a threatening manner during a community meeting, or any meeting come to that, would be up for commitment and likely voted out. This was the bedrock of individual safety at Grendon.

You could say almost anything you wanted to as vehemently as you liked as long as you didn't leave your seat and threaten, or commit, violence. A ripple of unease radiated around the room at Kevin's forceful words. I sensed that things could easily turn ugly now.

The chairman called for order and asked Damian to speak as he had his hand up. Damian was young and loud and as fucked up as Kevin in his own way. The joke on the wing was that Damian was evenly balanced only because he carried a chip on both shoulders. When he spoke there was anger in his voice. 'I tell you what, I ain't listening to this shit. If any man's got a problem with me I'm fucking ready. I don't give a fuck how big you are, you don't scare me.' Mel, who had been trying to calm Kevin, suddenly sensed that Damian had turned the spotlight on him. He looked at Damian across the length of the room and I saw the anger and confusion on his face. 'Is that directed at me?' he asked. Damian kissed his teeth loudly. 'If you want to take it as that. Deke told me you was talking to Kevin about "nigger this" and "nigger that", and how you used to bash up the black pimps in Bradford. What, you think 'cos you're big that I'm afraid of you?' The more timid members of the community began shifting in their seats, eyes glancing from face to face and beseechingly at the members of staff in the room.

The chairman and the staff looked stunned at how quickly the situation seemed to be heating up. I looked around at the stronger of the senior members of the community to see if anyone was going to step in and try to defuse the situation. Fred was sitting next to me but he looked disinterested and John, who sat opposite me, was making no move. I decided to step into the breach. I stuck my hand up and caught the chairman's eye. He looked very relieved. 'Yes, Noel, have you got a question?' I nodded. 'I notice Deke sitting there looking very smug, we've heard his name mentioned a couple of times as involved in this so I'd like to hear what he has to say.' The look on Deke's face was a classic. He went from smug to mug in a split second. Damian and Mel were still looking daggers at each other but their burgeoning argument had been sidelined for a minute.

Deke found a sincere face in his repertoire of looks-for-all-occasions bag and spread his hands as if in supplication. 'Ah've fuckin' nothin' ta hide,' he said. 'Ah heard Kevin and Mel talkin' aboot "niggers and Pakis" and ah didna think it was fuckin' right, so I told ma pal Bal and young Damian. Ah dinna think it's right, racism on the wing an' that. In fact, it's a fuckin' liberty, man!' I looked him right in the eye. 'Okay,' I said. 'If you thought it was such a liberty then why didn't you pull them and tell them that? Or go and report it to the race relations officer? Or put it in the book yourself?' Deke was on the ropes as all faces turned to him. He struggled for a moment and you could almost hear the cogs grinding in his brain as he tried to come up with a reasonable answer to my questions. I moved in for the kill. 'I'll tell you why, shall I? Because you're a snide melt. You don't give a fuck about racism really, you've got another agenda here, so why don't you tell us all what it is? Be a fucking man for once in your life.' Deke did the only thing he could do in the circumstances and threw it back on to me. 'Ah've got a better idea,' he said, a glint of malice in his eyes. 'Why don't you tell us where you stand in all of this? After all, you're Kevin's pal, are ye no? Surely he wouldna hang aroond wi' you if you were'ne partial to a bit of fuckin' racism yersel', eh big man?' I noticed that the angrier he got, the more Scottish his speech patterns became. Fred suddenly seemed to come to life beside me. 'Deke, let's have it right, eh? You've manufactured this whole situation because you don't like Kevin. There ain't no racist conspiracy, is there? You're just a sad geezer who's never happy unless people are kicking off around you. Just admit it and we can deal with it and move on.' Fred was so calm and reasonable, his voice acted like a sedative on the room despite his words. Deke's face started to turn red, whether from anger or embarrassment I didn't know and never would because it was in that moment of silence that Mel finally exploded.

I had heard rumours about Mel's explosive temper. It was said that it usually took around eight, or more, screws to slow him down whenever he went on a rampage in the system; seeing his performance that morning I could well believe it. He and Damian had been staring at each other since they had exchanged words the first time. Suddenly Mel pointed a sausage-like finger across the room at Damian and snarled, 'Who the fuck do you think you're screwing at?' Damian, being too young and angry to sense the trouble he might be in, kissed his teeth again. 'Fuck off you murdering bastard,' he said. Mel was very sensitive about his crime, so Damian's words bit deep. With a window-shaking roar Mel jumped up from his seat and began advancing across the room towards Damian. His eyes were slits of molten anger, his huge fists were clenching and unclenching and the veins were popping out on his neck and forearms like thick steel cables. He looked like the Incredible Hulk after he'd been on a course of steroid injections. Kevin tried to grab him and Mel swatted him away as though he were a fly. It was as though 50,000 volts of electricity had been pumped through the chairs in the community room as at least half of the community bolted up and got between Mel and the now worried-looking Damian. It was lucky they were sitting at opposite ends of the long room; any closer and Mel would probably have had another murder on his record. As it was it took ten community members and three members of the staff to stop Mel from getting across the room. At first he just shook them off as though they weighed no more than a packet of fag-papers, but soon he was covered in a mass of bodies. He was still advancing, but he was slowing down.

I had stayed in my seat and watched with interest. There was no way I was going to put myself in Mel's way, it wasn't worth the candle. If he'd been heading towards one of my pals I would have been obliged to get involved, but I didn't even like Damian. As the seriousness of what he had unleashed finally hit him, Damian was standing on his chair with his back pressed firmly against the wall. His eyes were bugged out in terror and his bottom lip was trembling, but he managed to squeak, rather unconvincingly I must say, 'Come on then. I'm not scared of you!' Mel was brought to a halt within about ten inches of Damian's throat, though I'm sure it was because he had come to his senses rather than the result of the efforts of the human blanket he was wearing. He stood still, arms outstretched and festooned with community members and uniformed staff, and shook his huge head. 'I'm all right,' he said loudly. 'You can get off me now.' Some people were not convinced, so Mel allowed himself to be steered out of the room.

In the relative silence that followed I stared around. There were about nine people left in the room. Those who hadn't jumped on Mel had run out in fright at what was happening. There were two broken chairs, one of which was no more than matchwood, that had got in Mel's way at some point. The chairman, vice-chairman, Deke the Sneak and Bal were gathered around a shattered-looking Damian, offering him words of comfort. Carrot Top was rooted to his seat, paler than ever. Even Biff looked as though he was in shock, though it was hard to tell with him as his face really had only one expression. Fred had jumped up with everyone else to get between Mel and Damian but sat back down again when Mel left the room. I looked at Fred. He scratched his nose and glanced around. 'Good here, ain't it?' he said, calmly. I smiled and nodded. The shouting

coming from outside the community room had all but died down and
any danger was now past. Me and Fred decided to go for a cup of sticky
in the 1s alcove and listen to what people had to say about the morning's
events. This was going to be discussed in groups for the next few days,
particularly group 3 as we had both Mel and Deke as members. On the
way out of the community room I stopped and looked at Deke. 'Happy
now?' I asked. He shrugged. 'A lot of good therapy got done here today,'
he said. 'A lot of people were able to air their feelings and nobody got
hurt.' As we walked up to the 1s landing someone was playing Phil
Collins's 'Another Day In Paradise' loudly on their stereo.

The fallout from the racism 'debate' was not as immediately bad as I
thought it would be. I think the physical aspect of it tired people out and
they knew it was one of those subjects that, the more you brought it up,
the longer it would take to go away. Nobody was up for starting it all
over again any time soon, but it wouldn't just be forgotten either. After
the community had licked its wounds, it would be time for a reckoning.
Mel would face a commitment vote for his violent actions, and Damian
too for provoking the situation. A 'wing special' was called later the same
day just to check how everybody was feeling about the morning's events.
Wing specials could be called by anyone at any time to inform the community about any important happening, or just as a forum to air people's
views about particular events. The mood in the special that afternoon was
particularly subdued, but to everyone's credit there were no absences.
Tom, the therapist, spoke at length about the importance of remaining
focused on our therapy and then asked how the community was feeling.
Some members expressed their shock and disappointment that the wing
had descended so quickly into violence. I hadn't been surprised at all. I
suppose it was because I was so fresh out of the system – I'd been on
C-wing for less than four months – where shouting, insults and violence
were everyday occurrences.

Deke approached me after the special and we had a little chat. I told
him straight that what he had done was bollocks, but I didn't hold any
bad feelings – well, nothing that wouldn't pass after a couple of days. On
the whole I liked Deke. For all his snakiness and attempts at manipulation
I saw him as just another ODC. But I warned him that he'd better not try
any of his snide moves on me.

A week later, after the dust had settled and cracked egos and damaged
psyches had had time to repair themselves, Mel and Damian appeared

before the community for their commitment votes. They publicly apologized to each other and to the community. Mel was particularly contrite as he had been in therapy for over three years and genuinely felt he had let everyone down. He had discussed his behaviour in our group. We had taken the view that he was allowed one mistake, but the incident proved that he still had a lot of work to do in therapy. In the end, though, it was up to the community as a whole whether he stayed at Grendon. The vote was a close one: he was voted to stay by a margin of 21 to 20. Damian was also voted to stay, but both men were given a period of community service for their behaviour. They spent the next six weeks emptying bins and cleaning out toilets. Kevin also came out of the racism débâcle with plenty of work to do in his group. I would speak to him in private and encourage him to start opening up. Mulling it over in my cell that night I acknowledged that Deke might have been right: if the racism row had brought up other things for people to work on about themselves, then maybe some good therapy had been done at that meeting.

9. Assessment

Assessments were one of the tangible ways we were able to measure our progress at Grendon. Six months after being allocated to a group you would have an 'initial' assessment. All members of your group, your facilitator, wing probation officer, psychologist and therapist would gather in a group room on the ground floor and question you on how you were doing in therapy thus far. The initial was always fairly light in tone, no really strong questions, just a gentle probing in order to get to know you better. Those at the initial, including group members, would suggest areas that it might be beneficial for you to work on and, if you had already started work on issues, encouragement was given to continue. My own initial was pretty standard. Brian opened it by asking me to give an account of what I thought about my first six months. I talked about my observations and feelings about C-wing and Grendon in general and explained some of my thinking on therapy: I had set myself no time limit for it, would take it slowly and see how it developed, not rush and drive myself mad looking for answers. Tom asked me if I had any issues in mind that I particularly wanted to deal with. I told him that there were many: my offending behaviour, my impulsiveness and recklessness, my inability to make relationships work and my guilt over the death of my son. Tom nodded. 'And what about your childhood?' he asked. 'Anything there?' I thought for a moment. I knew there were issues from my childhood that had made me what I was, but at this stage I wasn't yet ready to admit this in public, let alone discuss it. I shook my head. 'No,' I said. 'I don't think anything there would be relevant.' Tom smiled a knowing smile and wrote something in his notebook. I felt slightly uneasy.

I was asked by Dave to give a brief account of my crimes. This was more familiar and comfortable ground for me. I said I had been first convicted of armed robbery in 1977 and had spent most of the 1980s in and out of prison for various crimes until my conviction in 1988 for another series of armed robberies. Then I had escaped from jail in 1992 and committed more armed robberies, leading to another conviction in 1993 and a further fifteen years being added to my sentence. I explained how I had been released in 1997 after benefiting from a change in the law that allowed multiple sentences to be calculated differently, and had tried to go straight for four months, working as a road sweeper. I then outlined my descent back into crime, working with a gang of ex-jailbirds known as 'the Laughing Bank Robbers'. I had been involved in eight armed robberies across London and was arrested in 1998, just over a year after my release from my previous sentence, and was jailed for life. Brian asked what my role had been in this series of robberies and I had to admit that I had been 'the frightener': it was my job to wave the gun about and growl at people to scare them shitless and make them compliant. As I spoke about it I found myself becoming embarrassed and ashamed of my behaviour. Things that made me a face among others of my profession, that I had taken a sort of professional pride in, like being able to control a bank full of people and make them do my bidding, like having the 'bottle' to go armed and take the big prize, like being ruthless and violent, now appeared childish and wrong. As I spoke about my life in crime the words turned to ashes in my mouth. There was nobody here who would be impressed by my previous behaviour or stories of criminal derring-do. This was not an old lags' trip down felony lane, this was reality. I had never given a thought to my victims, to the innocent men and women I had casually terrified during my robberies. It had all been a game to me. But talking about it now made me feel sick. 'All I can say in my own mitigation is that I never physically harmed anyone on a robbery,' I finished, lamely.

When the hour-long assessment came to an end I was relieved. Everyone shook hands with me and told me to keep on working. The next step would be for the staff who had attended to type up their notes and observations on me and present a copy to me. Then I had to take the report to one of my group meetings and read it out to the group. There would be another discussion about what I thought of it. After that I had to take my assessment to a community meeting and read it out to the whole wing. Wing assessments were something to be feared. It was a chance for people to ask questions that they wouldn't dare ask anywhere else. If you had upset anybody in the community at any time or for any reason – maybe they didn't like the way you walked or talked, or how you ate in the dining hall or any number of other things – then this was when you would hear about it. Men who took the opportunity to have a pop on wing assessments were known as 'snipers' because they would stick their heads up, fire off a verbal shot and then duck back into the safety of the community. They could say anything under the pretext that it was a therapeutic question designed to help you understand your effect on others or just a personal observation that it might help you to be aware of. There was a handful of men on the community who were well known for their sniping and they would snipe indiscriminately at any assessment. It was easy to be prepared for these as you would be expecting something from them, but the hard ones were those who seemed to come out of nowhere and fire the verbal equivalent of a .45 pre-fragmented round straight at you.

One of the most notorious snipers on C-wing was my old pal Taff. Though never eager to talk about his own failings, he was guaranteed to point out other people's. He wasn't even a very good speaker and was quick to revert to personal insults when things weren't going his way. He had a bit of trouble with one of the guys who had come on to the wing just after me, Half-naked Dave. He decided that Dave, a north Londoner doing a two-strike life for manslaughter, had been giving him dirty looks, so he went up to his cell and tried to put it on him. He gave Half-naked Dave his mad-eyed stare and the intimidating speech that always started with the words 'I think you've got a problem with me . . .' But Dave was an old-school villain who had been around the system most of his life and wasn't in the slightest impressed. He showed Taff the door and gave him some advice in the form of 'Go and pull your act on someone who gives a fuck.' Half-naked Dave's treatment of Taff was cause for much amusement among certain people on the wing, myself included, and it was obvious that the Welshman was burning with humiliation over it. He never said a word but every time he was anywhere near Half-naked Dave you could see it on his face.

By the time of Half-naked Dave's initial assessment the incident had been forgotten by almost everybody, except Taff. He had spent his time waiting, polishing his sniper scope and selecting the verbal rounds he might fire. The assessment was going pretty well for Half-naked Dave; he was well liked in the community and had put in a lot of work on his crime. It had been a clear case of self-defence: he had been attacked by a bloke who lived a few doors away from him and had disarmed the man and stabbed him with his own knife in the ensuing struggle. He had been charged with murder but convicted of manslaughter by a jury. The trouble was that Half-naked Dave had a pretty violent record in his youth and that meant he had to receive a life sentence on his conviction.

Tom asked Half-naked Dave if he had made any plans for his future when he eventually got out of prison. Dave explained that he was taking various gym courses while at Grendon and hoping to make a career as a gym instructor on the out. Taff stuck up his hand. 'Yeah, I've been sitting here listening to everyone saying what a nice man you are and all that and what a great career you're going to have in the future, but what I want to know is, do you ever think that your victim might have had things he wanted to do with his life before you slaughtered him?' This kind of question was uncalled for but it was a typical snipe. The object of the snipe is to throw you off your stride and make you look bad in front of everyone. If you lost your temper, then the sniper would feign innocence and you would have damaged yourself in front of the community. How you handled snipers could show a lot about your character when under pressure. Unfortunately for Half-naked Dave he couldn't help but bite. 'Why don't you fuck off, Taff?' he said. 'You're just trying to dig me out because I mugged you off a couple of months ago. You vindictive sheep-shagger.'

That was enough for Taff. He now knew he could escalate the situation and come out looking good. Wearing an outraged expression that was as false as his pretence at reasonableness, he turned to Tom. 'That's racism, that is! I only asked him a question and he's fucking abusing me in front of everybody. You all heard it, he called me a sheep-shagger, that's a slur against my race, that is! I'm reporting this to the race relations officer.' Instead of sitting back and leaving Taff to look ridiculous as he should have done, Half-naked Dave lost his temper. 'Shut up, you fucking prick!' he shouted. 'You wouldn't last two minutes in another nick, you'd be run off the wing, you noncey cunt.' Taff stood up and looked at the chairman. 'I'm sorry, but I'm not going to sit here and be abused like this, he's already killed at least one person and I don't think he's dealt with that yet.' With that he flounced out of the community room.

Taff's performance at Half-naked Dave's assessment had worked a treat as far as he was concerned. As a lifer, Half-naked Dave would have to satisfy many criteria before he could be considered safe enough for open conditions or release. His burst of temper and abusive language on the assessment would be a setback and it would be noted in his lifer record. At the least, he would have to do more months in therapy working on this incident. At worst, it could hamper his progress through the system to release. Everything a lifer says and does is marked in his record and will be on the table when he eventually goes in front of the parole board. Manslaughter is a crime of violence and any loss of temper or control is classed as a risk factor. Wing assessments could be a minefield for the unwary. My own wing assessment was scheduled for early December and I was expecting the firing to be thick and fast, particularly from Taff.

In the meantime, life went on. Ray was doing well, he had been off heroin and cocaine for over seven months and was happy to be clean after many years of drug abuse. John had been given a job as a 'red-band', which was a big step for him after twelve years in prison. A red-band is someone who can be trusted to move about within the prison without a staff escort. To indicate this they are issued with a red cloth band, to be worn around the right arm. John had been a category A prisoner at the start of his sentence, which meant he could not even leave his cell without at least two screws, and a dog in some nicks, and his every movement was recorded in a little book. So to progress to a red-band was heady stuff indeed. Being a red-band is one step away from being trusted in open conditions. I was pleased for John, he had done most of his bird the hard way and now he was surely on the last knockings.

Daran, who still had over twelve years to go before he was eligible to even apply for parole, tended to just get on with things as though he didn't have a care. He intrigued me and I questioned him at length about his life. He came from a good middle-class family, but it had fragmented just as Daran was entering his teens and he ended up spending some time in care. From what I could gather, he had exhibited the classic signs of a psychopath in the past. His first criminal conviction was for kicking to death two dogs and a cockerel. He told me that one of the dogs had bitten him and he just got the urge to kill everything in sight. His father, who was apparently quite wealthy and influential, hired a top lawyer to defend him on charges of animal cruelty and he was dealt with leniently, receiving a suspended sentence. Soon after this incident Daran joined the Royal Navy.

Daran loved his time in the navy. He told me he most enjoyed the camaraderie, mixing with a bunch of good workmates, playing pranks on each other and going on the piss together. But he also liked the orderliness of military life, he felt right at home when he had a set of rules and regulations to govern his life. But despite all this, after five years in the navy Daran had outstayed his welcome. He assaulted a senior NCO in an argument over lateness and was given ninety days in the brig. It was a case of jump or be pushed, so he left. After drifting aimlessly for a year, he headed for France and joined the French Foreign Legion. The Legion is notorious for its brutal approach to basic training but Daran survived and went on to become a Legionnaire, wholeheartedly embracing its ethos. During his first period of leave he came back to England to visit family and friends and took his 'kepi', the Legionnaires' distinctive white pillbox cap, into his local pub to show them. It is one of the traditions of the Legion that anyone who disrespects the kepi must be dealt with severely. To a Legionnaire, insulting the kepi is like calling Allah a cunt in front of a devout Muslim – something you really shouldn't do. One of the drinkers in Daran's local made the mistake of thinking it would be a laugh to throw Daran's kepi on the floor. The retribution was swift and merciless. Daran beat the man to a bloody pulp and was arrested for grievous bodily harm with intent. His victim refused to give evidence against him. Once again Daran avoided imprisonment for an act of violence. But it would all soon catch up with him when he found himself charged with murder the following year.

When sentencing Daran to life imprisonment with a twenty-year minimum tariff for murder the judge expressed a wish that Daran should receive some sort of psychiatric help while in prison. His first examination by the psychology department at HMP Long Lartin led to the diagnosis that Daran suffered from a severe form of Asperger's Syndrome, a condition linked to childhood autism which can be encountered in some psychopaths. Daran was assessed for the Dangerous Severe Personality Disorder Unit at Whitemoor and found suitable. It was a voluntary programme where prisoners convicted of seriously violent crimes could be treated with a range of therapeutic measures. Daran lasted only a few months before pulling off the programme. In his own words, 'I didn't fit in there, it was full of strange people all talking about violence.' Instead, he applied for Grendon and despite, or maybe because of, the number of years he had left to serve, he was accepted.

Daran was a stickler for rules. I think that was one of the reasons why he found prison pretty comfortable: there was no shortage of rules. In many ways he was an innocent; he had no concept of personal danger. In prisons such as Whitemoor and Long Lartin, which hold some of the most volatile and violent prisoners in this country and where a word out of place could get you killed, Daran mixed with and talked to everyone.

He was so optimistic in his outlook and so naive in his understanding of prisoner politics that he became accepted as something different. But not as a threat to anyone. As a savage psychopathic murderer, and standing at a very fit and well proportioned 6 foot 2, Daran could have become the top face on almost any prison wing he stepped into. He had been taught unarmed combat and several ways to kill by the Foreign Legion but he just wasn't interested in conflict, which was strange given his military and criminal background.

I got on really well with Daran, he was always polite and outwardly happy so I couldn't imagine him committing such a gruesome murder as he was in for. For the first six months I knew him, seeing him every day, living a couple of doors away from him, I never witnessed Daran lose his temper or exchange a cross word with anyone. Sometimes I would try to wind him up just to see how far I could go. I had a terrible nagging urge to get at least a glimpse of the other side of Daran, the dark side that could cause him to spend hours mutilating the body of his victim, scooping out intestines and other internal organs with his bare hands and rolling in the blood. I tried to push him over the edge, by insulting the navy, the Legion, rules and regulations and Daran himself. Though he would get exasperated with me, he never once lost his temper. I knew there had to be a trigger, but I also knew that pushing it could be very dangerous. After some months I decided to stop trying. We were both doing well in therapy and, as I explored my own triggers for certain behaviour, I began to lose the craving to step up to the edge. Then Daran decided to give up smoking.

When he first mentioned that he was giving up smoking I just shrugged and wished him good luck. I've been a smoker since the age of thirteen and enjoy the habit so much that I have never even contemplated giving it up. My New Year's resolutions were always to smoke more. At Grendon the healthcare staff were very proactive in helping men to give up by supplying patches and counselling, and many men were able to stop smoking with few ill effects. Unfortunately Daran was not one of them. I noticed the first real change in him after he had been without nicotine for forty-eight hours. He seemed restless and agitated and he wasn't smiling so much. I put this down to his cravings for the weed and thought no more about it. On the third day of Daran's abstinence he got into an argument with one of the hobbits on the landing over some trivial matter. This was noteworthy as I had never heard him raise his voice to anyone. He locked himself in his cell and stayed there for several hours. I knocked to check that he was all right but he wouldn't open the door. This was very unusual as Daran was the most sociable man on the wing, especially with me. On the fourth day there were a few of us sitting in the 1s alcove drinking coffee and talking before groups when Daran marched past on his way to the shower room. 'Do you lot want to keep your fucking noise down,' he growled as he passed. The alcove went quiet and we all looked at each other. 'Was he joking, or what?' asked John of nobody in particular. Daran growling at people was a shocking development. As the day went on he seemed to become more angry and aggressive. He was like a pitbull with a pimple on its bollocks, snapping at people seemingly at random. Some men on the wing got frightened and went out of their way to avoid him.

On the fifth morning I confronted Daran about his behaviour and what I saw in his eyes was truly unnerving. His Jekyll to Hyde transformation was almost complete and the inner monster was in plain view for the first time since I'd known him. I tried to explain that his aggressive behaviour was starting to scare people and that it wouldn't be long before the staff noticed or someone reported it to them. He looked at me with utter contempt. 'Do you think I give a fuck what other people think?' he asked. Even his voice sounded different, harsher. 'If they don't like it they can kiss my arse.' This was so far removed from the Daran I thought I knew that even I was shocked. 'There are some cunts on this wing who need a fucking good beating,' he snarled. 'And maybe they'll get it sooner than they think.' As he spoke I noticed that his fists were tightly clenched. This was serious. Looking at Daran that day it became very easy to see him committing the savage and bloodthirsty acts attributed to him. I appealed to him. 'Listen, mate,' I said. 'Why don't you have a smoke, eh? Fuck all this giving up game, here, have one of mine.' I held out my tobacco pouch to him. 'Just one won't make a difference, will it?' He looked at my pouch. In typical fashion, when he had decided to give up smoking he had given away all his tobacco and smoking requisites. I saw his fists unclench and I was relieved. 'I've given up,' he said, but he sounded unsure. I put my pouch into his hand. 'Here,' I said. 'If you want one then have one. I'll be in my cell, I've got to write a letter. Drop my snout down after.' And I walked off, leaving him standing looking at the tobacco pouch in his hand. An hour later there was a tap on my cell door. When I opened it the old familiar Daran was standing there with a big smile on his face. 'Can I come in for a cup of coffee and a fag?' he asked. 'That's if you're not too busy?' He had already smoked half the tobacco in my pouch, one roll-up after another, and the infusion of nicotine had had a calming effect and brought him back to his old self.

I found the whole episode very strange. How could giving up smoking turn a man from a happy, outgoing and polite chap into a nasty ball of rage and spite? I wondered if this happened with other people who had given up, though I'd never witnessed it before, or if this transformation was unique to Daran. I could only assume that without the sedative effects of nicotine his darker nature worked its way to the surface more easily. When I asked him about it he had no answer other than, 'I found I got the hump more easily without the fags.' And that was as far as he was willing to comment. I made Daran promise not to give up smoking again as long as we were both at Grendon.

10. The Fight

The staff were aware of most of what went on on the landings of C-wing even though they rarely ventured off the ground floor except for the evening lock-up at 8.30. There was always someone who would slip into the office and let them know what was happening or put it in the book or raise it as a minute at a community meeting. In every other nick in the country anyone who went to the staff and told them what was going on would be declared a grass and be dealt with violently in short order, but at Grendon it was accepted by most as the norm. I never got to the stage where I could comfortably condone such actions – it always felt wrong to me – but I learned a degree of acceptance and not to look down too much on the men who did it.

One of my own prejudices that I did overcome at Grendon was actually talking to staff on a meaningful level. I learned to look beyond the uniform and see the human being behind it. In the system I addressed staff as 'guv' or 'screw', as did almost everyone else, but at Grendon it was all first names. Using someone's name makes it hard not to think of them as an individual and that was something I had always consciously avoided when dealing with prison staff. I didn't want to know anything about them because they were the enemy and we were at war. It is easier to do bad things to people when you dehumanize them in your mind. At first I felt really uncomfortable talking to staff and would go out of my way to avoid it, but their attitude to me was very friendly and accepting so I found it increasingly hard to stay aloof. The first time I called a screw by his first name I almost choked on it, but it became easier as the months went by. The first member of staff I had met when I came on to C-wing, Keith, was a great help on my journey towards mutual trust and respect between me and the staff. He would never miss the opportunity to engage me in conversation and ask my view on things that were happening in the prison system as a whole. We had many discussions about the rights and wrongs of the criminal justice system and, though we did not always agree, I respected his opinion. Unfortunately, Keith was a bit too liberal, even for a place like Grendon, and within a few months of my arrival on

C-wing he had taken 'long-term sick leave' and never came back. I never did find out the details of why Keith left, but there was a strong rumour that he had allowed an inmate out of his handcuffs at a family funeral despite being expressly told not to by the security governor. There was an investigation and Keith decided to leave before he was sacked. This was a rumour and maybe there were other reasons, but it would fit in with what I knew about Keith's character. He was a sad loss to C-wing.

One of the incidents that the staff never heard the full story on was 'the fight that never was'. The Hell's Angels MC have a motto: 'two can keep a secret as long as one of those is dead', which could have been thought of with Grendon in mind as it was the one place in the system where secrets were rarely kept. Usually any breach of the constitution, no matter how minor, would be reported by any number of people within minutes. So it was a major coup when two community members managed to have a stand-up fist fight on the landing and get away with it. But it did happen. Two of the men in my group, Abs and Dave, had never really liked each other. It was just one of those things. You can't like everybody no matter how much you try and some people take an instant dislike to each other. And this is how it was with Abs and Dave. They were civil towards each other and made an effort to work together in the group and not let their personal animosity get in the way of anyone's therapy, but it was fairly obvious that they were never going to be best man at each other's wedding. The funny thing was that they were very similar in character; they could both be loud, demanding and opinionated – usually all at the same time. I now think that this could have been the reason for their dislike of each other; maybe each recognized the negative character traits in the other. Anyway, one afternoon they argued and the months of keeping a lid on it all went out the window. They went from shouting to throwing punches at each other quicker than it would take Cyrano de Bergerac to snort a line of charlie. They fell through Dave's cell doorway in a tangle of arms and legs, gouging, butting and biting. The fight was witnessed by me, Fred, John, Ray, Fat Richie and Biff and it was a pretty brutal affair.

We managed to prise the pair apart and break up the fight very quickly, but the noise was attracting witnesses. Everyone, including the two protagonists, knew that their places at Grendon were now in jeopardy. They were quick to gain control and it was lucky that they had ended up off the landing and inside Dave's cell where they could be seen by fewer people. John went out on to the landing, first plastering a look of amusement on his face, and confronted the small crowd who had been alerted by the rumpus. Fred followed, pretending to be surprised by the crowd of would-be feedbackers. 'What's going on, lads?' John asked. 'Have they called a roll-check or something?' One of the crowd, Geek, a rapist who never missed an opportunity to feedback any breach of the rules in the mistaken belief that such behaviour would earn him brownie points with the staff, looked quizzical. 'There was a lot of noise coming from this landing,' he said. 'It sounded like someone was getting beat up.' Fred and John both laughed. 'You've got some fucking imagination!' Fred said. 'We was fucking about, that's all.' He pointed at John. 'Silly bollocks there knocked the bin over in the recess.' I walked out of Dave's cell and casually strolled past the small curious group. 'Stick the kettle on, will you, Fred?' I called over my shoulder as though everything was normal. 'Abs will make it if you get the water on.' People started drifting away, all except Geek, who was too snide and slippery himself not to be suspicious. He tried to walk past John and Fred to get a look into Dave's cell and they had to let him to avoid looking even more suspicious. What he saw was Abs and Dave sitting over a hastily erected chess board, evidently deep in concentration. Geek shrugged and headed back upstairs.

As soon as the crowd had dispersed we took stock and began a conscious effort at damage limitation. Both Abs and Dave were well liked in our circle and we didn't want to see them lose their place down to something so stupid if it could be helped. The first thing to do was make sure the boys were not going to commence battle again, but they were both contrite and shamefaced by now and agreed to shake hands and put their differences back on hold. Ray spoke to Fat Richie, who was adamant that he had seen or heard nothing and had nothing to feed back. Fat Richie had spent many years in the dispersal system and was as good as gold. My job was to speak to Biff, who had witnessed the whole incident. Biff was thicker than two short planks but he wasn't a snitch. I explained that he would not be able to say anything about the incident, not even in his group, and he agreed. We only had one problem left: Abs had taken a right-hander in the eye and it was now visibly swollen to about three times its normal size.

Participating in a cover-up of an act of violence went against everything that Grendon was supposed to be about. We had reverted to past behaviour in an instant. This was a serious matter that could get us all voted out, but it also told some of us that we had a long way to go in therapy and plenty of work left to do. Therapists and staff would interpret it as a return to our criminal behaviour, but I like to think we were doing no more than any group of friends would do for each other in a similar situation. The straight world was pretty alien to me but I was sure that straight-goers didn't always immediately inform on each other about everything.

Geek was a nasty bastard and more slippery than a bag of grease-coated eels so he suspected something had gone on and guessed it had been a fight and that it was being covered up. He mooched around the wing asking questions of everyone and generally making himself busy and it wasn't long before he spotted Abs's swollen eye and arrived at his own conclusion. His first stop was the office, where he voiced his suspicions to a member of staff and was told to go and report to Tom, the therapist. Soon afterwards Abs was called down to Tom's office for a chat. Tom asked him about his eye and Abs told him it was an old injury that sometimes became swollen and inflamed. During the time when he was a crackhead on the streets of north London Abs had been shot in the head by a rival with a sawn-off shotgun. He had nearly lost the sight in an eye and still had more than twenty lead shotgun pellets lodged in his skull. His injury was well documented, so Tom had no choice but to accept his explanation. He asked Abs straight out if there had been a fight on the landing but Abs denied it.

Deke the Sneak heard that Geek had been speaking to Tom about Abs and Dave possibly fighting and he decided to call a 'group special' to find out what exactly had gone on. A group special is when every member of a group is called together, usually with little or no notice, to discuss a matter of importance that has cropped up outside of group work hours. Any member can call a group special so Deke was within his rights to get us together. We gathered in our group room and sat there in silence. Deke demanded to know if there was any substance in the rumour that two group 3 members had been fighting. We all laughed the rumour off. Abs and Dave denied any fight had taken place and that was the end of it. Without witnesses or evidence the matter could go no further.

We had got away with it, but none of us felt good about it. There was not the sense of victory over the system that we would have felt in any other prison. Two of our number had fucked up and we had compounded that mistake by all getting involved and putting our own places at risk.

We had come to Grendon to get away from such behaviour, not to perpetuate it. Later I came to understand that our conspiracy had been much worse than the actual fight. The punch-up had been spontaneous and, in some ways, unavoidable, but we had been deliberately devious and corrupt in our dealing with it. We had all been compromised and our secret would surely come back to haunt us at some stage. It would be that little bit harder to be open and honest in our therapy and in our dealings with others knowing what we had done. I didn't suffer the slightest twinge of guilt at the time, I felt I had done nothing out of the ordinary, just the same thing I had been doing all of my life. And that was one of my problems. I had become so entrenched in the criminal/prisoner codes and values that I failed to recognize them as wrong. I was changing, slowly, but the last and hardest thing for me to lose was going to be my loyalty to my past life. This was to be my struggle.

On a cold Thursday at the start of December I entered the community room for my first wing assessment. I was slightly nervous going in and I was expecting a hard time from the snipers but I was surprised to note that Taff had not turned up. Taff and I were still actively engaged in the cold war that had started back in the summer and I guessed he would be looking forward to the opportunity of getting a few free shots in. The fact that he was not there did much to ease my mind and I felt ready for anything. I read out my reports to the wing, which were on the whole very encouraging and then sat back and waited for questions. The hour seemed to fly by as I answered everything with as much honesty as I could muster. I was asked about my crimes and how I felt about armed robbery now that I had given it more serious thought. I answered that I no longer saw armed robbery as a noble and victimless crime, and I explained how I had begun to feel a real empathy for my victims. I told them how I had become sick and tired of crime and prison and how much Joe's death had contributed to my change of attitude. I spoke from the heart and ended by stating my honest desire to live a normal decent life on my eventual release and that I was willing to stay at Grendon and engage in therapy for however long it took for me to consolidate that desire.

When the assessment was over I felt great. My friends all congratulated me on it and wished me luck with the rest of my therapy. I was slowly starting to feel as though I really belonged in Grendon. Things were not perfect, and probably never would be, but I could sense the change in myself, in my attitudes and thinking. I realized Grendon could work for me in a very real way and that was a relief. At the beginning I had worried that I would not 'get it', or get it and find it was not for me and waste another few years getting nowhere. Now I had a good feeling. I was never going to turn into a therapeuton, I think my personality is too strong to be erased completely, but I was willing to meet them halfway. And that would be a result.

11. Lights Out

For a prison that was only forty years old Grendon was in a terrible physical state. I had spent time in jails like Wandsworth and Dartmoor that, though well over a century old, had better fabric and amenities. It was as if no one had expected Grendon to last long at the time it was built so they used the cheapest materials and didn't put too much effort into its construction. In 1989 Grendon was condemned as 'unsafe for human habitation' by health and safety inspectors and every single inmate was transferred to other prisons practically overnight. The electrics in the prison were so bad that the inspectors wondered how nobody had been killed or seriously injured. Just turning on an office light switch at the wrong time could have blown the system and started a fire. With Grendon inmates taking up valuable places at other prisons it was considered a matter of urgency to get the jail up and running as quickly as possible so the contractors took shortcuts. Instead of 'wasting' time cutting channels for the new wiring and then plastering over them, they just laid plenty of conduit on the walls and ceilings. It made the prison look like a power station inside but at least it was quick and fairly safe. Within six months the whole jail had been rewired and was open for business again. Unfortunately the work was not to last.

In early December 2003 there was a power cut throughout the prison. It was around six in the evening and everyone was on association. The prison was plunged into darkness and in the few minutes it took for the emergency generator to kick in and power the emergency lighting there was a lot of good-natured banter. 'Put another shilling in the meter,' and 'Get your hand off my leg, I'm married!' could be heard from the darkness. I was sitting in the 1s alcove playing cards with Fred, John and Daran when the lights went out. Being veterans of prison life we knew that every now and again in most jails the electric went off in order to test the emergency generator and it never lasted long. When the emergency lights did come on we just carried on with our game. Twenty minutes later we started to wonder why it was taking so long to get the main lights back on. The emergency generator was only able to power the dim lights on the landings and in the offices, as well as the riot bells and other vital security apparatus, but none of the cells or wall sockets. Biff came up the stairs to the alcove and told us that a wing special had been called for five minutes' time in the community room. He said it was something to do with the power cut but he didn't know what. So we threw in our hands and made our way downstairs.

By the time we had all taken our seats in the dimly lit community room I noticed that some of the staff were looking worried. One of the governors addressed us: 'As you may be aware, we're having a problem with the electricity supply. The works department are doing their best to remedy the situation even as we speak, but they say it may take a while. We need everyone to go back to their cells for now, until it gets sorted, and I'm afraid we'll have to lock you all up.' There was a lot of muttering from the community and then the questions came thick and fast. 'How long are we going to be banged-up for?', 'What about the cell lights?', 'Are we getting Night San?' The guv had no answers for us but said the security department had ordered the lock-down and that it should be for no more than half an hour. In most other jails in the system there would have been serious unrest, possibly even a riot, if the screws had tried to cut association short and lock prisoners in pitch-black cells. Come to think of it, I would have been at the forefront of that unrest if it had happened to me in any other nick. But I went quietly to my cell just like everyone else. The policy at Grendon was openness and honesty in all things, and that was the same for the staff, so when the guv told us the lock-up would be for half an hour no one doubted him. When my cell door was locked the blackness inside was complete. My cell was at the end of a landing spur so not even the insipid glow from the emergency lighting, which was in the centre of the landing to illuminate the staircase, reached me. I groped my way to the window and looked out. Even the security spotlights that light up the grounds and perimeter wall after dark were out. My view, even when there was light, was of the wall so there was nothing for me to see out of the window.

I sat on my bed and wondered what I could do to occupy myself. Television was out, obviously, and so was the radio. Because Grendon has in-cell electricity I had stopped buying overpriced batteries from the canteen and just plugged it in instead. Now I wished I had at least kept a spare set of batteries for just such an occasion as this. I couldn't even resort to the old-fashioned cell pastimes that had been all but replaced by the electrical revolution in our prisons, reading or writing. I couldn't see the end of my nose, let alone the pages of a book. I lay back on my bed and waited for my eyes to become adjusted to the dark. Then I heard the 'window-warriors' start and I let out a deep sigh. Window-warriors are a fucking nuisance at the best of times, but thankfully they are a dying breed. Before prisoners were allowed to have television in their cells, and sometimes after, the thick-as-shit and easily bored among our number found their entertainment by shouting from their cell windows at night, sometimes well into the early hours. Window-warriors are the prison equivalent of an all-night rave party in the next door garden and the nutter who always sits next to you on the bus, mixed into one. A bad one can get everyone at it until half the prison is screaming threats and obscenities from their windows. Most times they try to preserve their anonymity by putting on fake accents and 'funny' voices while they are insulting and provoking people. There had been one or two window-warriors on F-wing while I was there but none on C-wing. Now it seemed the darkness and lack of any other form of entertainment had made some people revert to past behaviour. So I lay there in the dark and tried to ignore the cacophony.

I must have dozed off despite the noise, because the click of the electronic door lock made me jump. I got up, opened my door and came out on to the landing. The emergency lights were still on. I looked at my watch: 8.15. We had been locked in darkness for over two hours. All along the landing men were emerging into the weak light and squinting like long-buried moles. I walked to the alcove and saw around twelve uni-formed staff standing in a group. None of them was C-wing staff and they looked defensive and somehow ready for trouble. One of the females, a short, stocky woman with dyed blonde hair cut in a man's style and wearing a big pair of army boots, began to speak. 'All right lads, get some water and then back behind your doors as quick as you can. Let's go!' I was stunned. The show of strength, the attitude and the barked orders were what I would expect from screws in the system, but not at Grendon. There was a moment's silence, as though everyone else on the landing was as stunned as me, and then I shook my head. 'Who the fuck do you think you're talking to?' I asked angrily. 'We've just spent two hours in pitch darkness, we were told it was going to be half an hour, and you think you can come on here and give it the big 'un?' Others began to voice their anger as well and the screws closed ranks even tighter.

The screws, because that's what this lot were, were surrounded by angry prisoners. We had been willing to cooperate as long as we were told the truth and treated with a bit of respect, but the minute the regime reverted to type and tried to bully us all bets were off. After my initial outburst I took a back seat and allowed others to have their say. It was interesting to see usually placid community members in an angry mood. The situation escalated very quickly and I could see that the screws were shocked and worried by what was developing. Paul, who was usually a very nice and respectful fella, was shouting that if they didn't get the lighting sorted very soon they were going to have trouble like they'd never seen. Daran was looking quietly dangerous and even Fred was scowling. In these situations there is always the danger that someone will utter an ultimatum that will take everything to an even more dangerous level. In this case it was Fred. 'If you don't get it sorted, then I'm not banging up. Simple as that. So do what you have to do 'cos I'm not going back behind that door till it's sorted.' There were shouts of support and agreement from all sides. I didn't have to say a word; Fred knew I'd back him whatever he did.

This was now a very serious incident, about as serious as it could get in prison. We stood on the edge of an abyss and one wrong move could tumble us into it and start a riot. I had been in these situations before in other prisons so I knew every step of the dance to come and it was not something I wanted to be involved in if I had a choice. I pushed my way through the throng to stand in front of the screws and began to speak, calmly. 'Look, you can't reasonably expect us to be locked into cells with no lights. Number 1, it's illegal. The Prison Rules of 1999 state: "No cell shall be used to house a prisoner unless it has been certified for use under Section 14 of the Prison Act 1952", and that means adequate heating and lighting. And don't even get me started on the Human Rights Act. So let's all calm down, and you go and get a governor up here to explain by what authority you're trying to break the law.' The screws looked relieved that the shouting and growling had stopped, and that I had pointed out that they were not the ones responsible for this. I was glad of all those years I had spent studying prison law in order to get one up on the system. The screws saw their out and took it. 'Okay lads,' said the blonde spokeswoman. 'Do us a favour and please just get your water and we'll go and see if we can get a governor up here to sort things out.' With that, half the screws went downstairs.

There were still a lot of unhappy and irate men on the landing but they were confining their anger to muttering rather than shouting or violence. I looked at Fred and shrugged. 'What's the point of kicking off, mate?' I asked. 'Things go wrong here we could all end up with another ten-stretch on our sentences. Let's just see what they do.' Fred wasn't happy, but now that his first flush of anger was receding he was sensible enough to control his emotions. The five or six screws who had stayed on the landing were trying to make conversation with us and it was encouraging to see that in some cases they were succeeding. This was Grendon after all. I guessed that the first flashpoint had passed. Most of our anger was dissipating, but it would soon flood back if we thought we were being fobbed off.

Within five minutes the screws were back on the landing, this time accompanied by the wing PO and two SOs. The wing PO was liked and respected by the lads as a straight-shooter so when he spoke we were prepared to listen. He told us that it was now looking like it was going to take at least a day to sort out the electrics. There were groans and muttering in the ranks at this. 'But at least you've got lights in your cells now,' the PO said. We all looked at each other, puzzled. 'No, we haven't,' said several men. The PO smiled. 'Yes, you have. The power for the cell lights went on an hour ago.' Biff's cell was closest to the alcove so he went and pressed his light switch and, sure enough, the landing was flooded with light. Before banging up at six we had been told to make sure that all electrical cell appliances were turned off so that when the supply was reconnected it would not be overloaded straight away, and that included the cell light switches. We had been sitting in darkness and not one of us had thought to try the lights! There were relieved and shamefaced grins all around and the mood on the landing instantly lifted.

The next bit of news was even better received. It seems that the governor had used his influence and part of his budget to order a van-load of batteries that we could use to power our radios. He had phoned around and managed to locate a company in Leeds that were willing, on such short notice, to deliver the batteries to the prison and they were expected to arrive at any moment. Suddenly things were looking good again. We had gone from pitch-black cells to light and music, from the verge of a riot to an almost party atmosphere in the space of a few minutes. The PO informed us that if we got our water and banged up straight away the staff would go round the cells to supply us with batteries for our appliances.

We all agreed.

The PO proved as good as his word and later that night, with a hot cup of tea from my flask and waiting for *A Book at Bedtime* to start on my battery-powered radio, I reflected on how quickly the community had reverted to system behaviour. In the system we took it for granted that we were being lied to by staff and governors. In fact, a much used prison joke goes: 'How can you tell when a screw is lying to you? His lips move.' We expected to be treated like sub-humans. We became used to being ordered around and talked down to by the screws and we had our own personal set of behaviours for dealing with this. But at Grendon we were told to put all this behind us. We would be treated, if not as equals, at least as adults. For the first time in my life I had broken down that barrier between myself and the screws and I had started to believe there was another way to behave, but take away my light and start shouting orders at me again and I get straight on to the back foot and prepare to swing back. What I had achieved at Grendon was very fragile, I knew that now. I was making progress, I had no doubt of that, I had not taken the incident in the alcove the one further step it needed to go in order to erupt in violence, as I would have done in the past, but I had come close to it. On the plus side I believed I had done much to calm the situation that my outburst had been instrumental in starting in the first place, and that was personally encouraging. I would have to build on this foundation in the months and years ahead. Once again I felt good about being at Grendon. It was different, despite the occasional hiccups like tonight.

The next morning we all met in the community room at nine to discuss the events of the previous evening. We were informed that things were much more serious than had first been supposed: the works department didn't have the knowledge or the tools to restore the electricity supply to the prison. Apparently the jail had been overloading its electrical circuits for over a decade and now the system had just about burned out. We were told that it might take the whole day to sort it out and that the electrics would have to be turned off until it was. Luckily the pods where each wing did its cooking ran on gas so at least we were guaranteed a hot meal if nothing else. Because the emergency bells were going to be out no one could leave the wing to go to work or the gym, so we were stuck on a wing with no electrics and no heating for what would prove to be a very long day. Little was said about our mini-insurrection of the previous evening because there were now other things to worry about. The last time there had been this much trouble with the electrical system the prison had been closed down and everyone shipped out to different nicks, and there was no shortage of doomsayers to remind us of this fact.

By early afternoon the rumour mill that is a prominent feature of all prison life was starting to grind. Fuelled by boredom and paranoia the whispers came thick and fast. First was the story that G-wing, where the worst sex offenders were held, was the only wing in the nick that still had power. There were a couple of men willing to swear on their mother's eyesight that the nonces were living the life of Riley, basking in heat and light with tellies blaring. This story swept around C-wing quicker than a case of clap through a brothel. There was a lot of angry muttering from the various groups of men who had gathered on the landings to seek comfort from each other. I was on the ground floor talking to John and Fred when Biff became the third person to mention it. 'The fuckin' nonces have got electric! They're havin' it large on G-wing, the doorty fuckin' bastards!' I waved Biff over. 'Who told you they've got electric on G-wing?' I asked. Biff shrugged. 'I heard from Nigel, his mate had to go up the hospital and when he walked past G-wing he could hear it all going on.' Biff puffed his chest out in outrage. 'Do yourself a favour, Biff,' I told him. 'Stop spreading rumours, you silly cunt! The whole prison has no electric, and that includes G-wing. What are you, some sort of fucking melt?' Biff blinked hard. 'It's what I heard, is all. Divvent take it out on me.' And with that he turned and waddled off, no doubt to spread the poison elsewhere.

I took a walk around the wing and was not surprised at the mood of the men. We were no longer a community, but were quickly forming into several small gangs. The stories about G-wing had turned the mood nasty. Those whose crimes would be considered dodgy in the system were either flocking together in little groups or had decided to wait it out in their cells. Some of the groups of so-called ordinary criminals looked as though they might join together and march on Castle Frankenstein, torches burning and pitchforks waving. It was that kind of vibe, as if people were just waiting for a signal. I decided to stick close to my pals, and no matter what happened I would ride it out without getting involved. Around 3 p.m. word came from the staff that it was looking doubtful for the electrics to be restored to normal now. It was to be another night of light only in the cells. To be honest I didn't mind this, there was plenty on the radio to keep me amused and I had a good supply of books. The downside was that there was no heat and no access to Night San so we had to use pisspots again. It would be just like spending some time in the punishment block but with the bonus of being able to keep a flask and a radio and not have to sleep on a mattress on the floor. But some men on the wing had no block experience to fall back on and they found it hard to face the solitude of their own company without telly and PlayStations to distract them.

By 4.30 there was a rumour that Grendon was going to close down and that we were all to be loaded on to sweatboxes and shipped to nicks around the country wherever they had spaces. I found this one a bit worrying; after all there was a precedent for it. It would be just my luck to get this far in my bid for change only to be thrown back into the system. I knew what it took to survive in the system, I would have to be hard and staunch and put the mask back on. There could be no thoughts of victims, empathy or remorse in that environment, it would be survival of the fittest again. I had been out of the system for almost six months but I knew I would be able to slip back in. The thing was, I didn't want to. The rumour about ship-outs was so persistent that some people even started taking their pictures down and packing their belongings into their blue boxes. It seemed that every hour brought a new detail to the ship-out rumour. At 5.30 someone reported that there was a fleet of sweatboxes arriving at the prison gates. At six o'clock someone else had overheard one of the SOs on the phone to Whitemoor asking if they had room to take one hundred lifers. Like a lot of these rumours the one about Whitemoor was viable as there was a whole wing lying vacant there. D-wing had been emptied in 2002 and turned into a voluntary unit for dangerous prisoners with violent personality disorders. Unfortunately, few violent prisoners were going to volunteer for a place in an experimental unit inside a top-security dispersal jail, so the wing had plenty of spaces. The rumour about the Whitemoor move very nearly had me convinced and I was on my way to pack my kit when I met Fred. 'It looks like all the category B lifers are going to Whitemoor,' I told him. Fred, like me, was a category B lifer. 'What's it like there?' he asked. I told him what I knew about the gaff and we both decided that when we got there we'd pull out of therapy and get on to A- or B-wing where we both had plenty of pals. If I was going to take a backwards move into the dispersal system I might as well get the benefits of it, and Fred felt the same.

I went down to the office on the ground floor and sought out an SO to see if I could get any skinny first-hand. The SO, a straight-talking screw of the old school, was usually unflappable but was now looking flustered. This was a bad sign. I knew that if they were to close the prison down it would mean a certain amount of hardship for the staff as well as us. They would be sent on detached duties, which meant they would have to go and work in any prison where there was a space for them, sometimes many miles away from their homes and families. 'What's happening with this electric?' I asked. He sighed and shook his head. 'It's bad, Noel. It seems the whole jail has been living on borrowed time as far as the electricity supply is concerned, some vital part is burned out and the only thing to do is for the prison to buy a new generator. The governor's been on the phone all day trying to get authorization to spend the money, but the chances are slim.' I wasn't encouraged in the slightest by this revelation. 'Is it looking as though we'll be shipped out, or what?' The SO shrugged. 'I'd say it is a possibility. A very real possibility at this moment.' I left the office with a feeling of disappointment. It seemed my stay at Grendon was about to come to an end.

There was a noticeable change to the atmosphere and mood of the wing. Any feeling that it was a community was gone and in its place was something more primitive. I caught glimpses of feral eyes and hard faces in the semi-darkness and knew it would not take much now for someone to erupt into violence. Of the forty-two men on C-wing around forty of them were serious violent recidivists of one hue or another and all were capable of kicking off. It seemed that from the moment the rumour about being shipped back into the system started we all began to clip on our armour and reach for our weapons. We were reverting to the animalistic creatures we had been when we arrived at Grendon, but without the glimmer of hope that we had then. I felt it happening within myself, that hardening of attitude, bleak outlook and paranoia that are constant companions when serving a long prison sentence. I decided to seek out my friends on the wing and be ready for anything. Me, Fred, John, Ray, Daran and Kevin all gathered in the 1s alcove and discussed the situation. Kevin was convinced it was all a 'Commie plot' to get him removed from therapy and he went into a tirade about taking hostages if they sent him back to Garth prison. The rest of us let him rant for a few minutes to get it out of his system. We all realized by now that Kevin's response to any crisis was to lash out either physically, which he was getting away from since being in therapy, or verbally. I felt for him as I thought he was actually at a crucial stage in his therapy and going back into the system would hit him hard. I also knew that if the lifers were going to Whitemoor then Kevin, as a short-termer, would be going elsewhere. John and Daran were B-cat lifers and Ray was a fixed-term long-termer. Wherever Kevin was going, none of his pals would be going with him.

In the end we all realized that everything was out of our hands and we had little choice but to be philosophical about it all. There were arguments going on above us on the 2s and 3s landings and the sound of angry raised voices echoed down the stairwell and into the gloom. Give it another hour of this, I thought, and we'll all be at each other's throats. There was an atmosphere of parting among our group in the alcove as we made our plans for an unknown future. We all reassured Kevin and promised to keep in touch with him and Ray. We were just waiting for the word that we were on the move. It was getting late in the day for a ship-out but we all knew these were exceptional circumstances and the prison system could do anything at any time if they put their mind to it. The veterans of prison life had already packed a small bag with essentials: tobacco, Rizlas, matches, radio, a pen and writing paper, photographs and letters. We knew that ship-outs were usually rushed affairs and that the bulk of our personal property would be sent on at a later date. There was never room on the vans for property boxes.

Then there was a shout from the ground floor. 'Everybody please gather in the community room immediately!' This must be it. We filed down the stairs in silence. The mood in the community room was expectant as we all sat, grim faced, and watched the staff come in. The SO did the talking. First he apologized for the delay in getting us any information during the day, then it was good news. The governor had been given permission to purchase a new generator, at great cost, and it would be arriving at the prison at some time during the night or in the early hours of the morning. Wiring it up would take quite a while but the hope was that it would be switched on at some time during the following day. There was a spontaneous cheer from the more hysterical sections of the community and the relief in the room was almost palpable. There would be no ship-out now.

After the news about the generator there was a party atmosphere on the wing. Everyone was smiling and cracking jokes now and the cold and semi-darkness were ignored. The previous gloomy mood had been dispelled like a light mist on a breezy day. Men who, only minutes before, had been looking and acting as though they wanted to kill someone were engaged in lively banter with those who could have been their victims.

Fred, like the rest of our little crew, was cautiously optimistic. Our experience of the system left us all with the nagging doubt that this good news could be false, a means of keeping us calm so it would be easier to deal with us when the hammer fell. I remember reading an account of how the KGB used to carry out executions of prisoners whom they thought might become difficult at the time of death. They would take the prisoner from his cell a few days before the date of his execution and tell him there was good news, he had been granted a stay. While they were telling him this the executioner would hide behind the door of his cell and wait. The prisoner would be returned to his cell with a new spring in his step and BLAM! The executioner would put one in his nut just when he least expected it. And I have known the British prison system to use those tactics, though obviously on a smaller scale. Therefore cautious optimism was the order of the day for us veterans.

We had no need to worry. After one more night of minimal lighting and no heat the generator was hooked up and turned on. There was cheering all over the nick when the televisions came on for the first time in seventy-four hours. We had back all the comforts of home, including hot water and heating. I heard in the next few days that the regression I had witnessed among the men of Grendon had not been confined to C-wing; similar things had happened on the other wings. G-wing had had no electricity just the same as the rest of us, but it was interesting to note how they had been put up as scapegoats as soon as our society started to break down in the dark. When things go wrong humans always seem to look for someone to blame and possibly punish; prisoners are no different. Even at Grendon. Days later we also found out how close we had been to having the prison closed down and being shipped out. If the permission to buy the generator had been refused there was a contingency plan in place to ship us out. So that rumour, at least, was right on the button.

In the run-up to Christmas many men used their groups to explore the emotions and feelings that had been brought up by the electrical crisis, shamefacedly describing their descent into near anarchy and exploring what might be learned from it. What I personally learned was that I was becoming committed to Grendon and that I no longer felt the same longing to go back to what I had known. I needed Grendon and I was only just starting to realize exactly how much. We had our last group on 23 December and followed the Grendon tradition of having a small party for the final session. Each group member contributed a pack of biscuits or a tray of sandwiches and Brian brought the coffee and mince pies. We spent the whole hour and a half talking about things that had happened during the year on the wing and overdosing on caffeine and sugar. It was a good end to the therapeutic year.

My first Christmas in Grendon was very quiet. In other nicks Christmas was a time for kicking off in one way or another. There was always plenty of drink and drugs about for those who preferred to blot out the experience and there was no shortage of people looking for a fight. But at Grendon there was no drink or drugs and certainly no fights. Instead there were a lot of community competitions, such as bingo, quiz nights and gym-based contests. There were also the usual pool and card games. I spent most of the holiday in my cell thinking and writing. I worked out that 2003 was the eighteenth Christmas I had spent in prison, and as my birthday is on Christmas Eve it was also my eighteenth birthday spent inside. I supposed it was no wonder I had little feeling about Christmas one way or the other. My worst prison Christmas was in 1977 when I was serving a three-year detention sentence in Rochester borstal. I had tried an escape on Christmas Eve, breaking out of my cell and assaulting the night patrol with a steel bucket, and was captured and given the standard kicking. I spent Christmas, New Year and some months afterwards, in the underground strip cell of the punishment block. That's a Christmas I'd rather forget. There were no kickings or block cell for Christmas in Grendon, but there was a lot of quiet thinking time. It was okay to look back at my old life, but what I really wanted and what I was working towards was a new life. I couldn't wait for the holiday to be over so I could get back to building it. Though I didn't know it then, 2004 was going to be a very big year for me. In loads of ways.

12. Leah

While I was at Whitemoor I had written the first part of this autobiography – *A Few Kind Words and a Loaded Gun* – for which my friend and literary agent, the eminent writer Will Self, had managed to secure a publishing deal with Penguin. The book was accepted for publication just before I left Whitemoor, and from then until the actual publication date in June 2004 I spent a lot of time working on corrections, proofs, photographs and all the other things that need doing before a book hits the shelves. This should have been a pleasant and satisfying time for me, my first book about to come out, but due to the fact that I was a serving prisoner there were dark clouds gathering on my horizon. And they took the shape of those nosy, interfering bureaucrats from the Home Office. The restrictions on prisoners who write for publication are covered by Rule 34 of the Prison Rules 1999, and Standing Order 5b, and prohibit: 'material intended for publication or broadcast which is in return for payment, and concerns the prisoner's own crime or criminal history (unless it forms part of serious representations about conviction, sentence, or comment on the criminal justice system), or identifies individual members of staff or other prisoners, or which contravenes the other restrictions on correspondence'.

Up until 2003, the prison system had rarely bothered using Standing Order 5b unless it was to cover up their penchant for poking their noses into correspondence usually covered by legal privilege. I had certainly never heard of them using it to stop journalism articles, or even books, being sent out of prison for publication. And when you think of some of the high-profile prisoners who have had books published while in jail you may see why I tended to take Standing Order 5b with a pinch of salt. Valerio Vicci (the Knightsbridge Safety Deposit robber), the Kray twins and Charles Bronson ('Britain's Most Dangerous Prisoner') all had their life stories published from prison, and in the cases of Bronson and Vicci they did it from special security units. So if Standing Order 5b was not taken seriously by the staff and governors of the SSUs, then why should I worry about it? I'd been having articles published in newspapers and magazines from prison for over a decade and never had any problems with it. The only prison that ever tried to stop me writing was HMP Belmarsh, after I had won a couple of legal cases against their security department.

Despite all of this I did speak to Will about Standing Order 5b over a couple of visits at HMP Whitemoor, when the book was still in its early stages, and his advice was to keep everything straight and above board. So I had made a point of approaching the wing staff and telling them that I was writing a book about my life that was looking as though it might be good enough to publish. Their reaction was patronizing amusement. I guess they had all seen my personal file, which described me as 'below average intelligence', and couldn't take my revelation seriously. On the whole, the system saw me as a big violent thug and, luckily, the kind of publications I had written for in the past – the *Guardian*, *Independent*, *New Statesman*, etc. – were not the sort that would be read by the average screw – no tits or defrocked vicars. I think they viewed the fact that I was writing in much the same way as they would view a monkey who could play 'Greensleeves' on a penny whistle. It was still a monkey once the music stopped. And this attitude worked in my favour.

I made sure that when I sent out the pages of my manuscript I never used any subterfuge; it all went through the censor's office with the rest of the mail. Only once was I approached by one of the censoring officers who asked me if this book was for publication. When I replied in the affirmative he expressed a request for a free copy when it was published! And that was as far as the interest from the prison system went. Even so, I was relieved when the whole 500-odd pages of manuscript were in the hands of my publisher.

To my great surprise the serialization rights to *A Few Kind Words . . .* were bought by the *Telegraph*, a newspaper which I had no great affinity with, but they gave it a good spread in their magazine. While the *Telegraph* were preparing their feature there was an embargo on anyone else publishing reviews or extracts on pain of legal action, but the embargo was broken by the London *Evening Standard*, which printed a full-page review that was pretty scathing about the book and me personally. This before the book had even been released officially. Eventually the *Standard* agreed to pay compensation for their breach of the embargo, but in the meantime somebody in the Prison Service Press Office must have seen the paper's review and decided to have a poke about in my life.

About a week before the book was due to come out I was summoned to appear before a couple of governor grades at Grendon. I had never seen them, but that's not unusual these days. The structure of power in British prisons had changed after the 1987 Fresh Start initiative, which screws remember for putting an end to their very lucrative overtime payments. Before Fresh Start some screws would spend almost every waking hour, and some sleeping ones, inside their prison. They would start at 6 a.m. and sometimes not finish work until 10 p.m. or later. The government decided that the British prison system was becoming too expensive and that it was time for a complete overhaul. The screws tried to resist, mainly by working to rule or taking industrial action, but they also had to give up their right to strike.

Before 1987 there was one governor in control of each prison and the second-in-command was the chief, or 'bully beef', a uniformed rank who was in charge of the day-to-day functioning of the jail. Under these two were the assistant governors (AGs), who wore plain clothes and were in charge of each wing and the rest of the uniformed staff. With the changes the posts of chief and AGs were done away with and replaced with a governors' number system. So now you have the number 1 governor, number 2 governor, number 3 governor, etc., and just to make it more confusing each jail can have as many as four number 3 governors. So they now all have titles as well, like 'Head of Residence' or 'Head of Activities'. It's as though they gave the task of reorganizing the system to a roomful of drunken monkeys.

This is why the governors I now faced were unknown to me. One of them was in command of security and had the look of the rabidly ambitious anal-retentive that is commonplace among security staff. I was interrogated about my book: where had I written it? How much money was I earning from it? How had I got it out of prison? Had I done any work on it while in Grendon? I explained that everything about it had been done openly. I had written it at HMP Whitemoor and sent it out through normal channels, but as for the financial questions I told them they could mind their own fucking business. The security governor took exception to this and I could see in his eyes that I had made an enemy. After thirty minutes of questioning I was dismissed.

I was puzzled as to what had suddenly brought on this investigative zeal over something that had never been a secret. It wasn't long before it all became clear. It turned out that serial killer Dennis Nilsen, who had been convicted of killing and dismembering thirteen young men in 1983, had written his own autobiography, which had been seized by the prison system when he had sent it out for editing with a view to publication. Nilsen, quite rightly in my opinion, had appealed to the courts in order to get his manuscript back, but a judge had ruled in favour of the system. Nilsen was putting together a High Court appeal about the case, citing the Human Rights Act, and questioning the validity of Standing Order 5b. When the Home Office became aware of my own imminent autobiography, they panicked. The Home Office realized that Nilsen might use my breach of Standing Order 5b as an example of how he was being singled out if they didn't make a song and dance of all other prison authors. So the minions of the system embarked on an arse-covering exercise and I was caught in the net.

I was informed that the prisons minister, Paul Goggins, second only to Home Secretary David Blunkett, had ordered the investigation into my book and had sent a team to Grendon to nose about. Hence my grilling by the governors. I was raging over it. Here I was, attempting to turn my life around in every way possible, engaging in therapy, keeping my nose clean and starting to make moves to ensure I would never come back to prison ever again, and the hypocritical system was looking at ways to punish me just so as to save face in a court case that had nothing to do with me personally. It was a fucking liberty!

I took the opportunity to speak to Tom, the C-wing therapist, about how I felt and he appeared sympathetic. He told me that, having read the book, he was impressed by it and so was the number 1 governor, but that their hands were tied and events would now have to take their course. He was of the opinion that the Home Office would not take the unprecedented step of issuing an injunction on the book but might release a statement about it to the press. I spoke to Brian, my facilitator, and he was more optimistic, saying that he thought it was just a lot of hot air being blown by the Home Office because they had been caught on the hop by the Nilsen case.

A couple of days after the initial interrogation I was called in front of the main security governor. He went over the same questions about the book until eventually he seemed satisfied with my answers and informed me that no action would be taken against me because of the time that had elapsed since I had written the book. (Breaches of prison rules and standing orders have to be charged within forty-eight hours of the offence being committed.) However, he had been informed by the Home Office that I was not to do any more face-to-face interviews with the media. I was relieved that no injunction would be slapped on my book, but I told the security governor straight that I thought there was a good chance that I could have beaten any charge of breaching Standing Order 5b anyway, using the defence that the book was 'serious comment on the criminal justice system' as per the provisions of the rule. That was when he showed his true character. He sneered at me and said, 'You must be fucking joking, Smith. I've read some of it and I believe it's all lies and sensationalism. You've trashed a system that I believe in, and blackened the reputation of the Prison Service. If I had my way I'd burn every copy.' I nodded. 'Yeah,' I said, 'I bet you would. I've always thought that security screws were all book-burners at heart.' And that ended our meeting.

While all the trouble about the book was going on, I still had to engage myself in the therapeutic process every day and the events coloured my attitude. I spoke about my anger at the system for attempting to gag and stifle me and take away the one chance I might have for a straight career. It was as if they wanted me to stay in my place; I had always been prison fodder and that was how they wanted to keep me. That's why for a couple of months, when I should have been buzzing on my achievements, I was walking around like an active volcano. It did help that I was at Grendon and everyone, especially the wing staff, was very understanding of my feelings. If this had happened in any other jail I probably would have taken out my anger in acts of violence and destruction against the system.

I still had a serious mistrust of the system, knowing from experience how devious it can be on occasions, so I didn't completely relax until the book was released on 3 June. Once copies were in the shops it put me in a much better frame of mind. The reviews were fantastic, and even the people who had reservations about the morality of it still thought it was a good read. I saw the publication of my autobiography as a major step towards my full rehabilitation. No criminal who is intending to carry on pursuing a life of crime can put his life, past crimes and *modus operandi* in print for all the world to see. Once you admit to your mistakes, you would have to be an imbecile to go on making them. The book would help to establish me as a serious writer, which is the career I wanted to pursue in place of crime. *A Few Kind Words and a Loaded Gun* would also be a showcase for my bit of straight talent. It was only after publication that I fully realized how much I had invested in that book.

It first dawned on me that I might have a bit of a knack for the old writing game in 1992 while serving a nineteen-year sentence for armed robbery, possession of firearms and prison escape. I had been knocking up little poems for a mate of mine who had a lucrative black market card-making business at HMP Albany, on the Isle of Wight. Flushed by the success of this venture I answered an advert for 'prison writers' in *Inside Time*, the only national prisoners' newspaper in this country, and sent in a piece about an attempted escape using a JCB that I was involved in at HMP Wandsworth in 1990, and a couple of poems. Julian Broadhead, a Sheffield probation officer and author, accepted my stuff for publication in *Prison Writing* immediately and paid me a small fee. I thought it was money for old rope and set about seeing if I could do any more. I ended up writing throughout the rest of my sentence and took a journalism course. While I was in Whitemoor in 2001, serving my present life sentence, my son, Joe, died and this was instrumental in my eventual application for Grendon, but it also led to me writing my first book. I felt really bad about not even being able to contribute to the cost of Joe's funeral and it really distressed me. On a visit from Will Self, I discussed ways in which I might be able to raise some money. Will suggested that there might be a market for a book and that he was willing to act as my agent in the matter, and that was how it all started. I dedicated the book to Joe.

Soon I started to get letters from people who had read the book and wanted to tell me how much they had enjoyed it. I was well chuffed, and even more so when I started to get letters from women. It seemed that my story had struck a chord in the hearts of book-reading women all over the country. It was strange because in the book I describe what an absolute bastard I have been for thirty years. I document my violent and brutal past, both in and out of prison, and admit what a failure I have been in every relationship I've ever had, how I cheated on my wife and on all my many girlfriends, how I abandoned my children in order to pursue a life of crime, never giving a second thought to any of them until it was much too late. In short, I was a cold and uncaring brute, the sort of man that you would think most women would avoid like thrush. And yet, it appeared that there were women out there who could know all this and still see me as some sort of prize.

The letters I received were from women looking for various types of relationships with me, from casual sex to marriage, and at first I was quite flattered that there were women who found me attractive enough to put pen to paper. After all, my past behaviour aside, I was a forty-four-year-old, balding, overweight ex-villain with no definite release date. To put it bluntly, I would probably have had trouble getting a ride in a brothel (were I able to get to one) with a £50 note pinned to my jacket. But, being brand-new to the book game, I assumed that every author received these kinds of letters on publication. These women were probably hard-core book fans just eager to give good reviews, and the sexually explicit content of their letters was no more than a case of over-exuberance in celebration of the written word. But when they kept coming I began to wonder whether this was normal.

Some of the women sent photographs of themselves, and one or two sent other things. One morning I was called to reception to sign for a parcel which contained several pairs of knickers, all of them flimsy and some of them crotchless, from a woman in Hull who enclosed a note asking me to autograph them and send them back. The reception officer thought this was hilarious. All of the women who wrote seemed to be of a certain age – they all claimed to be in their thirties, though from the photographs some of them looked double that – and claimed to be single. I did get one letter from a woman who admitted she was married but she was enquiring whether I knew any 'hitmen' from my days as a criminal. I can only assume that she wanted her husband taken out of the game, as she slagged him unmercifully for two sides of A4.

Though flattered, I was very cautious about getting involved with any of the female letter-writers on any more than a casual basis. I figured that these women didn't really want me – not the real me anyway. What they desired was their idea of me, the fantasy that had formed in their minds as they had devoured the pages of my blood-spattered life story. Having spent most of my life as a fully paid-up member of what some tabloid editors luridly refer to as 'the London underworld' I was more than familiar with the kind of women who find a man with a sharp suit, a razor scar and a tough demeanour fascinating and attractive. We called them 'gangster groupies'.

Gangster groupies get turned on by criminals in the same way their spiritual sisters are turned on by pop and rock stars. In reality it is the infamy of the criminal that they find so attractive; the further up the outlaw food chain their target face is, the bigger the notch on the bedpost. I once spent the night with one well-known gangster groupie, who was working her way through south London robbery teams, and I overheard her discussing her conquest on the phone to her mate the next morning. 'Yeah, he was all right. No 357 Magnum though, more like a sawn-off shotgun, but not too bad.' Obviously, like the man from the *News of the World*, I made my excuses and left. So I knew there were women who were eager to take scalps in this way; I just never knew that any of them could read.

To this sisterhood of the con idol I must have appeared ideal, a big wild beast capable of almost anything, by my own admission, ruthless, strong and scary, the perfect fantasy alpha male. And yet, due to my incarceration and the length of my sentence, they could keep me at a distance. Though they said, or intimated, that they wanted to be dominated by me, in actual fact it was they who wanted control. Perhaps some, or all, of these women had been badly treated by men in the past and now, even subconsciously, saw the opportunity for a bit of payback? Maybe they would be able to satisfy some deep need in themselves and take the satisfaction they had failed to achieve through normal and real relationships? Giving these women any encouragement would be like entering a psychological mine-field for me and it could all blow up in my face. Anyway, if I were to try to regularly correspond with all of them I would never have time for anything else. I decided to leave it alone. I typed up a 'thank you' letter and sent copies.

Then, one morning in late May, I picked up my mail from the wing office as usual and noticed a letter with an Irish postmark. I was corresponding with my cousin, Marie Regan, in Dublin at the time so it wasn't unusual for me to get letters from Ireland, but I didn't recognize the handwriting on the envelope, nor the name and return address on the back. I went to my cell and settled down to read my mail. When I read the first line of the Irish letter I began to shake with a rush of sudden and unexpected emotion. At that moment my past caught up with me and my life was changed for ever. I read: 'Noel, I have written this letter over and over in my head for most of my life, and finally putting pen to paper with a good chance that you will read it feels strange. You knew my mother, Miriam Cotter, in London in the early 1980s, and I was born on 2 May 1983. I am your daughter.' My hands began to shake and suddenly there were tears in my eyes. The letter was from my daughter, Leah, whom I had last seen in 1983 when she was just a month old. She was now twenty-one years old and had two children of her own.

I started getting into trouble with the police at the age of thirteen, playing truant from school, fighting, thieving and generally being a nuisance. I was on the receiving end of some pretty strong beatings from the police and then from the screws when I was sent to a detention centre, but it wasn't all one-way traffic. I used violence as casually as most people used dialogue. My criminal behaviour escalated, and by the time I was sixteen I was standing in the dock of the Old Bailey being weighed off for armed robbery and GBH. I was a reactionary: the more you beat me the more I would try to beat you. Everything was about payback. I did my bird the hard way – slashings, beatings, psychotropic medication, padded cell, straitjacket and solitary confinement for three long years. Then they released me into the world.

I met Denise in 1979 soon after getting out of the borstal system and before I knew it she was pregnant with Dean and we were living together. But I was still running, trying to catch up on what I thought I had missed during the dark years. Instead of settling down and trying to be a father, I just carried on with my pattern of destruction. It's hard now to fathom how fucked up my thinking was in those days. I was twenty-one years old but I had spent a lot of the previous eight years in some very dark places.

In 1982 I met Miriam, when I was still an unbalanced young man, mentally scarred from my long years in the gladiatorial arena of the youth custody system and struggling to make my mark as an adult criminal. Miriam was an impish nineteen-year-old from Limerick, all wild dark hair and sexy twinkling eyes. There was something about her that captivated me from the start, a freedom of movement and attitude that attracted me, and I fell deeply in love with her. But, as with every relationship I've ever had, there were complications from the start. I was living with Denise and we had one child already and another one on the way.

I've never really understood people who think that it's impossible to love two women at the same time; to me it came naturally. I didn't love Denise any less when I was with Miriam and vice versa. I loved different things about each of them and gave them equal amounts of my attention and would have gone on doing so if circumstances had prevailed. Unfortunately, I've yet to meet a woman who shares my attitude, and I probably never will.

For a while I managed to keep my affair with Miriam a secret from Denise. Denise was pregnant with our son Joseph, and kept busy with our first son, Dean, while I was out living it up in the dives of south London, most of the time with the lovely Miriam on my arm. No one needs to tell me how much of a bastard that makes me sound now, and with the wisdom of years on my side I feel deeply ashamed of my actions. I could make excuses, but I won't. I was an arrogant man and truly believed I could have it all.

Eventually Denise began to suspect that there was another woman in my life. Throughout our relationship I had been pretty unstable when it came to keeping regular hours, I didn't work at a nine to five job, I was a thief, and that meant I was on call for twenty-four hours of the day. I would often be out all night, not returning home until the early hours and, though Denise was never happy with this, she had learned to accept it. But when I began disappearing for two and three days at a time things had to come to a head. It all became very messy when someone decided to whisper in Denise's ear about my indiscretions with Miriam. Denise had never been the shy retiring type, she had a bad temper, and when she was hurt it just fuelled her rage.

Trying to keep Denise and Miriam apart was a full-time occupation. At first I lied to Denise and tried to convince her that I was just 'working' at those times when I had been on the missing list, but she was no fool. I was under pressure but I wouldn't give up either woman. I was still seeing Miriam regularly and then coming home to the suspicion and rage of Denise, but I tried to shrug it off. Then Miriam fell pregnant.

Not even I could stand up too long to the pressure and earache I was getting from two pregnant hormonal women so I was forced to make a choice. I chose Denise, and Miriam, being a realist, decided to go back to Limerick. I didn't fall out of love with Miriam, I just didn't love her as much as I loved Denise at that time. It was hard days all round for a while. I missed Miriam and I felt guilty about her being left to raise a child on her own. Denise never forgave me for my infidelity and never missed a chance to bring it up whenever we argued, which was often, and our relationship was never really as close again. I chose to blot it all out by drinking and fighting to excess and redoubling my efforts at criminality. I was just an all-round bad guy. Though I may sound flippant about it now, it really was a dark period of my life which, incidentally, has not been short of dark periods.

On 2 May 1983 Miriam gave birth to a baby girl whom she named Leah Noelle Cotter. I spent that day as drunk as a skunk and ended up in the cells at Carter Street police station charged with a variety of offences ranging from assault to drunken driving and TDA. I saw Leah just once, when Miriam came over to England to visit some friends. She was a month old and I remember her gorgeous eyes looking up at me as I held her. Then there was nothing more for twenty-one years. Now, here I was being confronted by the reality of my past. It wasn't comfortable.

I was on a visit on the afternoon I got the first letter from Leah. My cousin, Joe Regan, and his wife, Sharon, had come to see me. I always looked forward to visits from them as they were very upbeat and full of news about members of the family I had been out of touch with. The first thing Joe said when he sat down at the table in the visiting room was, 'You look very pale, are you sick or something?' I told him about the letter from Leah. Sharon nodded. 'That'll teach you,' she said. 'Everything you do in this life has consequences for someone.' We spent most of the visit talking about Leah, Miriam, Denise, Lianne and Dean, and going over the old days. How would this development affect the family dynamic? Though me and Denise were no longer together we still had a pretty friendly relationship and I spoke to her and the kids every week. 'How do you think Denise will react to this news?' Joe asked. I shrugged. I half-knew how she'd react, she would kick off like a lunatic. Denise was the kind of woman who could hold a grudge for over two decades and keep it as fresh as a loaf of new-baked bread. Sometimes I wondered if there were any Sicilians in her ancestry. 'You've got to tell her,' was Sharon's parting shot. And I knew she was right.

After the visit, when I was locked into my cell for the evening, I reread Leah's letter a score of times. It suddenly dawned on me that if she had two children, then I was a grandad! I looked at the pictures she had sent and tried to see something of myself in her pretty face. She had my eyes, and my nose. I stared at the pictures of my grandchildren. Luke was nearly four and Jade was just a gorgeous little baby. I paced my cell for a while, my mind reeling. I would write back to her, there was no question about that, she was my daughter. I put myself in her place and wondered how I would feel about a father who had abandoned me and had made no effort to get in touch throughout my life. I knew I would be bitter and full of hatred. Yet, her letter, though naturally hesitant and uncertain in parts, did not come across as angry with me. That made me feel even more guilty and ashamed.

It was only when I banged my shin against the chair that I realized my cell was in darkness. I had been pacing for hours. I switched on the light and sat down at my word processor and began to write my first letter to

Leah. My heart was full of love for her, tempered by guilt and regret, and I felt really good about this new chapter in our lives. I knew that there would be rough times ahead, but forewarned is forearmed. My children had to be the most important thing in my life. I had failed them miserably in the past, but I vowed it would never happen again.

13. Kevin the Nazi

One thing I could never get my head around at Grendon was the fact that it is the only prison in the country, probably in the world if truth be known, that has no punishment block. In the past I had been no stranger to punishment blocks and solitary confinement, and in a perverse way I had welcomed the break from the grind of prison life that they provided. It had been a pattern with me that when I got fed up with it all I would cause a bit of trouble and be removed to a solitary cell. Usually I would get to this solitary space head-first and via a gauntlet of boots and batons, but once there I would relax and be happy with my own company for a few weeks. I know my need of solitary confinement was part of my institutionalization and probably some sort of desire to return to the womb. I even got used to being in the strongbox, or strip cell, which is a prison within a prison within a prison, a bit like those Russian dolls that fit inside each other. When I was in this space I could avoid all responsibility and be cut off completely from the rest of the world. I learned to close down and live only in my head for much of the time and this helped me to survive long sentences. But this was not an option at Grendon so I had to learn new coping strategies.

Eleven hours of group therapy a week could be pretty stressful. It's bad enough dealing with your own issues but when you also have to take on board the problems of forty-one other maladjusted men in a confined community it can be a real head-breaker. Having to sit there and listen to the most sickening and graphic descriptions of sexual and physical abuse can quickly become akin to mental torture. At first I was curious to hear some of these details, thinking that nothing would be able to shock me after the life I had led, but my curiosity was very quickly sated and the stories never stopped. Every time we got a new member in the group I braced myself up for some new atrocity committed by them or on them. I desperately needed a distraction from these horrors so I threw myself into education. I enrolled on a National Union of Journalists course, an ICS correspondence course on journalism and joined the editorial team of the Grendon in-house magazine, *Feedback*. I was also lucky enough to be able to buy a pretty decent word processor from a bloke who had finished his sentence and was leaving Grendon. Writing and education became my retreat and I spent a lot of my time in my cell. But I still had plenty of time to associate. Kevin turned up at my cell on a regular basis, usually in an angry state and looking for a sympathetic hearing.

After the racism row in the community Kevin had spoken a lot about his childhood and how much this had contributed to his development, or lack of it, as a man. It was unfortunate for Kevin that he happened to be in an unstable and very self-obsessed group. Group 2 consisted of Taff, a paranoid ball of fury at the best of times; Bilbo, a weird-looking serial rapist who had once been sentenced to death for killing a woman on Guernsey and was on his second life sentence; Chopper, a sixty-year-old Hell's Angel who was also on his second life sentence for murder; Mikey, an alcoholic serving life for murder; Daran, my psychopathic pal; Jip, a very needy Scotsman who lurched from one crisis to the next; and the Hedge-Jumper, a particularly nasty and obnoxious rapist. In this group, Kevin, being the youngest and the one serving the shortest sentence, was like a toadstool in a field of poisonous mushrooms. The only one of his group who really cared about him was Daran and they had been friends since F-wing. The others lost interest in Kevin very early on, and who could blame them? They all had massive problems of their own, and coping with Kevin, as I knew from experience, needed great patience. So by the time he began opening up the group had already washed their hands of him.

For Kevin, even admitting that his views and belief systems may have been wrong was a major step and it took a lot out of him. He became very emotional, which he considered a sign of weakness, and suffered even worse mood swings. He confided in me that he thought his group were not interested and were showing him very little support in his time of need. There was not much I could do about it except spend hours in my cell listening to him. As time went on Kevin seemed to get worse. He became louder and angrier as if to compensate for the humiliation he was suffering for revealing his emotional upheaval and not getting the response from his group that he had expected. Almost every day I would hear him shouting and raging over the most trivial of matters. He became very demanding of the staff, threatening all sorts of violence when he didn't get his way, and I pulled him aside a few times to calm him down. The lads tried to rally round him and help as much as they could but it was becoming a full-time job, and we all knew that he could not go on behaving this way without suffering the inevitable consequences.

I was still deep in a cold war with my neighbour, Taff, and every now and again it warmed up to a shouting match. As I've said, Taff had a big chip on his shoulder about the Irish, claiming that he had seen one of his friends killed by the IRA when he was serving in Northern Ireland as a squaddie. So he was hypersensitive to all things Irish. One night I was playing a Pogues tape in my cell, nothing contentious, just a bit of 'Dirty Old Town' and 'The Irish Rover', that sort of light-hearted folksy music, but Taff heard something completely different. The next morning he came out of his cell like a raging bull and accused me of playing 'rebel songs' specifically to wind him up. The man really was a sicko and I was starting to get the hump with his attitude. I told him in no uncertain terms to go away and fornicate with himself, but I knew that sooner or later I would lose my temper and end up doing him some serious damage. I needed to put a bit of distance between myself and Taff if I didn't want to end up on a GBH charge, so I set out to find a solution to the problem.

There were three cells on the ground floor of the wing. One of them was a 'safe cell', which had been modified to contain anyone who is identified as being in danger of suicide or self-harm. There are no sharp edges or anywhere to lash a noose. The other two are temporary cells, used only when there are new arrivals on the wing who have yet to be allocated to a permanent cell, or for people who have a medical condition that would need access to a toilet as both of the temporary cells are equipped with a sink and toilet. The ground-floor cells were twice the size of the upstairs ones and would have been an attractive prospect were it not for the noise and volume of traffic that passed them almost twenty-four hours a day. All through the night there would be gates clanging and phones ringing as the night patrol did their rounds, and in the daytime there would be streams of staff and community members in and out of the offices that adjoined the cells.

I had been diagnosed as a type 2 diabetic in 2000 when I reached Whitemoor, and I also had very high cholesterol and blood pressure for which I was prescribed diuretic medication, which made me urinate several hundred times a day. I presented this evidence to my facilitator, Brian, and asked for a move to a ground-floor cell on medical grounds.

Brian was agreeable but made it clear that he realized my request for a move had more to do with my feud with Taff than my medical problems. I had to get backing from my group and from the community as a whole before any move could be sanctioned. Everybody backed me but the therapist, Tom, called me in for a chat before any final approval. Tom questioned me on my reasons for the cell move and asked me how I was getting on with Taff. I lied and told him everything was fine and that the move was purely medical as up on the landing I was at the mercy of the Night San computer and sometimes I had to wait for two hours to be let out after pressing the button. Tom wasn't fooled and gave me a little talk on the therapeutic value of facing problems and sorting them out through dialogue. Yeah, I thought. That's easy for you to say, you don't live opposite a fucking fruitcake 24/7. My move to the ground-floor cell was completed in quick order and Taff was no longer in my face every day. I felt a lot better but our war was not over, not by a long shot.

By now I was settled well into group 3 and I actually looked forward to the group meetings. I got to know most of the other lads in my group very well and trusted them. I did a lot of therapeutic work on my criminal background and got ripped unmercifully about it. It was pointed out to me that I seemed to have a serious image problem and a massive ego, neither of which I had been consciously aware of. In the ego-driven and image-conscious world of the professional criminal and prisoner I had always been a bit of an oddity. When criminals and prisoners gather for a trip down felony lane the stories they tell are always designed to enhance their own reputations. Every robbery committed had a prize of a million pounds and every battle was won in style. But when it came to my turn I would tell of getting a good hiding from a couple of midgets or having a bag of money blow up on me on the way out of a bank. It wasn't really the done thing to lay out your failures for all to see but I really didn't give a fuck. I just told it as it happened, so it was a surprise when the group talked about my ego and image. But I promised to work on the problem.

Gradually I came to realize that how I saw myself was completely different from how other people were seeing me. I took a good look at myself and saw the shaved and scarred head, the broken nose and hard eyes, the wide shoulders, the tattoos and the flash swagger, and I understood how much my appearance and demeanour contributed to other people's perceptions of me. I could be very cold to those I didn't know well; I was abrupt, hostile and blunt to the point of rudeness and arrogance. But all of this had helped me to survive almost three decades in environments where an open smile was an invitation to take advantage. I had been wearing my thuggish exterior for a long time without even being aware of it, but now I needed to start shedding it. I began consciously to check how I spoke to people and make adjustments. I constantly reminded myself that there was no one here that I needed to intimidate or impress. And once I started doing this I began to relax even more. I knew it was working when, instead of going out of their way to avoid me, the more timid men in the community began approaching me for conversation.

With the summer of 2004 upon us I was doing pretty well: I'd had a book published, rediscovered a long-lost daughter and some old friends, and I was looking forward to the future for the first time in my life. Unfortunately, I was still in prison and at least three years away from any chance of release. I had kept in touch with a few of my old pals from the dispersal system and from the news in their letters nothing had changed in our top-security jails. It was still a daily round of stabbings, beatings and lock-downs, police investigations and conflict between screws and prisoners. In the past this sort of news would have given me a buzz and had me itching to get back into the fray, but now it just depressed me and made me glad that I had made the choice to leave that life behind for good. I had been at Grendon for almost a year, changing attitudes and behaviour that had been getting me into trouble for most of my life. I was delighted that I no longer saw violence as the answer to all my problems; I had learned to communicate and empathize with even the most unattractive of characters; I no longer saw all authority as my enemy and I had built friendly working relationships with most of the uniformed staff. I wasn't perfect by any stretch of the imagination, there was a long way to go and no doubt there would be the odd relapse and setback on the way, but I was able to see and feel progress within myself. And that gave me a real high.

Being in touch with Leah also contributed to my good feelings. I so looked forward to her letters that I would be buzzing for days after I heard from her. Leah sent me plenty of photos of my grandchildren, Luke and Jade, who are the two most gorgeous kids in the world, and filled me in on things that had been going on for her over the years we'd been apart. After a couple of months I received a letter from Miriam, Leah's mother, and we began a cautious correspondence. Miriam had changed immensely from the wild and carefree young girl I had known. Being a single mother had not been easy for her, especially as she had been abandoned by me while still deeply in love. When Leah was nine years old Miriam had married and finally put her past behind her. She told me her husband was a kind and gentle man and he had eventually adopted Leah. Miriam went on to have two more children, and, from what I could gather from her letters, she was very happily married. I was pleased for her.

Unfortunately, the reappearance of Leah after twenty-one years was not welcomed by other members of my family. Denise, as I had predicted, went into one, as usual. It seemed that the pain of betrayal had not diminished for her, and she vented her anger to me on the phone. I wrote her a letter to explain my feelings on the matter, which she returned unopened, and I also wrote to Dean and Lianne. Dean was pretty laid back about it, his attitude being what's done is done, but Lianne was not happy. It was clear to me that, while I was in prison anyway, I would just have to keep the relationships with my children separate. Once I was outside and able to mediate in a practical way I hoped things might be different. In the meantime I would do my best to keep in contact with all of them.

One afternoon I was in my cell writing when I heard a loud commotion coming from somewhere on the ground floor. I could hear Kevin's voice, raised and angry, but that had almost become the norm on the wing of late so I didn't take too much notice. A few minutes later I heard the blast of a riot bell. It had been so long since I'd heard one I didn't recognize the sound for a moment. Thinking that someone must have leant on the bell and pressed it by mistake I carried on typing. I knew that the staff would have to come running to the wing to answer the bell, even if it did turn out to be a false alarm, so I wasn't that surprised to hear the sound of running feet in the corridor outside my cell, but then it went quiet. There was a knock on my door and one of the uniformed staff, Derek, a Scouse ex-squaddie who was well respected on the wing because he would go out of his way to help anyone, was standing there looking worried. 'Noel, sorry to bother you, mate, but Kevin's gone into one, could you come and talk to him before someone gets hurt?' I walked out of my cell and was confronted by about twenty out-of-breath and nervous-looking uniformed staff from other wings. They had answered the alarm and were now blocking the corridor like a black-serge hedge. For a moment I was back in the ground-floor corridor of Albany prison, on the Isle of Wight, in 1994, when I had held a couple of dozen screws at bay in the narrow hallway with half a pool cue. I shook my head. They were all looking at me and I felt a twinge of fear. I still get nervous around gangs of uniforms – I've taken too many beatings from them not to. Derek walked to the SO's office along from my cell and I followed.

The door to the office was wide open and several staff were inside, including my facilitator, Brian, trying to talk to Kevin. Kevin had his back to the wall at the far end of the office. His face was contorted in rage and he held his clenched fists out in front of him. Eyes slitted and teeth grinding, he looked ready to kill someone. Anyone. I had seen men in this state before, usually just before their circuits really burned out and they exploded into severe unthinking violence. I could see that Kevin was ready for it. Brian tried to calm him down in a soothing voice but Kevin wasn't having it. 'I'll fooking kill you! Try and fooking touch me, put your fooking hands anywhere near me and I'll kill the lot of you!' he snarled, and I could see foam gathering in the corners of his mouth. Without thinking of the possible consequences I pushed my way into the office past the crowd of uniforms and walked straight up to Kevin. I put my arms around him and patted him on the back. 'Come on, mate,' I whispered. 'Let's go and have a cup of tea and calm down.' For a moment he was unyielding and the thought crossed my mind that he was too far gone and might attack me, but then he collapsed in my arms, his head on my shoulder, and huge sobs wracked his body. I comforted him for a minute until he got some control of himself and then led him gently out of the office and along to my cell. The staff parted for us and I noticed the relief etched on their faces.

I sat Kevin down and made him a cup of tea, all the while talking to him about anything that came into my head. He was visibly relaxing by the minute. Derek and Brian came to my cell door and asked if everything was okay. I put on a cheerful tone and made light of the incident and they were satisfied that the danger moments had passed so they went out and told the rest of the staff that they could go back to their wings as everything was now under control. I kept Kevin in my cell until he was more or less back to his normal self. He told me that he didn't know what had happened, one minute he was arguing with Derek in the office and the next thing he knew he was surrounded by staff and I was giving him a hug. Kevin had spent time in secure mental hospitals, seen dozens of psychiatrists in his life and spent years heavily medicated. He could be very violent when not on his medication and he had come off it when he arrived at Grendon. Though he was not actually serving his sentence for a violent offence, he did have plenty of violence on his record, including taking a screw hostage on a previous sentence. The staff knew that when he went into one it wasn't a game. Derek returned to my cell to tell Kevin that they wanted to take him up to the hospital wing for the night, just to make sure he was going to be okay, and Kevin agreed.

After he had gone, Derek and Brian approached me and thanked me for my help. I knew that in the system this incident would have ended very differently. The screws would not have hesitated, they would have piled into that office mob-handed and someone would have got seriously hurt. It is a testament to the caring and understanding nature of the staff at Grendon that they felt able to keep themselves in check and try an alternative method of defusing the incident safely. I had great respect for Grendon staff after that, and Brian and Derek in particular. That night I thought about how far I had come. In the system I would have egged Kevin on and urged him to attack the screws, and, if I'd got the chance, I would have joined him in the scuffle.

When Kevin came back from the hospital he was a lot quieter and I found out that they had put him back on his meds. He received a behavioural warning for the incident in the office and I knew then that he wasn't long for Grendon. The incident was only briefly talked about in the community meetings, and the general attitude was that Kevin was falling off the edge. The trouble was that the powers-that-be at Grendon had known that they were taking on a difficult case in Kevin. Grendon was his last shot before the system washed their hands of this difficult and deranged boy in a man's body, and now it was looking as though they had failed. The next step would be to 'nut him off', get him sectioned under the Mental Health Act and ship him to some secure hospital where he would spend his time heavily sedated, shuffling around with the rest of the living dead. It was sad, but there wasn't much else they could do. Kevin began dropping out of therapy, not turning up for groups, and no one challenged him. Behind the scenes, as became apparent later on, the therapists and governors were looking for somewhere that would be willing to take him, but having no luck. He was too needy and trouble-some for the rest of the prison system, even for taking up a space in a punishment block. So he drifted around C-wing like a noisy drugged-up ghost. His friends – me, Fred, Daran and Ray – became his points of contact, and he drained us on a daily basis as he lurched from high to low and then back again. Kevin needed help and though we gave as much as we could, listening to his constant rants, talking patiently to him and trying to help him sort out his problems, it wasn't enough.

Then one day, a couple of months after the office incident, Kevin received bad news. His sister, to whom he was very close, had been rushed to hospital with blood poisoning. The prison was informed that she was in intensive care in a hospital in Blackburn and that the odds were that she would be dead before the week was out. Kevin took it very badly. Once again his friends and the staff rallied round and tried to help him through this time of crisis. The doctor prescribed him daily doses of Valium and the staff put themselves out in order to convince the governors that Kevin should be given a compassionate visit to his dying sister. They were reluctant to let him out but after the staff argued long and hard the visit was granted. Kevin was taken to the hospital, double-cuffed and with four uniformed staff in attendance. When he came back that evening he was suicidal and his friends took it in turns to sit with him for several days and nights.

In the event his sister pulled through and beat the odds by making a full recovery. But when the doctor tried to cut Kevin's dose of Valium he became angry and demanding until, for want of a quiet life, it was decided to keep him on it. After a while he started once more to become angry and aggressive with everyone. I sat him down and strongly advised he come off the Valium and, as usual, he agreed, but he had no real intention of doing so. One evening Kevin went into a rant over something in the staff office, launched a heavy china mug at the wall and stormed off. Ten minutes later a member of staff found him sitting in his cell, perfectly still. He failed to respond to anything that was said to him and medical staff were called to the wing. Fred and I went to his cell and tried to speak to Kevin but he was in a catatonic state and made not a flicker of movement. We tried everything but he just sat there, eyes staring, as if he were made of wood. I guessed that he had finally had the breakdown that he had been heading towards for months. The nurse who came to examine him asked if Fred and I would help to get him to the hospital wing. We stood him up by physically pulling him out of the chair, and slowly walked him down the stairs and off the wing. He came where we led him, showing not a bit of interest in what was happening, silent as the dead and with a slack look on his face. I remember getting halfway up the long central corridor on the way to the hospital wing, just me and Fred on either side of Kevin and the nurse right behind us and the only noise our footsteps on the stone floor, when I looked down and noticed that Kevin had no shoes on and that his socks were flapping out in front of him with every shuffling step. He reminded me of a baby that had not been dressed properly and my heart broke for him.

At the hospital wing the duty nurse phoned the senior medical officer at home and asked him to come back into the prison. We sat Kevin down in a chair in the staff tearoom and tried talking to him, to no avail. The duty nurse made us all a cup of coffee while we waited for the senior medical officer to arrive, and more in hope she also made one for Kevin and put it on the table in front of him. We were sipping our drinks in silence when suddenly Kevin twitched and slammed his fingers into the boiling hot cup of coffee. We all jumped. He seemed to come back to life with the pain of the scalding liquid on his fingers and began to cry. Gradually he pulled out of his trance-like state. He seemed confused and told us he could not remember what had happened or how he had got to the hospital wing. Fred and I were relieved that the madness seemed to have passed for the moment. When the senior medical officer arrived he said that Kevin would have to stay in the hospital wing for a few days for observation. Fred and I went back to C-wing and collected some of Kevin's belongings. When we said our goodbyes to him that night both Fred and I were convinced that we would never see him again. We knew he needed more help than he could get at Grendon.

Four days later, though, Kevin was back on the wing, this time on an even higher dose of Valium. Tom, the wing therapist, told us in a community meeting that staff were working hard at trying to get Kevin a place in a secure unit but that things were moving very slowly. We all had to persevere. Some weeks passed, during which he just seemed to get worse. It was reported in the community meeting that he had been playing his skinhead music at full blast most nights and threatening newer members of the community with violence when they confronted him about it. People were walking on eggshells around him and he had even started to isolate himself from his true friends. It was clear that a lot of people were in fear of him and what he might do next. When the meeting was over, Derek approached me and told me that action was going to be taken immediately. A member of staff went to tell Kevin that the doctor wanted to see him up at the hospital wing. He had not attended the community meeting so had no idea that matters had reached a head. At the hospital wing he was informed that he was being shipped out of Grendon. Fair play to Kevin, he didn't cause any fuss. I think he had known for a while that he was on borrowed time. He asked if he could see me, Fred and Ray, and the governor agreed. We had not known that they planned to ship Kevin out that morning, we thought they would hold him in the hospital wing until a place in a unit could be found, so it was a surprise when we were told that he was leaving in the next half-hour.

Fred, Ray and I packed the essentials that Kevin would need for a ship-out — his tobacco, toiletries, radio and a few clothes, the rest would be sent on at a later date — and headed on the long walk up to the hospital wing once again. There were several uniforms milling around, most of the medical staff and a couple of governors as they had no idea how Kevin might react. Kevin was in one of the cells with the door open, sitting on the bed looking subdued and Derek was talking to him. When he saw us he brightened up a bit. We were allowed some privacy to say our goodbyes. He gave each one of us a hug and thanked us for putting up with him. He said he felt he had let us down, but he knew he was better off going. We all promised to keep in touch. Then Kevin was taken away to be double-cuffed by the escort staff and taken on the van to HMP Bullingdon, a category B local prison near Bicester.

Though we felt sad that Kevin was gone we all agreed that it would be better for him. Tom and Derek said that the plan was to keep him at Bullingdon for only a short while until he could be assessed by a psychiatrist and allocated to a secure hospital. The only other person who really missed Kevin and was genuinely upset that he didn't get a chance to say goodbye was Daran. That night I thought about Kevin, about how sad and damaged he was and wondered whether he would ever get the chance to live a normal life. I knew that he had been through a bad and abusive childhood, but guessed we had only heard about a fraction of it. I remembered how full of hope he had been when he, Ray, Daran and I had come through the induction process on F-wing, and I was thankful that I had not been so badly damaged by my own life.

Kevin had been searching for relief from his inner torment but he had not found it at Grendon. He was not a bad man. He was fiercely loyal to his family and friends, generous to a fault and very kind-hearted. He also had a great sense of honour and, when it was not suppressed by drugs, a marvellous sense of humour. Unfortunately, life had hurt and confused him and that pain and confusion had caused him to lash out in many ways. He had made it on to C-wing by saving the life of a stranger, but in the end he had been incapable of putting his own life back on track. I don't blame Grendon for Kevin's situation; he was a difficult case long before he reached here and nobody would have found it easy to cope with him. I do still have reservations about his group and how they seemed to give up on him so quickly. Maybe if he had been in a stronger group from the start things would have ended differently. Or maybe not. He had good friends around him and a staff group who genuinely cared about him, but it wasn't enough. In the system Kevin would have been 'sticked and nicked' for some of his behaviour, as he had been many times in the past, but at Grendon he was on the whole treated with patience and courtesy. Even his ghosting was handled in a civilized manner, when he was allowed to say goodbye to his friends.

Four months later Kevin was still in the punishment block at HMP Bullingdon. No place had yet been found for him in a secure hospital. He seriously assaulted three members of staff, putting two of them in the hospital, and was on a 'three-man unlock', which means the door of his cell cannot be opened for any reason unless there are three members of staff present. His sentence was due to finish in September 2005. Until then Kevin would live inside his own head, and, believe me, I know how lonely that can be.

14. Bad Memories

For me the most painful thing about being in therapy was the memories it was bringing up and the feelings that came with them. I had been able to commit some terrible acts in my life and then put them right out of my mind and feel no guilt or shame. I'd had little empathy for my many victims, simply because in my mind I had not seen them as real people. It was easier that way. I could shoot someone in the face with a shotgun, cosh or slash people and five minutes later be getting on with things as though it had never happened. But now that I was changing through therapy the reality of my past actions was assaulting me from all sides. I wasn't an evil man, I hadn't done all the bad stuff while being devoid of feeling, I had just been able to put my emotions into a box somewhere deep inside me and then firmly lock it. Now the lock was off and I had to deal with the emotional consequences of my actions.

One day I suddenly had a vivid memory of being thirteen years old and splitting another kid's head open with a tree branch for no other reason than he refused to fight me. His name was Steven, and I casually left him in a pool of blood and went off to play football with my mates. How had I become that callous and brutal at such a young age? I never saw Steven again nor thought about that day for the next thirty-one years. Then, after a particularly emotional group during which Fred spoke about his mother's death, I was sitting alone in my cell drinking a cup of coffee and the memory of Steven came to the fore in full colour. I remembered every detail, the feel of the branch in my hand, the vibrations in my arms as the wood made contact with Steven's face and the powerful rush of feelings straight after. Before I realized it was happening I was crying. Huge breathtaking sobs and floods of tears. After a few minutes I managed to get myself under control. When I thought about it afterwards I couldn't figure out if the tears had been for Steven or for myself. But I recognized that none of the emotions surrounding my past actions had been eliminated as I had believed; they were still there inside me, waiting to come out. The front that I had always shown to the world was beginning to crumble and I had to prepare myself mentally for the final breakthrough.

I knew that therapy was working for me and that there would be painful times ahead. I realized I was sorry for what I had done to Steven, and, though it was over three decades too late to be of use to him, it made me that bit more human. I could feel empathy for my victims and I was capable of feeling guilt over my actions, and this was all new to me.

As far as my long criminal career went I had always had trouble recognizing the victims of my crimes, particularly of my many armed robberies. In prison the armed robbers gravitate towards each other and are bestowed a kind of special status by almost everyone in the system. They are seen as top of the pecking order, a kind of criminal elite, and are treated as such. Most people are in awe of a man who has the bottle to put himself at the sharp end of criminality, in situations where, though the rewards are usually large, very long prison sentences and even death are almost inevitable. The police have little hesitation in shooting armed robbers, and they never shoot to wound but always to kill. As I have heard police officers explain in the past, when they are faced with an armed criminal they cannot take any chances. It's not a Hollywood action movie where the hero can shoot a gun out of someone's hand; in the real world they put you down as quickly as possible. And, if you should die in that situation, well that's just too bad. To know this and still go and put yourself on offer anyway is seen as a strange badge of courage in the criminal world. I had always subscribed to the blagger mentality that I was special, and that my crimes were on the whole victimless. I have heard it time and again from other blaggers: 'The only people we are really hurting are the banks and insurance companies and who really gives a fuck about them? Okay, so now and again you might have to give a leery guard a blast in the leg with a shotgun, or absolutely terrify every single person inside a jug in order to take the prize, but they'll get over it. It's not like you're going into their own drum and stealing their personal possessions that they've worked hard for, is it? People who work in banks, or even visit them, are not stupid, they must know that there's a chance the gaff will be robbed. I mean, they keep fucking cash there, don't they? What's the big deal? We come in, throw a fright into them for five minutes tops and leave with the fully insured cash. How bad can that be?' This is what we armed robbers tell ourselves and each other and anyone who will listen in order to justify our crimes. And the funny thing is we believe it. I had always classed myself as a 'gentleman robber' because I wouldn't shoot or cosh anybody on a robbery unless it was absolutely necessary. Three fucking cheers for me, Mr Nice Guy!

Being in therapy made me think long and hard about my actions. I began to imagine what it must have been like to have a gang of masked and armed lunatics burst into your life as you were peacefully going about your business, shouting orders and threatening to kill you. It must have been terrifying. I had been involved in over 100 robberies during my thirty-year criminal career, and that was a hell of a lot of victims who had been terrorized. I finally stopped thinking of it as a game and then the blagger's mantra seemed so crass and self-serving that I could no longer bear to hear it from people. I would no longer glamorize my life of crime, and I now felt ashamed of my actions.

Mark the Scouser was doing really well. He was well liked on the wing, honest about his shortcomings and always cheerful and up for a laugh. I really liked him and I think he would have done very well at Grendon were it not for his incredible loyalty. Unfortunately, when he reached C-wing one of his old criminal pals was already there and putting the two together was always going to be a recipe for disaster. Mark had known Sparky since they were kids and they knew each other's families. They had started out on their criminal careers together, committing hundreds of thefts and burglaries up and down the country before being separated by prison sentences. It had been some years since they'd seen each other but they had a strong bond. Sparky wasn't much liked by anyone on C-wing. Though he could be charming at times, the minute things weren't going his way he would switch and become a sulky bore who tried to intimidate those weaker than himself. He could be volatile and spiteful with it, so most people gave him a wide berth and kept him at nodding distance. He had 'little-man syndrome' and thought that shouting and sulking would make up for his lack of height, but all it did was alienate people. I have no doubt that Sparky had some serious mental problems, as, I suppose, we all did at Grendon. And there were probably traumatic incidents in his life that made him the way he was, but he seemed to revel in snide behaviour.

Sparky once tried it on with me in the middle of a community meeting but I wasn't having any of it and told him so in no uncertain terms. Sparky was tolerated by most people only because he was two-of-toast with Mark, whom almost everybody liked. Both of them had been heavy heroin users in the past and, while Mark was serious about trying to kick his habit, Sparky was still enamoured of his and was always ready to make himself busy when the occasional parcel did enter the prison. Though there was a strict no-drugs rule at Grendon, and there were long periods when the jail was absolutely free of drugs, every so often some arsehole junkie would take advantage of the situation and smuggle some in. They were usually those who had just come from other nicks and were soon sussed out and shipped out, but Sparky was the kind of bag-head who could sniff out a parcel of skag in a desert. And, maybe out of some kind of perverse loyalty, he would make sure he offered some to Mark. One day Mark called me into his cell and admitted that he had smoked heroin. He said he was feeling pretty bad about it, but it had been offered and he had found it impossible to resist. I found out later that it had been Sparky who had given Mark the skag and I was pissed off about it. As far as I was concerned friends were supposed to help each other, not prey on their weaknesses. I tried to tell Mark that Sparky was not his pal, not really, and no matter how much history they shared he should try to distance himself. But it was hard, they were both together on a wing that held only forty-three men and had to see each other every day. Besides, though Mark was smart enough to know that Sparky was bad news he still felt a strong loyalty towards the little man. There was nothing he could do.

A month later Mark was called for a piss test and it came up positive for opiates. He brazened it out, coming to the community and swearing that he had not taken drugs and that the test had been an anomaly. There was so much respect and liking for Mark in the community that people were willing to give him the benefit of the doubt. Even the staff admitted that tests had been known to go haywire in the past and give false readings, though this was very rare. In the end, after much discussion and Mark's repeated denials, the matter was dropped. But I knew the truth. The only good thing to come out of the whole matter was that Mark knew he could not risk another failed test and would have to knock the skag on the head. Sparky didn't really care, he was pretending to have a long-term back-pain problem and had managed to talk the doctor into prescribing him opiate-based painkillers. If his tests came up positive for opiates he always had an excuse in the medication.

One of the new members of the community was a Manchester kid named Cat, who was doing a five for possession of firearms. Cat slotted right in and started working therapeutically almost straight away. He was on Mark's group, group 1, and they got on well together. Cat was a good kid, a bit loud and leery in a harmless kind of way; he had a bit of bluster about him, but he was genuine in his desire to work out his problems and try to go straight. Mark took Cat under his wing and was always ready to listen to his problems, but Sparky took a dislike to him. Things were fine for a couple of months and when Cat had settled in he started going two-of-toast with Dave, the Milton Keynes drug lord who was on my group. The trouble was that Sparky disliked Dave even more than he disliked Cat, and the feeling was mutual. But both Dave and Cat got on well with Mark so peace, albeit a fragile and uneasy one, was kept.

During the evenings the community room was used for association. It had a television and a DVD player, and some evenings there would be a film on, but as we all had televisions in our cells these film nights were usually poorly attended. Mark and Sparky had bought a Game Cube between them and they had got into the habit of bringing it downstairs and plugging it into the television in the community room in the evenings because the screen was a lot bigger than that of the in-cell televisions. Sparky made sure to get to the community room first every evening so as to lay claim to the television, and they would sometimes invite a couple of others in to play 'Medal of Honour', a popular war game, on multiplayer. After a couple of weeks there was a bit of muttering from some people that they were hogging the telly, but this was mainly from the usual suspects, men who would seize on the slightest distraction so as to avoid focusing on their own problems. Anyway, nothing was done about it because Sparky would throw one of his strops and start getting all aggressive and intimidating. They always invited me along to play, but most of the time I was busy writing, though I did take up the offer a couple of times and spent an enjoyable evening machine-gunning pill boxes and blowing the heads off Nazis.

One evening Sparky was unavoidably detained and by the time he got to the community room Cat and a couple of others were settled in front of the television watching a film. Sparky, not one to shrug his shoulders and chalk anything up to experience, told the lads they would have to leave as he and Mark were going to be using the television for their game. Cat was having none of this and when, as inevitably happened, Sparky became aggressive he told him to fuck off. The general consensus in the community when the story came out later was that Sparky had had his bluff called. As he was a bit of a bully and used to getting his own way, his arsehole dropped out when Cat told him how it was. I'm not sure about this as I thought Sparky probably could have a bit of a tear-up on his own; he certainly had plenty of hate and spite inside him and that usually manifests itself in violence. Whatever his thinking may have been, his actions proved fatal for all of them. Sparky legged it back upstairs and went straight to Mark. Mark was not that tall but he was very broad, about 15 stone of mostly muscle, and he was very fit. Fred had been training me and Mark together and he worked us hard. We had a pair of mitts and a set of pads and our daily workout included boxing ten three-minute rounds on the pads. Having sparred with Mark I knew just how powerful he was. He was also no stranger to violence, though he had presented a calm and cheerful exterior ever since I had known him. I had marked him as one of those geezers who, once started, would be hard to stop in a ruck. Sparky knew all this and he also knew the strength of Mark's loyalty.

Cat, realizing that at best this would result in a bit of an atmosphere on the wing, headed upstairs to find Sparky and talk things out. In his naivety he couldn't have known just how explosive the situation had become. Mark, who had reached a critical stage in his therapy only that morning, was looking for a distraction from the pain he was feeling at raking over his traumatic childhood, so when Sparky came bursting into his cell with anger in his eyes and a tale of how Cat was trying to mug them both off by fucking up their evening routine, he was up for it. Just as they were coming out of Mark's cell, Cat happened to be walking up the landing looking for Sparky. Sparky steamed straight into Cat and floored him with a right-hander, then proceeded to kick him in the head several times. Other people who had been sitting in the alcove leaped up and tried to stop Sparky, and Mark interpreted this as an attack on his mate and went into one. Soon there was a ruck of legendary proportions going on. Staff, hearing the commotion, ran on to the landing and tried to break it up. By now Cat was off the floor and trying to defend himself. A couple of men came running from the pool room to see what was going on and Mark, gone berserk, had snatched a pool cue from one of them and began swinging it with wild abandon. The riot bells were ringing and the noise of the fight even reached my cell on the ground floor where I was chatting to Fred. We were both highly attuned to the sounds of prison and recognized it as trouble. In another nick we might have run up the stairs to see what was going on and maybe get involved, but we looked at each other and shrugged. From the sound of the bells going off it would soon be all over up there. So we just carried on drinking our coffee and mused on what might be happening and the implications it might have on the community meeting the next day. We hoped it didn't involve any of our group.

Meanwhile, upstairs two members of staff had bundled Cat into an open cell, away from Mark, and several men were trying to grab Mark and calm him down but he was still swinging the pool cue. He barged his way into the cell where Cat was and tried to hit him with it, catching a member of staff with a glancing blow instead. Then he was overwhelmed and pulled from the cell. Sparky, being the sly self-preserving slag that he was, had legged it as soon as the staff had appeared and had faded into the background. As the other two were being taken under escort to be locked up in their cells pending an investigation, Sparky was busy trying to cajole or intimidate the people who might know he had been involved. He did a good job because it took quite a while for the full story to come out. Twenty minutes after the fight ten members of the community knew all the details, including Fred and me. Any one of us could have approached a member of staff and spilled the beans on Sparky's involvement, but we didn't. I can only speak for myself, but I still could not bring myself to cross that invisible line that we call 'grassing'. I don't think I ever will, but I don't see that as one of my negative qualities. I came to Grendon to change some things, but not everything.

The rest of the evening was quiet. Cat and Mark remained banged up in their cells and Sparky almost tired himself out running all over the wing trying to put it on people to keep their mouths shut. Dave, Cat's best pal on the wing, had been in the showers when the fight went off and had heard nothing of it until it was all over. Now Sparky had to worry about whether there would be any retaliation from Dave. Sparky must have known that Dave, if he'd had the mind to, could have kicked seven bells out of him, so he avoided him. Dave was gutted for Cat, but he also knew how much work he had put in on his own anger and violence in the two years he had been at Grendon and he had no intention of getting involved. Dave banged himself up in his own cell so as to avoid seeing Sparky and doing something he would regret.

The next morning's community meeting was a charged affair. Mark wasn't there as the staff had kept him locked in his cell pending transfer, though we didn't know this at the time. Cat was there, looking suitably chastened, and he knew his place at Grendon was in the balance. Sparky sat at the far end of the room and managed to keep his face neutral. Cat was the first to be asked to explain himself and straight away some of us knew that Sparky had got to him, probably through his door after he had been banged up and Sparky was still out. Cat tried to play down the fight as a bit of boisterousness that had got out of hand, and he hardly mentioned Sparky's role in it. He stuck his hands up to committing an act of violence, which would be enough to get him shipped out. Others who had witnessed all or part of the fight then said their piece. The staff explained that Mark was being kept locked up for what they called a 'cooling-off period' because when they had spoken to him that morning he had told them straight that he would attack Cat as soon as he saw him. After about an hour of discussion the chairman called for a commitment vote on both Cat and Mark. Surprisingly, given the seriousness of the violence, the community voted for them both to be given a chance and keep their places. But the vote was close. It was obvious that the therapist and wing staff were not happy; they had obviously expected the vote to be a done deal as the constitution was very clear on matters of violence. Many people wanted to have their say and explain why they had voted the way they had and an extension was called. (Anyone in the community can request an extension to group or wing meetings if the reason is sufficiently serious and might leave the community unsettled if not discussed.) The fact was that both Cat and Mark were well liked by many people and that counted in their favour during the vote. If Sparky had been up for the vote, I believe things might have gone a lot differently. Some of us knew of his involvement but that old prison code of *omertà* stopped us from speaking up.

One person who did not attend the community meeting that morning was Caveman, who had an appointment at the outside hospital. Caveman was an awkward character. When I had first met him and heard that he was in for killing a child I'd had a strong impulse of wanting to kill him. But as I listened to his story in the group I began to understand him a bit more and found myself, against my better judgement, growing to like him. He could be a very personable fella and had a wry sense of humour, but I think what changed my opinion of him more than anything was his genuine sadness and remorse for his crime. He seemed to carry it like a heavy weight everywhere he went. He had not tortured or sexually abused his victim, he had lost his temper after a heavy night of drinking and drug-taking and punched the child once in the stomach. This does not make his crime any less horrifying or make him any less guilty, and I would be the last person who would make excuses for this man, but it was at least some mitigation. Anyway, Caveman was not the sort of person who would turn spaniel, so when Sparky had approached him on the previous evening straight after the fight and asked him to keep schtum, Caveman had refused and told him straight that he would be telling the truth about what he had seen. Unfortunately, Caveman was called up for a surprise hospital appointment, by coincidence, the next morning. The meeting ran an hour and a half over time and then the staff retired to their own meeting to decide on what was to be done. Sparky must have thought he had got away unscathed.

Though there is a form of democracy in the communities at Grendon, in the case of serious commitment issues the staff group always have the final say. On the whole, they will go with whatever the community decide in their vote, but if they feel the matter is too serious to be left in our hands they could go against our decision. That was what happened in this case. Thirty minutes after the extension ended a special was called by the staff and they informed us that because this was a serious violence issue they no longer felt the wing would be safe if the protagonists were to stay. Also, it would send out a message that C-wing was prepared to tolerate full-scale fights with no comeback for the offenders, and that could not be allowed. The staff group had decided that both men would be removed from Grendon at the earliest opportunity. Mark would be going that very afternoon and Cat would be off as soon as they could arrange a place in another prison for him. Cat was devastated and there was a lot of sympathy for him because the community knew that it had not been his fault. He had been attacked and yet he was being shipped out for violence. Mark, on the other hand, was apparently very light-hearted and philosophical about the whole thing. During the afternoon they allowed him to come down to my cell on the ground floor to say goodbye and I managed to have a chat with him. Knowing he was on his way back into the system Mark already had his prison armour and his war-face on but I could see he was fucking gutted to be going out this way. He admitted that if it had not been for Sparky he would not have been involved, but also admitted that he had gone too much over the top once he had. We embraced and promised to keep in touch, and then he was escorted up to reception where a van was waiting to take him back to

HMP Stafford. I was sad and sorry to see him go. C-wing seemed a little bit duller without him.

The next morning Caveman was in my group and was questioned about what he had witnessed of the fight. He put Sparky right in the frame. Cat, knowing that his days at Grendon were now numbered anyway, went to his group the next morning and told the whole truth: he had been attacked by Sparky with no warning and he felt as though he was now being punished despite having been the one attacked. It all came out on the feedbacks and a special was called for that afternoon. Sparky was put in the hot seat and grilled, not only about his role in the fight but also about orchestrating the cover-up. He blustered, threatened, sulked and flashed evil looks all round but failed to fool anyone. He was about to be put to the vote when he craftily pre-empted it by announcing that he was pulling out of therapy and that he wanted a move. This made it pointless to have a vote. It also meant that he would be able to get a progressive move rather than just a ship-out to the nearest nick with a space for him. The staff agreed to this and Sparky left the meeting happy. By jumping before he was pushed Sparky had got a good deal. While Mark went back to Stafford and Cat went to Bullingdon, Sparky got a move to a cushty C-cat privatized jail near where he lived called the Wolds.

Thinking about all this afterwards I realized that though Sparky was a spiteful little fucker he had only been behaving in the criminal way. He had been looking after number one when he was arranging the cover-up and this was the kind of behaviour that I too had been part of in the past. The difference between me and Sparky is that I had a bit more moral fibre and there is no way that I would compromise my friends the way he did. But I couldn't blame him for how he acted, I could only observe and try to learn something from it. In my own way I too was weak and still partly enslaved to that mythical criminal code. I had voted for both Cat and Mark to stay, despite the fact that I knew full well that they had committed a forbidden act of violence and made the wing unsafe. And I know that if it had come to a vote on Sparky I would have voted in his favour too. That wasn't anything to do with whether I liked him on a personal level or not, it was more about me and what I would allow myself to do within my own moral boundaries. I understood that it wasn't enough to just refrain from violence myself, though God knew how hard that was, but that I was also expected to look down on those who showed no such restraint. And I wasn't sure I would ever reach that point.

15. Hate-'em-all Harry

One of the blokes who came on to the wing in the next intake after mine was known as Hate-'em-all Harry. Harry was serving Her Majesty's Pleasure, which is the juvenile version of a mandatory life sentence. At the age of seventeen he had fallen under the influence of two older men who had taken him to the house of a suspected paedophile and got him to join in beating the man. Harry had a deep hatred of paedophiles and ended up cutting the victim's throat, killing him instantly. When the man, who incidentally turned out not to be a paedophile after all, died, the two older men turned on Harry and put all the blame on him. They both gave evidence against him in the subsequent trial and Harry was sentenced to HMP with no time limit. In the early days of his seemingly endless sentence Harry became a handful, forever kicking off. In the end, the prison system, as it so often does in the case of unmanageable prisoners, sectioned him under the Mental Health Act. Harry was subjected to electric-shock therapy, his head and body wired to a generator and a large amount of electric current passed through him – torture justified as an attempt to cure him of his awkward behaviour. When the mental health authorities had tired of experimenting on Harry, he was tossed back to the prison system and spent the next decade being shunted around top-security nicks, including a year in the punishment block at HMP Swaleside. Harry came to Grendon from Parkhurst, and he brought a message from my brother-in-law, Tony Hogan. It is common practice among long-term prisoners to send messages to each other via prisoners who are being transferred, and it is also a sign that the messenger is someone to be trusted. Nobody would send a message with a wrong-un so it was like an introduction. Tony was nearly twenty years into a life sentence for murder, and it had been his younger brother, Jimmy, who had received a two-strike life sentence for beating the nonce on the day before I left Whitemoor for Grendon. So I accepted Harry at face value instantly and I was never to regret that decision.

By the time he got to C-wing Harry, at twenty-eight, was already a prison veteran and very, very bitter. He had an almost pathological hatred of paedophiles and wrong-uns, so it was lucky that all the paedophiles at Grendon were kept on a separate wing, G-wing, or Harry would not have lasted long. He gravitated towards the 'normal' criminals on the wing straight away and was soon well liked despite his obviously sour outlook on life. I think it was over five months before I saw Harry smile. He seemed a lot older than his years and he had become hardened to the depressing disappointment of prison life. He soon became known as Hate-'em-all Harry. Harry was one of the most sarcastic men I have ever known and an expert at coming up with nicknames for people. Once Harry gave you a name it tended to stick. One day I was talking to him in the 1s alcove when Caveman walked by. 'Here,' said Harry, 'Britney's in your group, ain't he? How can you bear to listen to him talking about his crime?' I was puzzled. 'Britney?' I queried. 'Who the fuck is Britney?' Harry nodded towards Caveman, who was now on his way down the stairs. 'He's in for killing a kid, ain't he? You know, Britney Spears? "Hit me baby one more time"!' Though I wouldn't have taken odds on it during his first six months on C-wing, Harry was to become a Grendon success story.

When you spend years in jail you tend to miss women – unless of course you are a homosexual – and yearn just to talk to, or have some contact with, them. I was now in my sixth year of incarceration and I had gone through a five-year drought when the only woman I had any contact with was Denise, and she was always very businesslike in our weekly phone conversations. I had been having a relationship with a gorgeous girl named Lindsay when I was arrested, but she was too young and good-looking to throw her life away waiting for me to serve out my eight life sentences and I told her so. Soon after I was convicted and sentenced she saw the light and moved on. I wasn't bitter about it and I wished her luck. Since then there had been nothing.

The release of the book spurred some of my ex-girlfriends to get in touch, as well as perfect strangers and a lot of female prisoners. I went from drought to flood in a very short time. I had no plans to be tied down with any one woman if I ever got out again. I had a very poor track record when it came to relationships and I wasn't sure I could ever live with a woman again. I knew I was very institutionalized. The last time I had been out, in 1998, I'd had a large flat in Croydon but tended to live in one corner of one room. I wasn't used to having much space due to all the years I had spent in prison cells, and I didn't like people getting too close to me. That is what prison does to you. But I still hadn't given up hope that I might meet the right woman, one who could see beyond the 'Gruffalo' exterior and melt my villainous heart. If Grendon was teaching me anything, it was that there is hope for even the worst of us.

The book was selling well and due to be released in America so things were looking good on my proposed career front. But not so good family-wise. I had fallen out with Denise over my Irish daughter, Leah, and things were also a bit strained between me and Lianne, my other daughter. They hadn't really spoken to me since I had told them about Leah, though I did manage to speak regularly to Dean on the phone. C-wing had a Family Day coming up so I wrote and asked Leah if she would like to come over to England and meet me. Of course, she said yes and we set about making plans. Leah and I were exchanging letters, photos and tapes on a regular basis and found we had a lot in common, as you might expect between a father and daughter. She is a lovely girl and has a great sense of humour, but it was a real shock for me when she sent me a tape of her and the kids talking. To hear that lovely Irish lilt in her voice was strange, but nice. I sat there hearing the voices of my daughter and my grandchildren for the first time and I had a tear in my eye. I guess I'm just a big pussycat at heart. Though my many victims would tell you otherwise.

Rain or shine, good times and bad, therapy went on. We met every morning to discuss our issues. Tony the Stalker was proving to be hard work. He was very secretive about his life and appeared emotionless when describing his crimes. The group hammered away at him at every opportunity but it was like trying to break a mountain with a toffee-hammer. I found out that his obsession with his first victim ran so deep that he had changed his surname by deed poll to that of the victim's real boyfriend. This became my hammer with which to chip at him. I strongly suggested that his name change was just like taking a trophy that he could gloat over, and if he was serious about turning his life around he should start by giving up the name that tied him to his victim. Tony wasn't happy about this, but I was relentless. Every time he spoke in the group I made sure to ask him if he had changed his name yet. I could tell that this was annoying him and that somewhere deep inside that granite shell he was fuming, but I never gave up.

The small groups were pretty informal affairs. Once we were all in our seats someone might request a minute to talk about something that was bothering him and then this issue could turn into the whole group. We had to be perfectly open and honest for therapy to work and anyone who came into group 3 and tried to fanny us was in for a very rough ride. Group 3 had the reputation as the strongest one on C-wing, and with good reason. You could expect some stiff verbal challenges from the group if you tried to pull the wool. One man who was to find out just how challenging group 3 could be was a fella called Sandy. Sandy was serving a life sentence for beating a homosexual to death with a baseball bat. He had been transferred in from HMP Long Lartin, one of the top-security dispersal jails, and, as it turned out, he was a pathological liar. In my experience, limited though it is, pathological liars seem to come in two different flavours. The man we had nicknamed Chuck Norris when I was on F-wing had been one type, the kind who will tell outrageous and unbelievable lies. Chuck told us that he had been in the SAS as well as the Foreign Legion and that he had once parachuted out of a plane over the Atlantic Ocean and landed on the back of a whale! Chuck's lies were laughable. He believed his own stories, but few people who heard them would give them any credence, unless they themselves were as thick as two short planks. The other kind of pathological liar, however, is much more devious and dangerous, and I believe Sandy may have been one of these.

At first no one knew that Sandy was a liar except, of course, the therapist and the rest of the staff. In Grendon the policy is that, if there is anything important in your past behaviour to be exposed, it is up to you to expose it yourself. If you don't, they will pull you aside and advise you to do so or you might as well not be there. They can only work with honesty, anything less is unacceptable. Sandy came into our group hiding a secret. His tale was a harrowing one that emerged over several group sessions. He told us he had been sexually abused from the age of four until his thirties by the same man. He claimed the man had haunted him all his life, turning up to sexually abuse him and then disappearing again. Sandy said it was because of this that he had taken up weightlifting, boxing and martial arts, in order to be in a position to protect himself from this sexual predator. But even when he was thirty years old and working as a nightclub doorman his nemesis turned up again and sexually molested him. The way Sandy told it, this man had such a hold over him that he became frozen with terror whenever he appeared.

Sandy was very convincing, though I, being a cynical bastard, thought that some of his story just did not add up. I wasn't ready to challenge him on it yet, just in case it was all true and I caused him unnecessary distress. The group was emotional over Sandy's terrible tale and he got a lot of sympathy. He told us that eventually he plucked up the courage to confront his abuser and found out that the man frequented an out-of-the-way gay pick-up point in some local woods. Sandy drove there with a baseball bat in his car, though he was adamant he had no intention of using it, and found the man. He says he asked him why he had ruined his life and the man threatened him with violence and exposure. Sandy walked back to his car, followed by the man, who was verbally abusing him all the way, and was then attacked by the man. He managed to grab the baseball bat from his car and the next thing he knew he had beaten the man to death. He drove away but was caught in the police investigation some months later.

The thing that troubled me about Sandy's story was that he made no distinction between the man being a homosexual and a paedophile. A man who is attracted to a four-year-old is unlikely to find him sexually attractive when he is a thirty-year-old kick-boxing bouncer. Likewise, just because a man is a homosexual it doesn't make him a paedophile. Also there was the fact that none of this story came out during Sandy's lengthy trial for murder. If it had been true, and I'm still not 100 per cent sure that it wasn't, then at worst it could have been used as mitigation for his crime. At best, it could have swayed a jury to find him guilty of manslaughter or not guilty due to diminished responsibility. But Sandy only started to mention his abuse after mixing with men he met in prison who had been sexually abused. The cynic in me would say that he might have wanted to use this story in order to appeal his life sentence and an eighteen-year tariff and then had to get it documented by coming to Grendon and talking about it. But for a while I decided to give him the benefit of the doubt. I told Fred about my suspicions. Fred said that if Sandy's story was true and I questioned it I would end up looking like a bad bastard. He advised me to give it a few months to see if anything else came out. If it was still bothering me then I should voice my suspicions but in a diplomatic manner.

Sandy soon settled into the wing and seemed a pretty normal and likeable bloke. He became the charity rep after me and was full of enthusiasm and good ideas for raising funds for C-wing's chosen charity, the Banbury Young Homeless Project. I stayed on good terms with Sandy and he often came to me for advice on charity matters because I had done the job before him, but I never took him completely into my confidence on anything and I didn't spend a lot of time socializing with him. He made good contributions to the group and wasn't afraid to challenge other people. By now group 3 had changed. Deke the Sneak had been granted parole and was doing fairly well and going straight back in Birmingham. We knew this because it was a tradition for those who had been released from Grendon to keep in touch now and then by phone or letter. Sandy had taken Deke's place in the group. Abs had also been granted parole and had gone straight into a residential drug rehabilitation centre in Weston-super-Mare and he, too, was doing well. The man who took Abs's place in the group was a 21-year-old, straight out of Aylesbury Youth Offenders' Institute. His name was Candy and he was serving six years for raping his 59-year-old neighbour. Candy was small and slim with long brown hair which he invariably wore in a ponytail. He was very effeminate in his speech and mannerisms and a self-confessed cross-dresser. He told us he felt comfortable in women's clothes and was toying with the idea of having a transsexual operation. He was bisexual and had had long affairs with both men and women. He was also a drug user and had been addicted to both cocaine and heroin. Needless to say, Candy became a target for Sandy because he was a homosexual sex offender.

I was hard on Candy almost from his first group when he admitted that he had only applied for Grendon because he was terrified that he would be beaten up in any other adult jail. I was outraged by this since I had struggled long and hard with the decision to come to Grendon, and here was some cheeky pup telling me that he had come here to hide out. I told him, in no uncertain terms, that he would get no easy ride and if he tried to shirk his work I, for one, would have no hesitation in voting him out. I was annoyed with Candy but Sandy was almost dripping with hate for him and made sure everyone knew it. Whether this was a genuine hatred or just another attempt to prove that his own story was true I didn't know.

My suspicion that Sandy might be bullshitting the group hardened when he told us a story designed to elicit sympathy that was almost embarrassingly false. He spun his Mills & Boon tale with suitable solemnity of word and sadness of eye and I nearly burst into laughter on the spot. He claimed that the great love of his life had been a South American beauty queen with whom he had spent three short years and had fathered a daughter. The beauty queen had contracted an unspecified illness and Sandy nursed her at home for some months before she died in his arms. There was a deathbed declaration of love from her and a promise to always take care of the child from Sandy. As he was spinning this yarn I looked around the group to see who might be gullible enough to buy it and to my surprise everyone seemed absorbed. Surely I couldn't be the only one who was seeing through this? If Sandy's story had been the plot of a film it would have been a B movie reject. It was so corny all it was missing was the cob. Once he had finished, I was determined to get in there and challenge him on some of the details but it was the end of the group and time for feedbacks so I decided to wait for a better opportunity. I asked Fred if he believed it. 'It sounded a bit far-fetched,' he replied. 'Far-fetched?' I exclaimed. 'There was more truth in *Lord of the Rings*!' But once again Fred counselled caution. I knew he was right, there was always the slim chance that Sandy had led the life he had told us about. I suppose it can happen, though I was going to ask him where he had met a South American beauty queen when he had been working the door of a pub in Norwich.

It all came on top for Sandy when he was called in by a security governor to explain a telephone call he had made to his girlfriend. It turned out that he was arranging to have her up on a Family Day visit, when inmates' families are allowed on to the wing to look around our cells, and had foolishly talked on the phone about the possibility of them having sex in his cell. He also asked her to smuggle in some hard-core pornographic DVDs. This was a very serious matter. Maybe Sandy had got carried away with the relaxed atmosphere at Grendon and figured that no one was taping his calls but that was a bit silly for a prisoner who had already been in the system for nine years. Every phone call inmates make is taped as a matter of course and every con knows not to say anything on the phone that he doesn't want recorded and examined by the security department. Now they had Sandy on tape arranging two serious breaches of security. After the security governor had finished with him Sandy was called in to see the wing therapist. There was an investigation going on into what else Sandy might have arranged and it soon came to light that he had been making enquiries into the possibility of being able to play DVDs on the laptop computers that the prison supplied to those inmates who were taking degree courses. He had put himself down for a course and had a laptop in his possession. This matter was so serious that the security department immediately removed every laptop computer in the prison until further notice. There were a lot of irate prisoners who were at crucial stages of their course work when their computers were withdrawn. The wing therapist told Sandy that regardless of what happened in the security investigation his commitment to therapy was now seriously in question.

Apart from the removal of the laptops, the implications of Sandy's actions were very serious for C-wing as a whole. We had a Family Day visit coming up within two weeks and now security were saying that they might not let it go ahead. The twice-yearly Family Day visits were very important to everyone at Grendon. They were the times when men, some of whom had been prisoners for decades, got a chance to chill with their close family and loved ones. In the six-hour visit prisoners were able to eat lunch with their visitors in a relaxed atmosphere, and then show them where they lived and have a few photographs taken together. It may not seem a lot to people outside but for us these were the highlights of the year. After a six-month period of daily therapy the visits were the icing on the cake that helped to make it all worth it. Men could be arranging these visits months in advance, and to hear that we might now lose them because of the actions of one stupid individual made a lot of people angry. To say that Sandy was not the most popular man on C-wing, or even in the whole prison, would be putting it mildly. I had plenty of reason to be angry at Sandy. This Family Day was to be my first meeting with my daughter Leah. And now it was in jeopardy. I was raging and worried about it and didn't really want to even catch sight of Sandy's sorry face for fear that I might do something I would surely regret. Unfortunately, he was a member of my group.

The thing about Grendon is that if you stick your hands up about things, or 'own them', if you prefer therapese, then you are not considered to be beyond help. Sandy wasn't able to grasp this simple concept, probably because he had spent so long lying, so when he came into group 3 the next morning he tried to minimize the seriousness of his actions. This was a big mistake. Lying to group members was like calling us all gullible cunts and thinking we'd just swallow it. Sandy started by telling us that he had only been joking when he'd made the incriminating phone call. But it soon emerged that it had not been just the one call, but several, and that according to the tape evidence Sandy had made a concerted effort to convince his girlfriend to comply with his wishes. He was strongly challenged about his actions and his attempt to minimize them. I was quietly fuming, but I tried to get him to see that putting up a smoke screen was not helping his case. Unfortunately, it was like talking to a brick wall. He was asked if he had told the group any other lies but he said he hadn't, and there was no way we could prove otherwise so we just had to accept his word on that. Over the next twenty-four hours Sandy was in a very uncomfortable position as everybody on the wing went out of their way to avoid him. He had become a social pariah. I will say that he had plenty of front, he didn't stay behind his door in the dark but put himself about a bit. If it had been me I would have been too embarrassed to show my face on the wing, but Sandy was made of sterner stuff. We would see how stern when he had to face the whole wing at the next day's community meeting and be challenged on his actions by forty-two irate inmates.

The next morning Sandy took his place in the community room and got grilled like a rasher for the whole hour and a half. First he gave his version of events, just as he had told the group the day before, and still refused to accept any guilt. He said it had just been a running joke that got out of hand and that he'd had no intention of actually smuggling the DVDs or trying to have sex with his girlfriend. People weren't happy and they made this plain in their questioning. Then Taff piped up and said that Sandy was 'a fucking liar' and we couldn't believe a word he said. Sandy had moved into my old cell on the 1s opposite Taff and for a while the two had got on very well, but eventually they fell out over some perceived slight. I had come to realize that Taff was as mad as a hatter by now and that he was so paranoid he would hear personal insults in an empty room. I don't think there was anyone that he didn't fall out with during his time at Grendon, so it was no surprise to me when I heard that he had fallen out with Sandy. Like all bullies, Taff was a coward at heart, so instead of saying anything on the landings or in the privacy of a cell where he thought he might be in danger of getting a bang in the mouth, he would save his rage for the safety of the community meetings. It's true that this is what we were being taught to do, but Taff went about it in a very snide manner. He would save his ammunition for months and then let loose when he thought his victim was at his weakest, and disguise it under the thin veneer of therapeutic input. This time he had the feelings of the wing behind him because Sandy had been turned into such a hate figure, and he was firing on all cylinders.

Venom dripping from his voice, Taff described how Sandy had told him about his five-year stint in the army as a physical education instructor.

'He's never been in the fucking army,' he crowed. 'I caught him out because I'm the genuine article. He came out with a load of bullshit and I knew straight away he was lying, because I know, see?' At this stage I was tempted to question Taff on his own army tales, some of which did not ring exactly true, but Nobby, a former Satanist who was doing a discretionary life sentence for raping and torturing his own sister, jumped in with another example of Sandy's dissembling. Soon it had become a free for all, with people recounting outrageous lies that they had been told by Sandy and he was looking as if he would rather be in a strip cell in Wandsworth prison than sitting there hearing his lies coming back to haunt him. I looked over at Fred and caught his eye. He nodded as if to say, you were spot on. Mel asked Sandy straight if he had lied about his abuse but he was adamant that he had lied about nothing and he could explain everything. By now nobody was willing to believe a word that came out of his mouth. Half-naked Dave, who was the chairman, reminded us that it was almost 10.30 and called for an extension to the meeting as we still had not even reached the commitment vote stage. It was agreed that we should have an extension for as long as it took.

Whenever an extension is called for there is a fifteen-minute break to allow people to use the toilet and have a smoke. Fred, Ray and I congregated in my cell, which was almost opposite the meeting room, and had a smoke while discussing Sandy. We were all in agreement that Sandy was in serious trouble but that if he changed tack and started to admit his part in things he still had a slim chance of swinging the vote his way. What we didn't know then was that no matter how the vote went the staff group wanted him out. They obviously knew a lot more about the extent of Sandy's lying than we did, and they thought it had gone far enough. The phone calls had just been the means to bring it to the community and give Sandy the chance to come clean. When we were all back in our seats he was asked how he felt. He hung his head and looked ashamed. He admitted that he might have been thinking of getting a stash of porn DVDs and renting them out to men on the wing as a little business. He said it was not a definite plan, only that he had toyed with the idea and then rejected it. He denied everything else. This was too little too late as far as the community was concerned. After another twenty minutes of hammering it out the chairman called for the vote. In the end, it was surprisingly close – 23–19, in favour of Sandy going. I voted him to stay, but only because it was obvious that if anybody needed some serious therapy it was Sandy. He looked devastated that he had been voted out, but I don't know what else he could have been expecting. He gave a short speech in which he still refused to take any responsibility for his actions and that was that.

It was another week before security and the governor decided to give C-wing clearance to have our Family Day visit. Sandy was shipped to Full Sutton, a top-security dispersal prison in Yorkshire, and I, along with the rest of group 3, wished him luck and shook his hand before he went. The staff would never tell us just how far he had taken his lies but they hinted that there were things that they had been concerned about in his stories. To this day I do not know whether he was actually sexually abused over three decades by the same man, but one thing I am sure of, something must have happened in his life to make him turn into the character he was. As for Chuck Norris, the other type of pathological liar who was now on A-wing, he created his own dramas built from his lying words, but, fortunately, his lies were so transparent that even the dimmest A-wing resident had him marked down as a spoofer from day one so they were able to deal with him. Chuck did well at Grendon and at the time of writing he is on his way to an open prison. Sandy still languishes in Full Sutton but has applied to come back to Grendon. I hope that, if he does, he will be prepared to tell the truth this time.

I continued to make my plans to meet Leah on Family Day, which I was really looking forward to. I was now also in touch with her mother, Miriam, who was at first understandably very cautious about the whole thing. She soon came round when she realized what a strong bond Leah and I had already formed just through writing to each other and she agreed to the visit. Not that she could have stopped Leah anyway, she was twenty-one years old and a mother herself and she knew her own mind, but it was nice to have Miriam on board. Leah and I were writing to each other every week and by now my cell wall was plastered with photos of her, Luke and Jade. Miriam also sent me pictures of Leah during various stages of her childhood. I sometimes sat and looked at that sad-faced little girl in the photos and tried to imagine how it had been for her growing up without ever seeing her father. Leah recounted a few childhood experiences in her letters but she always put a happy spin on things. Reading between the lines I could sense the pain she must have experienced at being abandoned by me and to me it was fresh and intense. Leah sent me a poem she had written about me, and the words broke my heart as I read them. It touched me so much, I became terribly emotional. I kept this poem on the wall next to my bed for the rest of the time I was at Grendon. I know she won't mind my sharing it.

Dad

For all the times my heart was broken
and I cried a tear over a boy
For all the times I got upset
and wished that I would die
For all the times I was grounded
and sent up to my room
For all the times I had a fight
and was sent back home from school
For all the times my friends betrayed me
and we fought for weeks on end
For all the times I was sent to bed at 9
and snuck back out at 10
For all the times I was bullied at school
until the day that I fought back
For all the times I tried so hard
to get my life on track
I want to take the time
to fill you in on all those years
You missed the laughter and the fun
thank god you missed the tears
It's been a long, long time I know
and we cannot change the past
But after 21 years I've found my dad at last
If I could change one thing about you
I'd leave you as you are
You're my daddy and I love you
and to me you are a star

It is very painful to realize just how much I have neglected my children over the years. Of all my many sins this is the worst and one for which I believe I have no right to beg forgiveness. The fact that my kids grew up to be such loving and forgiving human beings has nothing to do with me but is a testament to their mothers, and for this I can never praise them enough no matter how much we have drifted apart. I know I can never get back the years I missed with my children, but, hopefully, if all goes well, I can earn their love and respect and get closer to them in the future. And now that I can see more clearly I am grateful to have a future.

16. Family Day

In the weeks leading up to the Family Day visit with Leah I was all over the place emotionally. Sometimes I was walking around with my head in the clouds and other times I was biting people's heads off at the slightest provocation. I had already had two Family Day visits since I had been at Grendon. On the first one Denise, Dean and his fiancée, Danielle, had come up and it had been great, though Denise had insisted on wearing a sour face for most of the day – I don't know why she hadn't just refused my invitation. My daughter Lianne could not come up on those first two visits because at that time she was still under eighteen and the regulations are strict about letting minors on to the wing. The second time it was just Dean and Danielle and we had a great visit. Lianne would be over eighteen and so eligible for the third visit, but since I had told them about Leah, Lianne had been refusing to talk to me. Being in prison puts you at a serious disadvantage when trying to work out problems with people who are on the out. I tried writing to Lianne but got no reply. I tried phoning and got one-syllable answers to everything I said, so in the end I decided to invite Leah and leave Lianne to cool off. I might have been fucking useless at it but I was her dad after all; we had to sort things out eventually.

In the meantime I was arranging the flight, hotel and various things for Leah with Miriam helping out. It would be her first time in England and I wanted everything to be perfect. I got in touch with an old pal of mine, Steve the Butcher, and arranged for him to be her driver for the four days she would be here. He was to pick her up at the airport and deliver her to her hotel, then take her sightseeing and shopping in the West End. The next day he would drive her down to the prison and hang about for six hours while she came in to see me. On the Saturday he would be taking Leah up to Stockwell to meet my parents and anywhere else she wanted to go. I chose Steve for this job because we had been good mates for a number of years, both inside and out, and I trusted him 100 per cent. In the end Leah brought her partner, Thomas, with her, though he did not come into the prison to see me but stayed in the car with Steve.

On the day of the visit I was as nervous as a long-tailed cat in a room full of rocking chairs. I changed my clothes three times and marched up and down my cell like a lunatic from 6.30 a.m. The cells weren't unlocked until 8 a.m. and the visits started at ten, by which time I was a nervous wreck. The first visitors came through the wing gates at 10.05 and I searched the female faces for anyone who looked like the photographs I had, but there was no one. I went back to my cell and tried to calm down. Everyone on the wing knew that I was meeting Leah for the first time as I had discussed my feelings about it in my group. Fred and Ray both poked their heads in and fired off words of encouragement, as did a few staff members, but I was in bits. Then I heard Jimmy, one of the facilitators, call my name. 'Noel, your visitor is here.' I flew out of my cell and almost bowled over Mel's mum, who was outside the door being greeted by the big man himself. I apologized profusely and headed along the corridor towards the wing gate where Jimmy and Brian were standing with big grins on their faces. When I got up close I saw a beautiful young girl with long auburn hair and a hesitant smile on her face and knew straight away it was Leah. I rushed up to her and we threw our arms around each other and hugged for the first time. Leah seemed so tiny and fragile that I didn't want to squeeze too hard in case I broke her. I held her away from me and looked at her. There was a lot of Miriam in her face and it took me back over two decades. I could also see a lot of myself in her features, though she was better looking than I ever was. After our emotional hello, I led her through to the space I had claimed for us in the community room. There were other visitors in there, but they were engrossed in their own conversations. It would not have mattered if they had been staring at us anyway because it was as though we were the only two people in the room. I couldn't take my eyes off her – here was my daughter, after twenty-one years. 'When I last saw you, you were about this big,' I said, holding my hands about eight inches apart. Leah laughed at this and it sounded like a mountain stream trickling over smooth pebbles. My heart was full of love for this girl and guilt for not having been around for her. Love and guilt battled back and forth inside me for the rest of the day and beyond.

I talked to her about the family and about myself and what I was doing at Grendon. It helped that she had already read my book and that we had been corresponding for almost a year. I told her a bit about how me and Miriam had met and how things had been. And Leah told me about her life and about Luke and Jade and her relationship with Thomas. In minutes we had formed a strong connection and it was as if we had known each other all our lives. The rest of the day went really well. We won a few prizes on the charity raffle, including presents for Luke and Jade, and we got our first ever photos taken together and ate our first meal together. During the afternoon I introduced her to a few of my friends – Fred, Ray and Daran – and also to Tom, the therapist, and several members of the wing staff.

The Family Day finished just before 4 p.m. and we were allowed to leave the wing and walk our visitors up the long corridor to reception. Leah and I were easy in each other's company now, like a father and daughter should be. I was sad that she was leaving but buoyed by the knowledge that we still had the rest of our lives to share. It had taken me twenty-one years to meet her and get to know her, but I understood that I now had to look forward and not back. The visit had been positive for both of us. I gave her a kiss and a hug goodbye and we squeezed each other tightly. Then she was gone, into the crowd of visitors flowing towards the next gate. I caught sight of her waving to me over the heads of the others and I waved back. I choked back tears and turned down the corridor towards the wing. I had met my daughter for the first time and no matter what happened in my life I would always have the warm memory of this first meeting.

When I got back to the wing many people came and asked me how it had gone and commented on what a lovely girl she was. That night, when my cell door was shut at 8.30, I sat in the dark and went over the day again in my head. I thought a lot about Leah and also about my other children, Dean, Joe and Lianne. I loved them all so much and yet I had caused each of them so much pain in their lives. Lianne was upset over Leah, and in a way I could understand why. Lianne had always been my golden girl, and she always would be, but how could I get her to see that? Being in touch with Leah wouldn't make me love Lianne any less. They were my two lovely daughters – you could tell they were sisters as they were both beautiful – and I vowed to do my best to bring them together when I got out. Dean seemed okay with the situation but he was caught in the middle as he was living in the same house as Denise and Lianne. Not for the first time I wished my poor Joe was alive. He would have been able to make sense of it all. That night I cried for all of my children and how I had fucked up their lives.

The atmosphere was always subdued after the Family Day visits, and this time was no exception. Men had spent the day with their loved ones, closer than some of them had been in years and now being able to express their true thoughts and feelings through being in therapy. It was emotionally draining for everyone involved. In a couple of days everything would be back to normal and inmates would be feeling refreshed and ready to tackle another six long months of examining their issues. The Family Day visits were the oil that kept the therapeutic machine running and some people would struggle to keep working without them. They were something I had certainly never experienced in almost thirty years of imprisonment and they reinforced in me the belief that I was doing the right thing.

A lot of the issues at Grendon revolved around drug abuse and many of the men were former junkies. Having relatively little experience of drug use in my own life I found it particularly hard to link into this and understand it. My frequently stated observation was, 'How the fuck could you start taking crack when it was so widely known that it fucked people up?' The way I saw it was that the dangers of addiction to heroin and crack had hardly been a secret over the last twenty years – there had been some very public campaigns about what can happen to the people who start on them – so what possessed these men to pick up the foil, needle or crack-pipe? I began to realize that I was not stronger or superior to those who had been addicted to drugs; I too had been addicted, to crime, and I had also known the dangers of my actions when I started out and yet chosen to disregard them. Once I had made that link I began to understand and empathize with the former drug abusers, and things became easier for me. We all run and hide from hurt and pain, but not always in the same way.

As for dealing, one thing that my forays into the drug world taught me is that I could never be any good at it. Every time I tried I ended up losing money and I didn't like the people who were involved in it. For many years I had been kicking myself for not getting into the drug trade on the ground floor in the early 1980s when most of my contemporaries in the underworld started earning fortunes from the cocaine boom. In those days I had yet to sample my first joint and thought anyone who took any kind of drug was a dirty junkie bastard who would sell you down the river in a hot second. Plus I was having too much fun getting my buzz from armed robbery and violence. I saw a lot of my friends become stinking rich on drug proceeds and then just laze around their villas in Spain and Malta while I was traipsing the wet streets of London trying to nick a few quid with my sawn-off and wondered whether I should have joined the club when I was offered the chance. But now I'm sure I was right. The drug game is not for me.

Back in Grendon I listened to the miserable stories of some of the poor fuckers who had been hooked on heroin and crack for most of their lives and thanked my lucky stars that I had never been tempted to try either. The way I see it now, as miserable an existence as it was, and notwithstanding the amount of damage I did and the victims I created, being addicted to armed robbery was something of a blessing in disguise for me. The high of what I was doing had been so good at the time that I was never tempted to try class A drugs. How much more terrible might my actions have been with a drug habit to feed? Drug addiction can turn the most mild-mannered person into an uncaring monster and drive him to do things that would be completely out of character otherwise. I was already a violent, damaged and ruthless individual; even so much as a taste of drugs would have made me ten times more dangerous.

Ray was one man who had been brought low by drugs. In his case addiction to cocaine had led to a mental breakdown during which he was walking the streets of south London with a loaded shotgun under his coat, hearing voices in his head telling him that everyone was out to kill him. It's sad to say but prison was the saving of Ray, and Grendon prison in particular. Grendon was the only place where he had managed to get clean and stay that way. He took a degree course in addiction and his aim was to become a drug counsellor and try to help others. After eighteen months at Grendon Ray was downgraded to category C and was allowed to go out to give talks about addiction and his own downfall to schools and colleges. I was really pleased for him that at last he was making something of his life and he became an inspiration to many of the addicts at Grendon.

John had also completed his time at Grendon and was granted category D status. This is a major achievement for a lifer and means that you are soon to be released. John seemed very stable and sensible and we all thought he would do well in his open prison. The night before his transfer to HMP Ford we gathered in his cell on the 3s to say our goodbyes. There was me, Fred, Ray, Daran and a few others and we all wished him luck.

John left the next morning and there was an air of optimism for him tinged with the sadness of seeing one of our own leaving. I thought I had come to know John pretty well since I'd been on C-wing. If anyone had asked me if I thought he would succeed in open conditions I would have told them that I was 100 per cent sure he would.

Unfortunately, John was only in Ford a couple of months before he was back in trouble. They let him have a home leave in order to acclimatize himself to the outside world after fourteen years in prison and he fucked up. Big time. John had received his life sentence after he was convicted of stabbing a man to death in a pub fight and he had been drunk at the time. Now, on his first jaunt into the outside world, he went straight to a pub and got drunk, despite the restrictions on his licence forbidding him to do so. Once drunk, he got involved in a serious fight in which he came off the worst. He was arrested at the scene and returned to prison, sporting heavy facial injuries for all to see. His category D status was immediately rescinded by the Home Office and he was transferred back into closed conditions.

We were all shocked when we heard the news and could barely comprehend how he could do such a thing after all he had been through. It was clear that John was a lot weaker than anyone had thought and that he had managed to hide some serious issues while at Grendon. When we, his friends, discussed it we could only take one positive from the whole sorry episode: it was a warning to us all that no matter how confident we became that we had dealt with everything that was troubling us we should never on any account grow complacent. It would take only one moment of our former madness to surface and we could be back where we started. It was a frightening prospect.

I vowed never to make the same mistakes John had made, but none of us is perfect and who knew what awaited me in life? I could only try my best and renew my determination to change and work on my issues. Grendon may not have been able to save us all but I was going to maximize my chances in any way I could to be on the winning side.

17. Scaredy Cat

Scaredy Cat was a horrible specimen. A nondescript kind of man, he tried to be even more so by projecting an aura of 'I'm-not-really-here' about himself. He was of average height, build and features; the only distinguishing thing about him was that he wore glasses. He kept his mouth shut most of the time and in two years I saw only two expressions on his otherwise bland face: false fear and fake sadness. Scaredy Cat got his nickname for his mouse-like demeanour whenever he was in the vicinity of so much as a slightly raised voice. When wing meetings became heated he would scurry out of the door as though he were so delicate that the slightest growl might cause him to drop dead on the spot. So it came as a surprise to me when I heard that Scaredy Cat was in fact serving a ten-year sentence for attempted murder.

One of the first wing assessments I had witnessed when I came to C-wing was Scaredy Cat's. He was asked to divulge the details of his index offence and I listened as he told a tale that seemed full of unfortunate accidents and coincidences. He had been living with his girlfriend but the relationship was going through a sticky patch. One night, after a particularly bad row, he had gone and got a can of petrol, thrown it over his girlfriend's head and then set light to her. I was horrified when I heard this and even more so because of the way Scaredy Cat told it. According to him, the petrol can had been sitting in the kitchen and he had not put it there nor had any idea where it had come from. He claimed that the petrol had merely splashed her shoulder, and he had only been playing with the lighter, thinking it was broken, when it had somehow set light to the poor girl. Instead of immediately phoning an ambulance for his terribly burned girlfriend, Scaredy Cat claimed he had panicked. First he had filled a bath with cold water and doused her in it – one of the worst things you can do for petrol burns – and then he had dressed her and taken her for a walk to a deserted playground. The poor girl, suffering from terrible burns and shock, could do nothing to get away from Scaredy Cat and must have thought she was dying as he tried to work out a story for the police and get her to promise that she would back up his lies. He kept her away from treatment for some hours until she collapsed into a coma. Only then did he call for an ambulance, claiming that she had been the victim of an attack by unknown assailants.

My own suspicions about this case are that Scaredy Cat had planned the attack, which is why the police found the petrol can in his kitchen afterwards. Nobody in their right mind would keep a full can of petrol in the kitchen next to the oven. Despite the image he tried to put across, Scaredy Cat was a crafty manipulating git and knew exactly what he was doing. I also believe that in taking her to the playground rather than the hospital, he was hoping that the girl would die of her injuries before she got a chance to tell anyone the truth. Unfortunately for Scaredy Cat she survived, though only just, and was able to tell the police what he had done. She had to have many operations for her injuries, including surgery to rebuild a semblance of a face from the charred ruin that was left. When I heard Scaredy Cat mumbling through the story on his wing assessment I became first hot then cold with furious anger. I studied his slumped shoulders and hands clasped as if in prayer, his downcast eyes and the trembling of his bottom lip and straight away I knew he was a fake. This fuelled my rage, but I managed to sit in my chair and not leap up and smash his teeth down his lying throat. When he had finished his performance and the chairman asked if there were any questions for Scaredy Cat, I took a deep breath to steady myself and told him straight that I thought he was a snide evil bastard and asked how he thought he could sit there trying to make light of this terrible act and expect us to believe a word he said. There was an audible intake of breath from the community and several of his group leapt to Scaredy Cat's defence. I took a verbal battering and because I was new to therapy at the time I became unsure about my reaction and position. I quickly figured that Scaredy Cat's group must know more about him than I was hearing and that I had been wrong to jump in feet first to something I knew little about. I was reacting emotionally when I knew that the idea was to remain dispassionate about people's crimes.

After the meeting was over Fred came to see me. 'See, you've got to stop reacting like that, mate. Sure, his crime is horrible and you'll hear a lot more of that sort of stuff if you stay here, but if you lose your head and start getting aggressive every time one of the bad fuckers starts talking about the naughty stuff you'll be on your way back to Whitemoor before you can say "nonce".' I nodded in agreement. 'The thing that got me

though, Fred, was I could see it was all an act. He doesn't even think that
he's done anything wrong. The little rat!' Fred smiled. 'What, and you
think you're the only one who spotted that? These people are not silly,
they're trained to deal with mugs like him and mugs like us. It's their job.
If he don't start admitting responsibility for what he's done he won't last
very long. Forget about him, let his group and the professionals deal with
him. You just concentrate on yourself.'

In time I learned to curb my fury at the crimes of men like Scaredy
Cat and followed Fred's good advice. Scaredy Cat himself kept a low
profile after his first assessment and avoided me at all times. Occasionally
I would look at him during community meetings and wonder what was
going on in his head, but I kept my own counsel. By now I was more
therapy-minded and, though I could in no way condone anyone's crimes,
including my own, I could understand a bit better how we had come to
commit them. I still thought that Scaredy Cat's group and the community
in general were too willing to treat him with kid gloves. I hoped the group
would stop pussyfooting around and challenge him on his crime, but it
didn't look like it was going to happen. Scaredy Cat was in group 1, which
was usually quite a strong, though quirky, group. Their facilitator was a
woman who was reputed to be the most educationally qualified person
in the whole of Grendon and, as such, not a lot would get by her. But it
was almost as if Scaredy Cat, because he projected such a quiet and timid
aura, got a bye in therapy. Listening to the feedbacks I would hear his
name about every four or five months using the group on something
trivial. Behind Taff, the paranoid psychotic woman torturer, I considered
Scaredy Cat to be the second most dangerous man on the wing. He never
accepted that what he had done was wrong and cast himself as the victim,
which meant that he was unable to learn anything from it and would be
likely to do it again. The problem that group 1 had was that another of
their members was one of the most difficult and attention-seeking men
on the wing: Billy Bullshit.

Billy Bullshit was a little round dumpling of a man with a head like a
cannonball and the features of a lump of fresh dough. He came from
somewhere out in the sticks, not far from Grendon in fact, and he was
serving a mandatory life sentence for stabbing a man to death. His story
was that he had got into an argument with the head yokel of whatever
town he came from and, after a stand-up fist fight during which he had
been soundly thrashed, had decided to wreak revenge on his enemy. Billy

legged it home, changed completely into black clothing, like some over-weight ninja, including a ski-mask, and lay in wait with a Rambo knife for the bloke who had given him the beating. When the man left the nightclub where the fight had taken place, Billy stalked him through the dark streets as he wended his drunken way home. Getting ahead of his target at one point, he allowed him to pass before jumping out and stabbing him several times in the back. The victim died on the spot and Billy was arrested some time later when he was overheard boasting about it. Billy was convicted of murder and given a life sentence with a min-imum tariff of eighteen years. After knocking about in the dispersal system for some time, he applied for Grendon and got here about six months before me.

The first inkling I got about Billy Bullshit's penchant for self-promotion was when I arrived on C-wing and someone asked me which jail I had been transferred from. When I replied Whitemoor, I was told, 'Oh, then you must know Billy Bullshit? He was running things there.' I didn't recognize the name, and as there were only two normal location wings in operation in the three years I was at Whitemoor I should have. I had known all the faces at Whitemoor and I was sure that Billy was not one of them. He was pointed out to me in the dinner queue. Though he looked vaguely familiar I could not place him. Either he had been running the nonce wing or he was just another nonentity who had slipped below my radar. I shrugged it off. I found out later that Billy had been on B-wing, while I was on A-wing, and had kept a low profile as he was way out of his league. He had been a runner for a pal of mine named Perry, who was well known as a good guy all over the system. 'Runners' in prison parlance are star-struck idiots who do all the running about for the real faces in jail. If I want to put a bet on with the prison bookie, or need some hot water for a cup of coffee, or someone to pick up my meal at the hotplate because I'm busy playing cards, I'll send one of my runners. It was muggy to admit that you were a runner, but there was nothing dodgy about it. I could understand Billy giving himself a bit of a rep to impress the rest of the mugs and I wasn't cruel enough to burst his bubble. But this was before I ever got to know him properly.

The trouble with Billy was that he started believing his own hype and was forever making up stories that cast him in a heroic mould just to boost his ego. When confronted with his bullshit's inconsistencies he would become petulant and stubborn and create another issue in order to take the dairy off the first. It was never-ending. Whenever Billy started talking you would see people yawn because they knew it was likely to be another round of self-aggrandizing bollocks. Everyone soon grew bored with him and this led him to try harder instead of just giving up talking crap and working on his real issues. While his group tried to get Billy to calm down and do his work, it allowed Scaredy Cat to become almost invisible in the group. Hardly a feedback passed by when Billy Bullshit hadn't pulled some stroke or told some tale that nobody believed. One of his stories was that when he was twelve he had seen a girl being gang-raped by a load of skinheads and he had come to her rescue and this is why he did not like rapists. A few days later he added with downcast eyes that he had not succeeded in saving the girl but had been beaten up and forced to participate in the rape. The next group heard how he had then been tortured and bullied by the skinhead leader for years afterwards until Billy had taken him on in a fight and beaten him. Every week he had a new story and a new crisis, anything to get in the spotlight. I think he called more specials than any other man in the history of Grendon.

Billy also had the 'distinction' of being put up for his commitment more times than anyone else. He never got voted out because I think everyone knew that he was in dire need of therapy and we hoped that sooner or later he would realize this himself and settle down. One commitment vote that was very close was over a serious incident involving a 'chiv'. A chiv is a crude prison-made knife or stabbing implement which can be fashioned from almost any item that you can put a point on. Billy's story was that he had been near a window working on his garden job outside the wing when he had overheard Nobby, the Satanist who had tortured and raped his own sister, slagging him off to someone else. Nobby weighed in at about 6 stone wringing wet and would make the average jockey look like a heavyweight bruiser. I can only imagine that his sister must have been even smaller than he was. Billy said he had been fearful for his own safety, aware of Nobby's penchant for torture, and had therefore decided to arm himself immediately in case Nobby was going to attack him when he came back on to the wing. He snapped a piece of wood about eight inches long and ended up with a chiv, which he put down his sock and smuggled back on to the wing. He claimed it was in his head to ambush Nobby before the latter got a chance to do it to him. After a couple of days of thinking about it and walking around with his chiv in his waistband, he thought better of it, broke up the chiv and flushed it down the toilet.

This was a typical Billy Bullshit yarn, there being no proof of any of it other than his own words. It served the purpose of making him the centre of attention once again. But this time it backfired on him. When he told this story to his group Nobby was outraged to be used in Billy's attention-seeking. Very few people believed for one minute that Billy had brought a chiv on to the wing since there was no way he would have been able to flush eight inches of wood through a prison toilet. Wood floats and prison toilets are a lot smaller than the average bog pan. But Nobby immediately put him up for commitment. Carrying a weapon on to the wing with the intention of doing violence was a very serious issue and Billy obviously hadn't thought out the implications in his rush for the spotlight. Here was a lifer, in for ambushing his victim and stabbing him to death, confessing to what was basically a fantasy about repeating his crime. Billy had put himself right in the hot seat. He got a hard time in the wing meeting and was strongly challenged on all past incidents as well as his present 'crime'. For perhaps the first time he did not look as though he was revelling in the attention he was getting. I almost felt sorry for him, but he was the author of his own misfortune so I saved my sympathy for a more deserving case. He was rinsed by the community, but that was the least of his worries as he was getting some disapproving looks from the wing therapist and the facilitators. As a lifer, he could ill afford this kind of incident on his prison record. A lifer has no automatic right to release, unlike a fixed-term prisoner. Life is classed as ninety-nine years and the parole board put great store in the applicant's prison record. Billy had well and truly knackered his chances of an early release.

Billy's commitment vote was very close and he was voted to remain at Grendon by only one vote. I think the majority of the community were fed up with him and wanted to send him the message – pull yourself together or next time you'll be out. Because he had not been voted out Billy was given community service: he had to paint the staircase that led from the ground floor up to the 3s. He did a good job and the scare of almost being voted out quietened him down for a few weeks. But the trouble with men like Billy is that they cannot help but seek attention. Through natural progression, group 1 had started getting some new, stronger members and they were not willing to put up with Billy's nonsense. Six months after he was almost voted out, he was again put up for commitment for wasting the group's time with his fantasy life, and this time he was not so lucky. Billy left Grendon for HMP Kingston as a much despised and ridiculed little man.

I could empathize with people like Billy Bullshit to a certain extent as I too had grown up with an inferiority complex. As a kid I'd always felt that I was insignificant in the overall scheme of things. I had been really skinny and wore big plastic NHS glasses, and we were so poor that I rarely had new clothes or shoes. Almost everything I wore came from a jumble sale. Kids set great store by these things. I think that was why I got into so many fights. When I was eleven years old I had a yellow satin bomber-jacket. It was the business, bright and shiny, with elasticized cuffs and metal popper buttons, and I felt like a king when I wore it. My mum had got it from a jumble sale at St Bede's school hall which was just across the road from our estate. When the other kids on the estate admired my jacket and asked me where I had got it, I told them that I had a rich uncle in America who had sent it over especially for me. Whenever we played football I always wore my jacket and swore that it made me run faster and score more goals than I ever had without it. I loved that jacket; it made me stand out in a crowd and all the other kids admired and coveted it.

Behind our council estate was a row of big private houses, with huge back gardens, cut off from the estate by a high wall with a chain-link fence on top of it. We could look down on the gardens from the top balcony of the flats and what we saw was pristine lawns, neat flowerbeds and ornamental ponds. These houses were where the 'posh' people lived. Posh people had things like gardens, cars and telephones; they always had enough to eat and didn't have to collect firewood from the common in winter. I envied them but not in a nasty way, I just wished that we had what they had. One day all the kids off the estate were playing football when the ball was accidentally kicked over the wall into one of the posh gardens. Me and a kid named Joey Finn climbed the wall and fence to try to get the ball back. It was a hot day and when we reached the top of the fence we saw that the family who lived in the house were outside relaxing in their garden. There were a couple of kids about our age and they were looking at us as though we were exotic bugs. Me and Joey straddled the top of the fence and, seeing our ball caught in the lower branches of a cherry tree at the bottom of the garden, I called out. ''Scuse me, mister. Can we get our ball?' The man looked up from his newspaper and smiled. 'Of course you can, but be careful.' Joey and I scrambled down the garden side of the fence and I grabbed the ball from the branches. 'Thanks,' I shouted and we turned to ascend the fence back to our own world. Then one of the boys in the garden piped up. 'Mother! Look! That boy is wearing my jacket!' I turned and saw that the boy was pointing at me and my yellow satin bomber. His mother smiled reassuringly at him. 'It's okay, dear. I donated it to the jumble ages ago. It was getting too small for you.' I looked at Joey to check if he had heard and my face burned with shame when I saw by his grin that he had. I scrambled up the fence as fast as I could with those casually spoken words ringing in my ears. I had been exposed, not only as a liar – there was no rich kindly uncle in America – but worse, as someone who wore jumble-sale clothes. Other people's cast-offs. The shame and humiliation of such exposure when you are a kid is indescribably terrible. Of course Joey couldn't wait to tell all the others on the estate and I became a figure of fun. They called me 'tramp' and 'dosser'. I had gone from the well-liked kid with the magical jacket to outcast and target of ridicule in very short order.

I ran off on my own up to Tooting Bec Common and just wandered around for a while wishing I was dead. I took off the jacket and stuffed it down a drain. When I got back home that evening I told my mum that I had lost it at the swimming baths. A week later I waited in the darkness of the porch in Joey Finn's block, and when he came out I hit him around the head with a cricket stump. I've had major problems with humiliation ever since. So I too, like Billy Bullshit, had set out to make the world take notice of me and to let everyone know that I was not some insignificant speck that could be pushed around. But, unlike Billy, I didn't just do it in a fantasy world. My way of getting noticed and putting my message across was through extreme violence and outrageous crimes.

Some of the men at Grendon were fantasists like Billy Bullshit, but that did not make them any less dangerous. Over half of those on C-wing were convicted murderers, and some, like Carrot Top, had more than one victim's blood on their hands. Sitting on wing meetings, listening to the seemingly casual introductions when the speakers gave their index offence – murder, manslaughter, rape, arson, armed robbery, grievous bodily harm, blackmail – I often wondered how straight-goers might view us.

Knowing that they were in a room crowded with men who were admitting such crimes with about as much emotion as you would put into a 'good morning', would probably have frightened and horrified the average person. I realized that I had spent the greater portion of my life surrounded by dangerous and sometimes evil men and I had fitted right in and thought little about it. What did this say about me? Before I had come to Grendon I had actually been more uncomfortable in the company of people who didn't have the odd dead body in their background. My literary agent, the author Will Self, had noticed this. He wrote a piece for the *Independent* just before my book was published and described our first meeting.

I had been out of prison about three weeks when ex-'Public Enemy Number 1' turned journalist, John McVicar, phoned me to say that he had passed one of my short stories to his mate Will Self, who was interested in meeting me. I had heard of Will while I was in prison and often read his articles and columns in the broadsheets and found them very amusing. His use of strange and unfamiliar – to me at least – words was interesting to a novice writer with a thirst for knowledge like myself, so when John phoned and asked me if I was interested in going to Will's house for dinner I said okay. I thought John was going to be there too, but when I turned up on that summer's evening, the day after Princess Diana died, he was not. Will was very charming, welcomed me into his home and introduced me to his wife and his guests, all straight-goers with good jobs in the literary world. I had not the slightest idea how to behave around straight people, I didn't know how to talk to them or interact on any level; I was lost. The only things I would usually say to straight people with good jobs – 'Hand over the money or I'll blow your fucking head off', or 'Not guilty, yer honour' – did not seem appropriate in the circumstances, so I decided to keep my mouth shut and say as little as possible. I must have been the dullest dinner guest ever. When Will wrote about our meeting six years later, I was surprised to see that he described me as 'painfully shy'. I had never thought of myself as shy, especially as I had spent my life crashing into crowded banks and taking over in a few seconds. I had just been so immersed in the criminal world, so deep in it, that straight people were like aliens to me. I had no understanding of them.

The good thing about having a book published is that it can broaden your social circle, even if you are locked up in jail at the time. I received a lot of letters from people who had read the book but had no connection with the criminal world whatsoever, other established writers and budding writers, normal straight-going men and women. And pretty soon it dawned on me that these were beginning to outnumber the criminals and prisoners I was in contact with. I was pulling away from my previous life in many ways, moving forward instead of looking back. This would be my world when I eventually was released, the straight world, and I was starting to acclimatize myself to it.

18. The Wall

After I had been at Grendon for over a year we were informed in community meetings that the Home Office had decided to take down the perimeter wall and replace it with a double fence. The wall at Grendon was in a bad state of disrepair, crumbling in some places, and they had been talking about replacing it for some years. Grendon is a category B prison and there is not another category B prison in the country that has fences rather than a wall so this led to the inevitable round of rumours. Without a wall how could Grendon remain a category B jail? It was unprecedented. And if it was to be downgraded to category C, what was going to happen to the vast majority of inmates who were category B? There has long been a feeling at Grendon, with some justification, that the rest of the prison system would rather see it disappear for good. Grendon was pretty much an embarrassment for the rest of the system as it had the lowest reconviction rates of any Category B prison and did its job without resorting to a rigid security regime, boots, batons and the liquid cosh. It didn't even have a punishment block. The message had been loud and clear for over four decades: you can rehabilitate the most violent criminals by treating them like individuals and getting to the root of their problems. But the system generally refused to hear it.

Now we feared that the removal of the wall was part of a plan to get rid of Grendon altogether. The system has previous for changing the direction of a prison at the drop of a hat. In 1993 HMP Send was a thriving open category C prison for men until one day everyone was shipped out to category B Highdown at a few hours' notice. HMP Send was closed down for a couple of weeks and then reopened as a female prison. The same happened to HMP Downview, which had been regarded by prisoners as one of the best category C prisons in the country, and that too reopened as a female prison. HMP Maidstone, which had been a category B prison for over 100 years, suddenly became a category C and the category B inmates were dispersed to other jails across the country. So it's not as if it had never happened before. The governors and staff assured us that, other than the wall coming down, there were no plans to change Grendon's regime or direction. Being a suspicious bastard myself I was not so sure. In any case, work on the wall and the new fences was going to mean a lot of disruption and a step-up in security. We found out afterwards that there had been some serious discussion about shipping everyone out until the work was completed as it would be too much of a security risk to have prisoners in a jail where this kind of operation was going on. In the event the security department were given a free rein for the first time in Grendon's history and, believe me, those anal-retentive fake policemen made the most of it. What they did was turn Grendon into one of the most restrictive regime prisons in the system.

The security department at Grendon usually had very little to do compared to their counterparts at any other high-security prison – and how that must have grated on them. The kind of people who are attracted to the security departments of prisons are those who tend to be suspicious of humanity by nature and see plots and intrigues wherever they look, particularly among prisoners whom they think are all criminal master-minds just waiting for their chance to rise up and slaughter the innocents. I have seen many examples over the years that confirm this belief, including one security PO at HMP Albany. Finding a prisoner who had died from a heart attack in his cell ten hours earlier, this screw insisted that he be handcuffed to the stiffening body for the ambulance ride to the local hospital 'in case it's some sort of escape plan'. The security department at HMP Belmarsh refused to allow a video of the TV programme *The X Files* to be shown to prisoners because it concerned telekinesis and 'They may gain the knowledge of how to dismantle locks with the power of the mind, and that would be a serious security breach.' These are the same kind of people who refused to allow bananas as part of the prison diet for over forty years because they thought that prisoners might dry out the skins and smoke them to gain an illegal high! When was the last time you heard of someone entering a rehab clinic to beat their addiction to banana skins?

The planned removal of the wall gave Grendon security staff a licence to spring to life and begin issuing diktats on our day-to-day life. We would no longer be able to take our daily exercise in the yard or play football or jog, but would be caged off in a space between each wing that looked like a bombsite. The visits garden, which had long been a feature of the relaxed atmosphere of visits in the prison, was to be closed until further notice. Red-band inmates, who had achieved a position of trust through their long and hard work, would in future be escorted in the grounds by a member of uniformed staff.

Even though all this and more was going on, the therapeutic work was still being carried out in the wings. Taff was up to his old tricks again. Since moving on to the ground floor I had had little to do with Taff. He was no longer in my face from the minute I opened my door in the morning and that suited me just fine. But he was a bully and bullies need victims to make themselves feel good. A little inoffensive Scotsman who would probably get blown away in a strong breeze was the weird Welshman's next victim. Wee Dog was the laundry man on C-wing. A sickly young fella doing five years for burglary, he had a lot of problems, suffering from every known allergy from hay fever to lactose intolerance. He could die just by eating a peanut. Wee Dog had probably never had a fight in his life but he did a pretty good impression of someone who couldn't be pushed about. He did the laundry for everyone on C-wing in a small room next to the main office and basically minded his own business. The rules concerning laundry on C-wing were simple: the laundry man did the washing of a different landing every day but in the evenings it was a free-for-all and anyone could use the washer and drier. Taff had a habit of strolling into the laundry room and using the machines whenever he felt like it and this jarred with Wee Dog who felt that the big Welshman was taking the piss out of him.

After telling Taff a couple of times he shouldn't be using the machines for his own wash during the day, Wee Dog got the hump. Emboldened by Grendon's no-violence rule he decided to lay it on the line for Taff, and told him in no uncertain terms and strong language that he should stay out of the laundry and let him get on with his job. Taff started his rolling eyes, don't-fuck-with-me-I'm-hard act and Wee Dog's arsehole dropped right out. Seeing that he was terrified was grist for Taff's bully mill and he couldn't resist grinding it a bit more, standing over Wee Dog in a threatening manner and verbally abusing and threatening him. Wee Dog was so terrified that he did not let on about the incident for weeks. But finally he told his group what had happened. Taff was put up for his commitment for a threat of violence and intimidation, and once more the C-wing community sat in judgement. The thing about Taff was that he was very crafty and manipulative. He had one third of the wing terrified, one third thinking he was just misunderstood and the staff on his side. I was one of the remaining one third who could see right through him like a just-cleaned window. Unfortunately, one of the things that worked in his favour was the fact that the people who knew what he was all about were also those who had lived their lives by criminal rules and the main one of these said that you didn't stick anyone in the shit with the authorities. In the system we would have quickly dealt with Taff ourselves without getting the authorities involved. He would have been cut or scalded and run off the wing to seek protection in the Rule 43 wing. But Grendon did not allow us to work in that way any more and their alternative did not sit comfortably with us, so the likes of Taff got a bye.

In his commitment hearing he managed to push all the right buttons, explaining his behaviour towards Wee Dog as a shameful aberration that had occurred only because he himself was struggling with difficult therapeutic issues. He shed a few tears and promised it would never happen again. Though I hated the man even I couldn't bring myself to vote him out, and the vote went in his favour. He had got away with it again. There is a strong school of thought among men at Grendon, one which I personally subscribe to, that the psychologists and therapists love a 'case'. That is, when they come across some anomaly in a prisoner that makes him an interesting case study, they are willing to bend or disregard the rules in order to allow them to study him at leisure. It doesn't matter what sort of mayhem he may be wreaking on the community as long as the therapists and psychologists can get a good long look at him and maybe write about it. I believe that this is how it was with Taff, Billy Bullshit, Kevin, Scaredy Cat and others. What fucked Kevin in the end as a case study was that he became overtly active and violent, but even then they kept him long past his sell-by date. But Taff's days at Grendon were numbered and he would soon be leaving. For me and others it wouldn't be a minute too soon. I had spent far too much time daydreaming about knocking on his cell door and weighing him in with a few choice punches and headbutts, and that wasn't healthy at all.

Fred was very into his gym and had passed many certificates in all aspects of physical exercise. He was now doing a degree in personal fitness training and part of his course involved him training people and showing results. He asked me if I would help him out by letting him train me and I agreed. I was forty-three years old, 17½ stone and smoked sixty roll-ups a day. The last time I had taken any regular gym exercise had been in 1992, when I had been twelve years younger and 3½ stone lighter, so I imagined Fred was going to have his work cut out for him. But I was willing to get back into shape if I could and I knew Fred was good at what he did, so I trusted him to take care of me.

When we started on our training regime Scouse Mark was also with us, but he got ghosted after a couple of weeks. Under Fred's guidance I was soon on a sensible diet and training five days a week. I liked the treadmill and rowing machine in the gym, but my favourite was the boxing training and sparring we did in an empty group room on the wing in the evenings. Ray, a keen boxer himself, had made a set of pads out of an old training mat and Fred had a pair of Lonsdale mitts we could use. I never felt more alive than when we were doing a good ten-round sparring session or throwing punches at the pads. Mark had a punch on him like a mule's kick and Fred, having boxed semi-professionally, was fast and powerful. I quickly regained my former love for physical exercise and pretty soon I was feeling better than I had in years and had lost 1½ stone in weight. But disaster was about to strike on the academic front and it would force me to put the training on the back burner for a while.

One day I was writing a letter to a friend of mine on my word processor and was just about to save it when the electricity went out. It proved to be a temporary power cut that affected the whole nick. When the power came back on I noticed that I could not access any of the work on my disk. I tried several different things but a message kept coming up on the screen that read: 'Disk incorrectly formatted or damaged.' This was a bit worrying as we were only allowed the one disk in possession – security rules again – and my disk had around ten months' work stored on it: seven chapters of this book, all my work for the two journalism courses I was doing, several short stories, five chapters of a novel I was writing and all my letters, as well as a couple of unfinished journalism articles. At first I didn't understand how serious this was. Not having a lot of experience with computers, I just assumed that anything could be retrieved. I spoke to some of the men on the wing, including Daran and Mel, who worked on the PICTA course about computers and their maintenance. After much trying, they concluded that my work was lost for ever. One of the instructors on the course unhelpfully suggested that he could try sending the disk to the FBI headquarters as they were experts in getting information from damaged disks. He said it could take up to four years and cost $10,000. I gave him the look I reserve for imbeciles and sentencing judges. There was nothing for it, I would have to start all over again, and that meant things such as my training regime with Fred would have to be sacrificed for now.

In the next three months I spent a lot of association time in my cell trying to catch up, which kept me out of most of the stuff that was going on in the wing. I still went to my group and community meetings every morning and I put aside an hour in the evening when Fred and Ray could come down for a coffee and fill me in on what was happening up on the landings. We had a couple of difficult characters in group 3 in Tony, the stalker, and Candy, the cross-dressing rapist, who were both in denial of their crimes and behaviour. In some ways the group managed a breakthrough with Tony, or so we thought, but he was such a deep and unfathomable character that it was hard going all the way. I think he particularly hated me and Fred because we asked him the most difficult questions. I had kept on at him for months to change his name back to the original name he had been given by his parents rather than the trophy name he had taken to remind him of his first stalking victim. Finally one day Tony announced to the group that he had instructed a solicitor and that he had signed the final form to get his old name back. Everyone saw this as a major shift in Tony's attitude and I was particularly pleased that my hammering at him had paid off. But Tony was a lot sneakier than we gave him credit for.

In order to get anything at Grendon – a new job, a reduction in category, a temporary release or anything else important – we had to go through a process known as 'backing'. First, you had to raise your request at a group meeting and be questioned as to why you wanted whatever it was you were asking for. If your group decided to back you, the next move was to take your request to the community and ask for backing from the whole wing. There would be more questions and then the chairman would call for a show of hands for the backing. If the community backed you, then it would be discussed by the staff group, and if they backed you too, you were home free. It sounds like a lot of palaver but it worked and helped to keep all decisions and requests open and honest. Most backings were mere formalities and it was only when you were asking for something unusual or therapeutically unsound that you could run into trouble.

One morning Tony asked group 3 for backing to apply for the education red-band job. While the wall repairs were going on, the red-bands who worked in the grounds had lost a lot of their freedom of movement but the education red-band was an inside job consisting of a bit of cleaning and helping out in the education block. Knowing that this involved working in close proximity with female civilian staff such as teachers and clerical workers, some of us in the group expressed concerns that Tony, with his history of stalking women, was applying for the post. He put up a good argument but I was not convinced and said so. Some of the group thought that he should be given the job as it would be a good test for him. I was adamant that he should not, and managed to put forward such a good argument that I split the group. In the end it was classed as a partial backing but that we should discuss it again at a later date. Tony wasn't happy and the way he glared at me I was glad that I wasn't a woman. But I thought no more about it.

A couple of weeks later I had to miss a community meeting due to an optician's appointment. As I was not there and our facilitator, Brian, was also off sick, Tony took this opportunity to try for wing backing for the red-band job. He worded it craftily, as though he were going for an education cleaner's job and only on a temporary basis to help out. He managed to get wing backing. When I heard that he had succeeded, I was nonplussed. I asked Fred how it had happened and he told me, 'You know what it's like when you go for a job backing on the wing, no one really puts up any resistance.' On a wing backing you only had to have a majority show of hands. I figured that the staff team would never give him backing anyway, but it turned out that Tony had picked his moment well to apply for their backing because not only was Brian missing but our wing therapist was also away on leave. And that's how he managed to slip into the job. But security knocked him back for the actual red-band and gave him the non-existent title of assistant red-band. Tony was happier than a dog with two dicks and I just chalked it up to experience. I had too much work of my own to worry about Tony.

Six months after Tony took up his post in the education department I started to hear things that were a bit disturbing: 'Have you seen Tony's office? Lord Tony's proper built himself a little empire down at the education block!' I decided to have a look when I went down to take my NUJ course on Monday afternoon. Sure enough, Tony had commandeered one of the smaller classrooms on the ground floor and turned it into an office, complete with his own computer, printer, desk, swivel chair and pin board. He even had a space to entertain guests, with a coffee table and chairs, and a kettle. Some people found it amusing, but having heard about his behaviour first-hand in the group I recognized it as a sign of a return to his old habits. By now I had been at Grendon long enough to have a good grasp of therapy and to spot certain behaviours in my fellow men and know that this could be a warning of something developing. As I mentioned before, Tony had a very officious and superior manner, having spent so long giving orders and being in charge in the navy. He didn't even class himself as a criminal and thought he was above everyone else in prison because he had come from a comfortable middle-class background. I noticed that sometimes when the likes of Fred, Dave and me spoke about our rough and ready childhoods in poverty and our criminal behaviour Tony had a disdainful look on his face as if we were some sort of Dickensian street urchins and he were a top-hatted toff with a silk hanky at his nose. I believed that deep down he had not one jot of remorse for his crimes and that he was still convinced he had been right no matter what anyone said. And because of his self-righteous beliefs he could quite easily make the same mistakes and commit the same crimes again without even a twinge of conscience. Tony was almost religiously fanatical in his beliefs and that was always dangerous.

There were a few females working in the education department but the one who stood out was the new girl, Sheryl, who was assistant to the head of education. Sheryl was young, around twenty-four, good-looking and a little shy. As you might expect, she was a bit unsure about working in a category B prison full of violent men, and it showed. She was the perfect victim for Tony and he made a beeline for her almost from day one. He wasn't the kind of predator who would jump out of a bush and attack a woman – not at first anyway. He was much more subtle than that. He interpreted mundane words and deeds by his victim as signals that only he could see and understand. For example, very early on Sheryl happened to ask Tony during a teabreak if she could try one of his herbal teabags. In Tony's mind this meant that she was interested in him and was trying to make an approach. This was how Tony's illness, because when you come right down to it that's what it was, an illness, worked. He had brought the teabag incident to the group and used it as an example of how he was now thinking in a different way from his past thought processes. He told us that far from the teabag incident stoking up his twisted ego, it had made him realize that he didn't have to take everything at more than face value. Despite the positive spin he put on this, I thought it was pretty sinister that he had even mentioned it at all.

Tony had so immersed himself in the day-to-day more mundane and tedious tasks that the staff were glad to see the back of, that he had made himself indispensable. Looked at from a dispassionate viewpoint, it was fascinating to see how he had infiltrated himself until nobody thought it strange that he had a fully equipped office in a pushed-for-space department and was issuing memos for supplies and for the works department to come and fit cupboards and shelves. He was also sending notes and memos to Sheryl, some of which were a bit flirty. It was clear that Tony, in his own mind at least, was no longer a prisoner serving a life sentence for stalking and attempted murder, but was an equal, if not superior, employee in the education department, and possibly on the verge of trying to start up an office romance with one of the juniors.

Out in the real world these first steps by Tony had inevitably led to rejection by the object of his desires, something he was unable to accept given the fantasies he had woven in his mind. With two of the women the result had been reigns of terror as Tony proceeded to stalk them, one for over eight years and the other until he burst into her home and tried to kill her. I can only assume, albeit from some strong circumstantial evidence, that he was lining Sheryl up as his next victim until events overtook him. One afternoon a couple of security staff took him from his office in the education department and walked him back to C-wing for a full search. One of the female teachers had been looking in Tony's office for some missing paperwork when she had come across a box of files, which turned out to be the CVs and personal details, including phone numbers and home addresses, of every civilian member of staff in the education department. Put this kind of information together with the average prisoner and you have the makings of a serious security breach; put it together with one of the most prolific and notorious stalkers in the country and it becomes ten times more serious.

In Tony's cell the search uncovered incriminating items that in any other nick would have seen him in a sweatbox out of the prison before his glasses had demisted: a notebook listing times that education started, radio call signs, exact timings of staff movements and observations on various education staff. Tony was suspended from his job immediately and an investigation was started. He was in for a rough ride from the group and I made sure I was at the forefront of it. Tony's explanation was that the whole thing was a mistake. He had no idea the box of files containing such sensitive information was in the room, he didn't know how it got there and he had never set eyes on it. We had noticed that whenever Tony was put under any serious pressure his face and neck had a tendency to light up in uneven red blotches and now he was glowing like a stop sign. I was determined to bring up the underhand tactics he had used to get the job in education in the first place and to find out if there had been anything untoward in his thoughts about Sheryl. Tony was dodging and jinking like a Premiership centre-forward, fending off every challenge and enquiry with protestations of innocence. In the end he started to get the hump with my strong questions and tried to give me the fish eye. I sat forward in my chair and stared at him. 'Listen, Tony,' I said, calmly, 'I've been intimidating people all my life. I done it for a living. So don't think you can stop this by trying to eyeball me. It won't work, I'm not a woman, so stop your fucking about and think about the shit you've dropped yourself in.' Tony realized that he had strayed on to dangerous ground and quickly took a step back. If I am to be honest I must admit that I quite enjoyed getting people like Tony on the ropes with a good verbal and therapeutic bashing. I was starting to enjoy it almost as much as I used to enjoy the physical fights I'd had. I knew that questioning and challenging from a therapeutic angle was supposed to help the recipient to understand his actions and that it wasn't supposed to be relished quite as much as I was relishing it. But I think I had a good balance; I was always calm and never really nasty in my challenges, did not rant and rave, but was firm and genuinely interested in the answers and I listened to them. I also expected to be treated in exactly the same way when I did unacceptable things. Some people find their way through therapy by pussyfooting around the issues but I preferred the head-on approach.

Tony took a verbal mauling from group 3, then another from the whole community, but he remained in denial. I half thought that the staff group might ask for a commitment vote on him once the investigation had been completed. The investigation could prove nothing solid against Tony, however, particularly as he was still not sticking his hands up to anything, but they sacked him from the education job and tightened up security even further. He had fucked himself no matter what the investigation said. His record as a lifer would be put in front of the Parole Board whenever he came to be considered for release and something like this never looked good or inspired trust. It didn't matter that nothing had been proved, just the suspicion was enough; it always has been for every prisoner. He had also shown that he still had a massive amount of work to do on himself in the group. And the group would not forget it. I would make sure of that.

One of Tony's closest friends on C-wing, Scaredy Cat, was also in trouble once again and this time he couldn't wriggle out of it by putting on his little-boy act. Some of the new and stronger members in Scaredy Cat's group were starting to flex their therapeutic muscles by challenging senior members of the group and Scaredy Cat was next in line after they had got rid of Billy Bullshit. One of the new members of group I was a big Northerner doing life for a gangland murder – Brian, or the Big Fat Fry-up-eating Geordie, as I was to know him when we became friends. Now Brian was weeding out the therapeutic weak links in the group. He put Scaredy Cat up for another commitment vote, citing his lack of work and interest in the group. Scaredy Cat was in serious trouble, but he only had five months left to serve on his sentence and then he would be released. When it came to the vote many senior community members remembered Scaredy Cat's previous chances, and he was voted out of Grendon for lack of commitment. This was one of the scariest times of Scaredy Cat's life. Now crimes against women and children are severely punished by other prisoners in their own special ways. Scaredy Cat knew, as we all did, that if he had to go into the system on normal location he would probably at the least be beaten up because of his crime. At worst, he could get a taste of what he gave his victim and have hot fat thrown in his face. Terrified, he really turned on the poor-me performance, complete with rivers of tears. But the community were not wearing it; we wanted him out. I suggested he should be sent to HMP Swaleside, a particularly violent category B prison in Kent, and he wailed in fear and despair. I had said it only for the crack, and because of that nasty spiteful little piece of me that still wanted to see men like Scaredy Cat get what they deserved. The meeting finished with him crying like a baby and shaking like a jelly, but it was very hard to feel sorry for him as he had been playing us for fools for over two years.

In a somewhat surprising development the staff team did not back the community's vote. They wanted Scaredy Cat to stay on C-wing because they had been monitoring him for some time and were in the process of engaging a top psychiatrist to assess his risk levels. This was serious. If the psychiatrist concluded that Scaredy Cat still remained a serious danger to the public, he could be detained even after his sentence had finished. In the meantime, the staff team arranged for him to have some intense one-to-one sessions with his psychologist/facilitator Helen. The community took the news calmly. It was a bit annoying that the staff had gone against our vote, but what they were proposing was much more serious. If Scaredy Cat didn't start catching up he could end up being held indefinitely. I wouldn't wish extra bird on anyone, but men like Scaredy Cat reap what they sow.

On a cold February morning in 2005 the peace of Grendon and the surrounding Buckinghamshire countryside was shattered by the sounds of mechanical diggers and dump-trucks rolling into the prison. The 42-year-old wall was coming down and we were in for five months of noise and disruption. Over the months the work on the wall went on, security became even more busy and intrusive. Gates that had previously been kept open to allow the freedom of movement on corridors and through the education department were kept locked. F-wing yard, which had so impressed me with its openness and freedom when I had arrived from Whitemoor, was caged off and became just a patch of concrete with no view other than the thick steel fence. For those who thought the removal of the wall was going to lead to a more open feel, all this was bitter disappointment and men became more and more unhappy. I was asked, by some of the lads on C and other wings, to put some of our feelings down on paper and convey them to the number 1 governor. Unfortunately before I had a chance to finish my plea for less interference from security someone on A-wing attempted an escape. The man, a lifer, had been tempted by the removal of the wall and had decided to dig out of his cell in a bid for freedom. Working through the night, he had made a hole in the wall using a metal radio aerial to dig the mortar from between the bricks. The cell wall was too thick to get through in one go, so he had covered the hole with cardboard and moved a chair in front of it to try to disguise it until the next evening, but it had been discovered during the daily fabric check. This was the first escape attempt at Grendon in four years and it couldn't have come at a worse moment. I could fully understand any prisoner's yearning for freedom and I could begrudge no one an attempt to escape as I had tried so many times myself in the past, but the hole in the wall was just what the security department needed in order to seize the reins.

Because of the incident there was the usual lock-down and plenty of rumours about full prison searches and ship-outs. During the lock-down

I carried on writing my plea for less security but I wasn't hopeful of getting an unbiased hearing for it now. Sure enough the prison was searched, including every cell on every wing, but there was none of the heavy-handedness and wanton destruction of personal property I had come to expect in other prisons. And when we were let out of lock-down we discovered that there had been several ship-outs, but all from A-wing. I had been worried that if it came to ship-outs I would definitely be top of the list because of my history, so it was nice to see that they were now dropping me out. It showed me that I was no longer as high profile within prison as I had once been and that was a good thing.

In March Grendon had a visit from Prisons Minister Paul Goggins, and he spent some time on C-wing for a Q&A session. According to the governor, Goggins had been the minister who had ordered the enquiry into the release of my first book. I decided to try to pin him down on a question that was in the mind of every category B prisoner at Grendon. 'Mr Goggins,' I said, 'we know that there are no category B prisons in the prison estate that have a fence instead of a wall, so can you tell us if you or the Home Office have any plans to change the direction of HMP Grendon and perhaps turn it into a category C prison?' The community room fell silent as we waited for his response. The minister assured us that the removal of the wall was just one more way in which Grendon would preserve its unique status within the prison system. He finished with these words: 'You have my personal promise that HMP Grendon will have no change in security classification after the wall is removed.' This was good enough for us. We knew all about not being able to trust politicians but I personally was reassured that he had uttered his promise in front of a reporter from the *Guardian* who was there to cover his visit. But the double fence and caged-off areas had changed Grendon and made it feel, somehow, more like a prison. To us it was further confirmation that Grendon could only get worse.

19. Addiction

One morning in my group I started to talk about my time in the juvenile prison system of the 1970s. My first taste of incarceration had been at HM Detention Centre Send, in Surrey, where I had been beaten, brutalized and humiliated by the staff as part of the short-lived 'short sharp shock' doctrine. I told the group, some of whom had similar experiences, how I had been punched around by the staff and made to stand naked in front of them for hours. I hadn't realized just how much this experience had affected my whole life and attitudes until I began to speak about it. I had rebelled at Send, attacking a screw with a shovel when I could take no more, and this had hardened my resolve to fight all forms of authority in any way I could in the future. At the age of sixteen I was sentenced to three years' detention in the borstal system and here too I fought authority. I was beaten on many occasions, injected with psychotropic drugs against my will, put in straitjackets and padded cells, as well as spending months in solitary confinement in underground cells. When I was finally released I tried to erase my pain and confusion by getting further involved in crime and violence, and by binge drinking.

In my autobiography I had somehow glossed over my drinking, but for four years between 1979 and 1983 drink was a major problem for me. I came from hard-drinking Irish stock – the kind of men who would class you as a dirty raving junkie for smoking the odd spliff but saw nothing wrong with knocking back eighteen pints of beer and fighting anyone who came into view. I had played down my drink problem, not only to other people but also to myself. With hindsight I understand that drink was one of the means I used to blot out my life. I wasn't a steady drinker, I would consume anything I could get my hands on as quickly as possible. And this led to many more problems. I would get steaming drunk and do some terrible things. Most of the time I was a vicious and nasty drunk. No singing and dancing for me when I was in my cups, rather I would be snarling and growling and looking to stick a glass in someone's face.

The worst thing about being in thrall to drink or drugs is that you just do not see it at the time. I didn't fully acknowledge the extent of my drink

problem until I started talking about it in therapy and began to hear what
others had to say about it. Once, on remand in Pentonville prison for a
drink-related assault, I did wonder whether I might be an alcoholic. I
decided to attend one of the Alcoholics Anonymous groups they held in
that jail, mainly because it was a chance to get out of the cell for an hour,
but also because I was curious. HMP Pentonville at that time had some
men with serious drink problems which bore no comparison to the one
I wasn't even sure I had. I sat there listening as men described how they
would crash head-first through off-licence windows in order to get hold
of a drink, or go into Superdrug and guzzle aftershave straight off the
shelves for its alcohol content. I left that AA meeting feeling that there
was no way I could be an alcoholic as I had never gone that far for a drink.
I failed to see that, in its own way, my drinking was just as much of a
problem. A lot of my fighting was done under the influence of drink and
I could become almost suicidal with it. I would think nothing of steaming
into three or four men at once, not because I was brave but because I was
uncaring about my own safety. Other times I would take a beating when
I didn't need to. I remember once calling on a fight outside the Charlie
Chaplin pub at the Elephant and Castle with a fella who was rumoured
to be some sort of karate expert and then just standing there and telling
him to take his best shots. I didn't even try to defend myself. I was so full
of self-loathing that I must have thought I deserved the beating. I can
now understand that drink didn't make me like this; it was already in me,
and drink just allowed it to come out. To use a psychiatric term, I was
very fucked up.

I hid in an alcoholic haze for years, wandering around lashing out at
anything I bumped into, including my own reflection. And then one day
I'd had enough. It may sound strange but getting back into serious crime
was the saving of me. If I had not once again become a professional
criminal, I could easily have become one of those men I had encountered
at the AA meeting in Pentonville and I might not be here today. Self-
destruction via alcohol had become too slow for me and getting back into
crime would speed things up. Of course this was not a conscious decision.
At the time I had no idea that I was trying hard to destroy myself, I just
carried on banging my nut against the wall, only I speeded the action up.
I guess returning to armed robbery was a roundabout way of putting my
life, or death, in the hands of someone else. I was fully aware of the very
real dangers involved in this career path. Every time I stepped out on to

the streets in possession of a firearm I was making myself a target for other men with guns. I can see things so clearly now: how I would spend every penny I robbed as if I was having one final party, how my armed robberies started coming at ever shorter intervals, until at one stage I robbed three banks in one day. How I would never simply stick my hands up and surrender when ambushed by armed police, I always had to push my luck and try for the getaway. I can remember just before I was due to be sentenced for the fourteen bank robberies I had committed while on the run from prison in 1992, I was being interviewed by a probation officer who had to make a report for the courts. She looked at the bundle of evidence photographs of me on various bank robberies and shook her head. 'You have a death wish, don't you?' she said suddenly. I laughed out loud and denied it, but she was closer to the truth than even I knew.

Working through therapy at Grendon allowed me to see all these things that I had kept deep inside me for the greater portion of my life. I came to understand my actions in a way that I never had. And just like one of those puzzles where you have to stare at a jumble of shapes and make out the picture within, once you can see the picture you can never again un-see it. Grendon was working for me. In the usual ebb and flow of prison life, a few of the lads I had come through F-wing with were either gone or on their way. Kevin was in Bullingdon, Ritchie was back in Long Lartin, Scouse Mark was in Stafford, Bug-eyed Bob had gone to Kingston, and Daran had put his papers in. Putting your papers in was another custom that was unique to Grendon. In most nicks you could leave in one of two ways: either by being ghosted for some real or perceived wrongdoing, or by getting a progressive transfer for good behaviour. Either way you would have little input into when or where you were going. You couldn't just wake up one morning and decide that you were leaving. But because Grendon was purely voluntary there was a process for deciding you wanted to leave and this was known as 'putting your papers in'.

Daran had a life sentence with a judge's recommendation that he serve a minimum of twenty years, so, realistically, he could expect to do at least five years over the minimum. He had been at Grendon for two years but he still had a minimum of ten years to serve and knew that there was no way he could be downgraded to even category C for a number of years yet. Plus he had always struggled to get his visits at Grendon, so he decided that it would be better for him if he were to apply for a transfer to HMP Kingston, which is in Portsmouth. As he was an ex-navy man, a lot of

Daran's old friends lived in Pompey and he would be sweet for regular visits if he was situated there. His partner, Clare, was still in the Royal Navy and was based in Portsmouth. I had met her on a Family Day visit and she was a lovely girl who must have had a serious commitment to Daran to still be visiting him after he had served over a decade in prison. Daran came to see me privately to tell me that he was thinking about leaving Grendon. He gave me his reasons and I had to agree that his thinking was sound. I told him that he had to do what he thought would be best for him; no one can do your sentence for you in prison. I would be gutted to see him go, I had become very close friends with this big psychopathic ex-Legionnaire and I would miss him. We said our goodbyes in that reserved and slightly ridiculous way that men of violence who have bonded do, by taking the piss out of each other with vicious banter, and Daran went off to call a special and inform his group of his decision.

Putting your papers in was a bit of a tedious process. First you had to tell your group and facilitator. Then you would be called in for an interview with the wing therapist who would want to know your reasons for wishing to leave therapy. The therapist would inevitably try his best to talk you into staying and cite the therapeutic work you had done and still needed to do. If you were adamant in your desire to leave, you would have to go back to your group and they would be given a crack at trying to convince you to stay. After that you had to take your decision to the full community in a meeting and be questioned on whether you were doing the right thing. You could usually judge someone's popularity on C-wing by the amount of time people spent trying to convince him to stay. Bug-eyed Bob, for instance, had put his papers in the month before Daran and the wing barely wasted ten minutes on him. It was all 'good luck' and 'if that's what you want'. With Daran things seemed to go on for weeks before the community finally accepted that he really had made his mind up.

The wing seemed a little emptier without Daran for a while, but prison life has a tendency to harden men's outlook when it comes to parting. In other nicks you could be talking to someone and ten minutes later they might be ghosted to another prison. In jail you quickly learn to treat any friendship as a transitory thing. But I knew that whenever I got out I would definitely be going to visit Daran and some of the other friends I had made at Grendon. Daran ended up in Kingston prison, but, unfortunately for him, both Bug-eyed Bob and Billy Bullshit were also there. It seemed as though Daran was one of those blokes who don't have a lot of luck.

By the time he left Grendon Bug-eyed Bob had become something of a detested figure on C-wing. The thing about Grendon was that spending enough time there tended to bring out your real character and personality for all to see. This is not too bad if you emerge even half likeable, but some people have no character and very little personality, and Bug-eyed Bob was one of these. He was snide, selfish, always moaning and had a kind of transparent rat-like cunning. One of the big things that turned the community against him was when he decided that it might be to his advantage to use therapy to try to get an appeal against his conviction. He carefully worked it so that he pretended he had been carrying a heavy secret in the eight years since he had been convicted and dropped enough hints to make his group curious enough to try to winkle it out of him. Over a couple of months he gradually brought out a story that was as see-through as it was ridiculous. He claimed that he had not committed the murder he had been convicted of and that in fact it was his brother who was the real killer. He maintained he had kept quiet through the trial and in all the years since out of a sense of family loyalty, but now he wanted to come clean and put the truth out there. Apart from the fact that Bug-eyed Bob didn't even know how to spell the word loyalty, his story had too many holes in it.

He claimed that he had admitted the murder to protect his brother, when it turned out he had pleaded not guilty at his trial. He even went so far as to say he was now willing to speak to the police in order to tell them what his brother had done and would be prepared to stand up in court and give evidence against him. The reasons for Bug-eyed Bob's new claims were twofold: one, he might be able to get a retrial if enough mud were thrown at his brother, or at worst a reduction in his tariff, and two, he envied the fact that his brother was doing very well, having settled down with a wife and family, while Bob was rotting in jail with no foreseeable out. But the group did not wear it for a second. Bob was severely questioned and challenged on his new story and it just did not add up. He spent a couple of long sessions in the therapist's office before coming to the group and saying that, even though he had been telling the truth, he was going to drop the story about his brother. Bug-eyed Bob tried to make it sound as though he was making some sort of noble sacrifice to protect his family, but as it was he who had brought the story up in the first place, that didn't quite ring true. After that he was finished in the community. Any man who would try to stick his innocent brother in the shit in the hope that he might reduce his own load was not worthy of anyone's respect or consideration. Bob saw which way the wind was blowing and put his papers in.

One of the new members of C-wing community was another terrible character we called the Mincer. The Mincer was an HIV-positive very camp homosexual, serving a mandatory life sentence for a horrific murder. Coming from an upper-middle-class family somewhere in the north of England, the Mincer had been handed every advantage in life on a diamond-encrusted plate. He had been given an expensive public school education, when he had discovered he had an amazing talent for both the piano and the violin. Recognizing this musical genius in their midst people had gone out of their way to nurture him. He had been accepted at a top music school and given every opportunity to make something of himself. Gifted not only musically but also academically, the Mincer had it all. But he decided to run away to the gay scene in 1990s London, where he engaged in unprotected sex and drug-taking. Which just goes to show that intelligence does not always equate to common sense.

Once the Mincer had been diagnosed as HIV positive he was given accommodation in a small block of flats that had been mainly reserved for pensioners who were nearing the end of their lives. The Mincer, always a weak character, suddenly realized he was in a position of power and set out to vent his bitterness and spite on those around him who were little able to protect themselves. He held all-night parties in the block with music blaring into the early hours of the morning, and if any of the old people complained he would terrorize them with his acid tongue and his gay junkie entourage. He was heavily into crack-smoking and always short of money to fund his habit so he took to banging on the doors of his elderly neighbours in the early hours of the morning and 'asking' to borrow money from them. One regular victim of the Mincer's extortion was his next-door neighbour, an 89-year-old woman whom I shall call 'Mavis'. One morning at around 5 a.m. the Mincer, having run out of crack, banged on Mavis's door and demanded money. By this time Mavis probably decided she had had enough and had not lived through the Blitz only to be bullied and robbed by the Mincer, so she refused to give him any money. He pulled a knife and proceeded to stab her over 100 times in the face and body. He then stepped over the old woman's bleeding body and ransacked her flat in his quest for drug money. Not content with the damage he had already inflicted the Mincer took another knife from the kitchen and on his way out stopped long enough to cut Mavis's throat where she lay already dying on her own doorstep.

In yet another example of how the judiciary of this country seem to favour the privileged class even when it comes to murderers, the Mincer was given a twelve-year tariff – ridiculously short when you consider the details of his crime. Perhaps the judge thought the virus would kill the Mincer long before he completed his time in prison, particularly given the poor state of healthcare in our jails. But he was wrong. The Mincer served six years on the protection wings of a couple of prisons before applying to come to Grendon. Almost from the minute he touched down on C-wing he was mincing about with his nose in the air. He had an air of superiority and self-importance about him, as though he somehow felt he did not belong among common criminals, but would suffer them under duress. It was no surprise to anyone when he immediately palled up with Tony the Stalker and they became two-of-toast. They were both middle-class men who felt that they had been accidentally tipped into a station that did not befit them. And neither of them could accept that they had done anything to deserve their situation. Their arrogance was breath-taking. The Mincer made few friends on C-wing apart from Tony, as most found his camp but haughty manner at best an irritant. He had an opinion on just about everything and once he started talking he barely paused for breath. The Mincer had arrived on F-wing with one of my brothers-in-law, Jimmy Hogan, and had apparently got on well with him. Jimmy was the one who had nearly killed the rapist in HMP Whitemoor and had been sentenced to life on the day I came to Grendon. He had applied for Grendon but had not managed to survive the rigorous selection process on F-wing and had been shipped back to his sending establishment. So out of politeness I welcomed the Mincer to the wing and had a chat about how Jimmy had been on F-wing. Because of the Mincer's medical condition he was placed on the ground floor in the cell next door to me. When I found out the details of what he was in for I was shocked and sickened, but I did not openly blank him. By this time I had learned to accept that there were men at Grendon who had committed monstrous crimes and instead of concentrating on them I should look to my own work. I knew that just by being here most of them were trying to face up to what they had done and change their behaviour.

In the first couple of months he was next door to me I made no overt attempt to be friends with the Mincer but neither did I treat him any differently from the rest of the men on the wing who were outside my immediate close circle. I said good morning to him when the cell doors were opened every day and replied whenever he spoke to me, which was not often. To be perfectly honest I was not aware of any tension building between us, but I was soon to find that he felt differently. One morning I brought my six-monthly assessment to the community and after talking for a little while about how I reckoned I was doing at Grendon and what work I still had left to do, the floor was opened for questions. I was expecting a snipe from Taff and had prepared myself for it. Sure enough, he jumped in with both spiteful feet: 'I hear you've written some book thing? I've not read it and I don't want to read it, but do you think that makes you special or something?' His childish attempt to rile me was inept and I batted it off with a question of my own. 'I don't know, Taff, do you think I'm special? And if so, in what way?' He was fucked with that and began mumbling and stuttering until someone else cut in and asked a sensible question. I was inwardly satisfied that I had managed to deal calmly with Taff and gratified that he was fuming. I believed he was my only real enemy on the wing. A few community members asked some very constructive questions and I was just starting to relax when the Mincer piped up.

'I've been listening to what you have been saying,' he started. 'And, quite frankly, I'm appalled. You seem to have no grasp of exactly how dangerous you are to society. You are a hardened criminal, a gangster, with a long criminal record, who can sit here and glibly talk about your plans for the future and how you now empathize with your many victims. Having observed you since I have been on the wing I would say that you have not changed at all, you stomp around the wing putting out an aura of intimidation and frightening people. I see you as a thug and I think you will always be one.' I sat listening to him, my face reddening and my heart racing. I had an instant urge to get up and grab him by his skinny neck but I fought it. I took a deep breath and forced myself to calm down. The room was silent for a moment. I relaxed and leaned back in my chair. 'Okay,' I said, calmly. 'That's your opinion, mate, but I think you've got a brass neck calling me dangerous when you could wipe out half the wing with just a nose-bleed.' I knew this was way below the belt, but I couldn't stop myself. 'I understand that you must be very bitter about how your own life has panned out and that's probably why you choose to focus on me rather than concentrate on your own shit, but maybe you should try to sort out your own issues before you start throwing inaccurate and ill-thought-out accusations at other people. It's just a thought, mate, but what's really going on for you?' The Mincer stared at me in silence for a long few seconds and then, almost in slow motion, his face began to crumple and he let out a wail of anguish and self-pity. He leapt from his chair and ran sobbing from the community room in a flood of tears. I tried very hard to find a small piece of empathy for this man, but all I could see was his victim.

After the community meeting my pals congratulated me on how I had handled the assessment. 'That goes to show that therapy really is working for you now,' said Fred. 'At one stage I thought you were going to get out of the chair and give him a couple of right-handers, but you did the right thing. That's what therapy is all about, keeping calm, thinking about things and coming up with an alternative solution to the problem. Well done, mate.' I knew I had turned a therapeutic corner and been seen to do so. Before I had come to Grendon anyone who had tried to talk to me like that in private, let alone in a room full of people, would have been picking one of their eyeballs off the floor in pretty short order. I had reached that almost mythical stage for a criminal of my pedigree, a stage where my first action in confrontation is not physical violence. I must admit I was pleased with my reaction and it reinforced my belief of how far I had come. For the Mincer the work was only just beginning.

Later the Mincer asked for a sit-down with me, during which he shed more tears but admitted that he had not liked me from day one. He said it was not really anything personal, just that he feared and hated men like me who were strong and confident in themselves. There was a lot of envy because deep down he thought that it was his due to be strong and confident and command respect; his background and upbringing had instilled this in him and it pained him deeply that he had not turned out that way. I got the impression that he was a confused and emotional man who was dealing with severe disappointment and bitterness. I couldn't feel much pity for him because, like myself and others at Grendon, he had been the architect of his own miserable downfall. Some men at Grendon had been terribly abused as children – physically, sexually and in some cases psychologically – and though this did not excuse their behaviour as adults it could be seen as mitigation. For men like the Mincer and to a certain extent me there is very little mitigation. We did what we did because we didn't really care about ourselves and therefore other people. I told the Mincer this during our sit-down and we parted on amicable terms.

Eventually he moved up on to the 3s landing, possibly to get far away from me or possibly to be closer to his bosom buddy Tony the Stalker. But he didn't seem capable of making a connection with anyone else on the wing and this left him pretty isolated. The more isolated he became the more his arrogance came to the fore and this alienated him further from the rest of the community. There was some emotional muttering from the community when the details of his index offence were first fed back by his group and I knew that his first assessment was going to be pretty traumatic, probably for everyone involved. And I was right.

As I've said earlier, the initial assessment is supposed to be a light romp in the therapeutic woods, turning over the odd small stone in order to mark out a direction you should be taking on your therapeutic journey. But the Mincer's initial was more akin to a Spanish Inquisition. He was roasted from the start and, to give him his due, I think he gave honest answers to the questions that were fired at him. He admitted that he thought himself superior to the rest of us in every way and that he gave not a jot for what we thought of him. He went further and said he thought we were all 'criminal scum' and that the great tragedy of his life was that circumstances had forced him to live among us. He spoke of his crime as though it had been an accident beyond his control and the only emotion he showed was self-pity. The community were outraged and baying for his blood – in a therapeutic manner, of course. I sat silent throughout this seething build-up of emotion and kept my thoughts to myself. The reasons for my silence were varied. I didn't want anyone to think that I was after a bit of payback for his actions during my own assessment, and, in truth, I wasn't. My days of needing vengeance for my own satisfaction were gone. Plus I knew that the community were well able to point out the Mincer's faults and inconsistencies without any input from me. Another reason was that I was interested in listening to what he had to say for himself; in a strange way I found him fascinating. I had been around some dark places but I had never come across anyone as close to being so completely evil as the Mincer. I couldn't get my head around his crime. I could understand the concept of killing for gain – in other circumstances I could easily have ended up shooting someone on one of my robberies – but it was the overkill which confused me. The slaughter of a helpless target for no reason other than the urge to do it. It made me wonder if evil was a real thing that could be deep inside some people, or maybe all of us. The community rinsed him and it all ended with the huge, whooping sobs of self-pity that had characterized the aftermath of his attack on me.

After his traumatic assessment the Mincer put his papers in and stated that he wanted to leave Grendon. But if anyone was a case it was the Mincer and the wing therapist invested a lot of time into talking him into staying. Ray was in his group and told me he was dreading having to work on the many issues that were bursting out of the Mincer. He figured there was a good five years' work there. I half wished he was in my group as I would have loved a crack at opening him up. But I rated the Mincer as one of the top three most dangerous men on C-wing, and my days of living dangerously were definitely over. I decided to give him even more of a wide berth than I had been doing.

20. Vice-chair

Another unique thing about Grendon, when compared to the rest of the prison system, was the democratic nature of the communities. Every three months the communities held elections and voted men into positions of authority, and the most important role was that of chairman. You couldn't be voted into the chairman's job directly. First you had to be elected vice-chairman and do a three-month stint in this position before taking over the chair. The job of the vice-chair involved taking minutes of every community meeting and group feedback and recording them in the wing book. It also involved being available to the community at all times, doing the legwork for the chairman – such as typing up paperwork and distributing it to each cell, reading the book issues to the community at the start of any commitment, and attending weekly staff meetings.

About a month before the June elections various members of the community started dropping broad hints to me about going for the chair. I had been put up for it during the last election but had politely declined, citing my heavy workload, exams for my journalism courses and family complications as the reasons why I felt I wouldn't be able to give the job my full attention. The community accepted it but I knew I was in their sights as chairman material and that I would not be able to avoid it indefinitely. A part of me was quite flattered that people thought me trustworthy and responsible enough for such an important role. It said a lot to me that it wasn't only what I used to call 'real criminals' who were suggesting it, but the kind of men I had spent my time beating and terrorizing in other jails. The reason I was somewhat reluctant originally was partly because I really did have a heavy workload, but also because I was afraid that not enough people would vote for me. I had seen some men put up for the job over and over and then have to sit there with only five or six votes. I didn't want that disappointment and humiliation; I still had enough of an image problem to not want to go through that. But now I had run out of excuses not to enter the election and the group were still at my heels. Getting elected to the chair was a major thing at Grendon and not to be taken lightly. It involved a lot of stress and it was often said that you never really knew how far you had come in therapy until you had done your time in the chair. So on 3 June I was nominated for the post of vice-chairman and accepted the nomination. Now I would really find out how much I had changed.

Though it is not meant to be, the election for the chair was always going to be somewhat of a popularity contest. Just like most elections. In the past I had always voted for the person I was most friendly with, or the one who was most likeable. Carrot Top, for example, had put his own name forward for the job on eight occasions and never polled more than four votes. Though the therapist and staff always stressed the therapeutic value of the job it still all came down to whether enough people on the community liked you enough to vote you in. And that's what worried me. Before coming to Grendon I had thought of myself as a likeable enough fella, but, through the work I'd done in therapy, I had come to realize that what I had taken for friendship and respect was, in a lot of cases, nothing more than fear and self-preservation. People didn't like me, they feared me and that's why they laughed at my jokes and offered to do things for me. I knew I had changed a lot since being at Grendon but the vote would be the acid test and I was a bit nervous about it.

One of the things about the chairman's job that made it attractive to a lot of men was the fact that, if you handled it well and in a mature way, it often led to good reports being written about you by the therapist and staff – reports that would be useful in the constant quest for re-categorization and even release. It was seen as a very important step for any member of the community. As long as I had been on C-wing everyone who did the chairman's job had ended up with positive reports and a progressive move to open conditions, which is a very attractive prospect, particularly for a lifer. Both John and Big Ritchie had been transferred to HMP Ford, an open prison in Sussex, soon after completing their time as chairmen. Dave, the Milton Keynes drug lord in my group, had been downgraded to category D after doing the chairman's job and was awaiting transfer to HMP Latchmere House, a resettlement prison in Surrey, and Half-naked Dave, who was the current chairman, had been recommended for category D, as had Hate-'em-all Harry who was the current vice-chair. It was a big responsibility, with tangible rewards for doing it right. Of course all this appealed to me – I didn't want to spend the rest of my life in jail – but I also questioned my ability to do the job properly if I got it. It would take only one fuck-up and then, instead of category D and progressive moves, I could be facing more years in therapy. All of this was going around in my head. No matter how irrational some fears might be in the cold light of day, they can still seem very real in the darkness of your own mind, but I decided that if I were nominated, then I would give it my best shot.

In the weeks running up to the election each group was given a list of the rep jobs, including the chair, and we had to put up the names of the men we thought would be suitable for the positions. Caveman announced that he was putting me up for the vice-chair. I was a bit surprised because he was hardly on my Christmas card list, though I had changed my opinion of him since the early days. That was part of my new ability to judge men by their personalities rather than their crimes. I had strongly challenged Caveman on his crime, attitudes and behaviours during many group sessions, but I had never made it personal. I asked the questions that I had a genuine interest in and that might be a pointer towards why he had ended up here. Nevertheless, it was a good feeling to know that my group as a whole backed the nomination. When all the groups had handed their nominations to the vice-chair I was surprised to hear that someone in each group had put my name forward.

After the June election the current vice-chairman, Hate-'em-all Harry, would be stepping up to the chair, and he seemed certain that I was going to be taking over the vice-chair. He came to see me after all the nominations were in. 'It's going to be nice working with you,' he said. I shrugged. 'That's if the community vote me in. Someone else could get it, H, you know that.' Harry gave a rare smile. 'You're fucking kidding, ain't you? You're well liked on here, most people will vote for you.' I was grateful for Harry's encouragement but I still wasn't so sure. It was odd as I had always been confident about most things in the past, but I suppose that was because I didn't give a shit about anything. Now I realized that I wanted to do well and I was afraid of failure.

There seemed to be a disproportionate number of Londoners on C-wing, considering there was a maximum of only forty-three men on a wing. There was Half-naked Dave, so-called because he always seemed to be in shorts and a vest, even in the middle of winter; Hate-'em-all Harry, Marvin the Blagger, Micky the Growler, all from north of the river; and me, Freddie, Kevin S, Big Frank and Ray Bishop from south London. Then word came down that another north Londoner was coming to C-wing. His name was Pickles and he had a reputation as a really bad junkie. He was one of those geezers who near enough had his name reserved on a cell in his local nick because he was in and out of jail so often. He was a nuisance thief, driven by his addiction to heroin and crack to commit at least one crime – and sometimes several – every single day. Pickles was a hoister, though not one of the more sophisticated operators in that profession, as he would be the first to admit. 'Hoisting', or shop-lifting, as it is generally known, can provide rich pickings for the pro-fessional thief and is a low-risk crime. It usually attracts a sentence of three to six months, but by a combination of avoidable circumstances and plain recklessness Pickles had earned himself the sobriquet of 'the Most Dangerous Hoister in the Country', and a sentence of eleven years' imprisonment.

One of the scams Pickles operated to get hold of his drug money was 'the Snatch', which involved sending a half-respectable-looking accom-plice into a jewellery shop. The front man would ask the jeweller if he could have a closer look at a particularly expensive watch or ring. Once the front man had it in his hands Pickles, who would be keeping an eye on the proceedings from outside the shop, would come to the door and hold it open for the front man to make his escape. They would have a car waiting at the kerb with the engine running and, in the normal course of events, they would be driving away before the shop-owner could get out from behind his counter. They would then sell the item for a fraction of its value and spend their ill-gotten on heroin and crack. This scam was working quite well for Pickles until he took on a new and inexperienced front man. They drove to a jeweller's in Highgate and Pickles gave the front man his instructions but, unfortunately for all involved in the following fiasco, both Pickles and his front man were 'clucking', suffering from withdrawal symptoms from the drugs, and this made them reckless and dangerous. The front man went into the jeweller's and asked to see a £900 diamond ring. He was handed the item by the jeweller, but when Pickles opened the door as planned, instead of having it on his toes pretty lively to the getaway motor, the front man froze. Pickles, never backward at coming forward and not one to leave a job half done, snatched the ring from the front man's hand. He popped it into his mouth, intending to swallow it if he had to – Pickles was never going to give up the prize – and then legged it back to his getaway motor. But a passer-by who had witnessed the whole thing decided to intervene.

At this point I would just like to say a few things about those misguided members of the public who, in the heat of the moment, suddenly believe that they can only be harmed by kryptonite and decide to tackle desperate criminals in the act. While I fully agree that it's good to be community-spirited and to try to lend a hand when you can, we do have a police force whose job it is to catch criminals. It can be great when you get lucky and get your picture in the local paper and a few pats on the back from your pals down the pub, but remember that the men you are tackling are desperate not to go back to prison and will do almost anything to get away. Have-a-go heroes can end up seriously hurt or worse. Leave it to the police.

Now back to Pickles. As he jumped into his car and threw it into gear, the brave/stupid passer-by jumped on to the bonnet and hung on to the roof aerial. Pickles, mindful that his fence and dealer were waiting less than three miles away, was not going to stop for anything, least of all the white-faced gentleman draped across his windscreen. He put his foot down. As the car picked up speed Pickles became more desperate to be rid of his unwanted passenger, but the man clung on all the tighter. At this stage I would imagine that the man would gladly have climbed down and walked away had Pickles had the decency and presence of mind to stop the car for a minute, but he didn't. What he did instead was to start swerving from side to side in order to shake the man off, and at fifty miles per hour this is exactly what happened. The man lost his grip and bounced over the roof of the speeding car and crashed on to the hard road behind. Once he had thrown the man off the car Pickles thought about him only for as long as he remained, broken and bloody, in his rear-view mirror and that was about thirty seconds. His all-consuming craving for drugs left little room in his consciousness for thoughts of anything else and he dismissed the incident by telling himself the man would be okay, just a few cuts and bruises.

Pickles drove to his dealer, cashed the ring in and thirty minutes after the robbery was lost in a drug-induced stupor. Pickles's victim ended up brain-damaged and in a wheelchair for the rest of his life. Four weeks later Pickles was arrested in a raid on a crack-den. In court eight months later he pleaded guilty to theft of the ring and GBH with intent to resist arrest and was sentenced to eleven years' imprisonment. To be fair to Pickles, in over twenty years of drug-driven crime this was the only time he had ever caused serious physical harm to anyone, and he stuck his hands up to it the moment he was captured. Usually he was comfortable in prison – it was his home from home after all – but this time was different. It wasn't only the length of the sentence, but a very real sense of guilt and remorse that started eating at him from the moment he was arrested and heard the extent of his victim's injuries. He carried on getting out of his nut on drugs every day, but he couldn't stop thinking about what he'd done, no matter how much skag he put into his body. Eventually he decided to apply for Grendon.

When Fred and a couple of the lads told me that Pickles was coming on to C-wing I had reservations. It didn't help that word came through that he'd been involved in a drug scandal while on F-wing: he'd stuck his hands up to smoking heroin. Pickles survived the scandal, though several other inductees were shipped out when they tried to wriggle out of it. Anyway, he came to C-wing and immediately palled up with the north London crowd. I was hopeful about him when I saw he was going two-of-toast with Half-naked Dave, as I'd known Dave since F-wing and classed him as a genuine geezer who had taken his therapeutic journey very seriously. Half-naked Dave was also an ex-junkie from north London, and was serving a two-strike life for manslaughter. He had grafted with Pickles in the past and I knew that if anyone could steer Pickles in the right direction it was Dave. I also knew that Pickles would vote for me in the election as I was well fancied for the chair by the London contingent.

The day of the election seemed to zoom up on me very quickly. Hate-'em-all Harry had been doing a bit of quiet campaigning on my behalf, although this was frowned upon by the therapist and staff group. Harry's campaigning consisted of slipping my name and the word 'chairman' into almost every conversation he had with anyone about the elections. It made me laugh to see how easily he could do it with no shame and with an angelic look on his devilish features. So in the weeks leading up to the meeting the London contingent had been subtly briefed by Harry, and I was sure of getting a good show of hands even if I lost the vote. I was up against the usual suspects in Carrot Top and Fat Rick, and a couple of outsiders, but my main rival for the vice-chair was Mikey, who was well fancied by a lot of the community. Mikey was from Southampton and a senior member of C-wing community, having arrived six months before me. He was a mandatory lifer with a sixteen-year minimum tariff. He had been a serious gambling addict and an alcoholic, and had got into an argument with his best mate during a drinking binge. He beat the fella to death with a lump of wood, but overcome by guilt had then handed himself in to the police. Though as black as Newgate's knocker, Mikey had been one of the first men on C-wing to welcome Kevin, the Blackburn Nazi, on to the wing and tried to befriend him. Mikey was well liked for his calm and sensible manner; he was perfect chairman material and at the right time in his therapy to do the job.

The first topic of business, after minutes and backings, on election day was the vote for vice-chair. I sat in my usual seat halfway down the right-hand side of the community room and felt my heart beat a little faster when the chairman read out the list of candidates. My name was top of the list, which meant I would have to give my speech first. I remembered when Daran, the ex-Legionnaire, was up for vice-chair on F-wing. He was up against a fella who was a very good orator and odds-on to talk himself into the post. The bloke was the first to speak and spent a good ten minutes outlining all the excellent reasons why he should have the job, and at the end the community were so impressed they gave him a round of applause. The chairman then turned to Daran and asked him to give his reasons why he should have the job. Daran smiled pleasantly and said, 'For all the same reasons as my opponent, which he has explained clearly and eloquently. Plus, I'm better looking!' The whole community cracked up in laughter, except his opponent, and Daran won the election by two votes. Now I would be going first and it was a bit nerve-racking.

The chairman, Half-naked Dave, turned to me and asked if I'd like to give my reasons for wanting the job. I hadn't really planned what to say as I'd always found that planning was not my forte; I'd forget some important detail and then struggle to make sense from then on. I always spoke better when I was winging it. I can't remember too much about what I said but I kept it short and sweet and ended with the inevitable: 'Should the community see fit to vote me in I will endeavour to do the job to the best of my ability. Thank you.' I sat back in my chair and immediately thought of twenty things I should have said. Carrot Top was next and his speech went on a lot longer than mine but I could see some people close to nodding off as he croaked on. Mikey was on third and he gave a brilliant speech about why he would be good for the job and the job would be good for him. I noticed almost everyone was listening with interest to what he was saying and inside my head I knew he was going to get it. I gave a mental shrug and decided that I would go for it again further down the line, depending, of course, on whether I got a respectable number of votes this time. I didn't hear a word of Fat

Rick's speech or the others as I was too busy planning my next campaign. Then it was time for the votes to be counted.

All the voting at Grendon is done by a public show of hands and on a one-man-one-vote basis. I figured that a decent vote would be around ten; that wouldn't be too embarrassing. The chairman called for the votes for me. All candidates are allowed to vote, either for themselves or any of the others, but I'd decided not to look too desperate by voting for myself. I planned to vote for Mikey. The hands went up but I couldn't bear to look. Instead I fixed my gaze on the polished floor in front of me. I heard the chairman count the hands and when he got to twenty-three I couldn't believe it. Even with the London vote that was a surprise to me. There were only forty-three men on the wing but, never having been good at maths, I didn't realize that I had won outright. Everybody had to vote so the chairman called for the rest of the votes. Carrot Top voted for himself, and was the only one. Fat Rick got two votes, including his own, and Mikey wiped up the rest including mine. I was pretty stunned when I realized I had won.

Then came the ceremony of the changing of the chair. Half-naked Dave, at the urging of the community, gave a short speech about how he viewed his time in the chair and the therapeutic value he had got from it. He then stood up and vacated the brown leather chair at the top of the room for Hate-'em-all Harry. Next I left my own chair and took up my place in the vice-chair next to Harry, and Dave went and sat in the chair that I had vacated. Harry handed me the wing book and a pen, and the ritual was complete. I was the vice-chairman of C-wing community.

I was strangely proud of winning the vote. It made me feel as though I was really going somewhere. I knew inside myself that I was changing and it was great to have confirmation of this from others. It was a great boost to my self-esteem and it also made me feel good towards the community for voting me in. I was determined to do my best and take my responsibilities seriously. One of the things that I had to do as part of my duties was to attend the weekly staff meetings. This would be a big challenge as never in my wildest dreams would I ever have thought that I would be able to sit in a room full of prison staff and feel even slightly comfortable. It was only later on the day of election, when I was banged up alone in my cell for the night, that I began to have doubts. I had a moment of panic when I saw my new self in the way my old self would see me. I knew my old self would call me a sell-out, a screw-lover, or even a fucking grass. It had been unthinkable to my old self that I would ever be in this situation, working with screws and suits as though they were not the enemy. I felt a great wave of self-loathing and shame. Then I looked at the other side: this was a chance for me, a chance to live a normal decent life, to start anew and try to counterbalance what I had done in my past. How good was it going to be to get out this time and know that I would never be a prisoner again? To be able to prove to my family and friends that I was no longer a fucking loss who would be gone again for another decade and another until I was too old to be of use to anyone? I wanted to at least try to make amends to my children, if only by being there for them, just in case. I thought of all the terrible things I had done in the past and how lucky I was to be even getting a chance. It was a bad night and I didn't get to sleep until it was nearly light outside, but I believe that I managed to finally shrug off the last doubts left in my mind about the validity of what I was doing at Grendon. My criminal self was fast fading into the background and taking his way of thinking with him. That way of thinking had served me well when I was immersed in the criminal culture but in my new life, the life I was planning and hoping for, it was redundant. The next day I felt a lot better.

I enjoyed my time as vice-chairman. Me and Harry had the same sense of humour and it was a joy to work with him. He had come to C-wing, like myself, as a bitter, violent and fucked-up man, but he had changed so much it was wondrous to behold. Don't get me wrong, he still held on to his biting sarcasm, which I suppose was one of his defence mechanisms, but he had matured beyond belief in a relatively short space of time. The prison system had had him for fourteen years of his life and taught him nothing of any value. He had entered prison as a boy really and it was only in Grendon that he found the space and help that he needed to grow into a man. I watched him daily as he sat down with people and helped them to work out their problems in a mature and sensible manner. He managed the staff meetings like an old hand, always speaking his mind and refusing to be steered in any direction that he didn't think was right. I learned a lot from Harry and I was glad that he happened to be the chairman during my time in the vice-chair. But Harry had also learned a lot from Dave when he was in the chair, and this is how it worked at Grendon – it wasn't enough just to gain what you yourself needed, there was value in passing it on to others who were on the same journey. And that was a lesson in itself for a lot of us.

21. Working for the Man

Being the vice-chairman didn't affect my work in group 3 and we still met three times a week. Unfortunately, sometimes we had to vacate our group room on the ground floor of C-wing and march up to the education block to have our meeting in one of the classrooms in the centre of the prison because the noise of the wall coming down was a real distraction. We still had Brian as our facilitator but the group had changed a lot since I had first arrived as a new member. Dave, the Milton Keynes drug lord, had been transferred to HMP Latchmere House. Tony the Stalker, after his trouble in the education department, decided to throw his dummy out of the pram and had pulled out of therapy. He refused to accept that he had done anything wrong and hated being questioned on it. He put his papers in some months later and was awaiting transfer back to HMP Swaleside. In a way I was sorry to see Tony pull out as I knew he needed therapy as much as anyone, but there was also a part of me that was glad, because he was fucking hard work. Fred was still in the group but he was in the middle of having reports written up for his try at cat D and everyone expected him to get it this time. Abs, who had once been a member of group 3 before being released on parole into a rehab, was back in trouble. We were pretty shocked to hear that he was now on remand in HMP Wormwood Scrubs charged with GBH on his girlfriend. Word gradually reached us that he had got back on the crack while still in rehab. We discussed it in one group and the consensus was that it was a shame for Abs but even more so for his poor girlfriend who had stuck by him in the hope that he would change, only to end up with a broken jaw for her trouble.

Failures, like that of Abs, really affected the group. The group became a surrogate family for most of us and we were happy when one of our number went on to do well, but we felt it keenly when one of us failed. We shared our innermost thoughts and feelings with the group and told each other things that we had never told anyone. What bound us together in trust was the belief that each one of us was equally determined to change and that we were all on the same road, albeit at different points along it. So when one of our number reverted to old behaviour it was like a smack in the face to all of us. We would examine the failure as a group and try to work out what it was that had gone wrong. If there was a pointer to be had then we wanted it to be clear so we ourselves would recognize it if it came up for us. We decided that in Abs's case it could have been that he didn't do long enough in therapy and didn't work enough on his crack addiction. Every failure was treated as a cautionary tale and wrung for lessons like a wet rag soaked in information.

In place of Tony the Stalker we ended up with a geezer called Phil the Pikey, and taking Sandy's seat was a blast from the past in the form of Silver. Silver was the young fella who had left group 3 and Grendon in my first year, after he had rushed into therapy too quickly and vomited up all his issues in one go. He had gone back to HMP Swaleside as an emotional wreck and we had heard that he had been involved in a violent incident there. It turned out that the rumour Silver had stabbed another prisoner in Swaleside was completely erroneous. What he had done was become a Muslim. The Silver who came back to group 3 after over a year's absence seemed to be much more together than the one who had left. He looked a bit strange as a white kid who insisted on wearing a Muslim robe and one of those little pillbox hats that some Arabs wear, and there were a few humorous comments about this, mostly behind his back. The trouble with Silver was that he had a lot of previous for jumping on bandwagons, particularly those of a religious nature. He had been a Christian, a Pagan, a Buddhist, a white wizard and into some sort of Chinese religion as well. But this time he solemnly told us that he had found the one religion that suited him and he would give his life to Allah. It was true that he was a lot more mature and serene than the last time I had seen him and I half-thought that maybe he had found his calling. But, being pretty suspicious and cynical of all religion and the people who 'find' it, I decided once again to reserve judgement.

Silver settled back into the group pretty smoothly and began to work on some of the issues he had brought up in his previous time here. Phil the Pikey, on the other hand, was a nightmare from day one. Fuck knows how he had passed the stringent assessment process and made it to Grendon, let alone down on to C-wing. Phil was a short, bald man of forty-six who claimed to be a genuine traveller, one of those people who live in caravans rather than houses and are linked to the real gypsies, or

Romanies. How true this was I don't know, because Phil let slip that he himself lived in a house and, having quite a few mates who are real travellers, I know that is one of the last things to admit. They actually call people who live in houses 'kennel bred', and it's a stain of shame for a real traveller to live in a house. Anyway, Phil was doing ten years for smashing his way into a drug dealer's house and attacking the occupants with a large machete. He held a woman down and deliberately cut her across the face, as well as cutting one of the men. His motive was robbery, of both drugs and money. Phil was a degenerate junkie, but he tried to dress his actions up in a story about the people in the house being police informers. Like a lot of criminals, he had an image of himself as some kind of noble character with a strong moral code, and the first day in the group he started by telling Caveman that he didn't think he would be able to work with him because he was a wrong-un. This angered me, probably because I recognized Phil's attitude having once had the same attitude myself, but also because I had come to know Caveman over the previous two years and had grown to like him.

It was unfortunate for C-wing that we happened to receive an influx of men over a period of about three months who had all known each other in HMP Bullingdon, the category B local prison nearest to Grendon. Because they had all been together, not one of them wanted to be the first to shed his prison image. They had survived in other jails by giving it the big 'un and now each thought that it would be a sign of weakness if he acted as though he really wanted to be in Grendon. So they formed a clique on the wing and tried to behave as though they were still in Bullingdon – noncing people off, trying to bully weaker members of the community and sniggering at the therapy. In groups they did just enough to make the therapists believe they were here for the right reasons, or they kept quiet. They told each other that the only reason they were in this wrong-uns' jail was to pull the wool and get parole or recategorization as quickly as possible. I could understand why they were doing it. I'd like to think that even if I'd come on C-wing with five or six of the lads I'd just been in Whitemoor with, I'd be strong enough to go my own way, but I can definitely understand the attraction of getting into a comfort zone. They couldn't see that what they were doing was actually a weakness. Because they were refusing to engage in the therapeutic regime on anything but a superficial level they thought that the rest of the community would be cowed by their behaviour, just like the men they had bullied in the system. What they underestimated was the collective strength of the community. They were getting a bye on their behaviour only because the community understood that it can be hard for some men to settle into therapy. The surprise for the newcomers would come at the point when the community decided they'd had long enough to integrate and it was time for them to shit or get off the pot. Phil was at the forefront of the newcomers.

The thing that jarred and amused me in equal measures about Phil and most of the newcomers was that I recognized them as fakes. They didn't realize that some of us on C-wing had actually been the characters that they now professed to be. They boasted to anyone who would listen about how they had bashed up nonces, attacked screws and done bundles of block time for their subversive behaviour. But not one of them had been to a dispersal jail, where the most troublesome prisoners are sent, and most of them were C cats who had rarely been further than their own local jails. They were like little children playing at being adults. Being in Grendon, with its no-violence rule, made them braver than they had ever been. It was as if they were in an arse-kicking contest with a load of one-legged men and sure to come off best. So they abused their position. Phil's oppo, a greasy-looking melt called Martin, who was doing seven years for a moody robbery on a sweetshop or petrol garage, was the most vocal of the newcomers. He started every sentence with 'When I was in the block for chinning a screw . . .' and ended every sentence with a declaration of how if he wasn't in Grendon he would surely be in some block chinning screws. He and Phil hung around C-wing like a bad smell, giving the evil eye to whoever they presumed were the weaker members of the community and talking loudly about nonces and wrong-uns.

Phil had a habit of leaving the door of the wing phone-box open whenever he made a call to his friends and family and shouting into the handset as though it were a can on a piece of string and he had to force his words physically down the line. The phone-box was on the ground floor about fifteen feet from my cell and I would often listen in amusement as he sought to big himself up to the other men who were waiting patiently in the phone queue. One evening I was waiting for the phone myself when he started telling whoever was on the end of the line that Grendon was 'full of mugs and wrong-uns' and that he felt like taking a table leg and 'weighing a few of them in'. Phil had never said anything to me directly and was always careful to exclude me from his comments about Grendon's clientele while in the group, but this evening I was in a bit of a bad humour and decided to take exception to his words. I searched my recent memory for my old skin and quickly slipped it on for a moment. When Phil came out of the phone-box I called him over. I gave him the clenched jaw and the hard stare and moved in close to him. 'Phil,' I said, softly but full of menace, 'did I just hear you calling me a mug on the blower?' His arsehole dropped completely out. It was one thing to be a big fish in a little pond but when a real shark appears you'd better come up for air. He apologized profusely and assured me that he hadn't been including me in his blanket statement. I nodded slowly. 'Okay,' I said. 'Just be careful what you say in future.' He couldn't wait to get away from me. I got a bit of satisfaction out of the incident, instant gratification, and it made me feel better, but I decided there and then that Phil needed putting in his place.

I didn't have to wait long. A couple of days after the phone incident Phil was in group 3 ranting about the kind of people he was forced to live with at Grendon when I told him a few home truths. I asked him if he realized that his crime, the deliberate slashing of a woman's face, would be enough to get him bashed up, burned out and run on to the numbers (protection wing) in a lot of nicks. He seemed shocked and the colour drained out of his face. I continued, 'If you turned up in Whitemoor when I'd been there and any of the lads found out what you were in for I would have been the first one into your cell to bash your head in, and I wouldn't be alone. See, far from being one of the chaps, you are, in fact, a fucking wrong-un to a large percentage of the prison population. You want to think about that before you go mouthing off about other people's crimes. You're doing a ten, and if you're not careful you'll be doing it alongside these people that you've been looking down on since you've been here. Only, in a real jail. Where you're likely to get a clump.' That shut him up. But fair play to Phil, he did go away and think about it. In reality he had a lot of problems in his private life, which he had originally come to Grendon to sort out, but there seemed to have been no previous thought about who he might find here and what he might have to do. I couldn't work out whether it was arrogance or stupidity. Now he was at the point where he was going to have to get into therapy or get out. I was glad to be able to help him kickstart his work, but only he could do the rest.

Another group 3 member who was becoming hard work was the

21-year-old bisexual cross-dressing rapist, Candy. Despite sounding very windswept and interesting, Candy was in fact one of the dullest people on C-wing. In groups he would sit in a corner and not open his mouth for weeks on end. Now that Sandy, his main enemy, was gone Candy had settled in for the free ride. He spent his days ensconced in his cell on the 2s landing, usually with Nobby and Fat Rick, his two best pals, playing on his PlayStation. Whenever I did hear him talking, usually in meal queues, it would all be about what level of 'Splinter Cell' or 'Resident Evil' he had reached. But if he thought his holiday could last indefinitely he was very much mistaken. As the new vice-chairman I was about to up my game, and Candy was in my sights. I was 100 per cent serious about therapy, and I wasn't about to carry any dead wood.

22. Expectations

By the time I took the vice-chair I had been at Grendon for twenty-three months. In the paperwork you get before coming to the prison it states that the minimum time you must dedicate to therapy in order for change to happen is eighteen months. But I always knew that because of my age and the number of years I had invested in my previous life, eighteen months probably wouldn't cut it for me. I came in with no real time scale in mind, I was prepared to stay in therapy for as long as it took for me to be sure that I had explored everything. Time was something I had an abundance of: as a lifer my actual sentence was ninety-nine years, and anything less was a bonus. But there were some people who set really strict time restraints on their work, either through impatience or because they tied in with where they thought they should have been in their sentence. A few men were so rigid in their thinking that they actually expected to be 'cured' of a lifetime of terrible behaviour at eighteen months on the dot! There were others, mainly lifers but not exclusively so, who would quickly start to regress if they did not get what they expected, be it recategorization or recommendations for parole. It was sad to see these men put in months of work only to fall the first time a small hurdle was put in their way.

The trouble with Grendon is that you can get a bit carried away with the whole experience. It breaks you down, smashes all the barriers you have spent decades erecting, takes your armour and your weapons, and leaves you weak and vulnerable before allowing you to start putting on the first layers of the new you. In my own case, for example, I came to Grendon as a hardened violent recidivist. I'd never had anything but the most cursory relationship with prison staff, they were 'the enemy', the front-line storm troopers of my main enemy, 'the system'. I detested authority of any kind and to show any weakness in the face of my enemies was unthinkable. In the past I had done my time in my own way, fuelling every moment with hatred for the system, for the screws, for other cons, even for the very fabric of the buildings that housed me and the walls and fences that contained me. Almost from the very moment I entered the machinery of the criminal justice system I became a different person. I had learned to cut myself off from the outside world completely, because I knew from bitter experience that whatever happened out there could not be changed by me. I was alone in prison, I didn't need visits, or letters or news. Prison became my world and I accepted it. I've seen a lot of men go mad over the years through trying to live in two worlds at once. They keep one foot on the out and one foot in jail and as a result they have the added stress of trying to balance both worlds. I think it was John Donne who said, 'No man is an island', but he'd obviously never done a bit of bird, because that is exactly what happens to the survivors in prison – we become self-sufficient islands. Some people may wonder how we manage to face each new day in jail with the daunting, depressing prospect of the years stretching out before us. I have often had straight-goers, and even short-termers, express astonishment at the length of the prison sentences I casually reel off. They always say that they could never do so long. But what is the alternative? You have to do your time in the best way you can, and usually it is by making prison your reality and quickly erasing every sweet thought of that other, real, world before it can take hold and weaken you. If I woke up every morning longing for the out, I wouldn't last a year without having a breakdown.

So that is how I had always done my bird, blanking the out or paying it only a detached kind of attention on the infrequent visits I allowed in or when I received a letter. But Grendon wanted to strip me of that defence. In Grendon I learned to question my motto about the prison system – expect nothing and you will never be disappointed. Speaking to Tom, the therapist, Lynn, the psychologist, and some of the staff, I was starting to be won over to another view. It was as though they were telling me that I had to really participate in my incarceration. In order to bring the rest of my feelings and emotions alive I had to be able to feel what was going on, or there would be an unfeeling part of me that could block my therapeutic work. Now that I was changing, instead of expecting nothing from the system maybe I should expect everything. When they told me this I was naturally sceptical but I started to buy into the idea gradually. I thought about it and decided to give it a try. I was already receiving more visits and letters than I had on any other sentence and my walls were covered with photographs of friends and family, so for the first time in decades I began to enter the outside world mentally mid-sentence. I would lie in bed at night and think about how it might be when I got out, what I would do and how I would go about starting my future new life. I thought about my plans for work as a writer, where I was going to live, how I would cope, what problems I might face. In the past it had been easy: the minute things went wrong outside I would pick up a gun and try to rob or shoot my way out of trouble. In the future I no longer wanted that option. After thinking everything through over several months I became more confident and optimistic. But imagining the future and being out was making my time in prison harder. Every day seemed like a week, every week like a month, and I could clearly see the bleak, barren vista of the years I had left to serve stretching out before me. I became very depressed. This was doing my time the hard way.

How I kept myself going was by trying to be positive about what I was doing. Luckily my life sentence came with a clear set of milestones by which I could measure how far into the journey I was. In theory there was no end to my sentence, but my actual tariff, the minimum period I had to serve for the purpose of retribution for my crimes, was eight years. But how much longer I served after that was open-ended. It was up to me to try and make it as short as possible. At the six-year mark of my sentence I was given a 'paper hearing' by the Parole Board. In a paper hearing the prisoner does not appear at the board, but a couple of Parole Board members take a good look at all his paperwork, reports, record, history sheet, etc., and then decide whether he is ready for open conditions. A move to open conditions for a lifer is a massive step and is rarely granted on a paper hearing, so I did not expect any result, but it would be good to read the Parole Board's written rejection as it would give me an inkling of how they might be looking at my case. A couple of months after the hearing I received my reply from the board. They refused to grant me open conditions, as expected, but they did give me a date for an early review in April 2006, by which time I would have served nearly eight years with almost three years in therapy. The reasons given for not granting me open conditions were my 'long criminal history' and 'the safety of the public', which was fair enough. But what buoyed me up was the timing. All parole reports are started six months before the actual parole date because they are so extensive and important, so my parole reports would be started in November 2005, just as I would have completed my six-month tenure as vice-chair and chairman. I started to think that I might have a real chance of getting a move to open conditions by the summer of 2006. As long as I did well in the chair, with no major blow-ups or fuck-ups, then surely along with my demonstrable change of heart and direction I would have lowered my risk factors enough to progress? The trouble with this kind of positive thinking is that when you get a knockback it can be very hard to swallow. All I could do was hope for the best and keep doing what I was doing.

As vice-chair one of my duties was to facilitate sit-downs between prisoners who had problems with each other, and during those unsettled months for C-wing, with the arrival of the Bullingdon crew, there were plenty of these. It seemed as though Harry and I were constantly sitting between warring factions who wanted to vent their anger and hatred for each other. Usually we would sit down with the protagonists in group 5's room on the ground floor, sometimes with a member of staff present if one was available, but usually just me and Harry and whoever had the problem. In an ordinary jail these differences between prisoners would usually be settled with violence. If someone thought that someone else had been giving them dirty looks or making snide comments, then it would be a case of getting together in a cell or the recess and duking it out, or slipping a couple of PP9 batteries in a pillowcase and catching them unawares. At Grendon it was all about expressing the feelings verbally, and everyone knew that this option was available. The rules on a sit-down were that each party could have their say without interruption, and verbally there were no holds barred. No one was allowed to leave their seat and, if either party made any physically threatening move towards the other, they would be put up for a commitment vote. It worked very well and it was interesting to see men absolutely tear into each other verbally and then, when it was all out, end up shaking hands and going about their business feeling better for having vented. The main job of the vice and chairman was to keep it safe, to get between the men if it looked like kicking off physically, to offer sensible advice and to make sure that both parties were going to be 'safe' with each other after the sit-down was over. Most times sit-downs ended okay but every once in a while they were not enough.

One typical sit-down Harry and I facilitated involved Silver and Tony the Stalker. They absolutely hated each other and in the group the civility between them was as thin and brittle as old veneer. Each was everything the other detested. For Silver, Tony the Stalker represented middle-class authoritarianism, hypocrisy and arrogance. Silver saw what he had always suspected, that those well-fed teachers, judges and magistrates who had been looking down on him for most of his life were actually nothing but black-hearted wrong-uns who could point the finger in public and then commit horrendous acts in their own lives. He saw what he believed was the truth of this theory every time he looked at Tony, and it burned him up. For Tony the Stalker, Silver represented what he viewed as working-class scumbags, young and cocky but confident and articulate, easy around most people and fairly well liked. In short, everything Tony was not, but would have loved to have been. They managed to avoid each other everywhere except in group 3, where they sometimes clashed. Their blow-ups in the group were usually short and bitter with both quickly reining in their true feelings for fear of giving themselves more work to do. But they weren't fooling anyone. Silver had the quicker and more fiery temper, and Tony was a slow-burner who could erupt after provocation, as you might expect from a man who had spent almost a decade getting his own back on a woman who had dared to spurn his advances and then tried to kill another who had done the same. C-wing was way too small for people to avoid each other for long, as I had found out during my protracted war with Taff, and one afternoon Silver and Tony bumped into each other and an argument developed. I heard all the shouting and went up to the 1s landing to see what was going on. Silver and Tony the Stalker were almost toe-to-toe and screaming in each other's faces. I calmed them down and arranged a sit-down. With Harry and me facilitating, we let the pair vent their spleen on each other for over two hours. Many times we had to give them warnings when one or the other got carried away and made moves to leave his chair, but eventually they tired themselves out with all the shouting. Just letting out their feelings about each other was enough for them to be able to go back to quietly hating each other with little danger of a physical confrontation. Until the next time the grievances built up to boiling point again, and we would deal with that whenever it happened.

Another south Londoner who arrived on C-wing and became a good mate of mine was a fella from Bermondsey called Nolan. Nolan was a tall, good-looking kid, serving eight years for armed robbery, and he could be a pretty strange cat sometimes. The trouble with Nolan was that he could be too open and honest for his own good. The first thing that got people talking about him was when he declined the privilege of having a television in his cell. It wasn't that unusual in itself as some people do prefer not having the old goggle box, either as a protest, like my pal Shotgun Shelley, or because they might be working on things like Open University degrees and don't need the distraction. But Nolan's reason, which he openly told people, was that he believed that televisions actually brainwashed viewers by flashing subliminal messages to them, making them do things that they would not otherwise do. Obviously by the time his reason did the rounds of the wing it had been contorted into 'The new fella thinks his telly talks to him and gives him messages!', which made Nolan seem like a bit of a fruitcake. Hearing Nolan was from south London I invited him into my cell for a cup of coffee and a chat. I had heard the 'talking telly' story but I had spent enough time in jail to take rumours like this as bollocks until proved otherwise. I found Nolan to be a pretty intense but interesting fella. He had had a windswept and interesting life, having left south London in his teens for the wilds of Devon and a life as a hippie. What had driven Nolan away from south London as soon as he was old enough to make it on his own had a lot to do with his family. With the exception of his mother, whom he trusted and loved unconditionally, the rest of his family were con-merchants and street-players, forever pulling strokes and working the corner. Nolan's dad was King Con, and he couldn't resist working his mind games and grifting any mark who happened to hove into view, including his own children. From a young age Nolan, because of his innocent looks and plausible manner, was put to work in the family business, which involved lying, story-spinning and trying to part suckers from their money and goods. He hated it, and by the time he reached the age of fifteen and saw that there were other options, he got on his bike and left it far behind him.

In Devon he lived among New Age travellers, took copious amounts of drugs and was a regular at all the festivals. He drifted along in an acid-and-cannabis-fuelled haze for many years, mixing easily with all those groups that seem to have a great life on the fringes of 'normal' society. He knew hippies, bikers, weirdos, potheads, acid freaks and pagan mushroom-gatherers. After the mean streets of Bermondsey, where every cockney wideboy is out to make a pound at the expense of everyone else and where greed, slyness and violence are *de rigueur*, Nolan thought he had found the perfect uncluttered peaceful life. But it turned out that he still had a lot of the Bermondsey boy left in him.

Each area of London has its notorious patch, the place that usually produces the fighters and the criminals. Just like New York had the Five

Points and Hell's Kitchen, London has Canning Town in the east, Fulham in the west, the Cali in the north and Bermondsey in the south. These are the 'manors' that have reputations among the criminal fraternity and the police. They are like throwbacks to the old Victorian criminal enclaves, 'thieves' dens': tough, usually run-down and impoverished areas that produce hungry people who are willing to take chances wherever they find them. Bermondsey has the reputation of being one of the toughest. Canning Town may have the maddest fighters, the Cali the most prolific thieves, Fulham the flashest villains, but in the last four decades Bermondsey has produced the cream of the armed robbery set. Gilbert Kelland, in his book *Crime in London*, claimed that in the 1980s Bermondsey blaggers were responsible for approximately 96 per cent of all armed robberies committed in the whole country. Maybe it's something in the water at Deptford Creek, but there is definitely a Bermondsey thing going on. And Nolan had it in him. The fact that he ended up convicted of armed robbery was no surprise, but how he reached that point was not via the usual route.

In Devon Nolan met a nice girl who had a young daughter and they settled down as a family in the hippie version of domestic bliss. Life was pretty good and Nolan provided for his new family with a little bit of drug-dealing and low-level rip-offs, 'nothing too heavy, man'. But eventually he began to hear the call of south London and decided that maybe it was time to move back up to the smoke for a while and introduce his new family to his old family. Maybe they would have mellowed out now that a few years had passed? So off they went. Unfortunately for Nolan, little had changed and once he was back in the fold the rest of the family exerted pressure on him to 'earn' and contribute. He had a flat with his wife and stepdaughter but his relatives would turn up unannounced and make themselves at home, taking proper liberties. In order to cope with all the agg Nolan began to snort a bit of cocaine, a drug he had previously had no use for, and pretty soon a bit turned into a shitload. His rip-offs got more ambitious and he slipped easily into the role of con-merchant and class A drug dealer. With constant pressure from his family and his coke-fuelled lifestyle driving him on he upped his game and started committing armed robberies on drug dealers, then jewellers, then banks. His mental health, never that robust in the first place, began to deteriorate seriously. He became severely paranoid and violent, given to extreme mood swings, and putting more Colombian marching powder up his hooter than Al Pacino in the final scene of *Scarface* wasn't doing him any favours.

Eventually one of his wife's relatives, perhaps noticing how wired Nolan had become, funded a holiday to Spain for him, his wife and stepdaughter. Right up until the plane took off Nolan was hoovering up the devil's dandruff and while the aircraft cruised at 30,000 feet he was flying just that little bit higher. A crash back to earth was inevitable for Nolan, and when it came it was bad. Two days into their Spanish holiday, while sitting on a lovely golden beach surrounded by other holiday-making families, Nolan's mind hit the hard ground and cracked in half. He became absolutely convinced that the rest of the holidaymakers on that beach were part of a massive paedophile ring and that they were out to kidnap his stepdaughter and sell her into slavery. When he listened closely he could hear them all whispering their plans and every time he glanced around at them he caught the sly and calculating looks on their demon-like features before they quickly changed their faces back to human. He tried telling his wife but could not find the right words to convince her, so he decided he had to act. He steamed into a young family close by, throwing punches and kicks at them, all the while shouting that he knew what they were up to. For Nolan, in his fractured state of mind, this was reality; he had no doubts whatsoever that what he was doing was right. He would not let them take his child and would fight anyone to stop it happening. But for the rest of the people on that beach he was a pale, wild-eyed lunatic who had suddenly begun attacking innocent people for no discernible reason. They rushed to help the family who were being attacked and overpowered Nolan before he could do any permanent damage.

Eventually Nolan was calmed down, though he was still deep in his madness and would remain so for the next few years. He was taken back to his hotel and the police were called. Once in his room he phoned the police himself and told them about the paedophiles who were infesting the hotel and the beach and how they were really demons in human form. The Spanish police didn't know what to do with this *loco Ingles* so they did nothing except give him a warning. The hotel manager asked him to leave and find somewhere else to stay. Nolan's wife took him to a Spanish hospital, but because they had no medical insurance the hospital didn't want anything to do with him. They advised him to go back to England. So he did.

Back home the family took him straight to hospital and Nolan voluntarily signed himself into psychiatric care. He later told me that he did it because his paranoia was so bad that a secure hospital was the only place he felt safe, where no one could get at him. In the hospital Nolan was sedated and given daily doses of psychotropic drugs and this seemed to help him to level out. He was still as crazy as a shithouse rat, but he was now able to hide and manage it better. After eleven weeks in hospital he felt well enough to venture into the outside world again, but deep inside he knew he wasn't right. None of his problems had gone away and they were all waiting for him. He got back into snorting coke as if he was in training for the drug-abusers' Olympics, and went back into armed robbery. This time he was caught, and it may have been prison that was the saving of him. After he was sentenced he ended up in Parkhurst around some very sensible cons, who suggested that he give Grendon a try, and within a short time he was ensconced in C-wing.

When I met him he had a bit of a God complex, thinking that he was the only person who could understand the meaning of life and the scheme of the universe. He also strongly subscribed to all sorts of conspiracy theories. Having a conversation with him was like trying to converse with Stephen Hawking after he had drunk three bottles of Polish vodka. You knew that somewhere inside him there could be a lot of sense and intelligence but wading through the gobbledegook was hard work. But I liked Nolan because of what I sensed about him – he was essentially a good-hearted kid with no real nastiness in him and, like most of us at Grendon, he had fucked himself up. A lot of the divs on the wing didn't understand him so it was easy for them to label him as a 'weirdo' and leave it at that. His group, group 1, focused on his eccentricities as a way of avoiding looking at their own work and he went through a bit of a hard time when his paranoia, never that far from the surface anyway, took over. I told him he could always knock on my door for a chat when things were getting too much for him, and we had some pretty deep conversations in which he tried to explain to me how he felt about everything from UFOs to religion. After a few months on the wing Nolan started to gain a bit more confidence and began to make real progress in his therapy. I was pleased he was settling in but I also had an inkling that his journey wouldn't be a smooth one, and I was right.

23. Work

Every Monday afternoon me and Harry had to sit in on a staff meeting in group 3 room. Attending would be Tom, the therapist, Lynn, the psychologist, Joanna, the junior probation officer for C-wing, Helen, the group 1 facilitator, and most of the uniformed staff up to SO grade. The purpose of the meeting was to discuss wing business. The staff would tell us who had been backed for various things and who had not, and the reasons for this. Then Tom would fill us in on what might be happening in the next week, whether any outside party – civilian psychologists, criminologists, law students, etc. – had requested to be allowed to attend wing meetings or hold Q&A sessions in the wing. Also there would be discussions on matters that might arise in the next week's community meetings, which men were due assessments, who had pulled out of therapy, who was due to be transferred out of Grendon, and anything else that might affect the running of C-wing. I wasn't looking forward to my first staff meeting. I still tended to get butterflies in my stomach whenever I was in a room with more than two uniforms, as in the past this meant it was about to kick off. I also wasn't yet comfortable with being part of the system and didn't know if I'd ever be able to dispel completely the shame and humiliation at what some small part of me still saw as capitulation. But Harry gave me a gee before the meeting. 'Don't worry about it, Raze,' he said. 'I felt the same when I first started the job. All you've got to remember is to be your own man and don't do or say anything that you're uncomfortable with.'

Harry handled the meeting like a pro and had them eating out of his hand from the first minute. It helped that he had already had three months of staff meetings as the vice-chair but I was glad he was there. He cracked jokes in his dry way and made everyone laugh, putting me at ease by asking for my opinion on certain matters. I could see that the staff group were relaxed and genuinely liked Harry, which was a bit of a revelation because I still thought they were just doing a job with us. In my mind there remained a bit of a divide between inmates and staff. I got on okay with most of the staff, and I did have real respect for and a friendship with the likes of Jimmy and Brian, but there was a certain level I could not go to with most of them. I had got Tom, the wing therapist, down as a bit of a cold fish, constantly studying us, weighing our words and emotions and filing away our body language for later examination. Now I saw he was quite a relaxed man with a good sense of humour. After the first meeting I felt a lot better and I knew it was going to get easier as time went on.

When not carrying out my duties as vice-chair or doing my journalism course work I was still spending a lot of time with Fred. Now that most of the old faces – John, Ray, Kevin and Daran – had gone, me and Fred were like a win double. Fred could be a bit manic when he was on a roll and he had a quirky sense of humour, often coming out with outrageous remarks. He would tell some of the staff that he was thinking about getting them into a headlock and running them head-first into the nearest wall, 'just for the fun of it', or he would coat people relentlessly until they had to walk away. Fred was a brilliant boxer, and almost without fear, but he had a terrible complex about his size and weight.

I remember once when he was training me as part of his fitness in-structor's degree he got it into his head that some big geezer from another wing was giving him dirty looks. I noticed that Fred was becoming distracted as he kept looking at this fella who was working out with weights on the other side of the gym. I could see he was fuming and asked him what the problem was. 'Does that big mug think I'm a cunt, or something?' he asked, rhetorically. I looked over at the bloke and didn't notice him doing anything untoward. 'Drop me out, Fred,' I said. 'The fella ain't even looking at you, he's just having a workout. Now turn it in.' But Fred wasn't having it. When he got into this mindset the next step would be showing the other man that he was stronger than he might look. 'I know what it is,' he told me. 'He's looking at little skinny me and thinking, "Look at that little cunt, how can he be giving orders in the gym, he's like a fucking fag-paper!"' This was serious because I could see that Fred had already worked it all out in his head and convinced himself that these were the man's actual thoughts.

No matter how long you stay in therapy there is still only so far you can go with it, and though it does help you to rationalize your thoughts and feelings in the search for better solutions and not always to succumb to your first impulses, sometimes you can just be having an off-day. Plus, with a lot, if not all, the men at Grendon, impulse control was a difficult thing we had to be aware of constantly. Let's face it, if you spend most of your life sticking it on anyone who you think might be taking a liberty with you, then it will become an almost natural response. What I'm trying to say is that every now and again almost everyone in therapy will have a momentary relapse. And Fred's complex about his size was his blind spot. Catch him on the wrong day and all the therapy in the world was not going to stop him throwing a right-hander. This doesn't mean that therapy didn't work for us – normal everyday citizens have the same problem sometimes – but the difference is that the reaction of a violent criminal can sometimes be a bit more extreme. My own blind spot was my insane jealousy about Denise and other men. I could tumble into a killing rage in seconds if I thought about anything like that. We all have our raw spots. We just have to work on them.

I climbed off the rowing machine and put my arm around Fred's shoulders, steering him out of sight of the man he had become fixated on. 'Listen, mate,' I said, reasonably. 'Get this shit out of your head. He ain't looking at you, he's just some melt going about his business, okay?' Fred wouldn't be swayed, and I realized that this hadn't just flopped on him, it had been building up for a while. 'No, Raze, he's been at it for weeks! Every time I come in here the geezer's screwing me out, and I'm starting to get the fucking hump with it. He needs a good one on the chin to sort him out.' I tried jollying Fred along, cracking a few jokes about how silly he was being. I told him not to fuck his life up. As a two-strike lifer he would be guaranteed another twelve months on his sentence just for chinning another con. Eventually, he took this on board, said he was okay and I got back on to the machine and carried on rowing myself to nowhere, happy that I had averted a disaster. I was somewhere in or around the pain barrier when I noticed that Fred had gone. I looked around in panic and saw him looking up at the weight-lifter with his hands on his hips. I jumped off the rower and nearly crashed into a weight machine as I tried to hurry across the gym floor on rubbery uncoordinated legs. But when I reached Fred he was calm. 'This is Jimmy,' he said in introduction. 'He's from east London. I knew one of his pals in Parkhurst.' I was relieved that no punches were flying and shook Jimmy's hand. 'You all right to get on with your bike exercises?' Fred asked me. 'Me and Jimmy are going to do a circuit.' I nodded. 'You sure everything's okay?' I asked. 'Sweet as,' Fred replied. So I shrugged and carried on with my workout.

What Fred did was set up a killer circuit, one that he knew he was capable of winning because of his fitness, and, under the guise of friendly competition, ran the muscle-bound Jimmy into the ground. Fifteen minutes later Fred was leaning casually against a weight machine chatting happily to the ruined east Londoner. Jimmy, his face redder than a Texan's neck, was on his hands and knees on a gym mat with sweat pouring off him, trying to get enough breath into his overworked lungs to reply. Fred had satisfied his own personal demon, proving that size and muscle aren't everything, and no one had been hurt. If you didn't count Jimmy's pride. On the way back from the gym Fred was his usual happy self. 'Thanks, mate,' he said to me, and I knew what he meant. Me and Fred had become great friends, but more than that, we had come to rely on each other to straighten each other out when it was needed. I would be sorry to see him go. It was more proof that therapy really did work – three years earlier Fred would probably have stuck a dumb-bell through Jimmy's face.

Fred was going through the process of his end-of-tariff reports. As a two-strike lifer he had a tariff of four years six months for GBH on his brother. Once that was up he was entitled to an oral hearing in front of the Parole Board to argue for release. With his record Fred realized that getting released, even though he had served the period the judge had passed on him for 'punishment and retribution', was never a real prospect. The best he could hope for was downgrading to category D and a period in an open jail. The report-making took almost six months and involved being interviewed by the wing therapist, the psychologist, the prison probation officer, the personal officer, the wing senior officer, the lifer manager and an outside probation officer. In some cases, such as with the wing therapist and the psychologist, there was a series of three or four interviews spread over a couple of weeks. These interviews were intense, most of them lasting a minimum of two hours, and involved a lot of repetition for the lifer. You had to go over your life, time in therapy, family relationships, resettlement plans and offending behaviour in great detail, and the process could be very draining. Then on the date of the hearing before the board you could be grilled by board members for anything up to six hours before they came to a decision. Of course, it wasn't that simple: you then had to wait for their answer. In theory the Parole Board should reply to your application within seven working days, but it was not uncommon to wait months. Half-naked Dave, for example, waited eleven months because the Home Secretary did not agree with the Parole Board's decision to send him to an open prison. And he was not the only one: Mel, the huge lifer in my group, waited for thirteen months and then got a knockback for another two years!

Just take a moment here and try to imagine the mental hell you'd go through while waiting for an answer from the Parole Board. Imagine you've served your tariff, say sixteen years, which is an average tariff for a mandatory lifer. You've done everything that's been expected of you, but you know you are not getting released just yet because the law says you have to serve a period in open conditions in order to be eligible for release. So you expect to do at least a further two years. You know that when you have been in an open prison for six months with no problems you become eligible for unescorted days out and then outside work in a real job, able to earn a real wage. This will be your chance to prepare for your future life, spend time with your family and gradually ease yourself into the outside world. It's what you've been dreaming of and praying for almost every waking moment since you first climbed aboard the sweatbox that brought you to prison. All those years never seeing something as simple as a tree, or a bus, or a view not dissected by a fence or a wall. All those heart-wrenching visits where you weren't allowed to hold your children or embrace your girlfriend without CCTV and the suspicious gimlet eyes of heavy-handed warders watching your every twitch. Those endless days toiling in prison workshops at menial poorly paid tasks, the nights of listening to the screams and roars of the other men or women enclosed in the boxes on all sides of you. The grim grey existence of closed prison is almost behind you now. You appear in front of the Parole Board, all shiny clean with your arguments fully formed and ready. You are grilled by the board for hours and then they say, 'Thank you very much, we'll be in touch with our answer in due course.' And the wait begins. How can you describe the stress of waking up every morning hoping that today might be the day when you will know your fate, only to be given no information whatsoever and starting all over again the following day? There is no one you can ask, no action you can take in order to speed the process up, and it can go on for months. Now imagine that the answer finally comes – and it's negative. Now you know you must go through the whole thing again next year. It is no wonder that some lifers are in favour of capital punishment. And yes, most of these men and women have committed crimes that warrant them being in prison, but let's not pretend that life imprisonment is a walk in the park.

Reading the newspapers and listening to some of the crap that's spoken, you might think that getting out of prison on parole is as easy as turning up in front of the board and saying 'let me out'. Far from it, we have a very rigorous parole system in this country, certainly when it comes to releasing lifers and long-termers. Many lifers who have even a hint of 'danger' left about them can spend years, sometimes decades, in prison over and above the minimum tariff set by the trial judge. The only time we ever hear tariffs discussed in the media is when some paedophile gets a squeeze or when some idiot juvenile murders a middle-class banker or city gent, and then the tabloids whip the public into a frenzy with their screams for longer prison sentences. All prisoners are lumped together under a tabloid umbrella marked 'Murderers, Rapists and Child-killers', or just 'Leering Lawbreakers' in the case of the *Sun*. Then some cowardly politician will pander to the mob and impose even more severe restrictions on the majority of prisoners to make himself seem tough.

Fred was pretty lucky since it took only nine weeks for him to get his answer from the Parole Board. He was granted category D status. That was the good news, but he had also been given a two-year knockback. That meant he would spend a further minimum of two years in prison before being allowed to apply for parole again. With almost four years in therapy, it made me wonder just how much store the Parole Board actually put in what we were doing in Grendon? Or maybe it was just Fred that they had reservations about? Either way, the kid was on his way. He applied for Springhill, the open prison right next door to Grendon, even though it had a reputation for being full of mugs and plastic gangsters serving minuscule sentences for crimes like drunk-driving and shoplifting. The trouble with these short-term petty offenders is that they have no real concept about doing bird and cause a lot of agg for long-term prisoners who just want to finish their sentences and get out. If you're doing nine months and have fuck-all to lose, what's to stop you acting the cunt? You can drink, take drugs, give it the big 'un all you like, you'll still be walking out of the gate on your date. But long-termers, and particularly lifers, have usually struggled for years to get to category D jails; the slightest bit of trouble and they can be shipped back to a closed prison for another couple of years. So for the lag it means gritting his teeth and walking a tightrope in open jails, trying to avoid the idiots who might want to earn themselves a rep by goading him into a punch-up because they know he has to swallow or take the chance of even more bird. Some category D jails, such as Latchmere House in Surrey or Blantyre House in Kent, accept only a more mature clientele of long-termers coming to the end of their bird, but the waiting lists for these jails are very long and Fred wanted out of Grendon as soon as possible. So he applied for, and was accepted at, Springhill. It was either that or hang about in Grendon for another year awaiting a transfer.

I was gutted that Fred was leaving. Of course I was happy that he was progressing in his sentence, and I really believed that he was going to make it on the out when they eventually gave him his chance. But I was sad to be saying goodbye to a good friend. The evening before he left we sat in my cell and spoke about the future. Fred had all his qualifications as a gym instructor and he hoped to be able to work with young kids, maybe teach them boxing. He knew he could never get his trainer's licence because of his criminal record but he had high hopes for the future. I wished him luck and told him that if he ever needed anything he only had to drop me a line. Then, realizing that we might be in danger of showing some emotion, we fell into the vicious but humorous banter that characterizes most male relationships in prison.

The next morning Fred came down to see me before I went into group. By the time I came out at 10.30 he would be over in Springhill starting the next phase of his journey. We didn't have to say anything, we just clasped hands and embraced. And that was that. I felt Fred's leaving pretty acutely for the next couple of months and got depressed a lot. I was lost on C-wing now; everyone I had started out with had moved on and I was the only one left. I felt unable to connect with anyone on a meaningful level and I ended up retreating into my job as vice-chair and immersing myself in writing. I still had friends on the wing, there was Nolan and Half-naked Dave, plus I had grown to like Pickles, though I couldn't take too much of him in one sitting as he had become very fervent and intense about therapy. I sometimes spoke to one of the new guys, Kung Fu Chris, but he was another deep character. I realized that what I was missing was someone with whom I could just relax and have a good laugh. Everything had become way too serious, and, as I've said before, my sense of humour is one of the things that has helped me to survive over three decades in prison. Fred had been my pressure valve, and now I was going to have to vent through something other than humour. I was about to enter a very rocky period at Grendon, and this is when I would find out just how much I had changed.

24. A Loaded Question

After my stint as vice-chair I took the leather chair and became chairman of C-wing community on 12 August 2005. Hate-'em-all Harry vacated the post with a huge sigh of relief and within five months he would be downgraded to category D and on his way to HMP Ford. I had learned a lot from Harry and felt more comfortable in my dealings with the staff group. I knew what I had to do and now it was just a case of getting on with it. Mikey, who had been my closest rival on the last vote, was voted in as vice-chair and I was happy for him. I would enjoy working with Mikey as he was an easygoing and sensible man. It would have been a bit more difficult for me if one of the needy crowd had been voted in as vice, but, as usual, they got mostly their own vote and nothing else. Being chairman was a lot more stressful than being vice-chair because I became, in effect, the first point of contact for anyone who had business with C-wing. It was also my job to run the community meetings, conduct all business, call for minutes at the start and end of each meeting and make sure everything ran within the time boundaries. I had be available to both staff and community members at all times, and meet any official visitors. Sometimes being the conduit between the community and the staff and governors called for a fine balancing act, but I managed it okay. Mikey was a big help and proved very sensible and calm under fire. He was particularly good at pouring oil on troubled waters during the occasional sit-downs. The chairman's job, however, reinforced in me the already strongly held belief that most of the governor grades at Grendon could not be trusted. One typical example of this was when all wing chairmen were called to a meeting with the dep and two other governors soon after I had taken the chair. We met up on G-wing and were offered coffee and biscuits and a lot of soft soap about what a great job we were all doing for the prison and our individual communities. Once they got to the point it turned out that, in order to save money, they had taken the decision to bring in early lock-up for all prisoners on Friday evenings and for two hours at lunchtime on weekends. The reason we were called was so that they could get us to break the news and sell it to the communities. It was a smart move. If, as should have happened, a governor had turned up at each wing's meeting and given the news, it was odds-on that they would have had to put up with at least an hour of questioning and flak from forty-odd men. This way we would have to announce it as a done deal and then move on to the next topic of business.

The dep swore blind that these new restrictions would be in place only for a maximum of three months and then we would go back to normal. The chairman of D-wing questioned this, saying, 'I was here four years ago, guv, when you told us that the early bang-up on Saturday and Sunday evenings was only going to be a temporary measure. Here we are, four years down the line, and we are still getting locked up at 4.30 at weekends. How do we know that if we sell this to the communities as "temporary", that you won't make us look like idiots in three months' time and make it permanent?' The dep smiled sadly and shook his head as if he was genuinely hurt by the accusation. 'I can assure you,' he said, sincerity dripping from every syllable, 'this is only a temporary measure. You have my word.'

There's an old prison adage that says, 'You can tell when a prison governor is lying, because you can see his lips move.' And in this case that was to prove very apt. When I left Grendon, almost two and a half years after that meeting with the deputy governor, the whole of Grendon was still being locked up at 4.30 on Friday evening and at lunchtime on Saturday and Sunday. So much for 'temporary measures'. But that was just one small example of how the governor grades at Grendon either ignored the therapeutic process or tried to use it for their own ends. Though I had a lot of respect for the wing staff and other professionals at Grendon, on the whole and with one or two exceptions I felt nothing like the same for the governor grades. As for the big cheese, the governor himself, I rarely saw him after the flurry of official activity over the publication of my first book.

I treated the chairman's job as a serious position, but I would be lying if I said that I saw no chance for personal advancement in it. Almost everyone who successfully completed the post had ended up with good reports and a progressive move to category D conditions. And, like all lifers, I wanted D cat. It was the last step before actual release. At the time of my six-year paper hearing, I was still a category B prisoner. My aim was to achieve category C status before the next paper hearing, which would be at the seven-and-a-half-year mark. But category C can also be granted to a lifer by the governor of the prison, rather than by the Parole Board, on the recommendation of his staff, and I was granted this security downgrade in July 2005. In all the years I had spent in jail I had only ever been downgraded to category C on one occasion and that was on a previous sentence. Within six weeks of being downgraded I'd made two attempts to scale the wall of the lower security jail I was in, and then actually did escape while being escorted by two prison officers. So getting cat C now was a major achievement for me. It also meant that within six months of the downgrade I would be entitled to apply for a ROTL (release on temporary licence), which meant a day out of prison to a local town, though escorted by a prison officer.

I can fully understand that any prison governor looking at my previous record might be a tad nervous about signing his name to a document that would allow me loose in the community with minimal supervision. After all, I had shown great reluctance to accept my previous periods of incarceration with good grace, and had proven myself a severe danger to the public. The last time I escaped from prison I had robbed fourteen banks, been involved in two shootings, and generally caused mayhem wherever I went. It took a squad of police, armed with machine-pistols, a helicopter and a high-speed car chase through the streets of rush-hour London in order to get me back safely behind bars. So, of course, I understood the trepidation this knowledge engendered in the governor grades. The wing and therapy staff had confidence in me, they had witnessed the changes in my character and behaviour during my time in therapy, particularly Glenda, who was one of the few who had known me in the past (at Belmarsh, though we hadn't exactly hit it off), so they recommended I should be given the chance to prove myself. But it was never going to be easy for me to get anywhere near the gate, let alone outside it, with my terrible pedigree. And my writing career proved to be another negative factor.

After the ministerial involvement in the 'investigation' into the publishing of my first book, I had agreed not to give any more interviews to the national press but I had been trained as a journalist by the prison system – in fact one of the few vocational training courses at Grendon was the NUJ course run by the education department which I had taken and passed with distinction – so I still wrote the odd piece for the *Independent*, *GQ* magazine and various others. But since I had managed to slide without charge from the book investigation it seemed that someone somewhere up the ladder, perhaps in Prison Service HQ, the Prison Service Press Office, or maybe even the Home Office, had decided to make me their pet project. I never did get to the bottom of who was actually behind the campaign to stop me writing, but I can assure you that it was a very real and concerted effort on their part. The number 1 governor was told to unhitch my wagon and slap me back into place. He handed over my chastisement to one of the governors. He was one of those who had worked his way up from landing screw to second banana in a cheap suit and couldn't stop boasting about it. I had my first dealings with him when a piece I'd had published in the *Guardian* about prison education angered the PSPO because Baroness Scotland, then minister for prison education, had taken the trouble to pen a defence to my accusation that the system had all but scrapped funding for higher education in favour of basic skills targets. Any prisoner who wanted to further his education had to seek funding from charities. I'm almost sure that Baroness Scotland herself didn't get on the blower to PSPO and order them to single me out; more likely it was some oversensitive soul in PSHQ or PSPO who was outraged that a serving prisoner had the audacity to elicit a public reply from a minister. But, however it went down, I was soon to receive a visit from the governor.

He started out by trying to impress me with his hard-man credentials. Apparently he had worked in a Special Security Unit back in the day when it was home to some of the most dangerous prisoners in this country. He dropped the names of a few well-known criminals and let me know that they all considered him 'firm but fair'. The usual bollocks. Then he tackled me on my writing. He wouldn't say who had asked him to have a word with me, though I asked him point-blank several times, or what was his reasoning behind the objections. First he tried the old Standing Order 5b route, asking me if I knew it was an offence against prison rules to receive payment for published articles. I told him I was well aware of this and that my fee had been donated to the NSPCC and I had the paperwork to prove it. With most of my published writings I had followed prison rules to the letter: I had sent my stuff out through the ordinary postal route, which meant it could be censored by prison staff, since all outgoing mail has to be handed to staff unsealed. My articles were covered by the exceptions to Standing Order 5b in that they were 'serious comment on the criminal justice system'. I wasn't given to frivolous accusations that had no merit. Realizing I had covered all the bases and that he had no leverage, the governor waffled a bit and then told me, in a veiled and roundabout manner, that the PSPO weren't happy, and they had got in touch with the number 1 governor and made him unhappy, which made his deputy unhappy, and if all these people remained unhappy, then I might want to reconsider my 'hobby' of writing for the press. After all, I was a lifer, and I had to rely on these people being happy with me if I ever wanted to progress in my sentence. I looked at him with absolute contempt. I was tempted to tell him to stick the PSPO and the governor up his arse and then follow them, but I said nothing. He seemed satisfied with my silence, probably taking it for compliance, and left.

The following month I wrote a piece for GQ magazine about the amount of female fan mail I'd had since the publication of my autobiography, and again I received a visit from the same governor. This time he dispensed with the tedious formalities and came right to the point: if I didn't stop getting my name into outside publications it could be very detrimental to my progress. I got the message and, realizing that these people had my life in their hands, I agreed, out of pure courtesy, to let the governor see everything I was sending out for publication. Not in advance, but at the same time as it went out. I was pissed off at myself for accepting this censorship via the back door as I realized that the management of the prison, the PSPO, PSHQ or the Home Office didn't have a legal leg to stand on in this matter. But where, in the past, I would have relished a good battle with the system over this, I now had much more to lose. I was starting to see an end to my sentence and I knew in my heart that I would never be going back to crime. I had a future on the outside and I wanted it. I couldn't do anything that would jeopardize my progress. He was satisfied with my concession and left.

As I had suspected would be the case, pretty soon the governor was back to press his advantage.

'Look, the governor is all for you writing, he doesn't want to stop you.' I managed to prevent myself snorting in derision at this. He continued, 'All we're asking for is that before you send anything out of the prison for publication we should be allowed to look at it in advance. Just in case we have to answer enquiries about it, at least we would then be able to say we knew about it and not be embarrassed. That's all.' I thought about it. 'So you want to censor me? Above and beyond the censorship every other prisoner's mail is subjected to?' He shook his head. 'Not censorship, just awareness.' We both knew he was pissing down my back and trying to convince me it was raining but I let it slip and set about refining the terms of this new arrangement. In the end, against my better judgement and with a heavy heart, I agreed to submit my writings in advance but sought, and received, firm assurance that any objections to what I had written would be conveyed to me in reasonable detail and in time for me to make changes and still meet publication deadlines. He left it at that for the moment, but a couple of days after our meeting he was back with a 'compact' for me to sign.

A week later, Will Self got in touch to tell me he had secured me a feature gig for a glossy magazine called *Men's Health*, who wanted a 3,000-word piece on prison healthcare. I duly set about putting this together well in advance of the publishing deadline and then submitted a copy to the governor, as agreed. I informed him of the publication deadline in my attached note and asked him to get back to me as soon as possible. I had no doubts the article would be approved as the contents were not contentious in the slightest and if anything gave the prison a gee. So I waited, and I waited, and every time I made enquiries over the next two weeks I was informed a reply was 'imminent'. I eventually got my reply two days after the deadline had passed. In a terse note the governor said that the article had been read by the Press Office and deemed 'not suitable' to send out for publication. No reason was given for the refusal and despite my many enquiries I never did find out what they thought was wrong with it. It was then that I realized that they didn't just want to censor my writing by cutting bits out, their intention was to close me down completely. It didn't matter if I was writing an article on flower arranging for the Women's Institute magazine. Someone, some-where in the vast machinery of the prison system did not want my name or views getting to the outside world. It was a good job I didn't suffer from paranoia any more. Much.

I spoke to Tom, the head therapist, who had been a witness to me signing the compact with the governor and told him what had happened. I finished by saying that as far as I was concerned the prison had broken that compact and it was now null and void. Tom sympathized with my position but told me that if I carried on getting my writing published he could foresee trouble with the governors. But I was adamant. I would submit no more of my work for approval.

For quite a while after the affair of the broken compact I just gave up writing for outside publications. I had plenty of other work to do and was kept busy writing *Raiders*, my second book for Penguin, and studying for my journalism exams. But some months before I became eligible for my first ROTL I was offered a regular column in *Loaded* magazine, the best of the 'lads' mags', and even though I knew the prison system definitely would not approve of this, I decided to do it. To be honest I quite enjoyed writing for *Loaded*, it gave me a chance to crack a few jokes and write articles for a deadline once again – good practice and experience for any aspiring journalist. I did nothing to hide the fact that I was writing for publication again, and I sent the columns out through normal mail channels where they could be stopped or censored at any time. The prison system would say I was defying them and daring them to stop me – not really the best attitude for someone who was in therapy in order to change – but I was breaking no rule or law and I believe that their attempts to gag and stifle me were wrong in practice and principle. I detest tyranny in any form and still say that challenging authority is not always a bad thing. I would change a lot of things about my character while at Grendon, but not everything – nor did I wish to. I would not become a shill for the system or an unthinking automaton who would 'just follow orders'. It was not in me. My writing was a big part of my individuality, and as it was one of the things that would help me to make the transition between my old life and the new one, I sincerely believe it should have been encouraged. But that was not the way of the prison system.

So 'Razor's Life Inside' became a regular slot in *Loaded* and was very well received by its readership. I even had a photo taken in the ground-floor corridor outside my cell for the byline, looking suitably con-like in my Ray-Ban Wayfarers sunglasses. My tongue-in-cheek columns of 750 words every month illustrated various aspects of my prison experience – such topics as prison escape, prison violence, the borstal system, illicitly brewed alcohol, sex offenders and prison riots. Some of the uniformed staff at Grendon were regular readers and would often comment on how my pieces made them laugh. But there would be very little laughing when my scribblings eventually came back to haunt me later on.

Then I applied for my first ROTL. You cannot imagine the excitement of a man approaching his first day in the outside world after years of incarceration. To walk along streets with people who are neither criminals nor prison staff, to experience myriad colours and smells, to eat real food with metal implements instead of slop with a plastic spoon, and to be free, if only for a few short hours and with a plainclothes guardian in tow – a definite frisson of freedom nonetheless. Like Christmas in heaven! But before all this could come true, there was the process to go through, and the prison system does not make it easy. As a lifer, the hoops you have to jump in order to get a ROTL are high and many. After serving a chunk of years and then waiting the six-month period after being granted C cat, the next step is to apply in writing for your day. A refinement of this move unique to Grendon is that you first have to get backing from your group, and then backing from the community. If this is granted, and I never heard of anyone on C-wing getting a negative from group or community, your application goes to the wing staff, who will discuss it with the therapy staff and wing PO. Next you appear in front of a ROTL board, which consists of your personal officer, therapy staff – Tom and Lynn – the wing SO and sometimes the PO. During this interview you are questioned on your past record, your progress in therapy, what you intend to do on the ROTL, whether you think you're ready for it, and whatever else takes the questioner's fancy. If this board is satisfied with your answers, you move on to the next stage, which is another board. You do not appear on the second board, usually held some weeks after the first one and attended by security staff and a security governor, who scrutinize your record and reports and finally make their recommendation. If they agree to your ROTL, you will appear on a third board attended by wing and therapy staff plus a governor. You will once more be subjected to many questions as to your intentions. Eventually you will be asked to leave the room and the governor will make his decision. If it is positive you will be informed of the date of your ROTL, with the codicil that the paperwork will first have to be signed by the number 1 governor. This whole process can take up to five months (exactly how long mine took) and every day you wait is an agony of hope and anticipation.

Glenda agreed to escort me on my first ROTL. Though by then I had mostly changed my views about Glenda, I was still a bit hesitant about her taking me on my first day out. But she had fully backed me in the board meetings and was tireless in her encouragement, so I swallowed the small doubt I still had about her and decided to see how she would shape up once outside the prison. I knew it was very important to feel comfortable about my escort; I didn't want the day to be ruined by her acting like a screw. I was aware that security would order her to keep me on a short leash but I at least wanted to be able to relax and enjoy the day. I began to count the days down. It seemed that some of the community were almost as excited as I was about my first day out. Of course my close friends were, but so were others who saw it as an example of what they, too, might be able to look forward to. After all, if someone like me, with my record, could get a ROTL, it proved that Grendon was not going to hold our past behaviour against us, and this gave a few people hope for themselves.

But three days before I was due to go out there was a security scare in the prison when the radio of one of the screws went missing. It turned out that it had not been stolen but mislaid, but, in time-honoured prison-system tradition, they decided to overreact first and ask questions later. With a stroke of a pen the governor cancelled all ROTLs as a 'precaution'. Don't ask – I believe I've already explained that the prison system and its minions are not very big on logic. It was very disappointing and frustrating for me to get this close to temporary freedom and then have it snatched away through no fault of my own. But all I could do was swallow and be patient. Once the screw's radio had been found – probably in his pocket – my ROTL was rescheduled. But then a lifer from A-wing, who had been granted his first ROTL, decided to leave his escort and head back to his home town of Manchester for another bite of the criminal cherry. Good luck to him, but his escape from an escort meant that all ROTLs were cancelled once again.

Then, just one day before I was again due to walk out of the prison gates, I was summoned to a meeting with one of the governors. As I walked into the room I knew this was not going to be good. I was told to sit down and then he held up the latest copy of *Loaded* magazine. My heart sank. 'It has been brought to my attention,' he said, 'that, contrary to prison rules and in spite of being specifically ordered not to do so, you have written for a national publication.' There was no way I was letting him get any further without correction. 'Just stop right there,' I said, a spark of anger igniting inside me. 'Number one: I was never specifically ordered not to write for any national publications, and two: I think you'll find that neither have I broken any prison rules.' He shook his head. 'You had an agreement with the governor that anything you want to send out for publication must first go through me and be okayed by us, and now we discover that, unknown to us, you have been writing a regular monthly column for a national magazine. Frankly, we are very disappointed. How do you think it looks when the number 1 governor gets a call from the

Prison Service Press Office asking how one of his inmates has not only been getting national exposure but also has his picture at the top of the column? Can you imagine the embarrassment it's caused when he has to admit we know nothing about it? It makes it look like we're not in control of our own prison!'

I shrugged. 'As far as I'm concerned I've done nothing wrong. We had an agreement and it was broken the first time out and I owe no loyalty to anyone. The fact that you and the prison system do not like my writing is neither here nor there as there's nothing legal you can do about it. So I don't know why we're having this conversation again.' He was fuming. He stared at me for a long moment without saying anything. Then, 'Well, I have to inform you that your ROTL has been cancelled until further notice.' Now *I* was fuming. 'For what reason?' I almost shouted at him. He pointed to the copy of *Loaded*. 'Because you have been courting publicity in a national magazine, because the opinions and attitudes you express in this magazine do not conform to the ethos of Grendon – you're talking about attacking sex offenders in one column! And because you have a photo of yourself, looking very like Charles Bronson, I might add, at the top of each column. This makes you "high profile" in the media, and we cannot take the chance that someone might decide to follow and photo you while you are out in public and then splash it all over the tabloids. That would be an embarrassment too far.' I knew there was no point in arguing with him. The other side held all the power and it didn't matter what I said. There was no way I would be walking out of that gate the next morning – or any morning if this mob had anything to do with it.

My anger quickly drained away as I examined and accepted the in-evitability of my situation. I sat back in my chair and sighed. I had to challenge him on what he had said, but there was really no enthusiasm in my questions. 'What the hell has my photo got to do with anything? What? You're really suggesting that you're cancelling my day out because I "look like" Charlie Bronson in my photo? Do you realize how mad that sounds?' He shook his head again and prepared to leave. 'Unless you have something constructive to add, then this meeting is over.' And that was that. Months of work and waiting for my first day out of prison in many years and I get told I can't go because I slightly resemble a notorious madman when I'm photographed in sunglasses. But even in the height of my misery I knew that he had a point about the publicity and that it would hold up in any legal argument about this matter. Also there was the fact that in one of my columns I had made a joke, albeit a bit of a black one, about attacking child molesters. I had been speaking about my past, but the subject matter was a bit insensitive given my present surroundings. I hadn't really done anything wrong according to the letter of the law, but I should have thought my position through a bit more carefully before rushing into things for instant gratification. At worst, it was a lesson learned. There was little I could do except wipe my mouth and move on. I used my group to air my feelings about the matter and decided to give up my column in *Loaded*. If I was ever going to progress through this sentence I would have to learn the art of compromise and keep a low profile. I decided to concentrate on writing books in the long term and keep my journalism work on the back burner until I was released.

I would apply again for my ROTL when the dust cleared over the *Loaded* affair. And though I had given up writing articles for publication, my war with the Grendon suits and the prison system in general over my writing was to rear its paranoid ugly head once more before I left the prison for pastures new. And next time it would be a full official investigation instigated by someone very high up the prison food chain.

Eventually I did get my trip to Banbury – about eight months after it should have been. I was escorted by Glenda, who was now my personal officer and group facilitator. The moment I stepped over the lip of the judas gate and into the free world was one to treasure. I stopped a few feet from the gatehouse, out in the car park and threw my head back to look at the wide expanse of grey sky with no walls or bars to cut off the view. It was pissing down with rain and it was wonderful to feel the raindrops on my face. I laughed out loud. Glenda was amused by my delight but I didn't mind. I suppose it was quite funny, laughing in the rain, but I felt really alive. Glenda drove one of the prison cars, and even though she was only doing 30mph down the country lanes, to me it seemed like the speed of light! It was nearly eight years since I'd been in the front seat of a moving vehicle and I became a tiny bit scared by the road seemingly rushing towards me. I kept pressing my feet into the footwell as though I was operating the brake and clutch when we approached bends – it was an involuntary reaction. Glenda seemed a different person outside the prison and not in uniform, and we chatted away with no uncomfortable silences. I was relaxed in her company, and we even spoke about the dark days at the start of my sentence when we had been on opposing sides at HMP Belmarsh. If someone had told either of us then that years down the line we would be going for a day trip to Banbury I would have laughed at them and Glenda would have ordered a drug test for them!

Banbury is a lovely little town, with a modern shopping centre right next to a canal and an old market place close by – it was a riot of colour and sound to me. I was fascinated by everything – people's clothes, mobile phones, shop windows, cars, traffic lights, trees, narrow boats – it was all fresh to my prison-dulled senses. I found a shop that sold CDs and spent most of my money on the goodies therein. We had lunch in a KFC – my choice, not Glenda's! – and then, all too soon, we were heading back to the prison. I was to have three more escorted ROTLs while at Grendon – two more to Banbury and one to that great swathe of concrete and neon, Milton Keynes shopping centre – but none was as exciting and life-changing as that first one. Being allowed out into the real world without sirens, armed police and 4lb of stainless steel hanging from my wrists was proof to me that my life was finally heading in the right direction. Going into therapy had been the right choice.

25. Trouble in Paradise

By the summer of 2005 the very fabric of Grendon had changed almost beyond recognition. The single wall had been torn down and replaced with double security fences draped with coils of sharp and shiny razor-wire, the previously open spaces between each wing were also fenced off and there were now no-go areas all around the prison. The erection of the fences appeared to usher in a new era at Grendon, just as I had feared, and the prison seemed to be being dragged into line with all other category B prisons. The pressure of overcrowding in the prison system as a whole was also beginning to impact on the kind of men who were ending up at Grendon, and we started to get junkies who were still detoxing when they reached F-wing. In the past the criteria for drug addicts coming into therapy was that they had to be clean at least six months before arrival and have passed at least three piss-tests. Now the local jails were just stuffing them on to the vans and sending them wherever the spaces existed. The rules governing almost everything began to be tightened up. For over forty years the rumour had been that Grendon was going downhill and now it really was.

Something that was to affect every inmate at Grendon was the fact that somehow the governors managed to lose over £100,000 off the yearly budget. As inmates we were not privy to the details of exactly how this could happen, but there was a persistent rumour about a dodgy accountant who fleeced the gaff and then did a runner before it all came on top. There may not be a jot of truth in that and the real reasons for the budget shortfall are probably as mundane as a miscalculation, but however it came about it had a direct effect on everyone. The first thing the governor did to pull the jail out of its financial hole was to slash healthcare cover. Grendon would no longer have medical staff on duty at night, so if anyone had a heart attack or became ill after 5 p.m. he'd have to hang on until a nurse could be called out to the prison. The first I knew of this was when I, along with a dozen or so other diabetics and epileptics, was called up to the healthcare centre. We were told that if we wanted to stay at Grendon and continue therapy, we would have to sign a disclaimer stating that we were happy to be denied twenty-four-hour healthcare! Fucking liberty! We were being blackmailed into endorsing the governor's cutbacks. We were told that if we refused to sign, we would be shipped out to whatever nick was available. Everyone signed, except me. I refused and told them I would go and pack. It was a bit risky calling their bluff like this, but I still retained enough of my old fighting spirit to do it. As I had hoped, the system backed down. They must have known that their behaviour was actionable by law and that I was just the man to take it all the way. Though I never signed their disclaimer they never mentioned it again. But it was a Pyrrhic victory as I was still left without twenty-four-hour medical care.

Another money-saver the governor foisted on us was the sale of our canteen. Grendon had one of the few prison shops that had not been sold to private profit-making commercial companies. Our canteen was not perfect by any means but at least we got a chance to see the goods before we bought them and had regular canteen staff to whom we could complain when stuff was out of date or overpriced, or even just to make enquiries to. The communities had discussed the possibility of a 'bagging-up' system on many occasions and always voted unanimously to keep the canteen as it was. Bagging-up is what they have in other nicks: you order your canteen goods a week in advance and instead of going up to the canteen the goods are delivered to the wing in bags and distributed by the staff. Commercial companies love the bagging-up system as it allows them to cut overheads. They don't need a canteen, and they have various tricks for increasing their profit margins, such as leaving at least one ordered item out of every bag but still charging for it. Once the bag has been handed over to the inmate the company refuses to accept liability for what may or may not be in it. Also, a lot of the goods will be past sell-by dates or damaged or part of a two-for-the-price-of-one offer but being sold singly and over the recommended retail price. Commercial companies are not coming into prisons and taking over these services for altruistic reasons, they are doing it, plain and simply, to make a profit out of a captive customer base with very little scope to complain about it and absolutely no chance of taking their business elsewhere. Despite the many community votes against it, the governor ignored us in his scramble to save money and sold us to a private company.

There was a lot of bad feeling and unease among the communities that things that affected our everyday lives and that we once had a say in were now being done behind closed doors. We had been given to believe that we had a forum where we would be presented with any changes, to discuss them in a healthy and open manner before being allowed to vote on them in a democratic way. This had always been 'the Grendon way', but now these things were being taken out of our hands and our arguments were falling on deaf ears. Many of the uniformed staff, and even the therapists, were also unhappy about the changes, but they seemed as powerless as the inmates when faced with a team of hard-line governors led by the number 1 governor himself. The mantra during these dark days became: as long as the therapy remains untouched Grendon will march on. But there were plans afoot to dilute even the therapy, the very core of why HMP Grendon had been so successful over the preceding forty-odd years. The governor decided that another money-saver would be to do away with the uniformed group facilitators and free them up for more mundane prison duties. This had a massive impact on the small groups as the uniformed facilitators had spent years building up relationships with their groups. Many men, me included, came to Grendon with a deep mistrust and hatred of uniformed staff, but seeing the same facilitator day in, day out, gave men a chance to get to know them as real people. I felt I could trust Brian with my most intimate secrets and feelings, but this didn't happen overnight; we built a mutual trust over a long and sustained period. Now the groups would be facilitated by any random member of staff who happened to be on duty that day.

The knock-on effect of scrapping the permanent group facilitators was that less real therapy was getting done. And for a therapeutic community this was a major setback. The fact was that, although a good percentage of the uniformed staff at Grendon were pro-therapy and intelligent enough to understand what was going on in the groups, there was also a significant minority who didn't have a clue and cared even less. These were the staff who had transferred in from hard-line prisons, like most of the governor grades, for a cushy ride, or inexperienced recruits who had been given Grendon as their first posting on a random basis. At least one third of the uniformed staff on C-wing were either ignorant of or uncaring about the therapeutic work. As far as they were concerned they were prison officers, screws, and not social workers or agony uncles. They were interested in searches, nickings and C&R training with batons and judo holds, not hearing that Chester the Molester had been raped by his grandfather and kept locked in a cupboard until he was sixteen which might be why he had become an abuser himself. The balance could work pretty well if these screws were not being forced to sit in groups but were just left to tend to general prison duties, but now they would be taking groups. It stood to reason that many men would find it very difficult to reveal their feelings and emotions, particularly those who had spent their lives as violent criminals in a macho environment like prison. But it is even harder to open up when you know that your screw facilitator is sitting there mugging you off in his mind, listening for juicy titbits he can share with the lads down the pub later, or openly yawning and looking at his watch while you are baring your soul. HMP Grendon was fast losing the things that had made it unique.

Personally, though, I didn't feel too bad. Things were going okay for me. I had a handle on my therapeutic journey and was working hard, I had reports coming up for the Parole Board that might see me attain category D status and a move to an open prison, and doing the chairman's job could only help my chances. Unfortunately, my chairmanship got off on a sour note as the first thing I had to deal with was a commitment vote. And it was the Mincer. Since our last run-in the Mincer had been keeping pretty much of a low profile, though he still managed to upset most of his group with his neat line in caustic comments about them. He also inveigled his way on to every Q&A session with students and trainee psychologists who visited the wing, offering his bitchy opinions on everything from the state of Grendon to their choice of shoes. But, as was inevitable, he couldn't keep his bald misshapen head below the firing line for ever. And it fell to me as chairman to facilitate his egress from Grendon.

After it came out that the Mincer had been having sex with an inmate at HMP Wakefield and that he had been half blackmailing him with that knowledge ever since, the Mincer became even more of a hate figure on C-wing. He seemed to feed on this hatred and spew it back in vitriol when people least expected it. He had a habit of waiting until someone in his group was at a sensitive stage of his therapy and then sticking the knife in verbally. Eventually group 5 had had enough of him and put him up for commitment. The reason cited in the book was 'failure to show commitment to the therapeutic process and group members'. My first action as chairman of C-wing community was to preside over this serious issue. I had little doubt that the Mincer would be voted out of Grendon on this occasion and I would have laid odds on the vote being a landslide. But once again I was to be surprised by how things turned out.

The Mincer took his place in the community room and Mikey read the book issue out loud. I asked the Mincer if he had anything to say in his defence, and I was definitely not surprised when he spoke, almost without drawing breath, for the next twenty-five minutes. He went from an outraged Dreyfus to Jesus on the Mount and back again in very quick order and many times over in the next half-hour. As I listened to him talk in that plummy, upper-class, self-pitying voice I was once again fascinated by this man. He seemed completely amoral and without a jot of shame, and the only remorse he felt was for himself. Once again I realized just how dangerous he was.

At the end of the Mincer's speech, in which he slagged everyone, reiterated his own superiority, and begged to be allowed to stay at Grendon, I called for the vote. There were forty-two men in the community room that morning and I, as the chairman, was the only one not obliged to vote. My vote would be used only in the event of a tie. 'Anyone who thinks the Mincer should go, stick your hands up clearly,' I said. There is always a small minority of men in the community who will not vote anyone out. These can be the pals of the man up for commitment, or just the hard-core who do not feel comfortable sending another man back to the system with a stain on his record. So I was expecting about two thirds of hands to go up. I counted, incredulous, and found that only twenty-three men voted the Mincer out. Just over half the wing. I couldn't understand it. He had as good as spat in everyone's faces and not for the first time, but there were still men in the community who obviously thought he deserved another chance. I called for a show of hands of those who thought he should stay – eighteen, including the Mincer himself. Even the staff looked a bit shocked by this, and I was later to find out that they had been so confident that the community would vote him out that they had already ordered a prison transport to take him to HMP Full Sutton. But still, he had been voted out. Now it was up to the staff group to rubber-stamp our decision, and they did, in very short order. The Mincer was told that he could reapply for Grendon in six months from his date of transfer. But it was to be over a year before he did return, and this time he would be D-wing's problem.

At the second meeting I chaired later that week I noticed that a couple of people were being disrespectful, talking among themselves in whispers, and when I called for minutes at least one man put his hand up and then pretended to be scratching his head when I pointed to him to speak. Then there was a sudden spate of men leaving the meeting under the pretence of using the toilet. They were the usual suspects, the liberty-takers who liked to see how far they could push the limits and test the boundaries of everything and felt safe doing these things in numbers. I knew they were testing me. I had been at Grendon a while now and had not punched anyone up in the air, I had become quiet and calm on the surface and these melts thought it might be fun to give me a poke. They were like spiteful kids at the zoo, spitting at and taunting an old lion who was safely secured in his cage. But this old lion still had a pretty powerful roar left in him. I knew that if I was to say nothing then it would just get worse with every meeting until they would blatantly take the piss. I had seen it happen to other chairmen and was adamant it was not going to happen to me. I waited until five minutes before the end of the meeting, and, in a lull in proceedings, I suddenly picked the wing book up and slammed it down on the table with a loud crash that jolted everyone out of their comfort zone. A lot of stunned and worried faces turned towards me, including staff and therapists. 'Right,' I began, 'I've noticed that some people in this room seem to think I'm some sort of old mug, and that they can take liberties. Well, I'm telling you all clearly now, there are going to be some changes around here. Number one: no fucking whispering among yourselves during the meetings; it's disrespectful to the person who is talking. Number two: when I call for minutes or a vote for any reason, you will raise your hand clearly. If I see anyone raise their hand and then pretend they are scratching their head or just stretching, I'll start questioning commitment and naming names. Also, nobody leaves this room once that door is closed. You're all grown men and should be sensible enough to have a piss before you come in here. It's only ninety minutes and if you can't hold yourselves that long then I suggest you report sick straight after this meeting and get a sick note. Now, any final minutes?' The hands went up clearly. After my little warning speech the community were on their best behaviour for as long as I was in the chair.

One of the new men who came on to C-wing soon after I became chairman was a kid from Manchester named Bart. Bart was almost as volatile as my old pal Kevin the Nazi, but he was not to reign nearly so long. Bart had gained notoriety in the tabloid press when he was nicked for kidnapping and robbing one of the 'stars' of a long-running Manchester soap opera. The soap star was rumoured to be a homosexual who frequented the roughest areas of Manchester in his quest for young rent boys, and this is where Bart bumped into him and ended up being launched on to the front page of the *Sun*. I do not know the ins-and-outs of the case, but Bart told us that he himself was not a homosexual and had certainly never been a rent boy, but then, as Mandy Rice Davies once remarked in another infamous case, he would say that, wouldn't he? Bart claimed he was just a street robber, another one of the growing army of youthful hoodie muggers, and that at no stage was sex involved in any of his crimes. Be that as it may, he was definitely an excitable kid, the sort who could start a fight in an empty room. He lasted only three months on C-wing, during which time he was up for commitment twice – once for threatening someone and once for playing his music loudly late at night. He had no social skills and could not have a conversation with anyone that did not quickly escalate into an argument. His end came when he threatened several of the staff over not being allowed to have a Manchester City football shirt that had been sent in to him. He left Grendon under a cloud but, like many others, he was back again a year later. This time he never made it off F-wing before threatening several members of staff with severe violence.

When thinking about Bart I was struck by the fact that I might have spent too long at Grendon. I was starting to see coming on to the wing the same characters with almost identical problems and personalities but with different names and faces. I sat in community meetings listening to the same speeches and queries that I had already heard during my first year on C-wing. It was like a constant déjà vu and I knew it would soon be time for me to move on. I was even more convinced of this when Bart's place was taken by ASBO Rob, a kid from Nottingham who was like Kevin and Bart rolled into one. ASBO Rob was young, loud, demanding, threatening, confused, hurt and vulnerable in equal measure. He was serving six years for a mindless and completely avoidable piece of violence where he had slashed the face of a passer-by after he intervened in a drunken brawl ASBO Rob had started. Like Bart, and Kevin before him, and no doubt a succession of such characters dating back to the first days of Grendon in 1962, ASBO Rob tested the patience and goodwill of everyone in the community, including the staff. For some reason I attracted these loud and vulnerable characters and seemed to become a father figure for them. It had happened with Kevin and, though I had tried my best, it had drained me emotionally. Bart was not on C-wing for long but at one stage the staff had asked me to have a talk with him and try to put him straight. He seemed to listen to my advice but, as is usual with these characters, he couldn't control his temper when it came to the crunch. I was determined that ASBO Rob was not going to latch on to me too, but he was put on the dining table right next to me, and soon I was pulling him to one side and trying to give him a bit of advice. Despite my resolve not to.

I suppose if I really analyse it, the reason I felt the need to help these kids was down to my son, Joe. I suffer a deep and inextinguishable guilt about not being around for him during his so short life. I feel it for all of my kids but for Joe in particular, and I suppose I saw some tiny spark of my Joe in these other fucked-up and lonely kids who felt the need to prove to the world how tough they were. So I invested in these lads the time and emotion that I should have given to my own son. If I were in any way religious I guess I would see this as serving a penance. But I'm not.

As it turned out, ASBO Rob gained the record on C-wing for most appearances in the wing book and most commitment votes. He was put up for his commitment no fewer than eight times, mostly for threatening and abusive behaviour, and survived each vote because people could see the vulnerability in him and the fact that he, more than most, needed therapy, or he would be back in prison with other victims to his name pretty soon after he was released. Unfortunately for ASBO Rob he palled up with a Scotsman who had come into group 3 for a while and the pair seemed to spark off each other in a bad way. Malky, the Scotsman, was a serious career criminal and heroin addict who had been set on a life of crime before ending up in the punishment block at HMP Wormwood Scrubs in 1996. At that time Wormwood Scrubs was just one of many prisons in this country that had a serious reputation for staff brutality. The punishment block was where all the really sick uniformed bastards worked. The inmates in the block had no one to complain to, and even if they did, then it was odds-on that no one was going to take the word of difficult prisoners who had been branded 'control problems' over that of the uniformed arm of the Home Office. The inmates were beaten on a daily basis. Malky was one such prisoner who had been tortured and threatened with death, and he was among the men who sued the Home

Office after the abuse came to light and several uniformed staff were suspended and twenty-seven charged with criminal offences. Malky was awarded the highest payout of £100,000 but the money could do little to fix his psychological state.

A week after being awarded his payout, Malky, deep under the influence of drink, heroin and crack cocaine, burst into a neighbour's home at 7.30 in the morning. He beat the man to the ground and stole goods worth less than £100. Malky was soon arrested and jailed for twelve years for aggravated burglary – back in the prison system where friends and colleagues of the Wormwood Scrubs screws were still working. Even the screws who had been suspended but against whom there had not been enough evidence to support criminal charges were now back at work and dispersed to prisons around the system. So Malky had about as much chance of doing his sentence quietly and in peace as he had of getting an apology from the head of the POA. And that was no chance. He was bounced around the system for a while, accruing several spurious convictions for breaches of prison rules, before applying to come to Grendon. Like the rest of us he was no well-adjusted citizen, but a bitter and twisted man with a vicious hatred of the prison system and a deep mistrust of prison staff. I think that Malky's reasons for coming to Grendon were 50-50. Part of him thought he might get a few answers to his problems, and the other half knew that it was probably the safest jail he could be in as the staff were not the sort to dig him out over a grudge that the rest of the system had with him.

So Malky came into my group and tried to do therapy for a while. He could be a very easygoing and erudite man, but he also went through long periods of black depression when he was just itching to dole out a bit of violence or pour his vitriol on to the nearest target. He took ASBO Rob under his wing, but instead of trying to steer the kid straight he fed Rob's own insecurities and temper. For a couple of months they bounced around the wing together and when they weren't arguing loudly between themselves or playing silly and spiteful practical jokes on each other, they were doing it to other people. Malky, with his deep-rooted problems, was never going to last long on C-wing and, sure enough, within three months of arriving on the wing he was voted out for threatening another community member and was sent back to HMP Swaleside. ASBO Rob was devastated that his pal was gone and had a couple of weeks of self-destruction when he tried pushing everyone's buttons. Half of the community had the hump with ASBO Rob and the other half were scared to say anything to him in case it developed into an argument. Despite hailing from Nottingham he was a mad Manchester United fan and was at his worst and loudest whenever they were playing. He would shout and stamp about, getting in people's faces when his team scored, and would be more belligerent when they were losing. If you supported any club other than Manchester United, you were guaranteed verbal abuse at any stage during any day from ASBO Rob. Plenty of the stronger characters on the wing chose to take offence at his verbal outpourings around football. Like in many prisons, it was a very emotive subject for some men. Insulting a man's football team was like insulting his mother. I had been a Chelsea fan since I was a kid and had been known to get into heated exchanges with armchair pundits who tried insulting the Blues, so I could see that ASBO Rob was pushing a lot of the wrong buttons and I decided to step in.

I sat him down and explained that he was on borrowed time at Grendon and that many people were starting to get the bollock-ache with his antics. When not surrounded by an audience, he was a pretty sensible kid and he told me that he knew he had to stop calling on arguments every five minutes but that he found it hard. He told me a bit about his life, how his older brother, whom he idolized, had died when he was still young, how he had been bullied from an early age. It was all the rage and bitterness for his previous life that was pouring out of him every day. I've noticed that many people who have been severely hurt and bullied as kids can become worse bullies themselves when their situation changes. ASBO Rob was one of these. His bullying was verbal and included everyone who entered his sphere of contact, but it was revenge-bullying just the same. His constant outbursts were challenges to the world. He was saying, 'I'm not the little fat kid who got pushed around any more, so let's see what you've got.' He seemed to listen to me and there were genuine tears in his eyes as he opened up about his life. I really felt for him and advised him to talk to his group about everything and to try to hold the shit in whenever it threatened to overflow; he could come and talk to me any time.

In the next few days I spoke privately to a few of the stronger characters in the community and told them that they should do their best to ignore any outbursts by ASBO Rob as he was not just an empty vessel and was willing to try to change. From that day on he quietened down considerably and I began to hear his work being fed back from his group. He could still be loud and aggressive on occasion and every now and then he would forget himself and call on a silly argument, but he was quicker to realize what he was doing and apologize. The downside for me was that once again I had felt the need to go to bat for another nearly lost soul and if he fucked up it would be brought to my door. I had vouched for him and now I would have to make myself busy every time I heard a raised voice on the wing for fear it might be ASBO Rob calling someone on. It was a worry, but not massive. I had come a long way since Kevin and felt strong and able enough to face the challenge once again.

As wing chairman I had to attend the odd meeting with some of the governor grades and grew to detest most of them. If they weren't blatantly lying to your face or spinelessly trying to wriggle out of some concession that had been promised, they were shamelessly covering their own arses by making knee-jerk reactions to every headline published by a tabloid editor. A couple of them were honourable and straight-talking men, but most were weasels who would personally execute every man in the prison if the editor of the *Sun* suggested it and it was endorsed by Prison Service headquarters. They would blindly follow orders and use that as an excuse for their actions. If Grendon had started out with these types in charge, it would not have lasted six months, let alone forty-odd years. I was to fall foul of one governor in particular and feel the sting of his spite in the months to come.

When I had first come to Grendon I had been struck by its openness and relaxed easy atmosphere. Now I could see just how much it had changed. More and more I began to look forward to moving on. I had learned a lot about myself at Grendon, but just by slowing down to take a good look at my actions and motives I couldn't help but start analysing other people's. I had always had a hatred for the prison system, though I had assumed that this feeling was for the faceless system as a whole. Now I began to understand it was more than this; it wasn't just the concept I hated, it was some of the actual people involved. Some of them were snide, petty and amoral, and the higher up the chain of command you went the worse the personalities seemed to get. I still hated the system per se, but now I could also detest individuals within it. Perhaps being forced to acknowledge some of my own failings gave me a better insight into these failings in others, and maybe this was a good thing as it diluted my hate to a certain extent and made me understand I should deal with people on an individual basis, even if they did all belong to the same gang.

On the writing front, I decided I could live without writing for the media at the moment, if that's what it would take to keep the peace. Instead I decided to concentrate on another book, this time about my teen years in a south London rockabilly gang. Surely the prison powers that be could have no objections to that? But, just in case, I decided not to inform them. I would not keep it a secret, but I wouldn't be shouting about it either. Little did I know how much damage this decision would cause me further on down the line.

26. Puce Papers

By the summer of 2006 C-wing was very different from the wing I had joined three years earlier. In fact the whole nick had changed. The wall coming down had a lot to do with it; suddenly there were those horrible green fences everywhere, most of them draped with coils of razor-wire. The regime had also tightened up, more in line with other category B training prisons, and we no longer had as much freedom even inside the main buildings. Exercise was held in a large cage, which was previously used for five-a-side football, and jogging was banned. Our two-hour exercise period at the weekends was cut to one hour, and we could no longer visit friends on other wings in the evenings. Each wing became a separate island state, and the overall community spirit disappeared from the nick. Governors, who had once been glad to visit the wings and sit in on community meetings, became shadowy figures who never left the 'top corridor', where their offices were, and instead we got a steady flow of edicts printed on pink paper and headed 'Information to Prisoners'. The 'puce papers', as we called them, were never about anything good or in our favour, but usually told us of some coming restriction. Many restrictions were supposed to be temporary, but we all knew that temporary measures tend to become permanent in prison, especially if they give the whip hand to security. That's just the way it has always been. As for C-wing itself, we had a few new staff and plenty of new inmates, and not all of them were in Grendon for the right reasons.

During my time at Grendon I was to witness first-hand the breakdown of its admittance system. For forty years Grendon had been unique in the prison system, not only because it actually did what it said on the tin – rehabilitating violent recidivists – but also because in order to get there you had to volunteer and submit yourself to a battery of tests and interviews. This process was perfect for weeding out the 'messers' and opportunists, men who wanted to come to Grendon because the visits were relaxed and they might be able to smuggle a couple of big parcels of drugs in before jacking it in and heading back to the system to live the life of Riley for a couple of months. Or men who merely had the urge to fuck things up, or who were looking for an easy ride away from the madness of the system, or who had got themselves into serious debt and wanted a place to hide out. The vast majority of these men never made it further than F-wing. For Grendon to work we all had to be serious about what we were doing and that meant that those 'bad apples' who did succeed in getting on to the wings were policed by the prisoners themselves. But when the admittance process began to break down, Grendon saw an influx of 'the wrong kind of prisoner'.

The reason for the dismantling of the admittance system was quite simply a case of Grendon becoming a victim of its own success. For four decades many experts on penology had been scratching their heads and asking, if Grendon works so well, why hasn't the system put more Grendons in place? And for a long time they got no answer. But then, in 2002, a private jail in Staffordshire, run by Premier Prison Services, called Dovegate, opened. HMP Dovegate, a new prison of six wings, modelled on Grendon and dedicated to the therapeutic process, had spaces for 240 men. Not to be put to shame by the private sector, though they had not in the least minded being put to shame by one of their own for forty years, the rest of the prison system suddenly woke up to the possibilities of rehabilitating prisoners by means of group therapy, and within a short while therapeutic units were being opened in HMP Gartree, Aylesbury YOI, Send women's prison, HMP Channings Wood, HMP Cardiff and many other jails around the country. When Grendon had been the only prison offering therapy, it could afford to be choosy about its clientele, but once other therapy units opened things changed. Men who would in the past have volunteered for Grendon now had the choice of going to a unit nearer to their home area, where it might be easier to get visits. Suddenly the number of men choosing to come to Grendon dropped. With so many new units the criteria for getting into them became weakened. It was a case of 'bums-on-seats', particularly at a time when the British prison system was dangerously overcrowded. Now all the therapeutic units were accepting practically anyone who even glanced in their direction. It has also to be said that in some of the other units the rules were not as strict as they were at Grendon. In Dovegate, for example, there was serious drug-taking and bullying in its first couple of years. I know this because quite a few ex-Dovegate men ended up coming to Grendon to get away from it.

This is why Grendon had to start accepting men who previously wouldn't have even made it to F-wing – just to keep the prison up to its CNA (Certified National Allocation). Some of the new intake on C-wing had not even had to take an IQ test, previously an essential part of the admittance process as men had to be of a certain level of intelligence in order to understand the therapeutic process. Where the average wait for a place at Grendon had been around eighteen months, we were now getting men who had been sentenced only two weeks before and had been sent to Grendon as their first allocation out of their local nick simply because they needed the space. Obviously this led to a few problems in the community. The Bullingdon crew were a prime example of what was happening. They had all been sent from HMP Bullingdon, an overcrowded local jail, because they had caused problems there. I have already spoken about Phil the Pikey and his oppo Martin, but there was also Dean the Scouser, a 6 foot 4 bodybuilder who bore more than a passing resemblance to Dolph Lundgren, the action-movie actor, and was serving eight years for kidnap and robbery. Then there was Jay the Rat, another Scouser but almost the exact opposite of Dean: he was about 5 foot 7 and weighed an obese 18 stone. Jay the Rat was doing eleven years for aggravated burglary and GBH in which he had broken into the home of an old woman and stabbed her in the chest when he was disturbed. The full extent of his crime didn't come out until much later, so he was accepted as part of the Bullingdon crew, and while they were sneering at the crimes committed by some of the men on C-wing little did they know that they had their own long-tail among them.

At this time the C-wing community was pretty weak. Most of the stronger senior members had moved on through natural progression – seventeen members in one four-month period – and the men who were left were either too caught up in their own personal therapeutic journey, or too cowed by what was happening, or too resigned to what they saw as an inevitable series of changes on the wing to bother kicking up much of a fuss. Nobody wanted to step into the firing line. My own feelings at that time were that I had lost all my good mates and I decided that the rest of the people on the wing were not worth fighting for. I could easily have put myself forward to challenge what was happening, I was certainly strong and capable enough, but I was going through a period of apathy. I also thought to myself, why should it be me who puts himself on offer? What's the matter with the rest of these people? In the past, one of my problems had always been that I couldn't resist jumping in and fighting for other people's arguments, but I was no longer willing to do that.

Maybe I was becoming selfish, but once my pals had gone I had to keep reminding myself that I had arrived at Grendon alone and I would be leaving alone. It was time to look after number one. So I cracked on and tried to get a bit of work done in my group.

Mel had pulled out of the group while he was waiting for an answer for his category D hearing. Everyone figured he would be gone soon; little did he or we know that he would still be waiting almost a year later. Fred had gone to Springhill, and Tony the Stalker had also pulled out and was waiting to be shipped back to a category B prison. Phil the Pikey was a different fella after our little run-in. He even occasionally did a bit of real therapy. He'd had a rough life, though a lot of it was of his own making because he had chosen to take heroin, no one had forced him, but I started to feel for him when he spoke about his children and how he had fucked their lives up. The trouble was that Phil could come into the group, offer a powerfully emotional bit of work, break down and swear he was going to change, but as soon as he left the group room and was back in the bosom of his Bullingdon buddies he would instantly become the same obnoxious character he had been before. So I was hot and cold about him most of the time.

Silver, on the other hand, was just as impulsive as he had always been. His new Muslim persona began to cause trouble on the wing, but only because he wanted it to. He became very demanding about his religious rights, and got more and more fanatical about Islam and his place in it as time went on. I could see that he would be fertile ground for Islamic extremists who might wish to mould him to their own ends. He had one of those personalities. I mentioned this to him in a group one day, and what I got back was a lecture on the Koran. He changed his name to Ahmed and gathered a small group of Muslim prisoners around him and exhorted them to stand up to 'the infidel' by being loudly vocal. The rest of the C-wing Muslims, three fairly young men who had all converted from Christianity, were very impressionable and looked up to Silver as their leader. It amazed me: here was this white kid, who less than a year earlier had been speaking fluent Mandarin and been a fully paid-up member of a Triad gang, now fully immersed in Islam and actually teaching others about it. Silver was adamant that he was a Muslim for life, that he had finally found what he had been searching all his life for, but knowing his previous for switch-hitting in religion he was seriously challenged by the group. He didn't like it, believing he should answer only to Allah (or 'Alan' as Phil the Pikey kept calling him!), and we all guessed that it couldn't be long before Silver decided that therapy was not compatible with his new religious fervour. After less than three months of coming back into the group, Silver's new-found calm composure disintegrated altogether and he started getting into loud arguments with other members of the community and staff. He put his papers in again and was quickly shipped back to HMP Swaleside, whence he'd come.

I liked Silver. He was basically a good kid, but he was very confused and impulsive. He couldn't stick at anything for long without getting antsy and wanting to try something else. I hope that one day he finds what he's after. But one kid who had barely a shred of decency was Candy. Apart from telling the group that he was at Grendon only because he had been told he would be beaten up in a normal adult prison, Candy didn't really tell us much else of any use. He was serving six years for the rape of a 59-year-old woman who had lived upstairs from him. As Candy described it, his crime seemed to be all about coincidence and bad luck. He minimized everything and felt hard done by because he was doing time for his actions. The prosecution in his case said that, after a bust-up with his girlfriend and a drink-and-drug binge, Candy had crept up the stairs and broken his way into his victim's flat. Finding the woman in bed, he stripped off, climbed in and raped her. This was the evidence he was convicted on, and for someone of his age – eighteen at the time – to get a six-year sentence shows the severity of the case. It is usual for rapists, particularly young ones, to be treated with undue leniency by the judiciary. A prime example is the 'DJ Rapist', as the tabloids dubbed him. He was convicted of a number of rapes of young girls and suspected of dozens more, yet he was given a two-strike life sentence with an eight-year tariff. Compare that to my own tariff of eleven years in the same court six months later and you can see that rapists, on the whole, tend to get more of a squeeze than common robbers by the old men in the wigs. But Candy wasn't wearing his rapist jacket too well. He claimed that far from breaking into his victim's flat, he walked up the stairs and happened to see her door wide open in the middle of the night. He says his first thought was to check that she was okay, so he went in. The rape, he claimed, was nothing more than consensual sex. The group members, having all been past masters of lies and deceit ourselves, were not going to wear that for a second. I took particular umbrage at Candy and his bullshit story and I tore into him

verbally and told him in no uncertain terms that if he didn't up his game
I was going to personally put him up for his commitment and vote him
out. I was hoping that the warning would liven him up and make him see
that we weren't playing games here. But all it did was make him more
devious.

The two new Bullingdon Scousers also ended up on group 3. Dean
was a bit of a bully. He used his size and physique to tower over people
he was trying to browbeat and had a handy line in hard expressions that
were also part of his bully kit. He came from a well-known crime family
in Liverpool, with his brother and uncles involved in 'looking after' the
top nightclubs and all the paraphernalia that went along with that scam.
He, like a lot of Scouse villains, got into coke and steroids, so while the
'roids built his body mass the charlie shrank his brain power. After a bit
of serious trouble, in which he robbed and beat the wrong people, Dean
had to leave Liverpool. He ended up eventually in Buckinghamshire,
where he set himself up in business dealing drugs and robbing other drug
dealers. He became well known in this quiet county and built himself a
reputation as a hard man. In Liverpool he had been just another tiddler
in the ocean, but in Bucks he was a barracuda in a puddle. The crime he
was now serving his time for was typical of his chaotic lifestyle and his
monumental temper. He sold half a kilo of stolen cocaine to a couple of
blokes in Milton Keynes but when he went to pick up his payment they
stalled and then gave him a bit of a runaround. After he had been hanging
around the concrete jungle of MK for several hours for his bit of dough,
the blokes finally turned up and he had to follow them in his car to where
the money was. During the journey the buyer's car drove at top speed
and Dean, trying to keep up with them, blew the engine on his new car.
He eventually got his money, but all the fucking about plus the fact that
he'd ruined a twenty-grand car, plus the coke, drink and steroids he had
consumed, only added to his almost perpetual rage, which was born of
arrogance and fathered by chemicals. He decided that these two 'flash
southern monkeys' needed a lesson in who they were dealing with. He
told them that they were going to give him a lift back to Newbury and
when they objected he produced a twelve-inch carving knife that he liked
to keep about his person for just such occasions. The two drug buyers,
now faced with a 6 foot 4 brick shithouse of an irate Scouser holding what
almost amounted to a sword and threatening to 'cut yer fuckin' 'eads off!',
decided that discretion surely was the better part of valour. On the journey

to Newbury Dean got on his mobile phone and, speaking in backslang so his hostages couldn't understand, he arranged for a few of his pals to form a welcoming committee. At the end of their forced journey the two unfortunate drug buyers were taken from their car, beaten and robbed of everything by Dean and his gang.

The two victims went to the police, but they told a story that left a few vital points out for their own protection. They claimed that Dean had been making a social visit to one of their friends when he suddenly became irate and kidnapped them for no reason, forcing them to drive to Newbury, where they had been beaten and robbed. In court Dean could hardly drop himself in it by mentioning the coke deal, but there were enough inconsistencies in the victims' evidence for the judge to express 'surprise and confusion' when the jury returned a guilty verdict on Dean and one of his pals. His very lenient sentence of eight years is a testament to the judge's surprise and confusion. Now Dean was in Grendon and in group 3.

The second Scouse addition to the group was an entirely different pot of mackerel. Jay the Rat was almost as tall as he was wide and had one of those gormless faces that are usually seen only on the terminally drunk or the morbidly obese. He had one front tooth in his tiny cupid's bow mouth and eyes that looked like a couple of raisins launched into a lump of dough with a slingshot. He had a habit of sitting with his hands folded on his lap and his mouth hanging open like the front door on a derelict house made from putty. His voice was a high-pitched nasal whine and the only time he was ever even partly animated was when he was eating or planning a sly move. Jay had made a name for himself on the Liverpool drug scene, and had had to vacate the area around the Mersey for pastures new, once he had fallen out with his drug partners. They had kidnapped and tortured him for several hours, and no doubt would have killed him and dumped his body had not the father of one of the gang arrived at their hideout at just the right moment. Knowing Jay's own father was a villain of some repute serving a long prison sentence at the time, the new arrival ordered his son and the others to release Jay. Against their better judgement the gang obeyed. They told Jay to leave Liverpool on pain of death and released him. After some weeks in hospital recovering from his wounds he went looking for revenge. For over eight months Jay the Rat crept around the streets of Liverpool after dark, wearing a bullet-proof vest and always keeping to the shadows as he tried to strike back against his former partners. He fired shots into their homes at dead of night, petrol-bombed their cars and stuck up libellous graffiti about them in their own manor. Eventually this guerrilla war took its toll on everyone and Jay left Liverpool for a rest.

A compulsive thief and burglar, Jay cut a swathe of broken patio doors and empty jewellery boxes from Cheshire to Dorset. He would steal and burgle not because he needed the money but just for the fun of it. Then one day he entered a small bungalow in the middle of the day and was disturbed by its occupant, a 64-year-old widow. Instead of running out of the gaff, which even a blimp like him could have easily done given the frailty of his victim, he stabbed her several times in the chest. It was only by a miracle that the woman didn't die. Jay gave himself up several days later and said he had been under the influence of crack at the time of the crime. Once remanded in custody, he found himself the target of other prisoners due to the callous nature of his crime. He knew the score, he had done a few bits of bird in the past for 'legitimate' crimes and had even been involved in beating the kind of men who were in for crimes such as the one he was now facing conviction for. Not only were prisoners who didn't know him gunning for him, but friends and members of his previous gang were also in jail and looking to settle old scores. For Jay the Rat, prison was even more dangerous than the Liverpool war zone he had left. After being sentenced to twelve years for aggravated burglary and GBH he made his way to Grendon.

To tell the truth I wasn't that enamoured of either Dean or Jay, and the fact that they were part of the Bullingdon crew and went two-of-toast with Phil the Pikey and the rest of that firm made me yawn. I couldn't be intimidated by anyone – after all that had been my game – but Dean tried it on a couple of times before realizing that an imaginary roll of carpet under each arm and a face like a dyspeptic pitbull didn't cut it with me. I'd faced real hard men and ran with the best of them and I knew that a lot of 'roid jockeys were no more than 9-stone weaklings covering their inner fear with fake muscle. Bullies like to look the part, but when pressed most of them find their arsehole dropping out. So I sat in the group and listened to the newcomers to try to discover some spark of sense and decency in them. Neither man was to last too long at Grendon. Jay got caught red-handed stealing from one of his mates. If there's one thing that prisoners hate almost as much as a nonce or a grass it's a cell thief. In most nicks the punishment for cell thieves is to hold their hand in a cell door jamb and then slam the heavy door on the offender's fingers. Jay the Rat was lucky to get off the wing with just a verbal mauling from the community. Dean put his papers in and headed back to Bullingdon when he found out how hard therapy was going to be.

Before Fred had left for Springhill I had given him my pal's phone number and told him to keep in touch by ringing her if he needed anything as I phoned her almost every day. Through my pal I found out that Fred was going through a bad time. Springhill was one of those category D nicks that was full of melts and plastic gangsters. I had thought that with all the time he'd spent in therapy Fred would have been able to handle it. I was wrong. Not knowing anyone over there, he started to get paranoid about everyone and spent a very uncomfortable couple of months trying to adjust to the relative freedom and the different class of prisoner. I sent word over to him to keep his chin up and not do anything silly. I wasn't worried that he'd do a runner but I did think he might chin someone if he thought they were taking the piss. I got him an invite to the next social evening on C-wing, though it was touch and go as security were now humming and hawing over whether to allow serving and ex-prisoners back into the nick for social evenings. It had long been a tradition at Grendon that men who had done well and traversed the therapeutic process could keep in touch with their wings via letters, phone calls and social evenings if they were in open prisons that would allow them to attend. The benefit was twofold: the contact with Grendon gave the ex-Grendonite a bit of a safety net, a lifeline of communication with old friends who were still in therapy and someone to talk to who could understand what they might be going through, plus it was good for those still in therapy to see men who had completed therapy and progressed through the system. It was an encouragement to carry on. So Fred, and Milton Keynes Dave and Ray, who were both at Latchmere House, were coming back for the C-wing social evening. It would be great to see them again and it would give me a chance to have a little chat with Fred about what was going wrong for him.

On the last social evening I had invited my old pal Jonathan Aitken to attend. I hadn't seen Johnny in the flesh since that morning in reception at HMP Belmarsh when he was being transferred to Standford Hill open prison and I was heading up to the Old Bailey for a retrial on sixteen counts of armed robbery and possessing firearms with intent. I had seen a lot of him on the telly and in the newspapers and I was glad he was making a new life for himself away from the dirty business of politics. We had kept in touch over the years by letter and he occasionally mentioned me in television and newspaper interviews when recounting his time in prison. I admire him a lot because he is one of those people who never forgets a friend. I know it will probably embarrass him if he reads this, but whenever he sent me a letter or a card he always included a postal order 'For your canteen spends'. He remembered from his own time inside just how useful the odd bit of money can be in prison. God bless him. After he had been out for over five years he finally succumbed to the many requests and penned a book about his time in prison. Entitled *Porridge and Passion*, the book immediately created a lot of interest and the *Daily Mail* bought the serial rights. Johnny wrote to me and told me that the *Mail* were going to use some of the passages about me in one of their issues and sent me a signed copy of the book. The *Mail*, perhaps a tad hypocritically for a paper with a reputation for tearing into leering lawbreakers at every opportunity, sensationalized Johnny Aitken's book and almost shivered in orgasm as it splashed his revelations about doing time in a top-security prison all over its centre pages for several days running. I could almost hear the collective gasp of the lower-middle-class readership at the bold headlines – SAVAGERY IN THE SHOWERS. DRUG DEALING IN THE CHAPEL. AND MY SHOWDOWN WITH A JAIL HARD MAN CALLED RAZOR . . . But, all in all, Johnny described his time in Belmarsh quite accurately and didn't try to pretend he'd been hard done by, unlike Archer, whose book about his own little holiday in Belmarsh was nothing more than a whinge-fest. In prison terms Johnny Aitken was an old-fashioned staunch con who took it on the chin, accepted his time and marched on.

Johnny accepted my invitation and turned up at the C-wing social evening, and he was a big hit with the lads. We had a long chat about our time together in Belmarsh, what we had been doing since (which in my case consisted of more bird), and our plans for the future. It was good to see him looking so well. Then he mooched about and got talking to a few of the men. He seemed just as at home back on a category B prison wing as he had been in the House of Commons. One thing I did notice was that many of the governors seemed to just happen to drop by the wing while Johnny was there. In the normal course of events you couldn't have dragged them near C-wing with a length of tungsten chain and six white horses, but stick a former cabinet minister on the wing and they started crawling out of the woodwork! It has always amazed me how uniform services, such as the police and prison, still seem to run on a system of 'knowing your place'. I have noticed this kind of obsequious manner in both screws and coppers – they don't just obey their superiors, they almost *worship* them. It reminded me of my favourite old prison joke: how do you get fifty screws into a phone-box? Make one of them a governor and the rest will crawl up his arse.

Something I was working on in my group was my criminal lifestyle and instrumental violence. I was absolutely sick of talking about my past life as a criminal and didn't really think there was much more I could get out of going over it again, but these things were an integral part of my risk factors, the things the Parole Board would take into account when it came time for me to go for open conditions or release. So I had to revisit them over and over, *ad nauseam*. I now understand that one of the reasons I had chosen such a high-profile crime as armed robbery was because I lacked self-esteem. It wasn't really that simple of course: other things also had to be factored in, such as my lack of education, growing up in relative poverty and my own indiscipline. As a child I had very little confidence in myself, I didn't have many social skills and this was due to the fact that my family were very secretive and we kids were told never to bring anyone home or have anyone knock at the door. While it was normal for other kids to have their friends back to their house, if any of my mates wanted me they had to shout up at my bedroom window, which was on the third floor of a block of flats. Imagine trying to explain to your mates, when you're ten or twelve years old, that they can't knock for you? I used to tell them that my mum was ill and couldn't be disturbed.

My father, God bless him, was a drinker not a worker, so there was never any money for luxuries such as paying the rent, gas or electric. We owed money in all the local shops and to every television rental company and hire-purchase outlet in south London. So a knock on the door at our house usually meant only one thing and that was debt collectors. In the event it was usually me who had to stand in the hallway and shout, 'Who is it?' at the shadowy figures on the frosted glass panel of the front door. If the reply was from an unknown voice who might be looking for 'Mrs Smith', then I would have to tell them that 'My mum ain't in and I don't know when she'll be back.' The door was never to be opened, no matter how much those shadowy figures cooed and cajoled. In those days bailiffs and debt-collectors would never try to force their way into a flat when the only person home seemed to be a young boy. Usually my mum, and sometimes my dad as well, would be crouched by the open living-room door whispering to me to tell them there was no one in. So that was my job, I was the keeper of the door. It's no wonder I grew up lying to anyone in authority and not trusting anyone I didn't know.

As a child, the shame of never feeling quite as good as other kids because most of my clothes were second-hand and came from jumble sales made my self-esteem about as robust as a house of cards in a hurricane. But deep inside I had a burning anger about this. I just wanted to blend in, but I started doing exactly the opposite. I don't think it ever was a conscious decision, but it probably had a lot to do with resigning myself to the fact that I was never going to fit in so therefore I would be even more extreme. To cover up my inarticulateness I became a fighter; instead of trading insults I would get the right-hander or the headbutt in at the earliest opportunity. Then I realized that being a fighter gained me, if not respect, then its close relation – fear. Kids who might have taken the piss out of my holed plimsolls or ragged haircut now wanted to be my pal, in case I clumped them. But deep down I was intelligent enough to understand this was somehow bogus, and I wanted people to like me for real, so I developed a jokey persona, cracking funnies, doing impressions of people and generally being up for a laugh. I didn't really like hurting people and always felt sorry for the kids I beat in fights, so being game for a laugh as well was my way of balancing things. I didn't want people to fear me, I wanted them to like me, but I wasn't sure how to go about it. Of course, when I reached my teens everything changed and having people fear me was very useful and desirable. In a nutshell I was a fucked-up kid who grew into a fucked-up adult who used violence as a tool to gain acceptance but felt guilty about it. Fuck, this therapy game is easy! Or maybe not.

27. Big Don

In my years at Grendon I had to sit through a lot of sad and horrific stories from men who had been horribly abused as children. Some of them made me physically sick and a couple of them gave me real nightmares. As I listened to tales of physical torture, sexual abuse and psychological torment, some of it beyond the realms of an ordinary person's imagination, I often wondered what sort of people could do these things to children? What could possibly drive a father to burn his own three-year-old son with cigarettes and then snap his legs and keep him locked in a dark cupboard for the next six years? Or an uncle to repeatedly rape his eight-year-old nephew and then sell him to other paedophiles for their own sick gratification? Or a mother to regularly electrocute her young son with bare wires whenever he was naughty? I had no answers and just knowing that such people were walking on the same earth as me filled me with, first, rage and then black depression. I can honestly say that the hardest thing I had to do at Grendon was listen to these stories and watch grown men who had previously been judged as hardened criminals and vicious killers break down and weep bitter tears for the traumatic experiences that had made them what they had become.

I hated it when a new member had to tell his story. I got a feeling of dread in the pit of my stomach and silently prayed that he would be just an ordinary criminal like me who had committed his crimes through greed and laziness, and not one of the ranks of the abused. But mostly my prayers went unanswered. I suppose it was something I should have expected – of course there were going to be a lot of psychologically damaged men in a prison like Grendon; I just never expected so many. I couldn't switch off any more, I was too open, felt too much empathy for others, and every time I had to sit through one of these terrible tales of perversity and inhumanity something inside me died a little bit more.

No story, however, was as harrowing as what I was to hear from a man named Don. Above all others, his story will haunt me for a long time. Don was a big fella, 6 foot 2 and weighing in at around 18 stone. He owed most of his bulk to a regular diet of anabolic steroid injections combined with pushing heavy weights in a succession of gyms around his old stomping ground of Liverpool. He was covered in tattoos – professional ones, not the old blue-ink-and-needle crap that a lot of jailbirds sport. He had the arrogant swagger that you see only in nightclub doormen, young villains and Flying Squad officers. In fact, Don had been a nightclub doorman for many years and was serving a discretionary life sentence for beating to death a fellow doorman who had been his best friend. From the moment Don walked on to C-wing he seemed to stir up a lot of animosity from other members of the community with his demanding nature. He was due to be lodged in a cell on the 1s landing which was empty, but he told the staff that he had a medical condition that meant he needed a cell with a toilet. The only two cells with toilet and sink were on the ground floor and I was in one of them. The other one was empty, having recently been vacated by an ex-Hell's Angel called Filthy Dave who had had a heart attack and was currently in Stoke Mandeville hospital recovering. A few community members had hopes of moving into this plum abode, so when Don was moved into it instead there were a few noses put out of joint and a muttering campaign started in certain circles about the 'brass neck' of this newcomer. I didn't really give a fuck who got the cell as long as it wasn't someone with a 200-watt stereo and a pile of jungle CDs, and as I watched Don move his possessions in I was pleased to note that he had neither. Once he was settled I went and introduced myself. He had heard of me since he had been in prison and told me he had read my book and enjoyed it, and I sensed that he was somewhat in awe of my reputation. I'm really not giving myself a gratuitous boost here, but some people just get that way around me at first. I think they half expect me to pull out a razor and start striping people for the fun of it. I used to get a buzz out of it – who wouldn't? – but now I find it a bit embarrassing and try to laugh it off. I spent about half an hour talking to Don about therapy and what he could expect from Grendon and he seemed genuinely interested. We shook hands and I went off to do something else thinking that he might be a nice fella.

In the next couple of weeks Don seemed to be intent on making as many enemies on C-wing as he could, and that included the staff. First, he went into the office and demanded that his cell be painted and that the furniture be replaced as he wasn't happy with its condition. These requests were fair enough, but it was the way in which Don delivered them and his obvious impatience that he was not getting what he wanted immediately that got the staff's back up. Don's arrogance started to be noticed by other people on the wing. In the words of the disgruntled mutterers, 'He's walking about like he owns the fucking wing!' And it was true to some extent, Don did have a bit of a superior and irritating manner, but so do a lot of people. I had a chuckle to myself when I heard the moaning, until, that was, Don approached me one morning and complained that I had had the volume on my television too high the night before. 'Yeah,' I told him, reasonably. 'That's because I'm a bit deaf in one ear. I damaged my eardrum by firing a shotgun off in a car when I was a kid.' He looked at me for a moment and then nodded. 'I know,' he said. 'I read it in your book. But do me a favour, keep the volume down, eh?' I sensed a challenge in his tone and smiled at him to show I wasn't biting. 'Okay,' I said. 'If it gets too loud just bang on the wall.' That night he spent twenty minutes banging on the wall between our cells before finally realizing that he was going to have to live with the loudness of my telly or move upstairs. For the next month he blanked me and would walk past me without saying a word. I was quite amused by it all. My protracted cold war with Taff had taught me not to stress out and take these things too personally. Life was bigger than that and if Don's only problem was a bit of noise from next door then he must have a perfect life. I dropped him off my radar and got on with the massive business of trying to sort myself out.

Don joined group 2, always the most dysfunctional one on C-wing despite having excellent facilitators, and soon settled into the routine of the wing. He made few friends and used to take minutes on almost every community meeting to complain about some aspect of someone's personal habits or behaviour. He did start knocking about with big Mel, who had been in my group for three years and was now awaiting transfer to a category C prison, but that was more because he took up the only available space in the dining hall, which was on a table opposite Mel. Another way in which Don tended to piss off some members of the community was with his almost obsessional hogging of the telephone. On each wing there was one telephone (until a second phone was installed in the autumn of 2006). With forty-three men on the wing, at least half of whom used the phone on a daily basis, we had worked out among ourselves that ten minutes had to be the limit. Men would queue up on the ground floor where the phone was situated and wait for their turn. Don, on the other hand, would be on the phone seven or eight times a day and sometimes breached the ten-minute rule, which did nothing to endear him to those who were waiting. He would apologize when pulled about it, but it didn't stop him doing it again. It would be safe to say that for quite a while Don was not the most popular man on C-wing.

As he began to work in his group his name would often come up in the feedbacks. That's how I learned that he had a young son, whom he loved very much, and it was him he was always phoning. Don had split with his son's mother some time before he was arrested for murder and he was desperate to keep some sort of contact with his little boy despite being in prison for life. No one with a heart could fault him for this. The muttering about him lessened. We also heard that he had been bullied as a kid and that was why he had taken up boxing, becoming a regional champion in the sport, and then body-building. This was also why he became a doorman. I know that, particularly these days when all doormen have to be licensed, working the door is a legitimate profession for well-adjusted members of society, and that the vast majority of doormen and women are nothing but professional, but, having had a bit of experience on the door myself, I knew that many of the men who took it up in the old days were really nasty types who had an absolute hatred for humanity. Some of them saw it as an opportunity to get their own back and dish out a bit of violence on the public. A lot of them were bullies who had themselves been bullied and were now looking for power and payback. I once worked for a while with a particularly horrible individual who made a habit of attacking men who were not only smaller than him but also incapable of fighting back because they were inebriated. One night I got him pissed on a bottle of brandy and then broke his jaw with my trademark one-pound ballpein hammerhead in a glove. Don was one of the bullied who became a bully and saw door work as an ideal opportunity to dish out a bit of hurt. It took him around six months of therapy before he admitted this.

After his first admissions in therapy Don became even more of a string vest on the wing and seemed to go out of his way to complain about everything and anything. I had seen this type of behaviour from many men at Grendon. It was as though the shame they felt at revealing bad things about themselves had to be obliterated and the only way to do it was by growling at everyone. It was like saying, yes, I do have guilty secrets, but that doesn't make me an easy target. It was all tied into image and pride, and Don was no different from the rest of us in that respect.

It was during this time that he had a run-in with Nolan that almost led to both men being shipped out. They got into a petty argument up on the 2s landing and Nolan told Don to go and fuck himself. Don, in his first display of physical violence since arriving on C-wing, grabbed Nolan around the throat and lifted him off his feet while growling into his face that he was going to break his neck. Nolan was no lightweight in the violence department himself, having grown up on the council estates of Bermondsey, but he had enough of his wits about him not to lash out. Knowing that against someone like Don fists would be next to useless, Nolan said the right things needed to calm the situation and internally vowed to get a tool and stick it into Don's neck just as soon as the opportunity presented itself. Don, perhaps realizing the implications of his actions, albeit somewhat belatedly, let go of Nolan's neck and was immediately contrite. Luckily, some people had witnessed the episode and a wing special was called to deal with it.

During the wing special Don apologized to Nolan profusely and expressed sorrow and contrition about the incident. But Nolan, still smarting from being manhandled and threatened, couldn't contain himself and made a few dire threats of severe violence to come, he said, when Don least expected it. The wing special lasted nearly three hours during which Don actually broke down in tears, perhaps of rage – nobody was quite sure – and Nolan walked out and came back again twenty minutes later. Eventually the matter was ironed out, meaning that both men had reached a place where they could be safe with each other on the wing and not have people wondering if they were going to attack each other. It ended with both men being put up for a commitment vote, Don for actual violence and Nolan for the very real threat of violence. The vote was held two days later at the next community meeting and both men were voted to stay at Grendon after a further hour of questioning and discussion by the community. Don was lucky. He was the first man I had seen at Grendon who had actually committed an act of physical violence and kept his place after a wing vote. He shaved the vote by two. Once again, though he wasn't very popular, I think Don managed to keep his place because we could see that he was in dire need of therapy. That, and the fact that the wing had lost many senior members to progressive transfers and the community was still young and unsure of itself. Had Don been up for commitment six months earlier he might not have been so fortunate. Nolan won his vote by eleven and

I think that was because the wing saw his threats as due to provocation. So both men stayed.

After the Nolan incident Don appeared to have a rethink. Maybe it was Mel who opened his eyes to the reality of his predicament, as I now often saw the two deep in conversation. Don seemed to wake up to the fact that he was serving a life sentence and if he ever wanted to get back to his son he was going to have to shape up and prove he had lessened his risk factors. Grabbing other members of the community around the throat just wasn't going to cut it. But now he seemed to go completely the other way and his ploy was so transparent it was almost amusing. Overnight Don became Mister Peace and Love. He became a Buddhist, joined the yoga class, gave up gym, and volunteered for every rep job available, paying special attention to the ones that would reflect his new direction – race relations rep, safer custody rep (who dealt with the wellbeing of vulnerable prisoners and self-harmers) and induction rep (going up to F-wing and talking to new arrivals about therapy). If there was a space on any committee, concert or conference, then Don would be in there batting for it. He stopped all his complaining and tried to show that he really had changed. Instead of making him more popular in the community, all this smoke and mirrors served only to make him the opposite. He was trying to pull the wool over the eyes of forty-two violent, devious recidivists who had used every ploy in the dodge book to their own ends in the past. He was fooling no one, but he cracked on as though if he were to show this face for long enough it would be accepted. Don wanted what all of us wanted, and what some of us had come to Grendon for, a shortcut out of his life sentence. And who could blame him? He had yet to understand that there were no shortcuts at Grendon.

Relations between myself and Don had been pretty cool and casual since our discussion about the volume of my television. We said hello to each other whenever we passed. I certainly had no animosity towards him and I believe he had none towards me. Then one morning, after feedbacks, there was a knock on my cell door and it was Don. He asked if he could have a word. I was a bit surprised but bade him enter and asked what was on his mind. He explained that he felt he was getting nowhere fast at Grendon and wanted advice on what he should be doing. As a senior member of C-wing community with over three years in therapy, I was used to men coming to me for a bit of direction and I always tried my best to steer them on to the right path, just as other senior members had done for me when I first arrived. Don and I spoke for over an hour and I advised him to slow down and stop trying to impress everyone with the fake nice-guy image. I told him that the only way he was really going to progress was by not being afraid to show his real feelings and personality. We could work with anger, even rage, we could work with almost anything just as long as it was honest. Don seemed to take this on board but admitted that he was absolutely terrified about opening himself up to the community as his past was pretty horrific and he was afraid of the rejection that might follow. He was also scared that by revealing himself as so damaged that might result in him spending many years over his tariff in jail. His deepest desire, the one thing that drove him, was the thought of getting home before his son grew up without him. He was the only good thing left in his life and if he lost him then he would have nothing. I really felt for Don. He was a very disturbed man but not beyond redemption.

The murder that Don was serving his time for had happened in the toilets of a nightclub during one of his nights off. When not working the door Don and the rest of the doormen of Liverpool, who all knew each other, would meet up in one of the clubs to snort cocaine, drink, talk about steroids and violence, and generally make a nuisance of themselves around the ordinary citizens. You can imagine the sight of twenty hyped-up musclemen in T-shirts deliberately two sizes too small, all the better to show off their steroid-enhanced physiques, fuelled by Colombian marching powder, German lager and 'roid rage. It would take only one comment about someone's pecs or abs to kick everything off at this manic narcissists' ball. Don got into a bit of a tear-up with one of his best pals and came off the worst for it. The two combatants then retired to the club toilets to wash the blood away and freshen up, but more heated words were exchanged and it kicked off again among the urinals. This time Don wasn't fucking about. He felled his friend with a massive right hook and then went to town, kicking and stamping on his fallen comrade's head with 18 stone of power and fury. The man died soon afterwards and Don was arrested for murder. At his trial Don was found not guilty of murder but guilty of manslaughter. The judge gave him a life sentence anyway, though a discretionary rather than a mandatory one. Either way he was serving life. And now he would have to prove to those in control of his freedom that he was no longer a risk to the public.

After Don gave up his weight-training regime his bulk quickly turned to fat, and with the loss of the body beautiful he also lost some of his arrogance. He no longer strutted around the wing flexing his biceps and giving everyone cat A stares or pretending he was Gandhi. He seemed to become genuinely calmer and more thoughtful. I was pleased for him when I began to hear more and more of his work coming out in his group's feedbacks. He was a lot more honest in his approach to therapy, and at the suggestion of his group he joined the psychodrama group, one of the two complementary therapies offered at Grendon – the other being art therapy. Psychodrama was run by a civilian facilitator called Martin and was held in the community room every Tuesday afternoon between two and four o'clock. It involved acting out scenes from your life or situations that you might find difficult to explain with just words and being able to get in touch with the emotional side of your character. Don seemed to flourish in the psychodrama group and pretty soon began to really open up about his early life.

The truth about Don was revealed to the community on his second wing assessment, after he had been on C-wing for over a year. He started in the routine fashion by reading out to the wing the written assessment of him by Tom, the therapist, Lynn, the psychologist, his personal officer and other members of his group. The reports were pretty standard but both Tom and Lynn's hinted at secrets about his childhood that Don might find healing to get off his chest. It was a pretty gloomy day outside, with low dark clouds as Don finished reading the reports and then began to tell us, in a choked and halting voice, about what he had endured. He and his brother, who was a year younger than him, had first been raped at the ages of three and four by their father. The two boys were kept imprisoned in their home, caged into the bottom bunk of bunk beds with no mattress, just bare springs, and naked. There they spent their days and nights wallowing in their own mess, occasionally being fed if one of their parents remembered to do it. But every night, when their parents came home drunk, the boys would be taken from their cage and used for sex. Sometimes the parents would bring home friends, mainly men, who would also have sex with the two young brothers. This went on until the boys were seven and eight, when their father left to live elsewhere leaving the boys in the care of their alcoholic mother. The night-time sex sessions continued, their mother bringing home a succession of men and women to have sex with both her and her sons.

Sometimes their mother would be alone and take her two sons into her bed and make them perform sex acts on her. As Don spoke about his horrific childhood the community seemed to sink ever deeper into a silent mire of horror, depression and disgust. We had heard some pretty tragic life stories in my years at Grendon but Don's attempt at steady dignity as he unfolded his grisly tale of terrible perversity was affecting everyone. The wind outside picked up and dashed raindrops against the window as if in sympathy with the mood inside.

Don's family lived in an isolated part of the country and kept pretty much to themselves. Neither he nor his brother went to school and they didn't meet anyone of their own age until their early teens, so they had no idea that what was happening to them was wrong. They accepted it all as part of their existence and even took to sexually abusing each other. When they were ten and eleven their mother moved in with her parents. But even here they were not safe from molestation as their grandmother also began to abuse them sexually. Once more they were locked up in filthy conditions and kept near starvation. Don told us the only time that he and his brother went outside the house was when his mother took them to the home of her best friend, an immensely gross woman of 18 stone, where the boys were made to perform sex acts on each other and on their mother and her fat friend. Both boys were subjected to bondage and sadomasochistic sex games, and their mother instructed them to slap and punch her while they were having sex. And all through these years they were regularly beaten with belts, straps and sticks at the slightest excuse. Don said that the only member of the family who did not join in the physical and sexual abuse was his grandfather. Sometimes he would sneak into the locked room where the boys were kept and give them little treats of sweets. But he was a physically weak and nervous man who was almost completely cowed by his wife and daughter.

When Don was fourteen he managed to escape from the house and was picked up by the police wandering the streets half-naked. Noticing the bruises and scars all over him the police contacted social services and Don and his brother were taken into care. But they refused to tell the authorities what had been going on in the house as they were terrified of their mother and grandmother and had always been warned that if they talked to outsiders they would be immediately killed. So no charges were brought against any of the family. For the next four years Don and his brother stayed in care, but were often allowed to visit their family, where the sexual abuse carried on unchecked. He was still abusing his own brother and both boys started abusing other kids in care. But Don was now witnessing other people's lives and beginning to realize that something was terribly wrong with his own family. At the age of seventeen he started his first relationship with a girl his own age, but having no experience of a normal relationship he showed his affection by beating her up and attempting to control her. At this stage he was still having sex with his mother whenever he visited his family. His mother's hold over him lasted until Don was twenty-one, and that was when he finally managed to break away from her influence. He took up boxing and body-building, secretly determined that no one would ever control him again. He had many relationships with women but couldn't stop himself from beating them and making unnatural sexual demands and every single relationship broke down. He heard that his mother had grown ill and that she was confined to a wheelchair and, against his own better judgement, he was persuaded by his brother to go and see her. The visit went badly as she taunted him about his lack of sexual prowess. Don cracked and dragged her from her wheelchair and beat her up.

As Don told us of beating his crippled mother and the great sense of relief and satisfaction he derived from doing it, his voice and set jaw almost defied us to find him wrong. But few of us in the room had any sympathy for the woman who had terrified, tortured and toyed with her children. At times in his story Don sobbed in real anguish and despair but when speaking of his mother, grandmother and father his voice dripped with real hatred. He told us how, when he heard that his mother was in hospital on her deathbed, he had to go and see her, not out of any feelings of love or sympathy, but to make sure she really was dying. He needed to see her suffering in agony in order to put some sort of cap on his own suffering and agony. But when he walked into her hospital room and saw that she had a picture of Don's baby son next to her bed he told us he came very close to losing it and putting a pillow over her sleeping face. He panicked, fearing she might somehow beat the cancer that was killing her and target Don's own child as her next plaything. Don loved his son – perhaps the only truly good and innocent thing in his life – and the thought of his mother getting hold of him brought him close to murder for the first time. His mother's life was spared only by the timely entrance of a nurse. Don took his son's photograph and slipped away from the hospital, and later that night his mother expired of natural causes. For the first time in his life he felt free. But, whether he knew it or not, he still carried a heavy load.

Forged by a lifetime of mistreatment and perversion, Don became a violent bully. And in the end he had to take someone else's life in order to have a chance to get his own life back. When he finished his story the mood in the community room was as sombre and dark as the weather outside. Don sat with his shoulders slumped and his eyes cast down, but, as he told me later, with great relief in his heart and a lightening of the weight he had carried for so long. This was the first time he had spoken about his life, ever. The community had been touched by his total honesty; we could sense that he had held nothing back. Even Nolan, who was the wing chairman at the time of Don's assessment and had been at the sharp end of Don's violent rage some months before, was obviously moved. He asked if there were any questions for Don, but there was only a chorus of quiet encouragement from around the room. It was only 10.20 but Nolan, in the silence that followed, told Don that if he needed to speak to anyone he was sure that we would all be there for him. He then dismissed the wing early, the first and only time this happened in my five years at Grendon.

I had always had trouble with the concept, put forward by many of those who commit horrific crimes, of the abused becoming the abuser, but during my time at Grendon it was a pattern I was to hear again and again, and I had to question my own scepticism. Perhaps we do create these vicious and soul-destroying cycles of violence and abuse by perpetuating them? Certainly, when I heard about the lives of men like Don it was easier to believe that he eventually murdered his victim as a release from the pain he had endured during his horrific tortured childhood. The alternative is to believe he did it for no other reason than a momentary loss of control and in the heat of anger, and this is how the law viewed it. But there was so much more. Who knows how many more Dons are rotting inside our overcrowded prison system or out there walking through life like time bombs just waiting for the right trigger to explode? It doesn't bear thinking about.

28. The Other Side

An essential ingredient of the running and success, or otherwise, of the therapeutic regime at HMP Grendon was the staff. The non-uniform therapy staff were all experienced and highly qualified civilians, some of whom had worked in other institutions before coming to Grendon. Tom, the C-wing therapist, had spent some years at Broadmoor. Lynn, the C-wing psychologist, had started out at HMP Swaleside, working with long- and medium-term prisoners. And Helen, the psychiatrist and group 1 facilitator, had a private practice on the out. The wing probation officers during my time, first Sue, then Joanna and finally Gill, all had plenty of experience of working in institutional settings with violent recidivists. And it was the non-uniformed professionals, rather than the actual prison staff, who had the biggest say over whether we, as prisoners, progressed through the system as individuals. In a standard prison progress was pretty simple: if you put your mind to it, all you had to do was keep your head down, stay drug-free and get no nickings for a period of time, and most prison staff would be happy to recommend you for a progressive transfer, as long as you were eligible.

But progress at Grendon was based on other things. Many men didn't realize that what they had volunteered for was not only a chance to change their lives but also to allow themselves to be judged by different criteria and a much higher standard than in the rest of the system. Whereas a typical system progress report would be pretty sparse and concentrate solely on whether the inmate posed a control or discipline problem, the same report at Grendon would be based on where you were in therapy. This could be very confusing for some men who felt that they deserved recategorization or a progressive move simply because they had achieved the standard set for the rest of the system. It could be a bit of a blow to be told that you could not progress because you hadn't done enough work on your relationships, impulsiveness or criminal values, and it was at these times that some men felt 'cheated' by Grendon in general and the non-uniformed staff in particular. You would think that if you had signed on to make a real change you would figure out that the reports were going to be a bit more in-depth and throw up different problems. I have to say that during my time at Grendon I was never asked to do the impossible; all therapeutic issues put to me were achievable as long as I was willing to put in the work. And that's what some men missed – therapy is not an easy cruise in calm waters, but a struggle through, sometimes, very stormy seas.

The main targets for the men who received knockbacks were Tom and Lynn, and on the whole they seemed to weather calmly the public outbursts of vitriol that occasionally came their way in community meetings. During my time at Grendon I had many one-to-one meetings with both Tom and Lynn, and I liked them both. Tom was tall, around 6 foot 2, and had blond hair and blue eyes and a quiet, posh voice. He was rarely dressed in anything but stylish, well-cut and obviously expensive suits and shoes that looked handmade. When not in one of his suits he would be equally well turned out in jacket and trousers that wouldn't have looked out of place in the pages of *Gentleman's Quarterly* magazine. Whether you imagined him speeding through the streets of St Tropez in an open-top classic Jaguar with an Audrey Hepburn lookalike laughing next to him, or striding the battlefields of the Second World War in a coal-scuttle helmet, Tom was the very epitome of sartorial elegance at all times.

Tom was a master interrogator, very serious but with a lot of charm and a sense of humour. He had a soothing, productive manner. He could ask the deepest questions and I somehow got the impression that no matter how I answered he would gain some small nugget of understanding from my reply. At first this was pretty disconcerting for me as I regarded every interview with anyone in authority as adversarial. I treated each interview as I would treat a cross-examination in the witness box by a prosecuting barrister. I knew he was an expert in body language so I kept mine as open and neutral as I could, and I would try to answer any question, no matter how innocent sounding, with a question of my own. This became somewhat of a strain to me, having to be on guard all the time, and eventually, as I progressed through therapy, I began to realize that Tom was not interested in catching me out. He genuinely wanted to understand what made someone like me do the terrible and reckless things I had done. I started to relax during the interviews. When I read the reports that Tom had written based on them, I was able to gain that much more insight into my own behaviour and the reasons behind it. I would say that overall I spent around thirty-six solid hours being interviewed by Tom on a one-to-one basis during my therapy. He also sat in on almost every community meeting and feedback, and facilitated my group when Brian or, later, Glenda was not in. Tom was also in charge of our six-monthly assessments, in which the whole group would gather and talk about an individual's progress and what work we thought he should be doing for the next six months. A couple of weeks after these assessments we would receive the written reports on them from Tom, Lynn, a probation officer and our facilitator, and they were a good indicator of progress, or lack of it, for each person. By the time I was ready to leave Grendon I felt I had come to know Tom pretty well, as much as I could in that setting, and not only did I have a great respect for him but I also liked him as a person.

Lynn, the psychologist, was viewed with great suspicion by most of the community. She was young, maybe mid-twenties, and very pretty. Bearing in mind she had to spend most of her days among forty-odd men who had been deprived of female company, in some cases for decades, and a small minority of whom were serious sexual predators, her style of dress was pretty understated and she never wore anything deliberately provocative. The problem was that, even if she had come to work in a quilted shroud, she could not hide the fact that she was a young, good-looking female and this will always arouse feelings in the average heterosexual male. While the more naive men sometimes had a crush on her, the more experienced prisoners harboured no illusions about having a chance with her and this made some of them bitter and hateful towards her. With monotonous regularity I heard wing rumours that Lynn was (a) a lesbian and lived with a bull dyke who had a moustache and tattoos, (b) (from the racist element) she was going out with a 6 foot 8 African pimp, (c) she was a crack whore at weekends and hated men, or (d) any combination of the above. The trouble with some men, and prisoners in particular, is that most of them are labouring under the misapprehension that they are irresistible to women, and when their not-so-subtle advances are ignored or rebuffed, they assume it must be because the object of their desire is at fault. If Lynn wrote a report for someone and didn't recommend them for recategorization, progressive move or a day out, it was never because that was her professional opinion, but always because she had ulterior motives. I quite liked Lynn. I found her charming and funny and very good at her job.

Psychologists are top of the power tree when it comes to decisions about lifers being released or recategorized. This is a fairly new development in the prison system. Ever since the late 1980s when anger management and cognitive thinking courses were sold to the government as tools of rehabilitation for prisoners, psychology has become very important in the penal process. It used to be that unless the prisoner was showing signs of blatant insanity that couldn't be cured by a good kicking and a regular dose of the liquid cosh, the system would call in a psychologist to see what they could find before loading the con on to the magic bus to Broadmoor or Rampton. But nowadays psychologists wield a lot of power and regularly become involved in the sentence-planning and report-writing of lifers and long-term prisoners; if they say that the prisoner is a risk, the Parole Board is very likely to accept their opinion. So a lot of lifers actively detest psychologists for the power they have over their lives. Me? I could take them or leave them. I came to acknowledge that as long as there was no personality clash between me and a psychologist, then all I could do was say my piece to put my case forward and hope for the best. For this reason I never really had any problems with Lynn. There was one time when I was up for Parole Board recategorization to open conditions eighteen months before my tariff, when I half-expected Lynn to write a report that recommended me, but she didn't and I had the hump about it and blanked her for a couple of weeks. But, on the whole, I was too much of a realist to carry it on for long. Besides, the law allows life-sentence prisoners to engage an independent psychologist to refute any claims made by the prison psychologists that are seen as detrimental to progress. So I could just let them fight it out between them.

The next most influential person on the wing totem pole was the prison probation officer, and we were lucky enough to have some good ones during my time on C-wing. The first one, during my first two years, was a very nice woman named Sue. Sue was from Northern Ireland and had worked at Grendon for nine years. She was very easy to talk to and always had a smile on her face. For my early reports I had interviews with her and always got on great with her. She was particularly interested when I first heard from my long-lost daughter, Leah, in Ireland. Leah lived in Galway and Sue knew the area very well and always asked how things were going with Leah. She came over to my table and introduced herself to Leah during the very first Family Day visit I had with my daughter. Sue was one of the few people who actually recommended me for open conditions in her report for my first parole review in 2004. Unfortunately, in early 2005, she decided to move on from Grendon and take up a post elsewhere. She was well respected and liked in the community and everyone was sad to see her go but wished her well.

The probation officer who took over from Sue was named Joanna. She was a trainee and not fully qualified, so a lot of men, particularly the lifers, were not too happy about her being allowed to write reports on them, and she became a bit abrasive as a defence mechanism when she sensed the animosity against her. Joanna was the probation officer during my period as chairman of C-wing and I saw a better, more caring, side to her so I got on okay with her. She didn't last very long, only about nine months, before being replaced by a fully qualified probation officer.

Gill, a petite Scotswoman from one of the islands, was more like Sue in outlook and demeanour. I remember my first meeting with her, soon after she came on the wing, and how enthusiastic she was about working at Grendon. She had been trying to come to the prison for some years. And, up until the day I left, her enthusiasm never seemed to wane. Gill was soon to be as well-loved and respected as Sue had been. Probation officers also have a very big say in a prisoner's progress, and though they have been getting a lot of bad press from those bastions of moral cowardice in the Home Office, usually via the tabloid media, they do a very difficult job and take, mostly undeserved, flak when things go wrong. Another good probation officer who worked at Grendon and sometimes made reports on lifers for the Parole Board was Emma, a nice woman who recommended me for D cat and release.

C-wing also had a fully qualified psychotherapist in Helen, the group 1 civilian facilitator. Helen was Scottish too, and was rumoured to be the most qualified and intelligent person working at Grendon, though these claims were invariably made by group 1, her own group. I never had any interviews with Helen during my time at Grendon, though I did have a few verbal jousts with her in community meetings. She was very professional, fiercely loyal and terribly protective of her group. She wrote each one of them such in-depth reports that occasionally half the time allotted for a wing assessment was spent just reading out her novel-length views and observations. In the early days I got the feeling that Helen didn't really like me. One time in my own wing assessment she commented, with some vitriol I thought, that I 'stomped around' as though I 'owned the wing'. I was surprised by the feeling she put into this statement but we can all take an instant dislike to someone for no discernible reason, so

I didn't let it bother me that much as I was not in her group and she didn't have to make any reports on me. I just kept my distance as much as possible. It was only towards the end of my time at Grendon, after I had read the chapter she contributed to a book about the jail called *Working with Dangerous People* (edited by David Jones, Radcliffe Medical Press), that I got a bit more insight into her real feelings. Helen, like most of us, was a very complex character and what you saw on the surface was not always the real person.

The two other members of the non-uniform staff were Debbie, who ran art therapy every Thursday, and Martin, who took psychodrama on Tuesday afternoons. I never really had much to do with Debbie, but she was a bit too New Age for my personal taste and I vowed never to go on art therapy.

Martin, and psychodrama, on the other hand, were more my cup of Tetley. Martin, middle-aged and bespectacled, had a penchant for the kind of casual clothes that probation officers and social workers find trendy. Check shirts, dark jeans and Cornish-pasty-looking shoes were his uniform, but his enthusiasm and unquenchable excitement for what he was doing were uplifting and inspiring for those of us who volunteered for the psychodrama group. Martin was a joy to watch in action out on the floor of the community room with a psychodrama in progress. He would gently lead the individual who wanted to act out some traumatic event in his life into the scene and then judge every move, every emotion, perfectly, knowing instinctively when to speak and what tone to use or when to fade into the background and just observe. I got a lot from my time in psychodrama and think it was the most intense and emotional experience I had at Grendon. It didn't matter whether I was ranting and raving in rage or sobbing my heart out in grief, Martin always knew when and how to step in and lead me back into the present.

The structure of uniformed staff on the wing was the same as on most prison wings, with one exception – three officers were designated full-time facilitators. The uniformed facilitators were in group 2, group 3 and group 4. Group 2's officer/facilitator was Jimmy, one of the most well-liked and respected officers on the wing, if not in the whole jail. Jimmy was a Scouser with a calm, helpful, friendly and efficient manner. The reason he was held in such high regard by the inmates was because he was not a bullshitter. He told everyone straight and he would not mess anyone around. If you asked Jimmy to do something for you, you knew it was going to get done if it could be done. He was a bit of a maverick, even among the staff at Grendon, and hated red tape and bumptious officialdom almost as much as the prisoners did. He had seen life before joining the Prison Service, having served with the Royal Greenjackets in various postings. Jimmy was so well liked that when Taff, who was a member of his group, came up with the idea of us inmates putting him up for a Butler Trust Award, the yearly awards for individuals who have achieved excellence in prisons and special hospitals, I even managed to swallow my hatred of the Welshman and sign a reference for Jimmy. It was very gratifying for us all when he won the award and went with his family to Buckingham Palace to collect it a year later. In the parlance of prisoners, Jimmy was 'good stuff'.

My first facilitator, Brian, was also one of the good guys. He had a very laid-back manner but could become passionate when talking about things that interested him, like art, hill-walking and therapy. Brian had a great sense of humour and did a fantastic job in group 3. It's essential for anyone in group therapy to have trust in the group because without it there is no way you can open yourself up completely and therefore you will inevitably miss out on some work. This means you must also trust your facilitator, who is a part of the group, and for some of us who were in groups with uniformed facilitators this was very hard. It was officers like Brian and Jimmy, who constantly strove to show us the human face behind the black serge, who allowed us to relax and trust for the first time. Being a group facilitator is a 24-hour-a-day job and these men never let us down or faltered in their commitment. Like most of us, they truly believed in what they were doing and this shone through. Unfortunately, after three years as my facilitator, Brian moved over to HMP Springhill, for personal reasons.

The uniformed facilitator who replaced Brian in group 3 was a woman whom I had a bit of history with. Glenda had been a wing screw at Belmarsh when I was starting my life sentence, and we hadn't got on very well. I was still in my hate-all-uniforms stage and Glenda had a bit of a reputation among the prisoners as 'awkward'. She seemed to take delight in fucking people over for petty infractions of the rules. I remember the first thing she said to me at Grendon was, 'What are you doing here?' To which my reply was to direct the same question right back at her. I don't think either of us believed the other's motive for being at Grendon was genuine: she thought I was there to work my ticket, and I thought she was there to fuck people over with little real comeback. We crept around each other for a long time, not quite trusting each other. Glenda was the facilitator in group 2, along with Jimmy, so we never really had much occasion for interaction anyway. But then, in the winter of 2006 there was a big staff shake-up and she took over from Brian as group 3's facilitator.

At first I was gutted. Not only that Brian, a man whom I had come to trust and respect, was going, but more so that Glenda was taking his place. Part of me just did not relish the thought of Glenda, who was, after all, one of 'the enemy' as far as I knew, taking over my group and I wasn't sure I would be able to open up with her in the room. But I soon found out that my previous impression of Glenda was wrong. She turned out to be a brilliant facilitator, and within a month I was as relaxed in her company as I had been with Brian overseeing group 3. By the time I became eligible for my first ROTL it was Glenda who I asked to take me. Outside the prison she was an excellent companion and I felt easy in her company. She took me for all three of my ROTLs, and by the time I left Grendon I felt that we were friends. Which goes to show how much I really had changed my attitudes and values during my stay there.

There were some other diamonds among the uniformed staff but there were also a few dogs. Some screws had never worked at any other prison than Grendon, and it showed in their stupid attitudes. Just like there were some lightweight cons who, on realizing the no-violence rule was being strictly enforced, suddenly became faces on arrival at Grendon, there were some screws of the same ilk. It's easy to go round giving it the big 'un when you know that nobody's going to give you a good dig in the snot for it. The dog screws who had never served on the landings of ultra-violent local jails and dispersal prisons where they would be in constant danger of being assaulted by the prisoners always seemed to grow an extra pair of balls at Grendon, one of the quietest and least violent nicks in the country. It was quite amusing to witness them getting all bolshy and rule-addicted when you knew that if they had tried the same behaviour in a real nick they would have been rumped, bumped and thumped in short order. Just like the inmates, some of the staff were good, some bad, and a minority were definitely mad. But it was a mix that seemed to work. Most of the time.

One major change that resulted directly from my time at Grendon was my attitude towards uniformed prison staff. I detested screws, full stop, and had never wanted to know anything about the person who was wearing the uniform, only how much abuse I could get away with, both physical and verbal. But at Grendon I found this deeply ingrained hatred being gradually eroded. In Grendon the staff were much more involved in the daily lives of the inmates and it was very hard to avoid them. They became – particularly the good ones, like Glenda and Jimmy – real people, with names, rather than just a uniform. I'm almost embarrassed to admit it, but I actually made a couple of good friends among the uniformed staff at Grendon. And coming from me, with my long and troubled history at the hands of the uniformed storm troopers of the Home Office, that's really saying something.

29. Biff and the Escape That Never Was

Geordie bank robber Biff was not exactly the brightest spark in the fusebox and should not really have been at Grendon. I don't believe for one moment that he would have been able to summon the necessary IQ score that was required for entry into the therapeutic community. But, like most criminals, he did possess an innate craftiness. On an emotional level Biff was like a child, often getting sulky and throwing his dummy out of the pram when things didn't go the way he expected. He would have periods when he would make good progress in his group, and then he would have a tantrum over some minor incident and fuck it all up. In his defence, though, not an awful lot seemed ever to go right for him. For example, there was a screw called Rambo, who was sometimes the facilitator in Biff's group, who seemed to take delight in inflicting what can only be described as low-level bullying. Rambo was one of those screws who looked forward to the monthly C&R training that all prison officers have to undertake. Though he was working in a prison where actual violence was almost non-existent he looked as if he had a longing for a bit of action and was always 'ready'. The ironic thing was that Rambo had never really worked in other prisons where physical violence was an everyday occurrence. I suspect, and told him this to his face on several occasions, that if he took his cocky attitude to, say, one of the dispersal prisons such as Whitemoor or Frankland, he would probably shit himself at the first sign of real 'action'. Screws like Rambo tend to pick easy targets, and unfortunately for him Biff was one of the easiest.

Listening to the feedbacks from Biff's group whenever he had done any work on his childhood was always hard for me. By the time I had sat through twelve months of group work and feedbacks I was starting to think I had become tempered and hardened to the horrific tales of abuse that flowed almost constantly from my fellow community members. But I was forever being proved wrong. Just when I thought I had heard the most unbearable things ever, some other poor soul would casually top it with an even more shocking story of man's inhumanity and depravity. On occasions I felt physically sick at what I was hearing.

Biff, it turned out, was to spend a very long time in therapy at Grendon, and he made little progress. He was already five years over his minimum tariff when he was finally downgraded from security category B to C. As a category C lifer he would be eligible for a maximum of three ROTLs per year. A lifer's first ROTL is a massive milestone in his progress and is granted only after many years of imprisonment. Biff's was granted after he had served almost nine years of his sentence and, obviously, he was very excited at the thought of going outside the prison walls. He planned a trip to Banbury, where he would spend the little bit of money he had managed to save out of his prison wages on a meal at KFC and then he would just walk around the town and take in the sights. It might not sound very exciting but imprisonment is a world of dull grey vistas and when you have been locked up for a few years even seeing a traffic light or a bus is cause for wonder and fascination. Most people on C-wing were happy for Biff, the consensus being that he might be a bit thick but he had been extremely hard done by. I don't think anyone believed for one minute that he was any sort of danger to the public, or anyone else, except himself.

There had always been a bit of needle between Biff and Rambo, and sometimes what passed for banter between the two could be more vicious than was needed. The trouble was Biff didn't understand the boundaries that exist between screws and cons, and he would sometimes say things to Rambo without being aware of the balance of power between them. And Rambo, though he tried hard to hide it, was a man who could hold a grudge. So maybe Rambo decided it was time that Biff was taken down a peg or two. A couple of days before Biff's ROTL Rambo decided to search his cell. Cell-searching on C-wing was done on a regular basis, as it is in all prisons, but usually a blind eye was turned by the staff to any petty rule infringements. In a regime as relaxed as Grendon there was really no need for the staff to strong it – no staff or inmates were being assaulted, there was no hooch being brewed, weapons or escape equipment being fashioned, or drugs being secreted, like in every other jail. The regime, though it was an unwritten rule, worked on a *quid pro quo* basis – you behave and comply with the therapy, and we won't nick you for having an extra pillow on your bed or having a floor mat in your cell that's two inches longer than the official allowance. Everyone knew that if it was nickings the staff were after, then they could easily have got them. But, on the whole, rather than resort to disciplinary hearings, at Grendon the men would be encouraged to deal with infractions via therapeutic channels – i.e. discussing things on the wing or in the groups. Nickings were usually a last resort, and only for serious offences.

So Rambo searched Biff's cell, and lo and behold he found a small piece of electrical wire that Biff had used to connect his TV and radio so he could have both plugged in at the same time. Most men on C-wing had the same arrangement in their cells as there were only two power points in each cell and we were allowed several electrical appliances. Of course, being in possession of this piece of wire was against prison rules, so Rambo nicked Biff. And an inevitable consequence of being nicked was that Biff lost his ROTL. The community were outraged when they heard, and many of the staff also thought that Rambo was out of order. But he was well within his rights and there was nothing anyone could do. Biff appeared in front of the governor for adjudication and was given a caution – the most lenient punishment the rule book allowed. He would be able to apply for his ROTL and start the process all over again in six months' time. It was devastating to get within spitting distance of a ROTL only to have it snatched away. It hit me hard, but it must have been doubly difficult for Biff because he was so immature – like a kid being told that Christmas has been cancelled after waiting impatiently and being good all year.

After the nicking Biff became very depressed and bitter. He rarely spoke in his group and spent a lot of time in his cell. Rambo, on the other hand, seemed to relish his new role as a dog screw and went from strength to strength, always on the lookout to nick someone, though he still picked the easy targets. It was as if he had finally come out of the closet and did not care that he was now detested by a lot of men on C-wing. Eventually he would gather a few like-minded acolytes from the new intakes of staff, and by the time I left Grendon there would be a noticeable division in the C-wing staff group. I still think he should have had the courage of his convictions and gone to work in a real nick. But that would have taken bottle, and I don't think he had it in him.

About three months after his nicking Biff was given a job as a red-band. He was allowed to walk around the prison grounds with a trolley and empty all the bins. He was working with a bloke from A-wing called Terry, who was a bit of a wide-boy by all accounts, and Biff seemed to enjoy the job. He still wasn't saying much in his group but he appeared much happier around the wing. He almost had a spring in his step as he

went about his daily routine. Then one lunchtime I happened to be talking
to him in the meal queue when a posse of officials entered the dining hall
and made a beeline for him. The uniforms looked as though they meant
business and were led by a grim-faced security PO, who put his hand on
Biff's shoulder. 'You're coming with us,' he said. Biff's face drained of
colour. 'What for?' he asked, nervously. The PO shook his head. 'Never
mind that, let's go.' And with that he steered Biff out of the queue and
the rest of the screws closed around him before hustling him out of the
dining room and off the wing. Everyone was stunned. This kind of thing
was unheard of at Grendon, so we knew it must have been something
serious. But no one knew what. Ten minutes later the wing chairman
came into the dining hall and announced that a wing special had been
called for straight after lunch.

When the whole community were seated Tom, the therapist, announced that Biff had been shipped out already and was on his way to
HMP Woodhill, a top-security prison near Milton Keynes. Or 'Milton
Keys', as Biff himself might have said. Apparently, acting on 'information
received', security had searched the shed where the bins were cleaned and
found two mobile phones and a pair of bolt-croppers. This was a massive
security breach and obviously pointed to an escape attempt. Now that
the wall had been replaced with fencing the bolt-croppers would have
been an ideal tool to cut out through the fence and the phones could have
been used to coordinate a pick-up by outside parties. As the only inmates
who had access to the bin shed were Biff and Terry, both were securely
in the frame and, as usual in the prison system, security had acted first
and would ask questions later. The community was in shock and opinion
was divided over whether Biff could be involved. He definitely did not
have the wit or resources for something like this if he was acting alone,
but Terry was more than capable. There was a lot of discussion in the
community about whether Biff was a completely innocent party or
whether he was maybe in on the plan with Terry as the instigator. I kept
quiet, but recalled how upbeat Biff had been in the last couple of weeks
and wondered whether this was because he planned to make his own way
out and fuck the ROTL process. It would be just the kind of idea that
might appeal to him after the way he had been treated.

Then Big Brian spoke up. He had taken Biff under his wing and it was
clear that he wasn't going to let his pal be tried and convicted without
some sort of defence. 'I'm not buying this for one minute,' he said. 'For

a start, if Biff was planning to escape there's no way he'd have been able to keep it quiet. I'd have known.' The community room was silent for a moment. Then Tom spoke. 'Well, did you?' he asked. Brian scowled. 'No, I fucking didn't. But maybe there's more to this than meets the eye. Let's not overlook some obvious points here. Number one, how the fuck could any prisoner smuggle in a pair of bolt-croppers? Mobile phones maybe, but bolt-croppers? I don't fucking think so!' A few people were nodding and looking thoughtful. Visits were pretty relaxed at Grendon, certainly compared to other category B jails, but there wasn't a snowflake's chance in hell that anyone could walk through with something as bulky as bolt-croppers. 'And another thing,' Brian continued, 'it's funny how this has happened in the very week that the security department are being audited.'

Brian was right. It did seem a whopping coincidence that a major escape plot had been discovered while Home Office auditors were in the prison to check on the security department's performance. Security breaches at Grendon were very rare, and I would imagine that with the new fences and the jail now being as tight as a drum the auditors might possibly be looking to downsize the security department. A major escape plot being discovered right under their noses would illustrate the need for more security. Plus nice brownie points for the security department who had proved they were obviously on the ball. Of course, this was all conjecture and supposition. But not beyond the realms of possibility. Tom raised an eyebrow. 'So, Brian, are you suggesting . . . well, just what exactly are you suggesting?' Brian shook his head. 'I'm not "suggesting" anything. I'm merely stating a fact. There is no way a prisoner could have smuggled in a pair of bolt-croppers, and security are out to impress this week. It doesn't take a lot of brain cells to make a connection.' There was a muttering of agreement from the majority of the community and one or two of the uniformed staff looked decidedly uncomfortable. Brian was one of my best pals and I decided to jump in and bring this conversation to an end as I could see he was getting agitated and I feared he might say too much and find himself the target of suspicion. 'Look,' I said, firmly, 'it's pointless us sitting here and speculating, the security department are not going to tell us any more than we already know. So I vote we bring this meeting to an end and await the outcome of the investigation.' Mark was also mindful of Brian's mounting anger and seconded my suggestion. The community agreed and the meeting closed.

Later in my cell Brian was able to let off steam about what he saw as the victimization of Biff. We all agreed that what had happened seemed very suspicious, but there was nothing we could do about it. I wasn't 100 per cent sure that Biff was completely innocent, but then I've always been a bit of a cynical bastard.

Both Brian and I were on a psychodrama session the next afternoon, and Brian used his time to talk about the way Biff had been treated by life and how pissed off he was about it. I was pretty new to psychodrama at this stage but finding it very interesting. I had been encouraged to become part of the psychodrama group by the therapy staff during every group assessment after my initial one in 2003, but I had resisted for quite a while. I couldn't see what I was likely to get from a lot of role-playing and talking to cushions, which was my first impression of it. I had also been put off by a story told to me by my brother-in-law Tony about his time on psychodrama while at Grendon. He has a hatred of nonces and was serving life for killing a man who sexually abused his daughter. Tony told me that he had been put through what was known as a 'hot seat' – which involved sitting on a chair in the middle of the room while being verbally abused by several sex offenders. According to Tony it was done to test his tolerance levels and to see if he could hold his temper in a stressful situation. Anyway, it turned out he couldn't. He ended up flying into a rage and attacking the lads playing the sex offender roles, and he was shipped out of Grendon.

But that was all before speaking to a few good friends who were already doing psychodrama, and spoke about the intense feelings it engendered in them. Psychodrama was about being able to express emotions physically as well as verbally, and once I had my first interview and taster session with Martin, the facilitator, I began to see the value of it. The psychodrama group I joined consisted of Brian, Roy, Christy G, Musa, Big Don, Pickles and Pete the Psycho. Martin facilitated the group. We met in the community room every Tuesday afternoon between 2 and 4.30. The first thing on our agenda would be the check-in, when every member of the group, including Martin, got to speak a bit about what they had been doing in the preceding week and how they were feeling. Sometimes this could be very light-hearted but other times members of the group would use the check-in to have a rant or get something off their chest. It could be something as simple as an argument they'd had with somebody on the wing, or something as serious as a bereavement in the family – you just

never knew what people were going to reveal. After the check-in Martin
would ask if anyone would volunteer to do a piece of work and usually
there would be several hands going up. If more than one person wanted
to work, we would discuss among us whose need we thought most
pressing. The man chosen would then go out into the middle of the room
with Martin and explain where he wanted to go with his issue. Martin
had a bag of cushions and pillows, along with odd-shaped bits of foam
rubber, with which the man working could set up simple scenes and
situations. For example, if I were working on a scene from my life I might
use chairs and cushions to stand for a certain room or situation, or even
to stand for thoughts and feelings. The rest of the group would sit on the
sidelines and observe, though we could stick our hands up and ask relevant
questions and offer advice.

Men often felt embarrassed at the start of a psychodrama, when asked
to describe intimate or violent scenes from their lives in front of other
people, and using cushions and pillows to represent feelings and people
can seem a bit silly at first. Once you get into a scene and begin to embrace
the real emotions behind what you are saying, however, it feels good and
you forget where you are and what you are doing. I myself have been so
caught up in psychodramatic scenes from my life that I really believed I
was living them again. A lot of the credit for us cynical criminals being
able to immerse ourselves in the moment must go to Martin, who is an
excellent facilitator and guided us through every step of the process. At
various stages during a psychodrama you can choose other group members
to play characters in your scenario. So I might have Brian as my brother
and Pickles as my mum, and Martin would encourage us to play the scene
as it was, and then as we would have liked it to have been. In this way we
would get to say to the characters the things that we had really wanted
to say at the time. After my initial fear and misgivings I found psychodrama
a big help, particularly in a non-verbal way. It was a more physical therapy
by which we could turn some words into deeds and, hopefully, exorcize
the lot. Or at least get some sort of closure.

Brian used the psychodrama check-in to lament the way Biff was being
treated by the system because, as Brian put it, 'he's an easy fookin' target'.
He ended up having another rant, and admitted he felt a lot better for
letting it out. In another nick Brian would probably have ended up in an
argument with the screws over it and maybe resorting to violence. And
that was an example of how Grendon and the therapy worked. Instead

of reverting to type when we had a problem, which would only lead us into more trouble, at Grendon we could sit down and talk about it, thus defusing the situation. It sounds simple, and that's because it is. If more people in the world were to talk and listen, then maybe we would have less need for prisons.

Some months later we heard that Biff had been completely exonerated by the investigation. Terry was not charged with anything either. An apparent escape attempt from a cat B jail and yet we heard nothing of the conclusions the investigation reached! It was all just quietly swept under the carpet, like a lot of things in the British penal system. Biff had been held in the top-security wing of HMP Woodhill and now he was applying to return to Grendon. There was no objection from the staff or security department, which was further grist for Brian's conspiracy mill.

Before Biff returned to Grendon several members of the community brought up his case in wing meetings and in their groups but these discussions only brought more questions than answers. The bottom line was that nobody from the prison system was prepared to say any more about the mysterious 'escape plot'. In the end Grendon's security department got their brownie points and no job or budget cuts. And Biff returned to C-wing, where he was to stay, even more chastened and disillusioned with his life than he had been before. He made little progress in therapy and seemed to lose heart. In 2009, his eleventh year of imprisonment and sixth year in Grendon, he decided to cut his losses and stick his papers in.

It strikes me as tragic that someone like Biff should spend the greater part of his life in prison for what are basically nonsensical nuisance crimes. Yes, he robbed two banks, but with a Hoover pipe! Biff was no more dangerous and in need of a top-security-prison place for a couple of decades than the average man on any average street. He was stupid, immature and had few social skills and little education – but, dangerous? A serious threat to society? A hardened criminal? I don't think so. The tragedy is that Biff will probably rattle around the prison system for the next ten years before someone is brave enough to sign his release papers. And worse – there are many more like Biff in our jails.

Grendon and the therapeutic process did not work for everyone. Some people cannot understand the concept of therapy; they just do not have the wherewithal to deal with it on anything but the most basic level. Still more cannot bear the painful feelings and memories that therapy brings to the surface, so they quit. And, of course, there are many who do not really want to change their lives. They're quite happy to stumble along from one crisis to the next, dealing with their problems through violence or other destructive behaviours. No, therapy doesn't work for everyone. But I was either luckier or more determined than most.

30. Diamond Geezers

I made a lot of good friends during my years at Grendon; I also renewed and strengthened friendships I'd made in the conventional prison system. In the early days I was having it with Fred, Ray, Kevin, John, Steve and Daran, but they were all to move on eventually and for a while I kept to myself. But the atmosphere and nature of the therapeutic community did not lend itself well to loners so I couldn't help but get involved in other people's lives. In the system I would gravitate towards men of my own kind – robbers, gangsters and other serious career criminals – and in Grendon I was no different. The therapeutic staff frowned upon and strongly questioned the formation of any sort of clique or firm on the wing, but they couldn't force anyone to mix with someone they didn't want to, so it was a question of balance. I made sure I was not openly hostile to anyone because of his crime and I was always polite to even the most unattractive of characters, but the people I had closest to me were the ODCs, most of whom I would have associated with in any other jail. I don't think this was in any way contradictory to the work I was doing at Grendon. I realized very early on that nobody was expecting me to hug sex offenders or suddenly become bosom buddies with people I didn't like. As long as people treated me with courtesy and respect, then I would treat them the same way. I would not physically attack anyone, nor would I openly discriminate against anyone because of their crime. But I chose the men I was really having it with. And they were some of the best.

Kung Fu Chris was a Scouser who had already served a long sentence for robbery with violence and was now doing ten years for bank robbery and possession of firearms. He was one of those genuinely hard and violent men who was also intelligent and had a quick wit. I don't suppose it would be much comfort to his many victims to know that Chris could have quoted Shakespeare or analysed Nietzsche while caving their face in – but he could have. When Chris arrived at Grendon a lot of people were frightened of him because of the image he presented of himself. He was around 6 foot 1 of pure muscle, though not the glossy look-at-my-pecs muscle of the vain bodybuilder, more the I-would-find-it-very-easy-to-rip-your-arms-off kind of muscle. He was a fighting machine – you could see it in his lumpy misshapen knuckles, in his wide shoulders, and in the brooding deep-set eyes that clocked your every move and analysed it instantly for any threat. He was the sort of geezer I would consider going against in a fight only if I was in possession of a serious advantage – like a sawn-off 12-gauge shotgun. And even then I'd want plenty of ammunition.

From what I heard on feedbacks from his group, and first-hand when we were both on psychodrama together, Chris had been a lonely, scrawny child who had been bullied mercilessly until he was fifteen years old and decided to fight back. He discovered he not only had a natural talent for fighting, but actually liked hurting people. His home life was difficult, and when he was seventeen Chris packed a bag and ran off to Hong Kong. Initially Chris's reason for choosing Hong Kong was because he fancied a girl whose father had been posted there by the army. Being very impetuous, Chris decided to follow his young love. But once there he found that life for a homeless and potless Liverpool teenager was never going to be easy. One of the few things that he had picked up from school was how to stand up to bullies and fight. So when he started looking for work in Hong Kong it was to the kick-boxing clubs and gyms he went. Over a few months he managed to pick up a bit of cash by fighting in illegal bouts against much more skilled opposition. The Scouse kid was never going to win but he put up a very plucky showing in front of the gambling crowds and became a favourite. He also picked up a bit of door work at the clubs and, eventually, a few strong-arm jobs, debt-collecting for local gangsters. After several years in Hong Kong Chris was mustard in the fight game and a bit of a champion kick-boxer. He was bright enough to be dissatisfied with the constant violence in his life, but he had no choice – the only work he could find always involved hitting people.

Eventually he drifted back to England and tried to settle down. Things went wrong pretty quickly and Chris found himself serving eight years' imprisonment for robbery and GBH. As you might expect from such a violent man, he was a troublesome prisoner. He couldn't settle into prison life and ended up being shipped around the system. On his release he began to drift once more, the trouble being that most people he associated with knew of his fighting prowess and propensity for serious violence and always wanted to use it for their own ends. From what I can gather Chris was rather a lonely character with few, if any, real friends and he was a man who felt trapped. He liked to fight but it wasn't the full extent of his character and he wanted more from life than blood, snot and broken bones. He met a girl and settled down at last to family life when children followed. But Chris always felt that he didn't quite fit in, and as he had no real skills other than fighting he felt inadequate as a provider to his new family. Desperate to do something – anything – in order to relieve his deep feelings of inadequacy and depression, he began to look to crime again. He went up to London for a meeting with some old criminal associates and ended up on a four-day drink and cocaine binge. Nobody wanted to work with him but he was given a sawn-off shotgun as a parting gift. For almost five hours Chris wandered the West End of London with the shotgun under his coat and an increasingly manic voice in his head telling him he should be a man and rob something. He told me that when it came right down to it he realized that the worst that could happen was that he would die, and on some level he told himself that might not be such a bad thing.

After much wandering and procrastination he chose a bank, went in and held it up. The robbery was destined for disaster from the start as the branch he had chosen had already been robbed twice in a year and the staff had learned their lesson. The moment Chris pulled the shotgun from his coat one of the cashiers triggered the alarm that sounded in a local police station. Chris left the bank with a bag of money but he was on foot and had given little thought to his getaway. He quickly became confused by the warren of streets and couldn't find a taxi anywhere. Meanwhile, the police had been very swift to cordon off the area and he found himself cornered by armed old bill. With many gun barrels trained on him he was ordered to drop his gun and give up. He was later to say that the thought of just shooting at the police crossed his mind. He knew he had once again fucked up his life and had to make a snap decision as to whether death would be preferable to spending years in the living death of top-security prisons. Chris told me that the only thing that stopped him doing a Butch and Sundance was the thought of his wife and children. He dropped his gun and lay down on the ground.

Chris was sentenced to ten years' imprisonment for bank robbery and possession of a firearm and once in jail he finally decided that he would have to change his life completely. He applied for Grendon and after some months was accepted. When he first came on to C-wing he was a terrible brooding presence, barely talking to anyone. He would spend a lot of time either working out in the gym or on the pads, or sitting in the corridor on the ground floor staring into space. In groups and wing meetings he would come to life and argue passionately about whatever topic or subject he felt strongly about. He was a formidable man when in full flow, voice raised, eyes flashing, daring anyone to contradict him. This was very frightening for the more feeble members of the community who felt unable to challenge him in any way. But all that Chris was saying, albeit in a scary and aggressive manner, was that he had come to Grendon seeking answers and would not tolerate dishonesty from anyone. I quite liked the fella and on the infrequent occasions that we did speak I was surprised by the range of his interests – philosophy, classical history and poetry.

Then one morning after groups I walked into the laundry to pick up my washing and found Chris in there with Marvin and Pickles. They were arguing over something that had happened in the groups and Chris was growing ever more irate. It was really none of my business, but I stuck my oar in anyway and told him to calm down. One thing led to another very quickly and before I knew it we were both shaping up to fight each other. To this day I couldn't tell you what exactly was said to make the argument escalate so fast, but it never takes a lot when those steeped in violence fall out. Chris made a move towards me and Marvin and Pickles tried to restrain him. At this point clarity returned to my own thoughts and I made the decision to go to my cell and get tooled up. There was no way I was going to be rolling around on the floor with this lunatic at my age! I had an empty coffee jar in my cell and my initial plan was to get it and break it so I had a jagged edge to stick into Chris if he decided to go the final step. But it's in this aroused state that the therapy really starts to kick in. On the short walk from the laundry room to my cell I managed to clear my mind and take a step back from the situation. Firstly, I reasoned that violence would solve nothing here, I knew from bitter experience that it could only make things worse. Plus Chris was in an emotional state and I knew that once he was calm again he wouldn't want to carry this on. I understood from what I'd heard from him that he was genuine about changing his life and violent ways, so if I walked away now I could approach him later and sort things out reasonably. I actually had the coffee jar in my hand for a few moments, and then put it back in its place. I felt a lot better about myself for not succumbing to my basic instincts.

Later that day I told Chris he had been out of order and that I was putting him in the book for his behaviour. He accepted this with a shrug, but I could tell he thought I was doing exactly the right thing. How you word incidents in the wing book affects how the wing views them, so I was careful how I put it. All I said was that Chris had lost his temper and as a result I had come very close to losing my own. I was playing it down a bit but it was the first and only time in my five years at Grendon that I put anyone in the book. When it came up for discussion in the wing meeting both me and Chris talked openly about our anger and how we sometimes still drifted very close to actual violence. It was a good bit of work and it proved to the community that no one had any need to be scared to challenge anyone else as long as it was done in the right way. After the book incident me and Chris became good friends, often plotting up in my cell in the evenings, usually for long argumentative discussions on everything from the real effect of therapy to the war on terror. We were also in the psychodrama group together for almost two years and I was always impressed with Chris's total honesty concerning himself and his lack of guile around other people's work.

We still had many loud and aggressive disagreements in wing meetings, but when Chris was finally given his D cat and transferred to HMP Ford I really felt I was saying goodbye to a very old friend. I do know that Chris must have got at least some of the answers he wanted from Grendon because by the time he left he was a completely different character, much lighter and more approachable. A good friend I am still in touch with.

Brian, the Bermondsey Butcher, was similar to Kung Fu Chris in many ways, and I was also to become very good friends with him. Originally from Sunderland, Brian had come to make his fortune, via drug dealing, in south London when he was in his early twenties. A huge man, weighing in at nearly 19 stone, he was a fitness fanatic who could benchpress double his own body weight. Though he looked a proper bruiser, he was really a very funny bloke. He could have a proper tear-up if there was no way out of it, and, having witnessed him working out on the pads with Kung Fu Chris, I knew he was the sort of fighter who would march on until either he or his opponent was out of the game. He could also take a good dig without folding. A few times when they were working out Chris would miss the pads and catch Brian a good kick or punch to the ribs or body and though he would wince in pain he wouldn't say a word. Brian was a tough man.

How he came to end up at Grendon was a bit of a horror story. Over about fifteen years he had risen through the drug-dealing ranks until he became an upper-middle-level supplier, mainly of cocaine, dealing in kilo weights. But Brian was just naturally criminal-minded and liked to dabble in all sorts of criminality, from strong-arming other criminals to forging documents and even minting his own fake pound coins. He stuck to south London but would move often between the boroughs. By the late 1990s he was living in Bermondsey and having it with a couple of brothers who were well-known heavy villains, mainly GBH and firearms merchants. One night he, the brothers and another man, also a criminal, went on an alcohol and cocaine bender and they all ended up back at Brian's flat in the small hours of the morning. There was some kind of disagreement between one of the brothers and the other man. No one will ever know what really happened that night except those who were involved and one of them is dead, but the survivors' stories differ greatly from each other. Brian says that the brother who started the argument pulled a revolver from his pocket and fired three shots into the other man. The victim was badly injured and tried to escape from the flat but was attacked by Brian and the second brother. Brian stabbed the man several times, then the first brother pulled a second gun and pumped several more shots into the victim. He died instantly.

It was decided that in order to keep the murder a secret for as long as possible they would cut up the body and dispose of it in several different locations. No one really fancied the wet-work but Brian had often hunted, skinned and butchered various animals for food in his youth, so he took on the job of dismembering the victim. Having spoken to Brian about this on several occasions I could tell that the experience had distinctly affected him though he spoke matter of factly about it and rarely showed any emotion. Once, after he had told me about the case in great detail, I asked him if, knowing all he knew now, he would do anything differently if he had his time again. He thought for a moment and then, a twinkle of amusement in his eyes, replied, 'Aye, I'd cut the fucking arms off last, the bastard torso kept spinning in the bath as I was sawing it in half. The arms left on would have made it a lot easier.' I laughed. Let's face it, what else could I have done?

So Brian, stripped to his boxer shorts, spent five hours in the bathtub sawing and hacking the body into manageable pieces. All three of the men bagged the body parts and then drove far and wide to deposit them in various dumps and landfill sites before returning home and retiring to bed. Brian flew to Spain two days later. While he was away part of the body was discovered and the murder hunt was on. Within a year both Brian and the brothers were nicked and went on to stand trial at the Old Bailey. According to the forensic pathologist at the trial the victim had been shot with three different-calibre guns as well as being stabbed and beaten. Brian and the older brother were found guilty of murder and given life sentences, and the younger brother was acquitted of murder but given eight years' imprisonment for helping to dispose of the body. Brian's minimum tariff was eighteen years.

At Grendon Brian was well liked by most people, though hated and feared by the original members of his group, group 1, which included Billy Bullshit and Scaredy Cat. Brian came into group 1 with a no-nonsense attitude and was soon challenging all the dead wood to put up or shut up. He was instrumental in Billy Bullshit's demise, and fell out with his facilitator, Helen, on many occasions because of his unwillingness to treat people as though they were wrapped in cotton wool. Brian liked to do his therapy the same way he had lived his life – hard, brutal and straight to the point – but Helen could be a bit of a Care Bear and loved her group to roll over and play spaniel. He was always talking about pulling out of therapy and just going back into the system, but he was one of the few people who had been on C-wing almost as long as me and he was still there when I left.

I have already spoken about Scouse Mark whom I first met on F-wing at Grendon soon after we both arrived. He was shipped out of Grendon in early 2005 after one of the worst scenes of violence seen on C-wing during my time there. I've described his fight with Cat, the Manchester kid, and how he very nearly brained a screw with a pool cue in the ensuing skirmish. He was transferred to HMP Stafford, where he stayed for a year before being granted D cat. Mark was doing a fixed-term sentence of only seven years, which is long enough, but relatively short when compared to other men in Grendon, and was considered a low security risk despite the fight. He went to HMP Ford, an open prison in Sussex, and it was less than a week before he decided to go on the run. Eight weeks after walking out of jail Mark was rearrested and charged with two more burglaries committed while he was unlawfully at large. He was sentenced to a consecutive three years' imprisonment, which brought his total sentence up to ten years. After some months in a local jail Mark once again applied for Grendon, and he returned in October 2006.

Before he came back on to C-wing there was a discussion in the community meeting about whether the staff and community were happy to have him back. As it had been a while since Mark had been shipped out there weren't many people left on the wing who knew him, but me, Brian and a few others argued strongly for Mark to be allowed to return. There are always men, however, who are frightened at the thought of someone who committed an act of violence while in therapy returning to the community. There were also people who didn't know Mark but had moral objections to having him back. But luckily his old facilitator, Helen, was happy to have him back in her group and the vote turned out in his favour. I was delighted. I really did like Mark and I also knew that the only reason he had got involved in the fight with Cat was because of his loyalty to his childhood friend, Sparky. Mark was not a naturally violent man. Yes, he would use violence when he felt it was needed, but usually only as the last resort. He was essentially a very easygoing bloke with a calm demeanour and a wicked sense of humour, and once he was back on C-wing without Sparky sticking his oar in, he became very well liked by the community.

Tony, on the other hand, was another big, violent man who effortlessly engendered fear in others even though he didn't really mean to. I had first met him when we had both just been sentenced to life imprisonment. We were both category A prisoners on Belmarsh's notorious Houseblock 4 and had a lot of mutual friends. Tony was from the East End of London, Custom House, and had a reputation as both a criminal and a fighter. At 6 foot 1 and 16½ stone he was fitter than a butcher's dog and as game as a brace of lions. A huge scar, stretching from the crown of his head down one side of his face to the jaw line, a souvenir of a knife-fight when he was in his teens, added to the air of menace that seemed to envelop him. He was serving a mandatory life sentence for a gangland shooting. When I first met Tony he had just been weighed off with life and was a very angry man, ready to bite the head off the world, so he was the last person I would have expected to see at Grendon. But like most of the ultra-violent men who volunteered for therapy, Tony had hidden depths.

I liked Tony from day one, though he was a bit younger than the rest of us in Belmarsh. A lot of men, even those who were seriously violent themselves, avoided Tony because of the barely suppressed rage that simmered just below his surface. Even when he was laughing he had the look of eagles about him, and it was understood that if you upset him he would march right through you and not stop until you were no more than a smear. The trouble with him was that he would be incredibly loyal to anyone whom he classed as a friend and his gameness and ability to go all the way inevitably led to him being manipulated by certain people for their own ends. Even the killing he was serving life for had not been his argument. He had stepped in to help somebody out and ended up doing a life sentence. And after knocking around in the dispersal system for almost a decade Tony, now older and that little bit wiser, finally came to the conclusion that he needed help. No longer satisfied with the man he had become, he applied for Grendon.

In his first twelve months at Grendon Tony was like a volcano, blowing his top at the slightest provocation. He was going through the emotional breakdown that most alpha-violent ODCs experience at Grendon – part of him embarrassed at being in a prison like that, mixing with that class of prisoner, having to deal with authority without the clearly defined rules of engagement that exist in other prisons. He constantly doubted himself and sought confirmation that he really was doing the right thing. Tony was on D-wing but would meet up with me, Pickles and a couple of other C-wing lads on the exercise yard every day, and the conversation was mostly about whether therapy in general and Grendon in particular were the right direction for any of us. I'm glad to say that I always encouraged Tony, and others, to march on and stick at it. Tony truly had a desire to change, and as I got to know him better I was pleasantly surprised to find that beneath the surface madness he was essentially a kind and caring man. His face always lit up whenever he spoke about his family, and particularly his god-daughter Danielle. When it came right down to it, Tony wanted what we all wanted – to be able to shed our violent personas, leave our offending behaviour in the past and start to live a normal life away from the lunacy. Like the rest of us, he had come to Grendon to try to make a start towards this.

Eventually Tony moved on to C-wing and before I left I introduced him to Brian and Scouse Mark, with whom he got on very well. Many men at Grendon didn't like Tony, but that was just a fear of his reputation and the way he presented himself. Once people got to know him and realized that he wasn't going to physically attack anyone, everybody seemed to calm down around him. Like all my friends Tony also had a good sense of humour and didn't mind taking the piss out of himself, in the right company. I could always get him to crack a smile, even when he was in the height of his madness and confusion. He had the habit of doing the accents of every character in whatever story he would be telling you; the only trouble was that he couldn't do an accent to save his life – everything came out sounding like a peptic Welshman with a mouth full of gobstoppers. I would wait until he was in full flow and then interrupt and question him on the supposed country of origin of his accents. 'So he was a Nigerian then, this fella?' I'd ask. Tony's face would screw up in frustration. 'No, I've said, he was Greek.' I'd look puzzled. 'But surely that was a Nigerian accent you were just doing?' At first Tony didn't see that I was getting him at it and he would become angry, putting more emphasis on the accent and speaking slowly. But in the end all I had to do was look at him and raise an eyebrow when he was attempting an accent and he would crack up. By the time I left Grendon Tony was well settled into C-wing and really making strides in his therapy.

Jonathan Aitken very generously described me in his prison memoirs as 'a man who would go to the wall with you', which is an American expression meaning a loyal friend who will always watch your back. And that is how I would describe all the men above. Looking at their criminal and prison records would give you only a fraction of their stories. On paper, and to their many victims and their families, these men are a bunch of murderous cut-throats who have committed horrifyingly sickening crimes. But there is a spark of decency and humanity in all of them. This is borne out by the fact that they have thought about their crimes, felt regret and remorse for them, and decided to try to do something about not repeating their behaviour and creating more victims. Volunteering to enter a regime like Grendon's and admit your weakness and failings in front of your peers and the authorities is not something anyone does lightly. There are thousands of violent criminals in our jails who will never address the reasons why they do what they do, who are not in the slightest bit interested in rehabilitation or changing their lives, and who, if the statistics are correct, will leave prison and create more victims. These people I now have no time for, but I truly believe that men like Chris, Brian, Mark, Tony and the rest deserve another chance, despite their terrible past deeds.

31. Kicking Off!

Though violence was absolutely forbidden at Grendon, and the penalty for breaking that rule was a commitment vote and, usually, a ship-out back to the nick you had come from, you cannot place a crowd of violent recidivists together in one small space and expect them all to become pacifists instantly. Every once in a while, someone would get pushed just that little bit too far and he would erupt. Thankfully it didn't happen very often, and most of the time there would be plenty of cooler heads around to defuse the situation before it got too far out of hand. But not always.

Warren was an ex-crackhead and aggravated burglar from Derby. Though he could be a nice sensible fella in smallish doses, he was also a bundle of insecurities and neuroses. His ego, like that of most criminals, was huge and this led him into some very serious egocentric thinking. He would hijack every group and community meeting and, no matter what was being discussed at the time, he would turn everyone to his favourite subject – the Life and Issues of Warren. For this reason he was detested by a lot of the community. Whenever he put up his hand to take a minute during a community meeting there would be a surfeit of eye-rolling, head-shaking and sighing from other members as they knew we were about to get another episode of the Warren Show – and it was bound to be a repeat.

Warren seemed to be oblivious to the fact that he pissed many people off with his continual neediness and self-promotion – either that or he just didn't care. He had been involved in a drug scandal when he first came on to C-wing, trying to buy opiate painkillers from one of the hobbits who had a bad back, but he had survived the commitment vote after admitting everything and throwing himself on the mercy of the community. Warren was another one of those people who obviously desperately needed therapy, and the community were always merciful in those cases. So Warren stayed in therapy, but it never lessened his egocentricity. Sometimes it seemed as though he just said or did whatever came into his head without a moment's thought for the consequences. As long as it further enhanced Warren's cause, then that was fine by him, and fuck anyone who might be hurt or offended. This didn't go down too well with other members of the community, particularly the more volatile ones.

One such was Sick. Sick was a young black gang member from Birmingham, doing eight years for his involvement in the drive-by shooting of a rival gangster. Sick was also a fairly intelligent and decent fella, but, like Warren, best in small doses. He was in group 3 with me and I quite liked him. He was bright, sensible and full of good ideas, when you got him on his own. But stick a few of his young pals around him and he instantly reverted to the 'bad bwoy gangsta'. The trouble with Sick was that, though he had a good heart and a real understanding of how he could fuck up his own life and other people's by his actions, he just couldn't help himself whenever there was an audience. I think that while he was desperate for therapy to work and stop his sociopathic behaviour, he just wasn't strong enough to allow this to happen. So he was classed as a bit of a 'switch-hitter' by most of the community – someone who could be today's therapeuton and tomorrow's RTU (returned to unit). How Sick dealt with problems or issues depended entirely on his mood and who was watching.

Me and Sick had a mutual friend in Musa. Musa was another one of those lost young men who had received HMP (Her Majesty's Pleasure – a life sentence given to juveniles) while still under the age of eighteen. He'd beaten his best friend to death with a hammer during an argument over a girl and was nine years into his life sentence when I met him at Grendon. He was tall, maybe 6 foot 3, thin as a whip and, like most young men who have spent their formative years in prison, could be as moody as any teenager. Though only in his twenties he was a very talented musician, having taught himself guitar in prison, and was pretty adventurous in his musical tastes. He was willing to give most things a listen – from trad jazz to hard-core rockabilly. We would often swap CDs and Musa would play me whatever piece of music he happened to be writing. He was a Muslim convert, one of Silver's group, but mostly hung around with Sick and another young black fella called Loony. Individually each of these kids was okay, but when they were together they could be pretty loud and sometimes even a bit intimidating to the more delicate members of the community.

One afternoon I was standing on the ground floor just outside my cell talking to Musa about Gil Scott Heron when Warren happened to walk by. Musa's face twisted into a sneer. 'I can't stand that geezer,' he said with feeling. I laughed. 'Yeah, he can be a bit of a melt sometimes,' I said, 'but he's not the worst.' Musa shook his head. 'I wouldn't be too sure about that.' I guessed there must be some bad blood between the two, but that was not uncommon in Grendon. There were many men in the community who absolutely detested the sight of each other, but who were 'holding it down' because of where they were and their desire for change. It was only later that I heard the full story and how personal it had become to those involved.

Musa was the catalogue rep – his job was to keep the official mail order catalogues prisoners were allowed to order their personal property from – and though he was almost always available if you wanted to get a catalogue, it was well known that he would have a lie-in on Sunday mornings and not get out of bed until eleven. It seems that Warren, looking for a clothes catalogue at 8 a.m. on a Sunday morning, decided that Musa needed to be woken up. Not content with knocking loudly on Musa's cell door, Warren decided to push his way into the darkened cell and grab the catalogue himself. Musa, already pissed off with all the banging on his door, jumped out of bed just in time to grab hold of Warren by the scruff of his neck and eject him from the cell. Obviously Warren's ego would not allow him to admit he had done anything wrong – or even out of the ordinary – nor would it allow him to simply walk away. A loud slanging match between Warren and Musa ensued, during which some very hurtful and offensive things were said by both parties.

As far as Musa was concerned Warren was now an enemy – and if he was Musa's enemy, then it just naturally followed that he was also the enemy of Sick and Loony. So for the next few weeks after the catalogue incident Musa, Sick and Loony could often be seen plotting together and looking daggers at Warren. Warren knew what was going on – he was a jail veteran and you cannot spend more than a few hours in prison without learning to recognize that what you are feeling is not always unfounded paranoia – but either he didn't particularly care that three more people seemed to hate him, or he was relying on the no violence rule at Grendon to hold back the hotheads. Musa spoke openly about his hatred for Warren in his small group, but the full venom of this revelation wasn't fed back properly to the community. And besides, hardly a week went by when an inmate didn't have a problem with someone else without it leading to actual violence, the logic being that to talk about it openly in the group nearly always led to a defusing of the situation. But this was different. Musa, not really a violent man despite his index offence, seemed to find strength and logic in the arguments of Sick and Loony and this further fed his rage at Warren. It's easy, with hindsight, to see how it could have escalated – all it would have taken was for either Sick or Loony to tell Musa that Warren had 'dissed' him in public and that everyone was laughing about it and that would have been enough to keep the hate going and for the plotting to progress to the next inevitable stage. After all, Grendon was full of very damaged men.

However it came about, the attack on Warren by Sick and Loony was the worst act of physical violence I was to witness during my time at Grendon. Matters came to a head one Saturday afternoon when Warren returned from a visit. The moment he walked on to the wing Musa was waiting for him and wanted to have it out. He invited Warren into group 5's room, which was on the ground floor, with the intention, he later told the community, of ironing out their differences. I've got to say I really did like Musa, but I believe he knew, or at least suspected, that things were going to escalate. For a start, Warren's reaction to any criticism was well known. There was also the fact that both Sick and Loony had now pulled out of therapy and were starting to get a bit loud around the wing while awaiting transfer back to the prisons they had come from, and never missed a chance to wind Musa up over being dissed by Warren. Sick and Loony didn't like Warren and they were both young and had been very violent in the past. Now, considering themselves no longer governed by the therapeutic rules of Grendon – including the golden rule of no violence – they were the loosest of cannons. Musa had spent the afternoon playing pool with his two confederates, who had suggested that he 'pull' Warren and put him in his place once and for all.

Without the influence and interference from Sick and Loony, the usually quite placid Musa would never have taken his issues with Warren any further than the therapeutic forum. But then, if my auntie had a pair of balls she'd be my uncle. Two minutes after Warren stepped into group 5's room at Musa's request, Sick and Loony walked in too and decided to add their voices and strongly held opinions to the argument. Warren, realizing that this was not a good situation to be in, did his usual: he told them all to go fuck themselves and walked out of the room. At this time of day, between the tea meal and the evening lock-up, there were not

many people on the ground floor as most men were up on the landings
getting water and showering before bang-up. I was sitting in the dining
hall with a good view of the hallway and saw Warren shouting something
over his shoulder as he walked towards the stairs. Then I saw Sick and
Loony come into view, moving purposefully and quickly towards him
with looks of anger on their faces. You didn't have to be more than a
casual observer to sense that things were about to kick off, big time.

I've been no stranger to violence in my life, particularly the short and
brutish prison type, but by this time I had been at Grendon for over three
years and the peaceful atmosphere that usually prevailed there had dulled
my reaction time. I saw Sick throw a powerful right-hander that connected
squarely with Warren's temple. It was a knockout punch, but before Warren
even hit the ground both Sick and Loony were all over him throwing
punches to his head and body. Warren collapsed and was set upon by the
two lads, only this time they kicked instead of punching. I sat there trying
to take in what I was seeing, shocked by the fact this was happening in
Grendon. The whole thing was over in less than a minute. The noise of
the attack quickly attracted other members of the community and Kung
Fu Chris and Brian – two of the biggest geezers on the wing – wasted no
time in copping hold of Sick and Loony and manhandling them away from
the unconscious Warren. A large crowd gathered. While Chris held the
two attackers at bay with a few choice words and a raised fist, Brian got
Warren into the recovery position. By now the screws had sussed there
was something wrong and someone pressed the alarm bell. As screws
came running on to the wing Loony took advantage of this momentary
distraction to break away from Chris and try to stamp on Warren's head,
but Brian managed to push him away before the screws intervened. Sick
and Loony were swiftly hustled up to their cells and locked in. I guessed
I wouldn't be seeing them again, and I was right. Warren was still sparko
with blood trickling from his nose and mouth so a medic was sent for. The
screws started to lock everybody up and I was one of the last to bang-up
as my cell was on the ground floor. The last thing I saw before my cell
door was closed was Warren being stretchered off the wing.

During the bang-up that night I thought about what had happened.
The sight of violence happening right in front of me had reawakened a
lot of old feelings. In the past I had given out, and been on the receiving
end of, many such beatings and had taken such incidents as just part of
life's rich tapestry, the coinage of the world I had chosen. I had never let

it bother me, locking out my feelings and emotions quickly and carrying on as if nothing had happened. But you cannot put off the effects of a violent life for ever and it doesn't matter how sorted you think you are, the feelings will creep up on you, usually when you least expect it, and have their day whether you like it or not. Sometimes they show themselves in ways that are not altogether obvious at the time. For example, I noticed that after particularly violent incidents in my own life I would become very careless with my safety – as if subconsciously I wanted to be punished for my actions. I would ride motorbikes through the night rain at 100 mph without a crash helmet, sometimes gunning the engine, closing my eyes and going through traffic lights on red. I would do terribly dangerous and reckless things, almost daring something bad to happen. Perhaps this was latent guilt? Depression and paranoia are also by-products of that kind of violent lifestyle. Some bury these feelings by using drink and drugs, which can only make things worse. I buried mine with more and more violent and outrageous acts – ploughing forward relentlessly with never a moment's rest to avoid having to fill a peaceful void with thoughts of guilt. My stay at Grendon had brought me to a shuddering halt and that meant time to think and feel. Having been on both sides of the fence at one time or another, I was well aware of how all those involved in the violence would now be feeling – like shit.

The next morning the whole prison was on lock-down for a couple of hours to give the screws time to ship out Sick and Loony. There were a lot of protestations and loud voices from the two departing bruisers, but no resistance. By lunchtime they were both locked in the punishment block at HMP Bullingdon awaiting investigation. When we were finally let out of our cells we were told by the staff that Warren was okay but being kept in the hospital with suspected concussion. Eventually he was cleared by the medics and returned to C-wing, bearing the bruises and marks of his beating. I have no wish to be unkind to the fella, but from that day on Warren absolutely milked everything he could from his attack. This was a man who had been no stranger to violence himself – his criminal career had been spent invading people's homes with intent – so when he started hijacking community meetings again to discuss the 'great wrong' that had been done to him and how much he was suffering, I had to suppress a snort of derision. What happened to Warren was wrong, but he wore his victimhood like a fucking badge. By the time I left Grendon nearly two years later Warren was still using minutes in community meetings to talk about the incident. I was to meet up with Warren some time later though, when we were both D cats and awaiting release, and was pleased to see that therapy had brought about a great change in him. He was an altogether more well-rounded individual. Hopefully Warren may yet prove to be another Grendon success story. Musa was put up for commitment for his part in the incident, but the community believed him when he told us that he had not intended a physical outcome for his initial confrontation with Warren. He survived the vote but was advised to take it as a warning of where ill-thought-out loyalties can lead. Once Sick and Loony were gone Musa seemed to go from strength to strength in his therapy and was eventually downgraded to category C.

The attack on Warren was the only real violence I was to see during my time at Grendon.

32. Last Knockings

By Christmas 2008 I had served almost ten years in prison, nearly half of that in Grendon. My tariff had been reduced to eight years by the Court of Appeal, but my first two applications for parole had been refused. I wasn't naive enough to think that I ever had a chance of serving the minimum and then being released, even though I had been out of trouble for a long time and was working hard to change my life for the better. The albatross around my neck was a big one – my past behaviour and previous convictions – and the criminal justice system has the memory capacity of a large herd of pachyderm, so I chalked my first two parole applications up to experience. I wasn't a whole-life tariff, thank God, so the system would have to consider me seriously for release at some stage, but I always knew it would be later rather than sooner. I had completed all targets set for me by the Home Office and prison system in order to progress through my sentence, I had voluntarily done almost five years in therapy, including eighteen months of psychodrama, and I had changed my thinking to such an extent that I no longer even thought of myself as a criminal. My plans for the future did not include crime or more imprisonment, and as far as I was concerned I was truly rehabilitated. Now all I had to do was get out of prison – much easier said than done.

Though I had quite evidently served longer than the minimum term that the courts had agreed should be my punishment, most of those who wrote reports on me for the Parole Board refused to recommend release. The only person who expressed the opinion that I was now of so little danger to the public that I should be released was the seconded probation officer – Emma – God bless her. The other report-writers – psychologist, psychotherapist, outside probation and all prison staff involved – recommended that I spend a period in an open or semi-open prison before release could be considered. I had been expecting this because my record for leaving prison and committing further serious offences was not designed to inspire confidence – so while I would be making a direct plea to the board for immediate release, as was my legal right, I was also prepared to go and do a few more years in yet another prison. It was a pain in the arse to know that even after a decade of porridge I still had a bit more to eat, but as pragmatic Hollywood Mafia bosses are sometimes heard to remark – this is the life we chose.

I hated the whole process of parole hearings, particularly at Grendon, because of the amount of in-depth reports required, which meant hours and sometimes whole days being interviewed by various staff. But the alternative was to opt out and have absolutely no chance of any sort of result from the board. So I persevered. The only trouble was that I seemed to have made some powerful enemies deep within the system and I wasn't exactly sure who they were. I know this sounds like paranoia, so I'll just lay out the facts and let them speak for themselves. In July 2007 I was up for parole with most report-writers recommending me for open conditions, but, two days before the hearing, I was handed a fax from the Home Office stating that the Secretary of State was strongly opposed to granting me either release or a move to an open prison. The reasons for this were contained in the attached form and consisted of a brief summary of my previous convictions and details of my index offences, and ended with the standard 'danger to the public' tag and a stern recommendation that I should remain in closed conditions. On this evidence the Home Office were never going to agree to my release or recategorization as long as I had a hole in my arse. My previous record and index offences were things that I could never change even if I stayed in prison for the rest of my life. This was a worrying development.

I have to say that a lifer getting a knockback from the Home Secretary was not really that unusual, but for the objections to leave not one glimmer of hope for the next hearing was pretty rare. But things were to get even more hooky at my next Parole Board twelve months later. On the morning I was due to appear before the board I was handed the Home Secretary's written comments on my case and once again it was a strong objection against any sort of progressive move on my part. I couldn't understand the reason as I had done everything asked of me by the prison system for almost my entire sentence, and volunteering for Grendon was above and beyond what they had asked for. I hadn't been nicked since I had been given a caution by the governor of HMP Highdown, for refusing an order, in 2002. I had passed eighty-three drug tests at Grendon. I had gained qualifications in my chosen profession of writing – a diploma from ICS on Freelance Feature Writing, and levels 1 and 2, with distinction, from the National Union of Journalists course. I had taken positions of responsibility in the community, including vice-chair, chair, charity rep, canteen rep, and running the 'pod', as the small wing kitchens were called. This time I had not wasted my years in prison fighting the system; instead I had sought out a way to genuinely change my life and behaviour. And all of this information was also contained in the paperwork clipped to the Home Secretary's objection. I had to ask myself seriously exactly what this Home Secretary – Jacqui Smith – wanted from me in order to allow me to progress through my life sentence. But no answers were forthcoming. Then things really did take a strange turn.

On the morning I walked into the Parole Board hearing with my legal team we were greeted by a somewhat confused board. The board, consisting of five 'professionals' chaired by a judge, immediately told my legal team that they were bound by law to inform us that they had received two contradictory opinions from the office of the Home Secretary. The first stated that due to my consistently good behaviour and positive reports during my years in therapy, the Home Secretary would have no objections to me being granted category D and being transferred to an open prison at the earliest opportunity; the second missive from the office of the fragrant Jacqui said exactly the opposite and objected to any recategorization, stating that I should remain in closed conditions for the foreseeable future. Both opinions came from the same office and were dated within three days of each other. Something fishy was definitely on the hook. The judge expressed the confusion and embarrassment of the board and said that, having reviewed the reports on my progress compiled by those at the sharp end, the board were minded to accept in principle the more positive of the Home Secretary's opinions. This was a massive relief to me because if the board had decided to go with the more negative one, then they might as well have cancelled the hearing and told me to come back in another year. As it was, I felt I had a good chance of getting some sort of result at this hearing.

As it turned out, after interviewing me and several professional witnesses, including an independent psychologist hired by my legal team, the board did decide to grant me a move to open conditions. But things could have been a lot different. At the very least, the two conflicting opinions could have led the board to postpone the hearing for months; at worst, it could have added another two or three years to my sentence. QCs are not usually given to showing puzzlement in front of their clients but when we emerged from the boardroom Jim Sturman shook his head. 'All I can say about this,' he commented on the two opinions, 'is that you must have made some very powerful enemies, at quite a high level.'

Thinking about it afterwards, I supposed that it might have been a simple administrative error, but it was hard to understand how someone – possibly the same person – could write two opposite opinions within a period of three days and send them both off to the Parole Board. I recalled the previous harsh objection and all the trouble I'd had since the publication of *A Few Kind Words and a Loaded Gun* – a book, I might add, which exposed the brutal and Machiavellian regimes in some of our prisons – and the fact that Baroness Scotland had had to issue a written reply defending the government's policy on prison education in a national newspaper after I had written a feature on the shortcomings of that policy in the *Guardian*. Add to that the fact that on previous prison sentences I had not been shy about causing as much agg for the system as I could manage, and I think it would be safe to say that I may indeed have made a few enemies in high places along the way over the years.

Still, despite all the shenanigans by the suits, I was now a category D prisoner – the lowest security category in the British prison system – which meant that after a period of risk assessment in an open prison I would be allowed to go out and visit my family without an escort, seek paid employment, and, eventually, be granted home leave of up to five days per month. It's hard to describe how it feels to reach this stage. You have to remember that on previous prison sentences my non-cooperation with the authorities meant that I had only once progressed beyond category B status. This was uncharted territory for me. When the written confirmation of the board's decision came through, six weeks after the hearing, the excitement of it all started to build in me. I figured that once I had proved myself in open conditions I could actually be granted release in the next couple of years. If I ended up serving twelve years of my sentence – bearing in mind my minimum tariff was only eight years – I would consider that as the final payment on my debt to society. My intention was to get out and never come back to prison. For me, now in my late forties and never having worked legally for any amount of time, the concept of being a straight-goer was new and exciting. And now that goal was really in sight.

In the meantime, life at Grendon went on. I gave my notice to Martin, the psychodrama facilitator, and tied up all my loose therapeutic ends in the final session. Tom and Lynn asked me if I'd thought about what I'd like to say to the community about my therapeutic journey during my final wing meeting. I hadn't really given it much thought but I would definitely urge those left behind to continue with their work and take hope and encouragement from my own example. There is no better spur to those who genuinely wish to change than to see one of their number progress after putting in the work.

Enemies in high places notwithstanding, I seriously believed I was well on my way to freedom. Even if I was just swapping my cell in one prison for a cell in another, the 'out' was finally within my grasp. But, for me, things never seem to be that straightforward.

33. Last Group

My time at Grendon was all but over. On 20 March 2008 I attended my final group therapy session. As I took my place on the blue chair and looked around I realized just how much group 3 had changed since my first session. In fact, the only things that had remained constant in the intervening four and a half years were the name – group 3 – the blue chairs and myself as a member. Brian, the facilitator, had been replaced by Glenda. Our group room was now a back dorm on the 2s landing instead of the large office on the ground floor. And every other member of my original group had been replaced, many times, over the years. I was now the most senior member of group 3. I had made the long hard journey from being a violent, impulsive hothead to some kind of therapeutic elder statesman to whom other members looked for advice and guidance. And I was mostly comfortable with that. My experience in therapy had added a new dimension to my outlook and for the first time in my life I was able to see everything clearly and articulate my thoughts without resorting to violence, anger or petulance.

The clarity with which I could now view myself meant I could also see seams of what I had once been running just below the surface of others. I recognized certain traits and behaviours being displayed by other members of my group, the wider community, and even the staff. And most of the time I could understand some of the reasons behind them. And while this could certainly be exhilarating, it was also a tiny bit frightening. It was as though a bright spotlight had been switched on inside my head, and my fear was that I might never be able to switch it off again. I wasn't sure I liked the idea of going through life automatically analysing everyone I met. I imagined that in the outside world people who are in one-to-one therapy usually see their therapist for one hour per week, an average of fifty hours per year. In Grendon I was doing over fifty hours of therapy in a month. After so much time in therapy it was almost like I had become, by osmosis, a therapist instead of a patient. I resolved to speak to Tom or Lynn about this before I left to check that this was a genuine phenomenon and not just my ego talking. And whether there was any way of toning it down a bit.

I looked around at my group. Seven troubled and complicated characters who had left countless victims behind them and were now serving a prison sentence of 100-odd years between them. Five of them were lifers, including three murderers, and the other two were serving double-figure sentences. I knew these men, in some cases, better than their own families had known them. I had spent many hours listening to their life stories, their intimate confessions and their deepest darkest secrets. There had been times when I had felt hatred, disgust, anger and pity towards some of them, and often exasperation, but there had also been times when I had been almost overwhelmed by pride at their breakthroughs and sudden understanding of their lives. Not only did we do our therapy groups together, but we also lived together 24/7. As a group we had become closer than friends or blood relatives, we were a therapeutic family. And like all families, we sometimes clashed.

The second longest-serving member of group 3, after me, was a burglar and con-man from Brighton named Roy. Roy was ten years older than me and had been a confirmed criminal since the 1950s. He had been in group 3 for over two years and he and I had had many therapeutic clashes. He was basically a decent man but his criminal and predatory instincts and values were deeply entrenched. He had come to Grendon from Parkhurst and was serving ten years for an aggravated burglary in which an elderly woman had been assaulted. Roy had all the shortcomings of most career criminals: he was obsessed with money and image, and was extremely egocentric. He was ruthless in his life of crime and, in turn, became just as ruthless in his therapy. I always had the suspicion that he had recce'd and planned his therapy in much the same way he'd recce'd and planned his many crimes, and was trying to present the image of himself that he thought was required in order to progress through the system. And I wasn't the only one. He was strongly challenged by the group, Tom, the therapist, and his psychodrama group on many occasions, but stuck doggedly to his line. He had been a heroin addict and prolific house burglar, and had the innate craftiness that goes with both. To be fair to Roy, I think that therapy began to work on him after a while and that he did genuinely achieve a desire to change, but he struck me as the kind of man who would quickly revert to type if things started to go pear-shaped for him. His resolve to create no more victims was questionable in my eyes and I wasted no opportunity to challenge him strongly. Sometimes with explosive results.

Roy was slightly deaf and had a tendency to speak very loudly even when calm, but when his buttons were pressed he would get very angry very quickly and end up shouting at the top of his voice. I found that the best way to calm him down was to keep my own voice reasonable in tone and level in volume. Another common criminal trait that Roy possessed in abundance was the ability to exaggerate and be over-dramatic, almost to the point of embarrassment. He would get so deep into telling a story from his past, physically acting out each character, that he would inadvertently let slip a dark and humorous nugget of information from the land of Roy deep within his mind. In the group we began to call these nuggets 'Royisms' and would examine them with comic fascination. This would often lead to Roy getting angry and reaching top decibel in his justification of what he had let slip. An example I remember was his absolute belief that he could smell money from a distance. He told us that when he was out burgling he would push open letterboxes and put his nose into the gap and that if there was cash somewhere in the house he would be able to smell it! Another Royism was that he had trained himself to flip coins and always have them come down heads up. Which begged the question of why he wasn't earning fortunes as a circus performer or betting on such a certainty? These and many other Royisms were the source of much amusement to the group, but of consternation and anger to Roy who seemed to actually believe what he was saying. He was the sort of man who could convince himself of the truth of anything he set his mind to, and if he really convinced himself he was rehabilitated, then the job would be all but done. Despite, or maybe because of, his shortcomings I quite liked him. He was the cranky old uncle of group 3.

The next longest-serving member on group 3 was Greg, a little Scotsman who was serving life for maliciously wounding an old woman whose only crime was being in the wrong place at the wrong time. Greg was another one of those men who wore a cloak of victimhood in order to hide the festering spite, hate and extreme violence that coursed through him. He had spent ten years as a category A prisoner, on various protection wings within the dispersal estate, before coming to Grendon, which was somewhat ironic. He was considered so violent and dangerous by the prison system that he spent a decade on the book, yet had to be housed on the numbers to protect him from his fellow prisoners. For Greg's violent streak to show itself he had to be drunk or under the influence of drugs, and he had to be presented with a completely helpless victim over whom he could have absolute power. In any other circumstances he was a mouse who appeared afraid of his own shadow. He was a very unattractive character in many ways. He was sly, selfish and quick to present himself as the victim, though brimming with rage and suppressed violence. But the truth was Greg *had* been a victim. We learned that he had been sexually abused from a young age. When he reached puberty he drifted into petty crime in order to get money for drink, in which he tried to find some kind of solace. After several arrests for theft, drunkenness and criminal damage Greg embarked on a campaign of harassment against his abuser.

Greg had never told anyone about the abuse he had suffered, so when he started to single out his abuser, attacking his home by various means, such as pelting it with eggs, smearing excrement on the doors and windows, emptying rubbish bins into the front garden, and spraying obscene graffiti, the locals and police saw only an out-of-control teenage thug and looked no further. This added to Greg's confusion and anguish. Subconsciously he wanted people to investigate his behaviour, to ask why this was happening. But nobody did. His next step was to look for victims over whom he could exert control and vent his rage. In the next few years he was arrested and imprisoned for attacking several people, often women. One night, on his way home very drunk, he spotted his abuser in the street. Greg attacked the man from behind, sexually assaulted him and then urinated on him. Greg was arrested for this and to add to his mental turmoil the local papers reported him as a homosexual sex attacker. In the small village where he lived everyone began to shun him. Having reached what he considered the nadir of his life, Greg finally worked up the courage to go to the police and tell them everything about how he had been sexually abused by his 'victim'. It was then that he found out that the man was known to the police and had previous convictions for sexually assaulting children. The local papers ran the story on the front page but did not mention that Greg was the victim. His abuser was eventually sentenced to eighteen months in prison after pleading guilty.

When Greg's abuser finished his prison sentence, he was resettled in a nearby town. Greg found out where he was living and one night decided that the only way to put an end to his mental torture was to confront the man. Armed with a 10-inch carving knife he waited outside the man's house for him to show himself, all the while going over in his head how rotten his life had become. But Greg was a cowardly man and when it came to it the thought of confronting his abuser face to face scared the bejesus out of him. What if the man were to overpower him and then rape him like he had in the past? No, Greg couldn't take the chance. But someone would have to suffer, someone would have to bear the burden of his pent-up rage and hate. Then, on the dark quiet street, he spotted a perfect target. Greg's victim that night was an 87-year-old widow who was out walking her dog before bedtime. He didn't hesitate and flew into her with all his hatred, slashing and stabbing. His victim was left with terrible facial injuries and lost an eye in the attack. She came very close to death, and Greg was arrested soon after. In group 3 Greg was often challenged by group members on all aspects of his personality, and he expressed what I believe was genuine remorse for what he had done. But whether he would not do exactly the same again were he to be released is anyone's guess. He was a victim who could only function by creating other victims. In the family dynamic of the group he was the slightly off-key distant cousin who would make an appearance only on special occasions and then had to be watched closely in case he slipped poisonous toadstools into the mushroom soup.

The next most senior member of group 3 was also the youngest. Westie was a south Londoner serving HMP for taking part with four other teenagers in a much publicized murder back in 1999. Westie had gone on to attempt another mugging that same night, and three days later he was arrested, along with the rest of the gang, and charged with murder, attempted murder and robbery. He was sixteen years old. On conviction for murder at the Old Bailey Westie was sentenced to be detained for life at Her Majesty's Pleasure, and given a minimum tariff of seventeen years. As soon as he reached the age of twenty-one Westie was shipped into the adult prison system at HMP Gartree. A likeable kid, but with an air of gloomy seriousness that belied his years, Westie was uneasy in therapy to begin with. Like me, he had spent his formative years in the juvenile prison system and certain skewed criminal values had been drummed into him. Showing any emotion to anyone, not immediately attacking people who stepped over your imaginary line, and even anything more than a casual association with the authorities were forbidden in that world. And breaching those rules would mark you out as prey. So the first work Westie had to do at Grendon was to overcome those years of indoctrination and learn to open his mind. As did we all.

Once he had managed to settle into group 3 and realized that his tough front was not needed at Grendon, Westie began to let his real character show through. In the eyes of the law, and no doubt to the families of his victims, Westie was no more than a vicious murderer convicted of a senseless killing, but as I got to know him I couldn't help but empathize with him. He was no more than a kid who had been caught up in a terrible series of events whose consequences would ripple through many lives and continue to echo down many years. At the time of the murder Westie had been attending college, studying retail and waiting for a place on an art and design course, the only one of the five who committed the murder who was actually trying to make something of his life. On the evening of the murder he had gone to the West End to buy his sister a birthday present, but met up with 'Jim', whose daughter had just died of cot death. Jim wasn't really a close friend, more an acquaintance, but Westie, seeing what an emotional state the man was in, decided to try to cheer him up. He spent the birthday-present money on alcohol and cannabis, and the two spent the evening getting drunk and stoned.

When the money ran out they decided, on the spur of the moment, to mug someone. They spotted two young men on Hungerford Bridge, and as they approached them they were joined by three other teenagers, including a girl, whom Jim knew. Nothing had been planned, and until that moment Westie had never laid eyes on the three newcomers. You have to wonder what malignant twist of fate, what truly outrageous misfortune, brought all of these teenagers together on that bridge at that exact moment? But from then on the tragedy was played out in less than five minutes. The two victims were quickly beaten and robbed by the five attackers, and then, as Westie was later to explain to group 3, someone shouted, 'Throw them over!' Westie said he never knew who actually uttered those words, but he was sure it hadn't been him. The words and the actions that followed them had haunted his dreams ever since. He told us that in his recurring nightmare he remembered in every single detail the terrified face of the youth that he had helped to throw from the bridge into the river below, heard his frightened pleading and his scream as he fell into the darkness. This man died; the other one barely survived.

As I've explained, criminals and prisoners are mostly cynical, hard-bitten bastards who can spot a spoofer or con-man a mile off. That's why group therapy at Grendon works so well, because it doesn't matter how many friends, family, jury members and prison psychologists you may have fooled with your lies and justifications, you cannot fool me. Because in many ways I am you. Every member of the group has had some of your experience and collectively we know who you are, and know how to challenge you when what you say does not sit right. And the group knew that Westie's remorse and guilt for what he had done were deep and genuine. I got to know Westie pretty well, both in and outside the group, and what struck me most about him was his total lack of real-life experience. He had come to prison as a sixteen-year-old kid, and had many years left to serve before the law and society considered his debt paid. He would be in his mid-thirties when released, if he was lucky. He had never voted, driven a car, been to a party, or done any one of a thousand other things that most people in their early twenties take for granted. One day he asked me, in all seriousness, what it was like to live with a woman. Of course it is right that those who commit the ultimate crime must pay for their actions, but sometimes I genuinely despair at how they are made to pay. In the group family Westie was the mischievous but essentially good-natured little brother.

Next was Seb, a tightly wound ball of paranoia and persecution complex from Grimsby. Seb was serving ten years for stabbing his ex-girlfriend in a frenzied attack that broke the knife he was using. For a long time I sincerely thought that Grendon could do nothing for him. In my opinion he was so seriously mentally ill that it was only a matter of time before he had a complete breakdown and had to be sectioned under the Mental Health Act. And I told him so on a couple of occasions. Like most of us, he came from a violent and dysfunctional background and his problems were deep-rooted. While he was at Grendon, his father, whom he described as an Arthur Daley figure, was jailed for four years for his part in a massive swindle involving fake cigarettes. Dad, it appears, was the typical lovable rogue, involved in many dodgy deals, sometimes on an international scale. The kind of man who would gamble the family's fortunes on some outrageous speculation, lose everything and then stand everyone in the pub a round of drinks before going home drunk to take out his misery and frustration on his family. Seb's father taught him that work was for mugs, the law was there to be broken, and women were to be taken for granted and slapped into place if they started yakking too much. Seb worshipped him, so he set out to emulate him, but it turned out that he had neither the charm nor the dubious talents for conning people that dear old dad seemed to possess. Seb was small-time, a waster who spent his days outside drinking, taking drugs and gambling, mainly on fruit machines – all paid for by his dole money supplemented with various petty scams. To Seb looking successful was almost as important as being successful, so he kept up a front, driving around in a nice car and wearing designer clothes – though the car was a ringer and the designer labels were cheap fakes. He lived in a fantasy world where the next big earner was always just around the corner.

But it was Seb's relationships with women that were to cause him real problems and lead him to prison. He became obsessed with girlfriends, possessive and jealous to the point of insanity. He was always testing them to see just how deep their feelings for him were. He didn't trust women and believed they would mug him off and leave at the first opportunity. And his treatment of them made this a self-fulfilling prophecy. He became bitter and ever more obsessive, sinking deeper into a madness of his own making, until, eventually, he cracked and attacked his latest girlfriend. When Seb came to Grendon he was in denial about his life and what he had done, and in order to deflect attention away from this painful truth he instead turned his obsessiveness on to petty incidents that were happening on the wing and in the prison in general. He would brood for weeks over insignificant words or actions, feeding his paranoia and his persecution complex until he could take no more. And then he would explode, usually in a series of detonations, a chain reaction of mini eruptions leading to the big one. He would first have a bit of a rant in the wing meetings, next corner individual staff and harangue them about the injustice of his situation, then it would be Lynn and Tom to whom he would tender his papers, expressing his belief that Grendon was 'shit' and he wanted out. Finally he would do something that could only bring things to a head. On one occasion he came out of his cell on Night San at three in the morning and launched his television up the landing, shouting, 'Is this what you want?' He woke the whole wing and was put up for his commitment.

But with the help of group 3 Seb eventually began to make a break-through by admitting his problems and issues and speaking frankly about his life for the first time. It was a long slow process but by the time of my last group he was doing well and starting to look like a more evenly balanced character. Once he managed to break the grip of his insanity, he turned out to be an intelligent and likeable man. He also had extra-ordinary writing skills, which I did my best to encourage. One day, if he can defeat his personal demons and harness the vast energy that used to

drive his madness, I believe he could express his talent. In the group family
Seb was the older brother who was okay most of the time but had to be
locked up during the full moon.

Next in line was Mark, a pretty insubstantial man in his mid-forties
from Oldham. Mark was very thin and would often miss meal times. Even
when he appeared in the dining hall he would eat very little. We used to
joke that he was anorexic, and maybe that wasn't too far from the truth
because I became sure that his lack of interest in food was related to deep-
rooted mental problems from his childhood. Mark's father had abandoned
the family when Mark was six, leaving him and his five brothers and sisters
with a mother who could not cope. The family lived in abject poverty
with never enough to eat and the children came in for plenty of stick
from other kids in the area for being scruffy and wearing second-hand
clothes. Mark became a thief and provided what little he could for his
siblings, feeding them and trying to make sure they didn't go hungry. It's
not hard to guess that Mark's attitude to feeding himself later in life could
be related to these early experiences. He would always offer his untouched
food to others. When he was ten Mark was taken into the care of the local
authority and here he was to suffer horrific and constant abuse at the hands
of the staff in a children's home. From then on his life followed an almost
predictable pattern. He drifted around, never working but stealing and
burgling between prison sentences. Though essentially a quiet, unassum-
ing man, and never violent in the commission of his crimes, not counting
his index offence, his fear and hatred of the authorities showed itself every
time he was arrested. He would fight the police until overcome by the
sheer weight of numbers, and had many convictions for assaulting the
police on his record. But once in prison Mark settled down and did his
time quietly and with no fuss.

When he finally came to Grendon, and group 3, Mark was into the
twelfth year of a mandatory life sentence for murder. He had killed a man
who had tried to sexually assault him when he was drunk, beating him
to death with a hammer. In the group Mark was very quiet and was often
pulled up by group members in private and told that he had to make more
of an effort. After about a year of near-silence, he began to open up
therapeutically and tell us about his life. It was slow going, though, and
by the time of my last group he was still moving at his own pace. Some
people just take longer than others and Mark was one of those. He was
well liked, both in the group and on the wing, and it was plain to see how

distressing it was for him to talk about the abuse he had suffered, so he was given more leeway than some. Mark continues to work in the group and I sincerely hope that one day he can reach a decent compromise between his past and his future. In group family terms Mark was the kindly uncle who sits in the corner saying little but smiling knowingly.

Lee was a Scouser, a career criminal serving an IPP (imprisonment for public protection), New Labour's latest version of a life sentence, for robbery with violence of a security van. By the time of my last group he had been with us only for five months, so I didn't really get to know a lot about him. What I did know, was due to his genuine eagerness to embrace therapy and attempt to change a lifetime of violent offending. He had grown up in Toxteth, never known his father, and had drifted into a life of crime and drug addiction by his teens. Lee was another one who had been taken into care and then found himself the target of sexual abuse by the authorities. By his early twenties he was a successful criminal, making vast amounts of money as both a mid-level drug dealer and sometimes armed robber – but he was never happy. He became a heavy user of his own supplies of both heroin and crack cocaine, which alienated his otherwise loyal family and made him violently erratic and careless. In one incident he went, with several others, to administer a knee-capping to another criminal for some perceived misdemeanour, and in the confusion Lee was shot in the stomach with a .38 pistol. He almost died, but it was while he was in hospital recovering that he received a visit from the woman who was to have a big impact on his future desire to enter therapy and try to change his life.

After leaving hospital Lee set up home with this woman and tried to go straight. But he was weak and was soon back on drugs and into a life of crime. He was arrested and convicted of robbing a security van team who were restocking a cash-point machine in a motorway service station. Lee went cold turkey in prison and by the time he volunteered for Grendon he had been drug-free for almost a year. In therapy he pulled no punches and held nothing back as he told us about his life. He was a welcome addition to group 3 and I was sorry I didn't have more time to spend with him. In the group family Lee would be the sensible older brother who might occasionally go off the rails.

The newest member of group 3 was Andy. By the time of my last group Andy had been with us for only three months, but it was long enough for me to figure out that he would probably not last the course. Andy was one of the Grendon intake who, before the dumbing down of the entrance process, would have been RTU'd after a short time on the induction wing. That's if he had even managed to complete the application process in his previous nick, which was doubtful. He was sentenced for torturing and beating a tramp to death in Leeds, for no discernible reason other than that his mate told him it would be a laugh. From a very young age Andy had been a sniffer – one of those people who get their kicks from sniffing solvents and various other things. He had started out sniffing aerosols, then glue, turps, paint, curtain-cleaner, before settling on petrol fumes for a couple of years. Only God knows how many billions of brain cells he annihilated via his nose over the years, but one thing is certain: there was no way he would have been able to pass the IQ test that used to be essential in order to get to Grendon. It was plain from the start that Andy did not understand the concept or practice of group therapy. He was highly suggestible and thicker than a skidmark on a wino's Y-fronts. As a group family member Andy was the newly adopted stepbrother who spends a long time locked in his room making strange noises.

That was the group 3 to which I said my goodbyes. A bunch of misfits and odd-bods with several murders and countless victims behind them – these had been my surrogate family, and despite how unattractive they might sound to others, I was going to miss them. Also, I realized, I was going to miss Glenda. I had grown to like and respect her in my time at Grendon. And that was true for a couple of other members of staff. That's something I'd never have thought possible before coming to Grendon.

My last group was spent in the time-honoured Grendon tradition – with a little party. Although in these circumstances we tend to use the word 'party' in the very loosest sense of the word. Glenda brought in, at her own expense, some fresh bread, butter, cheese and a few snacks – the sort of things you don't usually get to taste inside a prison – and we all ate, drank coffee and took a little trip down felony lane. I spoke about my first ever group and some of the changes I'd made in my life since then. I encouraged each member of the group to stick at his therapy if he thought he could actually get something from it. We all shook hands and everyone began to drift out of the group room and downstairs to get ready for feedbacks. I looked at Glenda. 'I just want to say, thanks, you know, for everything . . .' I was feeling a bit awkward saying goodbye, but she completely surprised me by giving me a little hug. 'Take care,' she said, and I suddenly felt very emotional. 'I'll phone and let you all know how I'm doing,' I said.

That night, during association, I slipped upstairs and into the empty group room. I sat in my usual chair and looked around. I was committing my surroundings to memory and realized that though I had spent many traumatic hours in this room I had never really looked at it closely. It was a long room, stretching the width of C-wing, with a set of two identical barred and dirty windows at each end – one lot looking out at the bulk of B-wing just across the garden, and the other end giving up a view of the old sports field that had been shut down after the great escape of 2002. The walls were painted in a faded yellow pastel, the carpet tiles were a dirty mix of blue and grey, and, of course, there was the untidy ring of blue cushioned chairs. I'd never noticed it before but, even devoid of group members, the room was slightly depressing. I wondered how much of the horror, sadness and misery that had been spoken in this space had been absorbed into its fabric. I had learned a lot about myself in this room, but, to tell you the truth, I was glad to be leaving.

That night I began to pack my property up for transfer. I had made it through Grendon and I was on the verge of starting the next phase in my life. I wasn't free yet, there would be a good few months left for me to serve in prison before the Parole Board and the Home Secretary considered me fixed enough to be let back into society, but I was getting close and I was ready to move on. But the best laid plans . . . and all that jazz.

34. The Final Sorry Chapter

In March 2008 my D cat was finally endorsed by the then Home Secretary – Jacqui Smith – and I was ready to be on my way. I made an application for HMP Blantyre House, a very progressive category C/D in Kent, the nick that had been recommended to me by both Erwin James and Jack Murtah, two ex-prisoners who had spent time there. Erwin (real name Jim Moynihan) worked for the *Guardian* and had been on day-release from Blantyre House when he had come to Grendon, along with photographer Jimmy Smith, to interview me in 2004 when my first book was released. Jack Murtah had been out of prison himself for over a decade when he came to Grendon to film a day in my life, but he had plenty of good things to say about Blantyre House, where he had spent time in the 1980s. It was from there that he managed to break into a video and television career (as opposed to cash strongboxes, which were his usual forte) which led to presenting jobs for Channel 4 and the BBC. Jack, along with cameraman and technician Dave, spent a couple of fun-filled days interviewing and filming me at Grendon for a slot about my life on the Prisons Video Magazine. PVM are a very professional small firm, run by a fella called Antonio Ferrara and funded by charity, which makes regular films about various aspects of life in prison and then shows them in every jail.

Though endorsing my D cat, the Home Secretary had seen fit to set my next parole review fifteen months away, in June 2009. The Parole Board had stated clearly that I had 'no more core work' to do on my offending behaviour, and the reason they sent me to a D cat, rather than releasing me straight away, was to allow me to set up a 'robust release plan' and get a bit more experience of resettlement – more days out of prison and overnight stays at my mum and dad's place, where I was planning to be released to. Most of which could have been done in six to eight months. It was a slightly sour note, but I was just happy to finally be on the home stretch. It had been a long ten years and I was looking forward to settling into a normal life for a change. I knew that, barring some major catastrophe, when I went in front of the Parole Board in June 2009 they would have little option but to release me. So, in effect, my next parole review would be my release date. I swallowed the fifteen-month wait. Let them have their final spiteful dig. By June 2009 I would have served just shy of eleven years, which was the original tariff given by my trial judge. So the decision by three court of appeal judges to cut my tariff to eight years, as eleven years was 'manifestly too long in the circumstances', didn't amount to a hill of beans. Make no mistake, what the criminal justice system gives with one hand will surely be clawed back with the other.

I was now also eligible for my fourth ROTL and planned a day out in Banbury to buy a few things I might need in D cat. I applied, appeared in front of the board, and was granted my day out on 5 March. I gave the good news to various members of my family and a few friends, and, like me, they seemed relieved that this terrible phase of my life was just about over. I had a lot to thank Grendon for: it had given me the time and space to reassess myself and weigh up what I really wanted from the rest of my life. I had learned a lot and gained a much greater insight into my life and behaviour than I would have if I had just spent the previous five years in a top-security jail, smoking dope, drinking hooch, and taking trips down felony lane with the rest of the jailheads. Of that I have no doubt.

Unfortunately, though I was finished with Grendon, Grendon wasn't quite finished with me. On 3 March 2008 I was once again ambushed by a posse, in the form of a governor grade and a security PO whom I didn't recognize, though I was more than familiar with his ilk. I was sitting in my cell, with Mark and Brian, just shooting the shit and having a laugh. The fact that I would shortly be moving on had given our daily get-togethers a slightly melancholy atmosphere, which we smothered in the usual time-honoured Grendon manner, by making our banter that much more vicious and cutting. We may have been veterans of therapy, where the display of our emotions was not only accepted but expected, but we were still men and prisoners. I had said goodbye to a lot of great friends over my years at Grendon – Fred, Ray, Kevin, Daran, Pickles and Christy G, to name but a few – and it was always the same. We hid our sadness and sense of loss behind a cloak of biting machismo coated with caustic wit, and laughed long and gruff while inside some small part of us wept and died in silence. Most of us had had many friends in our lives, but few real friends – men who, knowing all our shortcomings and our dirty secrets, would still stand by us and wish to spend time with us. Outside prison I had only one real friend – and I'm not talking about family here – on whom I knew I could rely to stand in my corner when things got rough. And that's not a lot for a lifetime of socializing. At Grendon I made some real friends, men whom I would be in touch with for the rest of my life. Maybe it was the shared experience of therapy, the stripping away of all our previous baggage and the feeling of rebirth you get when you reach your inner core and begin to become a new person, that makes us feel a closer bond to those around us.

Brian had recently purchased a pair of the most hideous sandals on the face of the earth and insisted on wearing them, so he became the butt of our acid humour that evening. Both Mark and I were laying it on thick and fast when my cell door was pushed open by Ginger. This usually happy and most easygoing of screws looked serious. 'Razor,' he said. 'The governor wants to see you. He's in group 5 room.' I was a bit surprised as it was early evening and we hardly ever caught sight of a governor this late in the day. On the short walk from my cell to group 5 room I asked Ginger what it was about and his reply did little to reassure me. 'I can't say, but it's bad. Just don't lose your temper.' With that I was ushered into the room where the governor and the security PO were waiting. Ginger came in behind me and shut the door. This was starting to look ominous and a bit like an adjudication, of which I had much experience, what with the suit and three uniforms lined up in front of me. I was invited to sit down and the PO cleared his throat. He was typical of the breed, short, fat, and with a look of mock sincerity lightly plastered over his otherwise smugly suspicious features. 'Noel,' he began, 'I have to inform you that we have recently intercepted one of your outgoing letters under PSO 4411. The letter will not be allowed to leave the prison, and has, in fact, been confiscated.' I stared at him for a moment in silence. I'd had agg from the system before over my writing and I could half guess which letter it was. But I asked anyway. 'Who is the letter addressed to and why has it been stopped?' The PO glanced down at a sheet of paper he was holding, then replied, 'It's addressed to a Mr Rick Lyons, a reporter at the *Star*. And I think you know why it's been stopped.' And there it was: my crime had been to write a letter to a newspaper reporter.

I had met Rick Lyons on a visit about a month before. He was the crime reporter for the *Star on Sunday*, and had written to me after reading my third book – *Warrior Kings* – asking if he could come to see me. Rick was planning a piece on teenage gang violence and thought it would be interesting to contrast the brutal violence of today's teenage gangs with that of the gangs of my era, the late 1970s, which I had written about in my book. We had a long chat during the visit and he promised to give the book a good plug in the paper. About a week later he wrote me a letter asking me for a couple of quotes for the article and whether I had any information on what the state of play was once gang members were jailed. I did a bit of research, mainly chatting with former gang members at Grendon, and sent Rick a letter with all the information he needed. And it was this letter that led to me sitting in front of a governor and his storm troopers.

I looked at the governor. 'Can you tell me the exact reason this letter was stopped? Is it illegal or against prison rules to write to the press? Is there anything in the letter that is untrue? Why exactly is it being stopped?' The governor blinked at each of my questions and had the good grace to shift uncomfortably, though the good grace did not extend to answering any of my questions. 'You know why it's being stopped, the PO has just informed you. And as a result of this I have no option but to cancel your ROTL.' I felt the fire begin to burn in my belly and my heart started to speed up. 'What the hell has this letter got to do with my ROTL?' I asked, getting a bit agitated at the leap from one thing to the other. 'How are the two things connected?' The governor refused to look directly at me. 'All I can say is that you have been warned in the past about contacting the media and the consequences of doing so. It has also come to our attention that you have had no fewer than three books published while at Grendon, and you were also warned about the consequences of that. PSHQ have ordered an investigation into how you have managed to do this, which is very much against prison rules, without permission from the governor.' I was astonished. It was true that I'd already been under investigation at Grendon for my first book, and that I'd had bundles of agg over my journalism work, which led to me stopping work for newspapers and magazines, but I had never kept it a secret that I'd written and had published two further books. The fact that the prison system had made no fuss whatsoever, though all my books were quite widely publicized and on sale to the public in most good bookshops, and that I had not smuggled them out of prison but sent them quite openly through normal channels, had led me to believe that knowing I was breaking no laws the system were choosing to ignore my literary career. It now seemed that they had just been biding their time and awaiting the optimum moment to pounce when they could do me the most damage.

I smiled, bitterly. 'Are you trying to say that you've only just found out that I'm a writer and that I've got three books on sale?' The PO jumped in first. 'PSO 4411 specifically forbids contact with the media by prisoners, and also publication for money. You have obviously chosen to ignore this and an investigation into your conduct has now been initiated . . .' I put up a hand to stop him. This conversation was going the way of most verbal or written communication with anyone in a position of power in the prison system – I was asking specific questions but getting replies that bore no relation to the questions I was asking. 'Forget the waffle for a minute,' I said. 'Just tell me what PSO 4411 is? Because I've never heard of it.' I was intimately familiar with Standing Order 5b, the rules covering prisoners writing from prison, but this PSO, or Prison Service Order, was a new one on me. The PO glanced down at his paperwork. 'PSO 4411 is available in the prison library if you wish to read it.' I shook my head in exasperation. 'Well, you're obviously holding a copy of it in your hand, so if you let me have a look then maybe we can clear this up.' The PO clutched his paperwork that bit tighter and frowned. 'A copy is available in the prison library for prisoners to read,' he repeated. Though I shouldn't have been surprised by his childish attitude, I was, but I had to laugh. 'You people really are something else,' I said. 'Okay, then. Can you at least tell me when this PSO was issued?' He frowned again. 'I don't know,' he said. 'But it's been out for a while.' I could see I was going to get little from him so I turned to the governor again. 'All right,' I said. 'I've had enough of this gaff anyway. Keep the ROTL if you like, I'm down for a transfer to Blantyre House, so I'm formally requesting that you get me out of this nick as soon as possible please.' He shook his head. 'I'm afraid that while the investigation is ongoing your transfer has been cancelled and a report will be sent to the Parole Board informing them of the latest developments.' It was as though someone had punched me hard in the stomach. I felt breathless and sick. 'What?' I almost shouted. But the governor and PO were already standing up and preparing to leave. 'Is there anything else you'd like to ask? Any questions?' I was too gutted to reply straight away and by the time I came to my senses they were gone out of the door and back up the hill to the admin block, no doubt to write up the meeting on my record.

This was about as bad as it could get for me. I knew that there were people running the prison system who had long memories and that I had never been flavour of the month in certain quarters due, in part, to my past behaviour in prison, but also because I had pulled no punches in my first book when describing the way the British prison system conducts its dirty business behind closed doors. Of course, deep down, I had known that the book business would come back to haunt me. I'd had enough warnings about my writing, though I still believe I had broken no prison rules or laws and that the system wouldn't be able to sustain a cogent argument in a court of law. Now it was time to put that theory to the test. I had what I sincerely believe was the best legal team in the country in my corner, and I knew they'd love to get their teeth into this. I went back to my cell and immediately drafted a letter to my solicitors – Ian Ryan and Mark Pritchard – informing them of what had happened. Both Ian and Mark had worked on my parole hearings, along with barrister Andrew McGee and my old QC Jim Sturman, and had done an absolutely sterling job. If anyone was capable of firing a terrifying broadside across the bows of the prison system, it was this bunch of legal eagles. It was time to unleash the big guns.

In the next couple of days the C-wing community heard what was happening to me and I received a lot of support, even from the men I had not been particularly friendly with. Most agreed that it was a liberty that was being taken and nobody seemed happy. I also got support from some of the uniformed staff. I had been due to come into a final community meeting to give the traditional speech of encouragement usually given by members who had successfully completed therapy and were moving on, but after much thought I decided that given what was happening there was no way I could say good things about Grendon, nor encourage others to carry on at this time. I still believed in the work being done at Grendon, it was just the people who were in charge that I had no faith or confidence in. It would have been hypocritical of me to sit in front of the community and try to pretend that everything was okay, when it quite obviously wasn't. I informed Tom, the therapist, that I wouldn't be able to do it, and this was accepted.

For the next four weeks I was like the ghost of C-wing. I had pulled out of all therapy groups and spent the mornings banged up in my cell, usually working on letters to my legal team. I missed the therapy – after all it had been part of my daily routine for almost five years – but my mates would drop in after groups and in the evenings and keep me up to speed on the comings and goings of the community. A couple of times I managed to brace one or other of the governors and question them on how the investigation was proceeding, but they would tell me nothing. It was truly Kafka-esque, the way they were behaving. They point-blank refused to tell me who was carrying out the investigation, the time limit, if any, or the parameters of the enquiry. Then I found out that before they had even approached me they'd had people from Grendon phoning and e-mailing my publishers and asking questions about my third book – *Warrior Kings* – how much I was being paid for it, etc. The staff at Apex Publishing Ltd started wondering why they were getting so many enquiries from the same source and refused to answer any more questions about me or the book. Finding out that all this had been done days before I'd been called to the meeting made me even more suspicious that someone somewhere was out to get me.

My solicitors, Mark and Ian, briefed Andrew McGee and Jim Sturman on my case and they put together a letter of intent which was issued to Grendon, naming two governors as potential defendants in a judicial review case. Our case was that I had broken no laws or rules with my writing and had at no time made a secret of it during my time at Grendon. I had discussed it openly in my therapy groups and had used the success of my published books in my representations to the Parole Board. Therefore the decision of the prison to start an official investigation into my writing career at this stage was 'perverse'. The letter finished by informing the governor that if I were not transferred to HMP Blantyre House before 4 p.m. on Tuesday 19 May we would initiate proceedings in the High Court.

Towards the end of April I was called to a meeting in the C-wing office with a governor and a woman who told me that she was a governor from outside Grendon and would be in charge of the investigation. Mark Pritchard had already told me that if I were to be interviewed, I should answer all questions truthfully and if there was anything I didn't like the sound of then I should ask for the interview to be delayed until he could get to the prison. I wasn't worried because I truly did have nothing to hide. The woman from the Home Office/PSHQ (she wouldn't actually tell me where she was from) turned out to be quite reasonable. She started by telling me that she had read my books and thought I was a good writer! Then it was down to business. I was asked how much money I was making from my books and I refused to answer this question without first taking legal advice. I was asked how I had managed to get my manuscripts out of prison. I told her I did it through the normal channels. She asked me if I'd had permission from the governor to send stuff out for publication. I told her that I didn't need permission. She refused to concede this point despite the fact that she could produce no written rule that proved it. Then she pulled a piece of paper from the bundle she was holding and asked if I had signed a compact giving them the right to see anything I was sending out for publication. I looked at the governor sitting in the corner saying nothing. His face showed nothing. I explained how the compact had come about and my reasons for claiming it as worthless and broken after the system refused to honour their side of it. 'Besides anything else,' I finished, 'if you check the wording it concerns only journalism work for the national press, and not books.' She shook her head and told me that it was her understanding that it concerned all writing for publication. We argued this for a few minutes but got nowhere. With that she said she was finished with her questions and asked if I had any of my own. I proceeded to ask a bunch of questions about who had ordered the investigation, for what reason, when it had actually started and when it was going to finish. None of which was answered except with, 'I'm afraid I'm not allowed to tell you that.' I could see I was getting nowhere fast again so I finished with, 'I suppose you realize that my legal team are going to take this in front of a judge if I'm not transferred out of here without a stain on my character by the nineteenth of next month?' She chuckled indulgently. 'I think you'll find that the prison system will welcome a court case on this matter. And I wouldn't get your hopes up about getting a transfer, certainly not for a while yet.' And with that, she was gone.

For the next couple of weeks there was nothing for me to do but wait them out. Rationalizing the matter, I knew that if we ever did get into a court of law I was almost certain to win the case, since the position that the prison system was placing itself in was indefensible. Even as I was being investigated for writing to the press and getting books published from prison, my old mate Chaz Bronson was splashed all over the centre pages of the *Sport* giving an interview for his latest book in which he listed and named sex offenders whom he would like to kill! Chaz was being held at that time in a cage deep in the bowels of HMP Wakefield, under twenty-four-hour watch and 'exceptional risk' category A conditions. His every fart was bagged, tagged and analysed by prison security staff, and yet they seemed to turn a blind eye to his writing career. I say good luck to him and more power to his writing hand, but don't then try and stand up in court and persecute me for the same thing! If it got to court I would absolutely slaughter the prison system by pointing out their hypocrisy. So I wasn't that worried about the legal aspect of what was going on, but I did have a nagging fear about what the prison system might do behind the scenes to fuck me up. If the investigation were to clear me of any wrongdoing then there would be a lot of red faces, possibly at senior management level, and that could mean a bit of quiet payback from one or more of them. It would be easy enough to 'find' some illegal item in a search of my cell or property, and all it would take was one nicking for me to be put back two or three years. Even writing a bit of unfounded poison into my security file would be enough to get the Parole Board looking askance at my application for parole. It didn't take much effort for those in charge to fuck up a lifer's chances, and they were well aware of this. It was definitely a worry. I could only hope that when the prison system had gauged the strength and seriousness of my legal team it would scare them into letting the old sleeping dog lie.

On 14 May I was once again called in front of a governor. This time he was accompanied by a security SO. He told me that the investigation had been completed, and while I was not to be charged with any offence against prison rules, I was to be under no illusion that the prison system didn't take a dim view of my activities. I was no longer permitted to have any contact with the media without permission from the governor, nor was I to have anything – books, articles or opinions – published without first receiving permission. I sat back in my chair and listened to this sternly delivered twaddle but I couldn't resist smiling at him. Once he had finished speaking, I leaned forward and looked him in the eye. 'So,' I said, 'bottom line is that I didn't do anything that warranted my D cat being put at risk or my transfer to open conditions being delayed. Which is what I told you six weeks ago! Just how much taxpayers' money and manpower have you lot wasted on this? Just out of interest, give me a ball park figure.' He looked uncomfortable and muttered something about it being none of my concern. 'Well,' I said, 'you have five days to get me out of here. And I'd like you to know that my QC and solicitor are really eager to get this case to court, and the fact that I've now been cleared will not diminish that eagerness. On the contrary, in fact.' He looked as though he had a freshly cut lemon stuck under his tongue – he pursed his lips and shook his head. 'That's up to you,' he said, prissily. I knew that the judicial review would now not go ahead but I just wanted to rub it in a bit. I stood up. 'Have me out of here in five days or I'll be seeing you in court,' I said, then left the room.

Despite the confidence I'd had in being cleared, I was still relieved to hear officially that it was all over. Brian, Mark and Tony were the first in to congratulate me, but most of the rest of C-wing were not far behind. But later that evening I was again visited by the security SO. This time he looked somewhat embarrassed. 'The thing is,' he began, 'the place that you had at Blantyre House has been given to someone else, so it's looking as though you may have to go back on the waiting list for your transfer to open conditions. Is there any other D-cat prison you'd like to go to instead? We could probably get you a place across the road at Springhill.' I laughed out loud. HMP Springhill was jointly run by the same set of governors who were in charge of Grendon. I couldn't believe the brass neck of the geezer. Once I had finished laughing I shook my head. 'No,' I said. 'I wouldn't voluntarily go to Springhill even if one of the governors was to promise to give me a piggyback over there himself!'

Over the next four days I went about packing up my personal property, most of which I got sent to the HMP storage depot at Branston, and giving away the stuff that was not on my property card. It is a long-standing tradition in prison that anyone who is leaving – either to freedom or to open conditions – will give away personal items to friends who are left behind. Most of the good stuff I had at Grendon had been bought on the black market from other prisoners and was therefore not entered on my official list of in-possession property. In most jails this would not matter but at Grendon there were a few dog screws on reception who would take delight in going through a departing prisoner's property and confiscating unofficial items, so I was leaving behind my Sony stereo system, PlayStation 2, electric fan, electric lamp, electric clippers and bundles of clothing. The lads were glad of these little gifts and they too would pass them on to someone as they left. Nothing is wasted in prison – except youth and time.

I still wasn't sure I was going to be moving on the nineteenth, since anyone from the governor grades that I spoke to said that I was going nowhere and that there was no space for me at Blantyre. But I was all packed and ready to go anyway. Then on the eighteenth one of the reception staff gave me the whisper that I would be on my way the next morning. I wasn't told officially until 8 a.m. on the morning of the nineteenth. Refusing to tell me of the move until the last minute was just one more spiteful dig, but this time, thankfully, a parting one. Brian, Tony and Mark helped me to carry my bags up to reception. We said our goodbyes and promised to keep in touch. And then it was over. My property was checked, I signed all my paperwork, and was taken into a waiting room until the van turned up. As I sat down in one of the familiar blue chairs I noticed that it was the same room I had been put in on the day I had arrived at Grendon in July 2003. It hadn't changed much. My thoughts drifted to the poor deaf-and-dumb fella I had been so worried about on that day. He had slashed himself across the stomach with a broken coffee jar a couple of weeks after going on to F-wing and been shipped out to a psychiatric hospital soon after. Just another disturbed and broken man in a long line of many.

After a while the transport turned up. It was a cat A sweatbox! I couldn't believe it. I was the lowest security category a prisoner could ever achieve and I was still leaving Grendon in a bomb-proof cell on wheels. Jimmy smiled at me. 'Sorry lad, it's all they had available at short notice. Still, you should be used to travelling in one of them.' I had to laugh. I shook Jimmy's hand and climbed aboard. The escort locked me into the tiny cell and I settled into my moulded seat. Through the tiny dark-tinted window I watched the gatehouse slip by as I left on my way to a brand-new episode of my life. Was I ready for the world? I believed I was, and whatever my future now held I would be facing it as, hopefully, a better and more evenly balanced man. I knew it was going to be a struggle, but my bridges had all been burned to ash, there was no going back. I still had time to serve in prison before I would be finally released, but for the first time in my terrible life the future was at last looking bright.

At 4 p.m. on that day, Tuesday, 19 May, I was sitting in my new cell at HMP Blantyre House. And that's a whole new story.

Grendon Glossary
A Guide to Therapese (and some other stuff)

Acting out – To act out fantasies in real life, or to kick off in therapy and behave in a contentious or sometimes violent way as issues are recognized. People struggling with therapy and becoming difficult to deal with are said to be 'acting out'.

Art therapy – One of two complementary therapies offered at Grendon, the other being psychodrama; a means by which men can express themselves through art.

At it – Someone who is 'at it' in therapy is someone who is not ready or willing to change but pretending in order to gain any advantage that might be on offer – a spoofer or con-merchant.

Bad space – Emotionally challenging mood, talking about unresolved issues. In the early stages of therapy there are usually plenty of 'bad spaces'.

Buying into it – Becoming involved in someone else's issue or problem and making it part of your own.

Comfort zone – Any place or position where you feel most comfortable. Therapy is about knocking you out of your comfort zone and making you face change, no matter how uncomfortable it becomes.

Commitment – Everyone who voluntarily enters the Grendon regime is expected to show commitment to changing their destructive behaviour at all times. If someone calls your commitment into question it can lead to a wing vote on whether you stay at Grendon or are shipped back into the system.

Community – Prisoners and staff committed to therapy and operating as a group. The whole of Grendon is a 'community', but each separate wing is also a smaller community in its own right.

Double – A term used in psychodrama. To 'double' someone is to volunteer to play a version of them during a scene, and sometimes to speak or act from within that viewpoint.

Empathy – A much used word at Grendon and the first thing that those in therapy should strive for, meaning an insight into the feelings of others.

Facilitator – A member of staff who has been trained in psychotherapy and will sit in on every group therapy session to facilitate. Both uniformed and mental-health staff can facilitate.

Family Day – Every wing community at Grendon hosts two Family Days per year. Prisoners' families are allowed on to the wing for a six-hour visit, during which they will be served dinner and be treated to a charity raffle. Family Day visits are very important for prisoners in therapy and are a chance to renew or strengthen family ties.

Feedback – A daily reporting back to the wing community of therapeutic work done in groups. Prisoners from each small group take it in turns to report the feedback.

Feedbackers – Informers, those who would slip into the office and tell staff of anything untoward going on.

Flagging it up – Pointing something out – usually a contentious issue which has been kept hidden.

F-wing – The induction and assessment unit at Grendon. Holding a maximum of twenty-five new arrivals for anything up to twelve weeks in order to assess whether the volunteers are suitable for therapy on one of the main wings.

Governor grade – Non-uniformed staff with direct responsibility for a section of the prison – security governor, residential governor, discipline governor, etc. Governor grades are numbered 1 to 5 in order of responsibility, with the number 1 governor responsible for the whole prison and reporting to Prison Service HQ and the Home Office.

Nonce – Common prison term for anyone accused or convicted of sexual crimes against children. It originated in HMP Wakefield before the advent of protection wings for prisoners in danger of being seriously assaulted by their fellow cons. All sex offenders were held on normal location but were locked in their cells while other prisoners were out. In order to inform the staff which cell doors were not to be unlocked, the abbreviation NONCE was chalked on them – it stood for 'not on normal courtyard exercise'.

Not doing it justice – 'I'm not doing this justice' is the standard utterance of any difficult feedback. Meant to denote that the speaker is uncomfortable – or has forgotten – the details of a group.

ODC – Acronym of 'ordinary decent criminal', used to describe a prisoner who has no record of crimes of a sexual nature, or against children, women or old people.

Owning it – Admitting guilt and taking responsibility. To 'own it' is a good thing and proves you are moving on.

PO – Principal officer – the next step on the promotional ladder for an SO and the highest grade any uniformed officer can reach. The PO has overall responsibility for the day-to-day running of his wing. All officers and SOs report to the PO.

Psychodrama – A complementary therapy in which volunteers form a group to talk about and re-enact scenes from their lives with particular significance for them.

Putting papers in – Quitting therapy, usually in the middle of a particularly painful patch. Grendon is the only prison in the country where prisoners can decide to leave if they don't like it because the therapeutic regime is entirely voluntary.

Rep jobs – Every member of the Grendon communities is expected to put his name forward for at least one 'rep job' at the quarterly wing elections. Rep jobs range from 'paper rep', collecting and distributing the daily papers, to 'charity rep', writing hundreds of letters to commercial businesses requesting prizes for the charity raffles held on Family Days and social evenings. In order to become a rep you must be voted in by the community via a show of hands.

ROTL – A system of 'release on temporary licence' whereby those prisoners who have served the greater portion of their sentence and have been recategorized to security category C, may be granted a six-hour escorted town visit. A maximum of three ROTLs can be granted in any twelve-month period, but only after vigorous risk assessment of the prisoner. HMP Grendon is the only category B prison which allows category C lifers this privilege.

RTU – To be 'returned to unit' is to be sent back to whatever prison you were transferred to Grendon from. Approximately one third of F-wing receptions are RTU'd before reaching a wing community. Men can be deemed unsuitable for therapy for any reason, from drug-taking to lack of commitment.

Run with it – Seizing the moment and not trying to avoid anything, being honest. Usually said as an encouragement by other group members when a life-story recital begins to falter.

Small group – Each wing community at Grendon has five 'small groups' of eight or nine prisoners and a staff facilitator who work together. The small group is where most of the therapy is done.

SO – A prison officer who has put in several years on the job and success-fully passed the exam for promotion to 'senior officer'. SOs are in charge of less senior officers and the daily running of a wing.

Social evening – Held twice a year on each wing community and open to any professional body or individual connected to prison rehabilitation or the criminal justice system. A buffet is provided and usually a charity raffle, and prisoner volunteers are on hand to explain the workings of group therapy and their own community to visitors.

The Book – A large blue ledger into which the minutes of every community meeting, group feedbacks and votes are recorded. When not in use by the vice-chair the book is kept in the wing office, where any-one can peruse its contents or enter an issue for discussion or vote. Commitment issues start with an entry in the book.

Therapese – The unofficial language of therapy. Some people who have been in therapy for a long time begin to use the hackneyed and clichéd words and phrases much heard in a therapy setting. Be prepared to hear plenty of 'bad spaces' and 'owning it', and also to be knocked out of your 'comfort zone'.

Therapeuton – A prisoner who has overdosed on therapy to the extent that it governs every move and feeling in his life. Someone who talks therapy all the time and tries to impose it on every person he meets. The therapy version of a religious zealot.

Therapy break – Each community at Grendon has three therapy breaks per year, which coincide with public holidays – Easter, Christmas and summer. Therapy breaks last two weeks but there is a weekly half-hour community check-in meeting, and anyone can call a wing or group special at any time during therapy break if an issue comes up.

The system – In Grendon every other prison is referred to as 'the system', denoting Grendon's place outside it. This 'them and us' mentality helps to foster a unique solidarity and sense of belonging in the prison therapeutic community and allows volunteers to give themselves permission to behave differently from how they would in a conventional jail, to drop the 'image'.

Throwing your dummy out – Acting in a childish manner, as a baby throwing a dummy from the pram in a fit of temper.

Town-hall clock – A disparaging term used at Grendon to denote a propensity to switch views and allegiances, as in 'That geezer's got more faces than a town-hall clock.'

Using the group – Presenting an issue to the group.

Winged – To be 'winged' is to be put in the book and called before the wing community, to be interrogated by forty-odd prisoners and some staff and to explain your actions in an open forum where everyone has the right to speak and to vote you out if necessary.

Wing special – An emergency community meeting at which attendance by every member of the community is compulsory. 'Wing specials' are only to be called in urgent circumstances, such as possible violence brewing or the discovery of drug-taking.

After Grendon

The Good Guys

Ray

Ray successfully completed his therapy at Grendon and received a progressive move to HMP Latchmere House, where he seemed to be doing well. He was released in 2006 and started up a scaffolding business with a couple of old friends. He also met a nice woman, an addiction counsellor, and they set up home together in Dorset. Unfortunately, Ray's own addictive personality came to the fore again. He started taking steroids, which led to other substances, and he found himself back in prison for breaching his parole licence. He spent a further seventeen months behind bars. These days Ray still lives in Dorset and runs a café. He is also boxing again as an amateur, and doing pretty well.

Fred

Fred also completed the remainder of his sentence at HMP Latchmere House, after spending some months in HMP Springhill. He was released on parole in 2007 and works in south London as a fitness instructor.

Daran

Daran is still in HMP Kingston and has some years left to serve before completing his minimum twenty-year tariff. He plays for the prison football team and is still a smoker, thank God. We write to each other a couple of times a year and I'm hoping to get to visit him soon after my own release. I will encourage him to make good on his promise to return to Grendon to complete his therapy in the future.

Kevin the Nazi

Kevin never did get the psychiatric help that the prison system promised. He was released from HMP Bullingdon, direct from the punishment block, in 2006 and went back home to Blackburn. In September of that year he was viciously stabbed by a former friend and almost died. I managed to speak to him on the phone soon after he came out of intensive care, but that was the last contact I had with him.

Mark

Mark completed his therapy at Grendon and was released in 2009. We have met up for a drink or two a couple of times. He is a very talented artist and I hope he can finally find the resolve and impetus to do something with that talent.

Hate-'em-all Harry

Harry was downgraded to category D and transferred to HMP Ford. He was finally granted parole in 2007.

Steve

A very old friend, Steve was always one year ahead of me in his life sentence. He completed Grendon, then went on to HMP Blantyre House, in Kent, where he qualified as a plumber. Granted parole in 2008, he now lives quietly in Hampshire.

Mickey

Mickey left Grendon and was eventually paroled from HMP Blantyre House in 2009.

Half-naked Dave

Dave was granted parole, but after suffering a personal tragedy he was recalled to prison for breach of his life licence. I hear he is now out again and looking forward to a nice quiet life.

Musa

Musa was at Grendon when I left, and was doing very well in his therapy. We have kept in touch and I was delighted to hear that he is being recommended for category D at long last.

Westie

Westie is still serving his life sentence but doing his best to change his ways and maximize his chances of leading a good and peaceful life when he is eventually released.

The Not-so-good Guys

Terry
Terry, the rapist I met on my first day on F-wing, has escaped on two occasions, though never staying at large for long. The last time was in 2007 when he escaped from a hospital in south London where he was being treated for heart problems. The press reported that after his recapture the police wanted to question him about the murder of an elderly woman which occurred close to where he was caught. Like a lot of sex offenders, Terry is a very dangerous man, particularly to the vulnerable members of society.

The Mincer
The Mincer served two stints at Grendon and failed both times. He is still in prison and, to be perfectly honest, I hope he stays there.

Taff
Taff was released from prison in 2006. I have no idea what became of him but I sincerely hope he did learn something during his time at Grendon and will create no more victims.

Carrot Top
Soon after I left Grendon I heard that Carrot Top was downgraded to category C, though whether any Parole Board or Home Secretary will ever take a chance on authorizing his release is very doubtful.

Candy
Candy, the cross-dressing rapist, pulled out of therapy when things started to get a bit warm for him. He was called before the community to explain himself when he was overheard telling someone that he was definitely going to rape again. He became a hate figure on the wing but finished his sentence and was released.

Bug-eyed Bob, Billy Bullshit and Tony the Stalker
All still in prison serving their life sentences.

'Billy'

Billy was finally convicted of the murder of a pizza delivery girl in 2006, and was jailed for life. It was in order to try him again on the murder charge that he had escaped the first time around that the 'double jeopardy' law was changed.

As for the rest – some of whom I would much rather forget – if you ain't mentioned anywhere in this book it's because there's not enough space. As we say in therapy, get over it!